JOSEPH SMITH

JOSEPH SMITH

The Rise and Fall of
an American Prophet

JOHN G. TURNER

Yale

UNIVERSITY PRESS

New Haven and London

Published with assistance from the foundation established in
memory of Henry Weldon Barnes of the Class of 1882,
Yale College.

Yale University Press books may be purchased in quantity
for educational, business, or promotional use. For
information, please e-mail sales.press@yale.edu (U.S. office) or
sales@yaleup.co.uk (U.K. office).

Set in Janson type by IDS Infotech Ltd.
Printed in the United States of America.

Library of Congress Control Number: 2024949130
ISBN 978-0-300-25516-4 (hardcover : alk. paper)

A catalogue record for this book is available from the British Library.

Authorized Representative in the EU: Easy Access
System Europe, Mustamäe tee 50, 10621 Tallinn, Estonia,
gpsr.requests@easproject.com

10 9 8 7 6 5 4 3 2 1

Contents

Acknowledgments

"FRIENDSHIP IS THE GRAND FUNDAMENTAL principle of Mormonism," Joseph Smith observed in a July 1843 discourse. Historians who study the Latter-day Saint movement embody that principle to an unusual degree. Scholars from a wide variety of backgrounds share ideas, sources, feedback, and encouragement. I am grateful to the many friends and colleagues who have extended that generosity to me as I have worked on this book. Matthew Bowman, Bryan Buchanan, Xandy Frisch, David Golding, Jaimie Gunderson, Robin Jensen, Patrick Mason, Spencer McBride, Ben Park, Courtney Peacock, and Chris Thomas read all or portions of the manuscript in draft form. They and so many others—Mark Ashurst-McGee, Kevin Barney, Todd Compton, Matt Grow, Andrew Hedges, Sharalyn Howcroft, Joseph Johnstun, Barbara Jones Brown, Elizabeth Kuehn, Lachlan Mackay, Mike Marquardt, Mark Staker, Colby Townsend, Jeffrey N. Walker—shared insights over meals, phone calls, and emails. Thanks also to Brigham Young University's Maxwell Institute, which hosted me for a summer and gave me the chance to talk with some of this field's smartest and wisest individuals about Joseph Smith.

Archivists and librarians make the entire enterprise of history viable. Many institutions, including county and state archives and local historical societies, helped me obtain needed documents and photographs. Two deserve special thanks. Rachel Killebrew of the Community of Christ Library and Archives welcomed me in Independence and also sent scans of documents with remarkable efficiency. The Church History Library of the Church of Jesus Christ of Latter-day Saints provided cheerful and quick assistance with answers to reference questions and the digitization of documents. Brian Passantino was a consistently helpful and friendly point of contact.

Two individuals supported this project with patience from conception to manuscript delivery: my agent Giles Anderson and my editor Jennifer Banks. I am thankful for both of them.

I am most grateful to my wife, Elissa, who listened to countless stories about Joseph Smith, read the entire manuscript with the sharpest possible eye, and rooted me over the finish line. "Men are, that they might have joy," teaches the Prophet Lehi in the Book of Mormon. Writing books is fun, and finishing one is satisfying. Sharing my life with Elissa is joyful.

Introduction

J OSEPH SMITH IS A WHITE whale for a biographer, captivating but maddeningly elusive. Smith cut a bold figure in Jacksonian America, bursting onto the scene with the Book of Mormon and calling his followers to a succession of new settlements. He readily attracted attention but purposefully shrouded key moments of his life in mystery. It is easy to grow obsessed with the mysteries left behind by this slippery subject.

Joseph Smith isn't a mythical figure like Jesus or the Prophet Muhammad. We have letters written in his own hand, and transcripts of his sermons. Scores of Americans met and wrote about him. Newspaper editors across the United States knew that their readers wanted stories of Smith's latest exploits.

Smith was audacious and sometimes outrageous. He appeared before adoring crowds in resplendent military uniform. He visited the White House and even ran for president. He inserted himself into state and local political campaigns and appeared—sometimes voluntarily, sometimes against his will—in countless courtrooms. Smith remains an irresistible figure for many who encounter him, whether they see him as a prophet or a scoundrel—or a bit of both.

Put me in the last camp. Smith styled his life after those of biblical prophets. "Joseph has the spirit of all the prophets," his brother Hyrum Smith once observed.[1] Joseph Smith imitated Enoch, Abraham, Joseph, Moses, Solomon, and other ancient figures. He was a sojourner, a dreamer, a lawgiver, a temple builder, and a man with many wives.

I

Whether God actually spoke to Smith is a matter of faith, not history, but there is no question about his prophetic self-conception.

Many of those biblical figures acted in duplicitous and morally dubious ways at times. Abraham told convenient lies. Moses killed a man. Joseph and Solomon worked slaves to death. On occasion, Smith also took David as a model for friendship and loyalty. The Bible describes this great king as "a man after [God's] own heart," but David committed adultery with a woman and arranged to have her husband killed in battle.

Smith likewise had flaws. I wouldn't trust him with my money, my wife, or my daughter. Smith told women that God would slay him if he didn't take additional wives. He asked trusted followers if he could marry their daughters. In a few cases, he proposed to the wives of other church leaders. Smith also pressured friends and followers to give their money and property to him or to the church, and he wasn't always a careful steward or a wise business leader. The communities he built collapsed as quickly as they grew, first and foremost because of the schemes of his enemies, but also because of his own stumbles. He talked of binding the Saints together for eternity, but some of his actions tore apart their relations on earth.

And yet Smith endeared himself to people, even to many who didn't share his religious principles. If you showed up at his door and needed a bed for the night, you could have it and a hearty breakfast, and Smith would enliven the conversation with his humor and good cheer. If you challenged Smith to wrestle, he'd be game, and he'd probably beat you. You might find him poring over a King James Bible, a guide to Hebrew grammar, or an Egyptian papyrus, but you'd just as likely meet him chopping wood in the forest. "I suppose you think that I am a great, green, lubberly fellow," he told one fresh convert.[2] Those who wanted a holy man were surprised and sometimes disappointed, but hundreds of men and women were pleased to find a prophet who shared their limitations of education and wealth. He was a "rough stone," as Richard Bushman, his foremost Latter-day Saint biographer, emphasizes. Even those who had heard every scurrilous tale about Joseph Smith usually liked the prophet when they met him.

Several aspects of Smith's skill as a religious leader stand out. Smith wasn't the best preacher in his church, but he grew into the role, and his people understood him as a font of heavenly mysteries and knowledge. Smith was also an American creator of scripture and ritual par excellence. Church members hungered for his revelations, which they received as messages from the Lord, and they embraced his ritual innovations, such as baptism for the dead. Smith's religious talents, and the texts, communities, and missions they created, drew thousands of individuals on both sides of the Atlantic to embrace his church.

Smith succeeded in large part because he provided compelling and provocative answers to questions many American Christians were asking. Which of the churches is true? Or are they all wrong? What must I do to be saved? How should I prepare for Christ's imminent return? How can I be with my loved ones forever? Joseph answered these and other questions by drawing first and foremost on the Bible, but also on contemporary ideas and cultural practices, from dietary fads to Freemasonry. Smith wasn't just a religious magpie, though.[3] He took inspiration wherever he found it, but he brought these ideas and practices together into an original, attractive system.

That system of doctrine and ritual became the basis for something that persisted and grew. Today the Church of Jesus Christ of Latter-day Saints claims more than 17 million members around the world. It is among the five biggest religious denominations in the United States and, because of its concentrated strength in Utah and surrounding states, possesses a cultural and political clout above its raw numbers. A host of smaller religious movements, from the progressive Community of Christ to polygamous sects, also trace their origins to Joseph Smith and his early followers.

Smith's enduring success was unlikely in the extreme. He grew up in a downwardly mobile family and received only a smattering of formal education. As a young man, Smith worked as a farmhand and as a treasure seer, someone who discerned the location of buried objects by seeing them through a magical stone. No one could have imagined that Joseph Smith would establish a church, publish what became the most widely printed piece of American literature, found a city that rivaled Chicago as the largest in Illinois, hold political and military offices, and achieve such notoriety that scores of enemies would conspire to murder him.

How does one make sense of Joseph Smith? Boston's Josiah Quincy, who visited Joseph shortly before the latter's death, described him as a "phenomenon to be explained," but Quincy didn't have an explanation.[4] Five decades ago, the scholar Jan Shipps referred to Smith as an "enigma" and "puzzle." Wisely, Shipps recommended that scholars move beyond portraits of Smith as either a fraud or an anointed prophet and search for an integrated understanding of the man comprehensible to skeptics and believers alike.[5]

Leaving aside the question of whether it would be possible to craft a biography of Joseph Smith that satisfied believers and skeptics, such a goal isn't inherent to the biographer's task. Can one explain Joseph Smith? Not fully, and not through the lens of a diagnosable condition, as some scholars have attempted.[6] Especially in the last five years of his life, Smith exhibited characteristics of megalomania in his obsession with power, disregard for danger, and penchant for grandiose plans and pageantry.

Rather than a psychological diagnosis, though, this observation speaks to the basic truth that the events of Smith's life shaped his personality and character. Smith tried harder than most individuals to master and transcend the circumstances that he encountered, beginning with his family's poverty. Once he began to gather communities around him, however, Smith repeatedly encountered challenges he could not overcome. He would back down temporarily and then double down on his ambitions. Oftentimes, people within and beyond the church advised Smith to behave more cautiously. He ignored them. Smith thirsted for excitement, reveled in risk, and gloried in persecution. He was "continually rising," he told his followers, despite everything and everyone that tried to hold him down.[7]

Any biography's starting point is documenting an individual's life with the greatest possible accuracy and context. Over the last twenty years, the Joseph Smith Papers project of the Church of Jesus Christ of Latter-day Saints has published generously annotated transcriptions of thousands of documents created or received by Smith. It is thus a propitious time for a fresh portrait of Joseph Smith. The most prominent critical biography of Smith remains Fawn Brodie's *No Man Knows My History*, published more than seventy-five years ago. Richard Bushman's *Rough Stone Rolling* appeared at the outset of the Joseph Smith Papers project. Written from the perspective of a believing Latter-day Saint historian, *Rough Stone Rolling* carefully situates Smith in the culture of the time but treads lightly on some of the most controversial terrain, particularly Smith's polygamy. Unlike many prior biographers, I have no current or former connection to the church Smith founded. And although I am a historian of religion in the United States, I am especially interested in the ways that Smith intersects with the chronologically and geographically broader trajectory of Christian thought and practice. Smith was an American seer and prophet, but he engaged questions—about salvation, about revelation, about the organization of human communities—that Christians have asked in many times and places.

The proliferation of documents about Joseph Smith has made the biographer's task easier but not easy. "Evidence is always partial," observes the historical novelist Hillary Mantel. Painfully partial. "History is not the past," Mantel continues. "It's the record of what's left on the record. . . . It's no more than the best we can do, and often it falls short of that."[8] Contemporary evidence is lacking for a number of key developments in Smith's life, such as the translation of the Book of Mormon and the nature of Smith's many marriages. Smith wanted it that way. As the historian Ronald Barney observes, "Joseph Smith never desired to be completely known."[9] He established secret councils and arranged secret liaisons, and some of his most noteworthy visions and revelations took place quite literally behind a veil. Where evidence is lacking or contradictory, I both give my best judgment and acknowledge elements of uncertainty.

Indeed, there are questions that historians cannot answer. We can analyze Smith's accounts of his experiences but can penetrate only so far into their marrow. Writers have spent considerable time assessing Smith's sincerity. Did he believe in his own visions and revelations? Was he making it all up? Was he making some of it up? Did he, as Fawn Brodie maintains, proceed from "conscious artifice" to a "very real sincerity?" Alternatively, as Richard Bushman suggests, if we narrate Smith's life from his own perspective and from those closest to him, is it "hard to doubt Joseph's sincerity," even when it comes to gold plates and revelations?[10]

Smith displayed elements of heartfelt piety. In an 1832 letter to his wife, Emma, he described going into the woods to pray. He stressed his desire to be with Jesus Christ. At other moments, by contrast, Smith seemed ungenuine, such as when he scribbled a revelation on a scrap of paper and tossed it to a man who was opposing him at a city council meeting. But we easily could deceive ourselves or be deceived. Smith anticipated that other men and women would read his letters. Perhaps he wanted to emphasize his piety to them, or to Emma. And if Smith understood himself as God's prophetic mouthpiece, perhaps he thought the Lord wanted him to compose a hasty warning. Smith knew that church members and outside critics constantly scrutinized his actions, searching for signs of sincerity or deception.

In the end, historians cannot differentiate between genuine and insincere religious experiences with confidence. "Fact is," says a character in Herman Melville's *The Confidence-Man*, "when all is bound up together, it's sometimes confusing."[11] It is better to narrate and interpret what

Smith preached and practiced instead of pretending to discern his inner feelings at any given moment. Like Benjamin Franklin or Andrew Carnegie, Smith was engaged in constant acts of self-creation.[12] Smith sold books, land, and merchandise, but he was also a relentless religious innovator, bringing forth new scriptures, rituals, buildings, communities, and councils. Inspired by the men he read about in the pages of his Bible, confirmed through visions and revelations, and affirmed by a growing number of followers, Joseph Smith made himself into a latter-day prophet.

Smiths abound in this story. For clarity, and for the sake of familiarity and convention, I refer to the subject of this biography as "Joseph" in the pages that follow. Also for clarity, I have standardized spelling and punctuation in quotations.

CHAPTER ONE

Very Low Circumstances

(1805–1816)

Joseph smith jr. grew up in a family that was often at the precipice. Hopes kindled. Dashed. Rekindled. They moved on to the next town, the next farm, the next chance. As a biblical proverb suggests, poverty stalked them like an "armed man," an enemy they could evade for a time but never escape.

Joseph Jr. was born on December 23, 1805, in the township of Sharon along the White River in eastern Vermont. Preceded by his older brothers Alvin and Hyrum and a sister named Sophronia, he was the fourth living child of Joseph Smith Sr. and Lucy Mack Smith.[1]

After their 1796 marriage, the couple had lived in nearby Tunbridge, Vermont, on an eighty-three-acre farm jointly owned by Joseph Sr. and his father, Asael Smith. The land consisted of a marshy fen, a meadow, and some rocky hills. The Smiths raised cattle, tended apple orchards, and grew crops such as cordgrass and hops. Four decades later, an acquaintance described Joseph Sr. as "rather tall and big boned and heavy muscled." In his prime, he was strong and fit for the hard task of wringing a living out of moist and stony land.[2]

Lucy's brother, Stephen Mack, and his business partner, John Mudget, had given her $1,000 as a wedding present. It was a handsome sum, which Lucy set aside for the future. Joseph and Lucy didn't want to spend their whole lives eking out a living on their farm. They had siblings who had advanced themselves by trading in land and goods. Stephen Mack owned and leased several farms in the county; he and Mudget owned a store in Tunbridge. Jesse Smith, Joseph's brother, also operated a store in the township. Why not follow their path to prosperity? In 1802, Joseph rented out his Tunbridge farm, leased a store in East Randolph (about ten miles to the northwest), and borrowed $1,800 from a group of Boston merchants to purchase merchandise.

Then Joseph caught ginseng fever. Americans like John Jacob Astor had made fortunes shipping ginseng to China, and the root grew abundantly in northern New England. Other central Vermont merchants were engaged in the trade and talked up the potential windfall. Joseph likely hired men to locate, dig, and wash hundreds of pounds of the root. At this point, a more experienced merchant, Elkanah Stevens of Royalton, offered him $3,000 for the lot. Joseph thought it would fetch considerably more in China, so he demurred. Instead, Joseph journeyed to New York City in the spring of 1803. He contracted with a ship captain named William Howell to sell the ginseng on his behalf in Canton. Howell's vessel was owned by none other than Astor himself. If all went well, Joseph Sr. would receive tea and other valuable Chinese products in return and could sell them for a tidy profit.

It was a risky proposition, reflecting Joseph's inexperience in business. If he didn't like Stevens's offer, Joseph could have sold his lot to another merchant or ship captain. Now his prospects relied on the safe passage of Howell's vessel, the vagaries of an international market, and the character of the men who would handle his transaction.

Elkanah Stevens's son also went to Canton on Howell's ship. For reasons that are not entirely clear, it was he who brought the proceeds of Joseph's shipment back to Vermont the next spring. The news was grim. Young Stevens told Joseph that the ginseng sale had been a "perfect failure." It had fetched only a small chest of tea. According to Lucy, the younger Stevens was a swindler. The sale actually had succeeded, but Stevens had stolen her husband's profits and soon absconded to Canada.[3]

Lucy may have blamed the disaster on Elkanah Stevens's son in order to make the disaster less embarrassing for her husband's reputation. The whole story is a bit strange. Why didn't Joseph go to New York himself to collect his goods from Howell? Why didn't he pursue legal remedies against either Stevens or Howell? It seems that the venture and the scale of his loss overwhelmed him.[4]

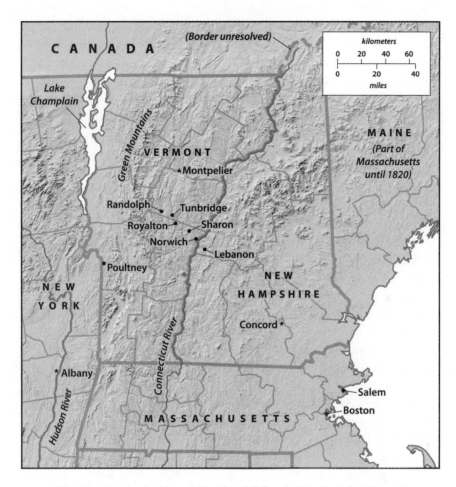

The New England of Joseph Smith's childhood. (Map by John Hamer)

What is clear is that Joseph was ruined. There was no windfall from the ginseng, and his store wasn't profitable. In order to pay what he owed to the Boston merchants, Joseph sold the Tunbridge farm, and Lucy contributed the $1,000 she had received as a wedding gift.

Lucy was now thirty years old, her husband a few years older. They started over on a farm in the township of Sharon owned by Lucy's father, Solomon Mack. Joseph Sr. cultivated the land in the summer and taught school in the winter. A few years after young Joseph's birth, the couple moved back to Tunbridge, and then to Royalton. Lucy brought three more sons—Samuel, Ephraim, and William—into the world during these years.

Tax records document that as of 1811, Joseph Sr. and his family were cultivating a thirteen-acre farm in Royalton. They owned two horses and a cow.[5] Their success was modest, but Lucy remembered that during these years they were "gaining gradually" and "in quite comfortable circumstances." They never stayed in one place for more than a couple of years, though, probably because of their precarious position as tenants.[6]

Alongside poverty, death also stalked the Smiths. The first ten years of anyone's life in that era were tenuous, and the first hours and days even more so. Lucy and Joseph's first child, an unnamed son, perished at birth. Their sixth child, Ephraim, lived only eleven days.

Lucy had her own brush with death early in her husband's ill-fated merchandising operation. Soon after the family's 1802 move to East Randolph a doctor told her—probably incorrectly—that she had consumption, or tuberculosis. The disease had killed two of her older sisters in young adulthood. It was a terrifying diagnosis, not just because of the thought of leaving her two young sons without a mother, but because she was not spiritually prepared for death. When her sisters had died, she had "determined to obtain that which was spoken of so frequently from the pulpit, namely a change of heart." The phrase reflects the fires of revivalism that repeatedly swept through the region. For Protestants inclined toward the revivals, salvation hinged on a deeply felt, emotional repentance followed by an assurance of God's forgiveness. Now, as she contemplated her own demise, Lucy was in agony because she had never had such an experience. "It seemed to me as though there was a dark and lonely chasm between myself and Christ," she later wrote in a history of her life. She begged God to let her live and "covenanted" with him that if he did, she would "endeavor to get that religion that would enable me to serve him right." She recovered.[7]

Prompted by the covenant she had made with God, Lucy dragged her husband to Methodist meetings in Tunbridge. The Methodists were the fastest-growing religious movement in the early American republic. Their itinerant ministers wore out countless horses making circuits among small churches in the hinterlands of New England, the plantations of the South, and the new settlements of the western frontier. These evangelists, like the long-haired and unkempt Lorenzo Dow, preached at revivals renowned—or notorious—for their emotional fervor. Methodists sharply rejected the Calvinist theology of their Congregational and Presbyterian counterparts, with its talk of predestination and God's sovereignty over human salvation. Instead, salvation was readily available. If individuals accepted Christ's offer of forgiveness, they would be saved from their sins. If they didn't, they faced God's eternal wrath.

Joseph Sr. had kept himself aloof from this sort of heaven-or-hellfire Protestantism. Back in 1797, he and his father, Asael Smith, had declared their membership in the Tunbridge, Vermont, Universalist Society. Universalists asserted that all men and women would be saved. Other Protestants denounced them as encouragers of wickedness. Without the threat of eternal damnation, why would people strive after righteousness? The declaration of Universalist membership exempted the Smiths from paying taxes in support of Tunbridge's Congregational Church.

Asael Smith paid his son and daughter-in-law a visit after he got wind that they were attending Methodist meetings. Asael "threw Tom Paine's *Age of Reason* into the house and angrily bade [Joseph] to read that until he believed it." Paine had gained acclaim in the United States for his pamphlet in support of American independence. His later publications were far less popular. *The Age of Reason* mocked the Bible as full "of lies, wickedness, and blasphemy." Paine became a symbol of irreligion in the early American republic, but Asael Smith regarded Paine's skepticism as common sense, at least as far as Methodism was concerned. Joseph ordered Lucy to stop going to the Methodist meeting. She was "very much hurt" but obliged.[8]

The backwaters of Vermont had a reputation for irreligion, that its farms and villages were populated with "nothingarians." The fact that the Smiths rarely attended church, however, doesn't mean that theirs was not a pious, Christian household. When Joseph Jr. told the story of his upbringing, he noted that his parents "spared no pains to instructing me in the Christian religion." They prayed with their children. They read the Bible to him and taught him to read it. They were eclectic and uncertain Christian seekers, but Christians nonetheless.[9]

The Smiths and the Macks didn't hear many sermons, but they sometimes heard directly from God. Lucy's sister, Lovina, recounted a vision of Christ in which Jesus urged her to "warn the people to prepare for death." Solomon Mack, Lucy's father, published an account of his late-life conversion. While suffering from rheumatism and spiritual agony, he saw a series of bright lights and found passages from the Bible imprinted on his mind. Mack prayed that the Lord would relieve

his suffering, and he was "entirely free from pain that night." His physical afflictions returned, but he was spiritually unburdened. "Jesus is
mine," he wrote, "and I am his / In union we are joined." It was the conversion experience Lucy had sought.[10]

Lucy also had visions, some of which she included in a history she
compiled several decades later. One day she went into a grove of cherry
trees and prayed that the Lord would influence Joseph Sr.'s heart. God
was silent, and she went home depressed. That night, though, she
dreamed of a magnificent meadow bisected by a "pure and clear stream
of water." On one bank of the stream, she saw two trees, one surrounded
by a "bright belt, that shone like burnished gold." When a breeze arose,
the tree with the belt "waved its beautiful branches in the light air,"
and its glory increased. The other tree remained still despite the storm.
Lucy's interpretation was that the unmoved tree was her brother-in-law
Jesse Smith; the "more pliant and flexible" tree was her husband. The
wind was the "breath of heaven," which would eventually incline Joseph
Sr. to accept "the pure and undefiled Gospel of the Son of God." That
was Lucy's hope for her husband and for her family. But where could
they find it?[11]

Lucy also recorded a number of her husband's visions. Shortly after
their son William's birth, Joseph Sr. had a dream in which he "seemed to
be travelling in an open, barren field." He could see nothing but fallen,
dead trees in every direction. He found that he was accompanied by an
"attendant spirit" and asked him to explain what he saw. "This field is the
world," the spirit replied, "which now lieth inanimate and dumb, in regard
to the true religion." The spirit directed Joseph Sr. to a box and told him
to eat what was inside. He located the box and began to consume its contents, upon which "all manner of beasts" rose up on all sides and began
"tearing the earth." He awoke trembling. Joseph had declared his hope in
universal salvation but couldn't shake his fear of looming judgment.[12]

In 1812, the Smiths moved to Lebanon, New Hampshire, twenty-five
miles away from Royalton. It was another fresh start, motivated by renewed hope that industry would result in comfort. Lucy, Joseph, and
their six children lived in a small rented home near the sawmills along
the Mascoma River, which flowed into the nearby Connecticut River.

Alvin, the oldest son, turned fifteen the next spring, so both he and
Joseph Sr. hired themselves out. Hyrum, two years younger, attended
Moor's Charity School in nearby Dartmouth, and Joseph Jr. and Sophro-

nia went to a local schoolhouse. Previously, the children had enjoyed or endured next to no formal schooling, a "deficiency" Lucy was eager to redress. Much of the children's education took place in the home. Joseph Sr. had taught school, as had Lucy's mother, Lydia Mack. A later neighbor recalled that the Smiths "had school in their house, and studied the Bible." It is unlikely that seven-year-old Joseph Jr. and the other children would have learned more in village schoolhouses.[13]

"We settled down and began to congratulate ourselves upon our prosperity," Lucy recalled. They were "perfectly comfortable." The embarrassment of the ginseng debacle had faded, and Joseph Sr. and Lucy could dream of better futures for their children.[14]

Those hopes collided with typhoid fever. The disease, circulating in the region, swept through the household in the winter of 1812–1813. "One after another was taken down," Lucy wrote. A typical course began with fever and proceeded to malaise, weight loss, and diarrhea. Nine-year-old Sophronia, stricken first, remained sick for three months, to the point that the doctors abandoned hope. Lucy recalled seeing her daughter "motionless with her eyes wide open with that peculiar set which most strikingly exhibits the hue of death." She and Joseph fell on their knees and begged God to spare their daughter, but she stopped breathing. Lucy wrapped Sophronia in a blanket and carried her back and forth. Finally, Sophronia let out a sob and started breathing again.[15]

Just when it seemed that the family had dodged the worst, seven-year-old Joseph was seized with a severe pain in his shoulder. A doctor dismissed it as a sprain, but two weeks later found an abscess "between his breast and shoulder," which he drained. The boy's ordeal was only beginning. Soon Joseph's left leg began to swell. It was acute osteomyelitis. The typhoid fever bacteria had penetrated Joseph's left tibia. His pain was excruciating and continued for several weeks. A surgeon came twice and made an incision in order to relieve the swelling, but to no avail. The doctors recommended amputation. A battalion of physicians from Dartmouth Medical School arrived for the grisly procedure.[16]

Lucy intervened. "Can you not try once more," she pleaded, "by cutting round the bone and taking out the affected part?" Then the sound portion would heal over it. The suggestion almost certainly did not originate with Lucy. She was describing a method pioneered by Nathan Smith, remembered by Joseph as one of the physicians who attended him. The experimental procedure was not without its risks. If the operation failed to stop the infection, Joseph could lose his life rather than a limb.[17]

Joseph was relieved that the men would not cut off his leg, but everyone knew that the procedure would be excruciating. As Joseph Sr. looked upon his son, and considered his wife's "intense anxiety," he "burst into a flood of tears and sobbed like a child." In a time before anesthesia, they could only offer brandy or wine to dull the pain that lay ahead. According to Lucy, however, Joseph refused the offer, refusing also to be bound for the operation. His father stayed by his side.[18]

The doctors bored into both sides of the affected bone and then broke off large pieces. Lucy, who had withdrawn a hundred yards from the house, rushed back in when she heard Joseph's screams. There was blood everywhere, and Joseph was "pale as a corpse."[19]

The operation succeeded. With the infected portion of the bone removed, Joseph began to heal. Bone fragments worked their way through his skin, and Lucy carried her son around the house until he could walk on his own. His uncle Jesse took him to Salem, Massachusetts, the farthest from home he had ever traveled, in the hope that the sea breezes would benefit his health. Still, it was a slow recovery. Joseph used crutches for several years, and even as an adult walked with a slight limp.

The bouts with typhoid fever cost the family its economic progress. Medical expenses left them in "very low circumstances," wrote Lucy. There was one more mouth to feed after the 1813 birth of Catherine, the couple's seventh living child, and their resources were dwindling. In 1814, the town of Lebanon assessed Joseph Sr. about one-fifth the taxes he had paid the previous year, indicating newly straitened finances.[20]

As the Smiths always did in such situations, they moved, this time back over the Vermont border to the town of Norwich. It was the fourth time the family had moved during nine-year-old Joseph Jr.'s lifetime. Joseph Sr. rented land in Norwich, but their crops failed, first in the fall of 1814 and then again the following summer. They sold fruit from the trees on the farm and scraped by.

In March 1816, a Norwich constable served the Smiths with a "warning out" notice, ordering them to leave the town. New England cities and towns in the early nineteenth century routinely warned unwelcome newcomers to leave so that they did not become a drain on a community's resources. The notice makes plain the place of the Smiths in the social order. They were indigent vagrants.[21]

The Smiths were already thinking of leaving of their own accord. Joseph Sr. vowed that if the crops failed yet again, "he would go to New

York where the farmers raised wheat in abundance." New Englanders had been infected with "York Fever" for decades by this time. Land in the western portion of New York was far cheaper and much more fertile than in the upper Connecticut River Valley. Several of Joseph Sr.'s siblings had already left Vermont.[22]

Joseph Jr. had recently reached the age of ten. He was regaining his strength, but his leg still hampered his ability to help in the fields. None of his efforts would have made a difference, however. Nothing grew in 1816. A volcanic explosion in faraway Indonesia led to an intense period of global cooling. In Vermont, there were frosts and heavy snow in June and again in September. The unusually cold weather "well nigh produced a famine," remembered Lucy.[23]

Like thousands of other Vermonters, the Smiths took the "year without summer" as a sign to head west. Joseph Sr. joined a man heading for Palmyra, a rapidly growing township about twenty miles south of Lake Ontario. Lucy stayed behind to settle debts. Then, sometime in early 1817, she and her eight children followed. (Another son, Don Carlos, had been born in Norwich.) Here was a lesson Joseph Jr. learned from his parents. In the face of failure, it was better to move on than to remain mired in unfavorable circumstances.

Before he left, Joseph Sr. had hired a teamster named Caleb Howard to transport his family. There was not enough snow to travel by sleigh, but what snow there was made for a muddy and slow journey. To make matters much worse, Howard was a callous scoundrel. He made Joseph Jr. walk in the snow next to the wagon for many miles each day despite his lameness. When Hyrum and Alvin tried to intervene, Howard struck them with the butt of his whip. Indignity followed indignity, until one day Howard tossed their goods out of the wagon and made to leave them near Utica, a hundred miles from Palmyra.

Lucy took matters into her own hands again. She seized the horses by the reins and forbade Howard from departing. In front of witnesses, she accused him of swindling her. Was he so low that he would abandon a mother and her children? She declared that she would take the horses, the wagon, her children, and their goods. "As for you, sir," she concluded, "I have no use for you." Lucy's strong will prevailed. The Smiths left Howard behind.[24]

In order to pay for lodging along the remainder of the route, Lucy sold bits of cloth and a pair of Sophronia's earrings. Eventually, the fam-

ily was reunited in Palmyra. The Smiths were out of money but full of
joy. They were ready for yet another fresh start.[25]

Joseph Jr. learned a great deal from his parents' fortitude in the midst of
poverty and illness. The Smiths believed in a porous border between
heaven and earth. Joseph Jr. inherited his parents' expectation that humans could call on God and receive divine assistance and guidance. At
the same time, he also absorbed their determination to trust their own
instincts above those of the ministers and physicians who thought they
knew better. The Smiths were a tight-knit family, unafraid to show their
affection for each other, and convinced that through their tenacity they
could overcome adversity.

    Some purported acquaintances of Joseph Smith Sr. later recalled that
"he used to tell about [Joseph Jr.] being born with a veil over" his face.[26]
Many early Americans believed that babies born with the "veil" or
"caul"—the amniotic membrane—covering their heads would develop
gifts for healing or treasure seeking. The story is probably not true, as
Lucy mentioned nothing of the sort in her history.

    Joseph Jr.'s childhood was mostly ordinary. His family was like many
others in northern New England: on the move in search of their fortunes,
never in one place long enough to put down roots, and divided and uncertain about religion. The only time that young Joseph intrudes into his
mother's history of the family is during his dramatic battle against typhoid.

    Joseph Jr.'s second dozen years would prove far more remarkable.
Born with the caul or not, he developed a reputation for visions and the
ability to see buried and distant objects. These gifts eventually resolved
his parents' religious disunity and freed him from their very low circumstances.

CHAPTER TWO
Light (1817–1825)

THE VILLAGE OF PALMYRA lay on the planned canal route that would connect the Hudson River with Lake Erie. Construction began in 1817, the summer after the Smiths arrived. The project, which President Thomas Jefferson had once deemed "little short of madness," catalyzed the entire region's growth. Palmyra's churches, mercantile stores, newspapers, and tanneries all prospered as the population more than doubled over the next decade.[1]

The Smiths settled into a small house on the village Main Street. Lucy, the family's most successful entrepreneur, painted and sold oilcloth table coverings. Her proceeds "furnished all the provisions for the family," and they began to replenish their stock of furniture. The family also sold pastries and root beer at a "Cake and Beer Shop."[2] Joseph Sr. and his oldest sons—Hyrum and Alvin—hired out and began earning the money that would enable the family to purchase its own land. Young Joseph did his part. As a twelve-year-old boy, Joseph earned 25 cents for a half day's work gathering and hauling hay, and he took a pushcart with the family's goods to town gatherings and camp meetings.[3]

In addition to the hodgepodge of work, Joseph Jr. received some formal education. In September 1817, Palmyra teacher Philander Packard included a "Joseph Smith" on the list of fathers who sent their children to his school. Joseph never credited Packard or any of his childhood teachers with a significant role in shaping his intellect. The instruction—

Eastern view in Main-street, Palmyra.

Palmyra's Main Street, ca. 1825. (Courtesy of the New York Public Library)

practical and spiritual—that he received at home was far more important to his development.[4]

According to Lucy, Joseph Jr. "never said many words upon any subject but always seemed to reflect more deeply than common persons of his age upon everything of a religious nature." Orasmus Turner, an apprentice printer in the town, remembered Joseph as "lounging, idle . . . and possessed of less than ordinary intellect." Turner's comments are probably tinged by Joseph's later notoriety, but he conceded that Joseph possessed at least some of his "mother's intellect." He joined a "juvenile debating club" that met in a Palmyra schoolhouse and enjoyed "portentous questions of moral or political ethics." As Joseph grew a bit older, he became less pensive, more jovial and given to mirth, but he never tired of intellectual debate.[5]

The most notable thing about "Young Joe" and the whole Smith family was their destitution. Pomeroy Tucker, a local printer and publisher, and a later critic of Joseph Jr., recalled his simple clothing and "vagabondish appearance." More well-to-do residents of Palmyra looked down on the family. Lucy Mack Smith recalled a tea at which a lady commented that she deserved a "better fate." Lucy replied that she had no reason to envy wealthier individuals.[6]

The Smiths weren't ashamed of their poverty, but they aspired to overcome it. They trained their eyes on a hundred-acre property that straddled the townships of Palmyra and Farmington in a portion of Farmington that soon belonged to the newly created township of Manchester. They built a cabin next to the tract on land that was owned by Samuel Jennings, a local merchant. Lucy described the cabin as a "snug log house." Snug indeed, with ten Smiths crammed into two main rooms, with two attic rooms above.[7]

In the summer of 1820, Joseph Sr. and Alvin together contracted to buy the land. They struck the agreement with Zachariah Seymour, a land agent for the heirs of Nicholas Evertson, who had owned the property prior to his 1807 death. The price was around $700, payable in several installments, with the final payment coming due in 1825. If they failed to make the required payments, the land and any improvements on it would revert to the Evertson heirs. Richard Bushman observes that the joint purchase indicates that twenty-two-year-old Alvin had become the "auxiliary family head," supplanting his downtrodden father. Regardless, the purchase was a landmark for the family. For the first time since the ginseng scheme that had cost Joseph Sr. and Lucy their Tunbridge, Vermont, farm, the Smiths were landowners.[8]

The Smith men set to work clearing the land, an arduous task for which Joseph Sr. was now ill suited. Thanks to Alvin and Hyrum's vigor, though, it went quickly. They soon had thirty acres ready for planting corn, wheat, barley, and other grains. As they felled and burned trees, they could sell the remains to manufacturers of potash. The Smiths also tapped trees to make maple sugar, producing a thousand pounds each year.

The Smiths needed to clear a bit more than $100 per year in order to make the payments on their land. It proved difficult. Prices for crops such as wheat had fallen sharply in the wake of an economic panic that began in 1819. Seymour cut the Smiths some slack when they couldn't make the entirety of the first payment. As the second payment came due, Alvin hired out, toiled on other farms, and earned the money. Going forward, that could have been the recipe for the family's financial salvation. The industry of Alvin, Hyrum, and Joseph Jr. could have secured title to the land.

The Smiths never made the final payment. In July 1822, Seymour died, and further transactions had to wait until the Evertson heirs appointed his replacement. In the meantime, the Smiths decided to build a new home on the property, a frame house rather than a log cabin. Alvin took "principal charge" of the project, which would provide his parents with a fitting residence for their old age. According to Lucy, the house frame was raised in November 1822, and they hired workmen to finish the home. Town assessors accordingly revalued the property the next summer, pegging its worth at $1,000, a $300 increase from prior years. Although the land agent's death postponed the family's quest to obtain title to the farm, the house was a tangible sign of their industry and progress.[9]

The Smiths had a measure of prosperity in their grasp, but religious certainty remained elusive. Around 1818, Joseph Sr. dreamed that he was walking toward a meeting house, alone and fatigued. He saw crowds of people rushing to get inside, but when he reached the door, it was shut. When he knocked, an angelic personage told him he was too late. He began to pray, but his flesh withered on his bones. "Oh Lord," he cried out, "I beseech thee in the name of Jesus Christ to forgive my sins." He felt strengthened and his flesh returned, then he awoke as he passed through the door. As a young man, Joseph Sr. had subscribed to Universalist principles, but his hope that God would save everyone did not eliminate his spiritual anxiety. Yet Joseph Sr.'s visions did not induce him to join any of Palmyra's churches.[10]

The Smiths had moved to what the renowned Presbyterian evangelist Charles Finney later called the "burnt district," a region marked by the repeated fires of revivalism. At camp meetings, such as those to which Joseph Jr. had taken his family's pushcart, individuals experienced intensely emotional conversions, sometimes characterized by wild physical manifestations of the Holy Spirit. They might writhe under Satan's grip or collapse when God wrenched them free from the power of sin. Detractors considered the meetings spectacles of fraud, madness, drunkenness, and debauchery.[11]

Soon after his family's move from the village to their log home, Joseph remembered, "there was in the place where we lived an unusual excitement on the subject of religion." A Methodist minister named Aurora Seager recorded that at an 1818 "camp-meeting at Palmyra" there were twenty baptisms, and forty men and women joined the church. Two years later, in June 1820, the *Palmyra Register* reported that a drunken Irishman had died after attending "a camp-meeting which was held in this vicinity." Revivals were a regular occurrence in the region. Joseph had ample opportunity to watch men, women, and children throw themselves on God's mercy—and sometimes upon the ground when the Spirit overwhelmed them.[12]

Joseph grew spiritually apprehensive. "My mind became seriously impressed," he wrote, "with regard to the all-important concerns for the welfare of my immortal soul." Joseph was "convicted of [his] sins," but he didn't know where to find forgiveness and salvation. Decades later, he told a friend that he "wanted to get religion too, wanted to feel and shout like the rest, but could feel nothing." For several years, Joseph's anxiety mounted, then reached a breaking point.[13]

There are multiple accounts of what happened next. One version became iconic scripture for Latter-day Saints.[14] In it, Joseph recounts his frustration that each church claimed an exclusive path toward Jesus Christ. "Who of all these parties are right," Joseph asked himself, "or, are they all wrong together?" Joseph felt the most attraction for the Methodists and their fervent promise that sinners who asked Jesus Christ for forgiveness would receive it. But how could anyone be certain?

Not knowing which way to turn, Joseph followed the Bible's advice that those who lacked wisdom should "ask of God." On an early spring day in 1820, the fourteen-year-old boy went to a secluded place in the woods and knelt to pray. Americans in the eastern United States no longer saw the wilderness as full of beasts and potential enemies. Instead, nature was a tranquil place where solitary individuals might encounter God. Camp-meeting hymns encouraged troubled souls to seek forgiveness and salvation in "silent groves."[15]

Joseph's grove didn't remain silent. When he tried to pray, he felt "seized upon by some power which entirely overcame" him, bound his tongue, and enveloped him in darkness. Joseph had seen afflictions like this at camp meetings, and it was more terrifying than he could have imagined.

Joseph called upon God, who delivered him from Satan. The darkness cleared, replaced by a "pillar of light . . . above the brightness of the sun." As the light rested on him, Joseph saw "two personages," bright and glorious, standing above him in the air. One pointed to the other and said, "This is my beloved son. Hear him!" It was God the Father, asking Joseph to listen to Jesus Christ.

Joseph got a hold of his faculties and asked his question. Which church should he join? The Christian Savior had a stark answer: "None of them, for they were all wrong." Jesus offered no advice about what he should do instead. When the vision ended, Joseph found himself lying on his "back, looking up into heaven." The light slowly departed.

This youthful experience became known among the Latter-day Saints as Joseph's "First Vision." In recent decades, scholars and others have pored over the several accounts of the vision, often with the motive of either buttressing Joseph's reliability or casting doubt on his credibility.[16] For instance, in Joseph's earliest, handwritten account, he cries out to God first and foremost because he wants forgiveness for his sins. He sees one divine being (Jesus Christ) rather than two. Observing such inconsistencies, Fawn Brodie dismissed Joseph's vision as either a "half-remembered dream stimulated by the early revival excitement" or "sheer invention." Richard Bushman, by contrast, suggests that as Joseph grew more confident, he shared more detail and emphasized different aspects of the experience.[17]

Whether or not heavenly beings appeared to Joseph is a matter of faith, not historical inquiry. It is impossible for scholars to penetrate the marrow of anyone's religious experience. At the same time, regardless of its particular content or exact date, there seems little reason to doubt the story's core: that a spiritually distraught young man sought, saw, and heard the Lord.

When Joseph told a Methodist minister about his experience, the man treated his story with contempt, saying that "there was no such thing as visions or revelations in these days." Of course, any minister would take offense at the notion that his church, like all of the others, was "wrong," but here was another fault line within American Protestantism. As they divided on the ecstatic scenes at camp meetings, so Protestants disagreed about visions. More educated and elite ministers disliked the disruptiveness of visions, which threatened to relocate authority from churches and scripture to individuals. Despite such misgivings, many American Christians had visions and dreams of Jesus Christ, or of Jesus at the right hand of God the Father.[18] Joseph Sr. and Lucy believed that God had communicated with them in this manner. Now young Joseph realized that he too had this gift.

After the minister's rejection, Joseph mostly kept the vision to himself. What might have marked a new beginning instead became lost amid the distractions of work, schooling, and other pursuits. "I pondered these things in my heart," Joseph later wrote, "but after many days I fell into transgressions and sinned in many things."[19] The vision's fleeting impact also was not unusual. For some Americans, an emotional camp-meeting

experience proved a decisive turning point, but for others, spiritual ecstasy soon faded. So it was for Joseph Smith.

Joseph discerned that he possessed other gifts, also disreputable in the
eyes of many elite Americans. Former neighbors later mocked the
Smiths as "money diggers," deriding them as fools or frauds—or both—
for having used divining rods and seer stones to search for buried treasures. Both in the hardscrabble settlements of Vermont and on the
almost frontier of western New York, many people engaged in these pursuits without any sense that they conflicted with Christianity. Indeed, for
some individuals these were deeply spiritual practices. It was a matter not
just of divining the location of buried gold or silver, but also of accessing
the spiritual power that would allow one to take possession of the riches.

At some point in his adult life, either in Vermont or shortly after his
move to Palmyra, Joseph Sr. began "dowsing" or "witching" with a rod.
How did this work? The dowser held a witch hazel rod, usually forked,
in his hands. When the rod dipped, it pointed the dowser in the right direction. It was common for individuals to hire a "water witch" when selecting the location of a new well. Peter Ingersoll, one of the Smiths'
neighbors after their move to the Palmyra-Manchester line, remembered
Joseph Sr. cutting "a small witch hazel" and showing him how to hold it.
Joseph Sr. also taught his sons to dowse. Isaac Butts, who went to school
with Joseph Jr., remembered that his classmate "had a forked witch-hazel
rod with which he claimed he could locate buried money or hidden
things." As day laborers, the Smiths plowed fields, built and repaired
fences, harvested hay, and dug wells. For the latter task, the fact that
Joseph Sr. and his boys used the rod made them more attractive to em-
ployers.[20]

Joseph Jr. soon grew attracted to another form of divination. Rather
than a rodsman like his father, the young man became a "glass-looker,"
someone who located objects by seeing them in a stone, referred to as a
"seer stone" or "peep stone." It started with neighbors who lived near the
new Smith farm in Manchester. Sally Chase, a young woman about Joseph's age, lived with her family just over the hill from the Smiths. The
Chases were active Methodists. Sally was also a glass-looker. According
to Lucy, Sally "found a green glass, through which she could see many
very wonderful things." When Sally Chase let Joseph look in her stone,
he saw a stone of his own. According to a later secondhand report, it
was a "great way off," along the southern shore of Lake Erie near the

A seer stone belonging to Joseph Smith. (© By Intellectual Reserve, Inc.)

Pennsylvania line, up a stream and under the roots of a tree. Several years later, Joseph journeyed to retrieve it. The details of the tale seem unlikely. Joseph wasn't in a position to travel 150 miles, and no other records suggest that he did. Nevertheless, wherever and however he found it, Joseph's first stone was dark brown and smooth, the size of a small chicken egg.[21]

In 1826 testimony, Joseph stated that he "had a certain stone, which he had occasionally looked at to determine where hidden treasures in the bowels of the earth were." On one occasion, Joseph directed his father and a group of men to dig into a hillside. According to two brothers who lived near the Smith property, the men dug a fifty-foot-long tunnel, prompted by young Joseph's vision of money within. Their exertions were in vain. But it is clear that the Smiths had neighbors and friends who believed that Joseph had the ability to see buried objects, and both they and Joseph himself persisted in such belief even when their attempts didn't produce any treasure.[22]

Joseph's own response to setbacks was to seek a more powerful stone. Possibly by peering into his brown stone, he divined that the desired stone lay buried on the Chase property. In or around 1822, Joseph, his older brother Alvin, and Willard Chase (Sally Chase's brother) joined together in this quest. Under the pretense of digging a well, they started tunneling down. "After digging about twenty feet below the surface of the earth," Chase recounted a decade later, "we discovered a singularly appearing stone, which excited my curiosity." Chase picked it up, emerged from the well, and showed it to Joseph, who "put it into his hat, and then his face into the top of the hat." Joseph claimed that "he could see in it." Both men wanted the stone and asserted a claim to it. Joseph had chosen the spot, while Chase had found the stone. In the end, Joseph persuaded Chase to lend it to him. The stone's light color made Joseph think of the Book of Revelation, in which Jesus promises a "white stone" and a "new name written" on it to those who "overcome" the world. As Joseph told neighbors about his new stone, news of the young Palmyra-Manchester seer began to spread.[23]

While Joseph searched for stones, divine beings kept seeking him out. The budding seer dated another remarkable vision to September 22, 1823. In the night, an "angel of the Lord" stood at his bedside. The angel told Joseph that the Lord once again had forgiven his sins. Then came the big reveal: there were "plates of gold" buried near his home. Joseph later identified the visitor as Moroni, an ancient inhabitant of the Americas and one of the authors of the engravings on the plates.[24] The angel recounted to Joseph "a history of the aborigines of this country, and said they were the literal descendants of Abraham." He added that Jesus Christ had delivered "the fullness of the everlasting Gospel" to these ancient Americans.[25]

Some elements of Joseph's vision were fairly standard fare. Many Europeans had speculated that at least some Indigenous peoples of the Americas had Jewish ancestry and could be the descendants of the ten "lost tribes" of Israel. The idea that ancient Americans had become Christians through an encounter with Jesus Christ was more original. And, of course, the most distinctive claim was that this history was recorded on gold plates buried near the Smith farm. By "plates," Joseph meant thin sheets of metal engraved with writing, perhaps akin to what many printers were using by the 1820s.[26]

Moroni appeared three times that night. According to what became the church's canonical account, on the third visit the angel warned Joseph that Satan would try to tempt him "to get the plates for the purpose of getting rich." Moroni's caution was well placed. Joseph had searched for treasures buried in the dirt, and his family was dirt poor. Why wouldn't he view the plates as his family's earthly salvation?[27]

Joseph was in a spiritual haze as he worked alongside his father the next day. Joseph Sr. noticed something was amiss with his son and told him to go home. The younger Joseph agreed, but while clambering over a fence on the way, he lost his strength and collapsed. As he lay on the ground, he again saw Moroni, who instructed him to tell his father about the vision. The elder Smith, accustomed to visions, advised his son to obey the angel and locate the plates.

Joseph related that he followed Moroni's instructions and "knew the place the instant that [he] arrived there." But Joseph also told people close to him that he divined the spot by looking into his white stone. The destination was on the west side of a hill, a couple of miles south of the Smith home. (The place later became known to Latter-day Saints as the Hill Cumorah.) He found a half-buried stone box and used a lever to pry off the top. Inside, the plates rested on four pillars.[28]

In his earliest history, Joseph explained that he made several attempts to take the plates but somehow could not. The angel appeared to him, informed him that he had allowed himself to fall under Satan's power, and urged him to repent. Joseph conceded that he had "sought the plates to obtain riches." As with his earlier vision of Jesus Christ, Joseph later told this story in greater detail. He took the plates, then put them down to see whether anything else valuable was in the box. The plates vanished. Moroni reappeared and chastised him for his disobedience, but permitted him another look at the treasure. He saw them back in the box, as before. When he made another attempt to retrieve them, something hurled him to the ground.[29]

As with his other treasure digs, Joseph went home empty handed but not discouraged. For those who sought buried treasures with rods, seer stones, or other means, locating the object of their desire was only the first step. Spirits guarded treasures and demanded precise compliance with their instructions. And when one was on the brink of success, the treasure might disappear or slip away to another location. The dream was deferred rather than denied, however. Moroni told Joseph to return in exactly one year and to bring his brother Alvin with him.

The angel's command proved impossible. In mid-November 1823, twenty-five-year-old Alvin suddenly fell sick with what Lucy called "the bilious colic." It might have been appendicitis. The family's usual physician was unavailable, so a doctor came from a nearby village. He prescribed a strong dose of calomel, a mercury compound, which lodged in Alvin's stomach. As when Joseph Jr. had been near death a decade earlier, a group of physicians came to help, but this time to no avail. Realizing that he would die, Alvin called his siblings one at a time to his bedside. Young Lucy, Joseph Jr.'s two-year-old sister, tightly clasped her hands around him. Only with difficulty could her parents unclench her. After Alvin died, the little girl wrapped herself in a white shroud and lay beside her brother's corpse.[30]

Joseph Jr. was seventeen years old when Alvin died. He never stopped mourning his eldest brother, whom he idealized as a handsome, strong, and sober young man. "I remember well the pangs of sorrow that swelled my youthful bosom," he commented two decades later.[31] Alvin remained in Joseph's thoughts—he would appear in his dreams and visions as well.

Joseph retained a lasting bitterness toward incompetent physicians. "Doctors won't tell you where to go to be well," he once alleged. "They want to kill or cure you to get your money." In particular, Joseph warned that a "calomel doctor . . . does not stop to know whether the stomach is empty or not."[32]

Alvin's death dashed the family's hope of renewed prosperity. Lucy, Joseph Sr., and the entire family had pinned their aspirations on their eldest son. It was Alvin who had helped arrange the land purchase, earned the money for the second payment on the property, and pushed ahead with the construction of their new home. Now, as Lucy put it, their happiness was "blasted."[33]

Neither Hyrum, now twenty-three, nor Joseph Jr. matched their late brother's industry, and fifty-two-year-old Joseph Smith Sr. was well past his prime. At some point, moreover, the elder Joseph began to drink to excess with at least some regularity. A number of neighbors remembered him as a drunkard. Those recollections were tinged by religious animosity, but Joseph Sr. himself later expressed remorse that he had "been out of the way through wine." Without Alvin the family struggled to move forward.[34]

Ten months after Alvin's death, Joseph Sr. published a notice in the *Wayne Sentinel*, one of Palmyra's newspapers. He complained about "harrow[ing]" rumors that Alvin's corpse had been stolen and "dissected," presumably by body snatchers who would have sold the corpse to anatomists shortly after its burial. In order to refute the rumors, Joseph and his neighbors went to Palmyra's cemetery, removed the earth at Alvin's grave, and found his remains undisturbed. Presumably young Joseph accompanied his father on the macabre errand. If so, he gazed upon his beloved brother's decomposed corpse, which despite its missing eyes and nose still would have been identifiable as Alvin. In the early nineteenth century, it was not entirely unusual for families to seek out opportunities to look upon their "mouldering" loved ones. The sight was horrifying, but even a decayed corpse could kindle fond memories and provide reassurance of the enduring connection between the living and the dead.[35]

The incident marks a rare appearance of the Smith family in the historical record during these years. The exhumation occurred only several days after Joseph Jr. was to return to the hillside with Alvin in order to meet Moroni. The conjunction seems unlikely to be a coincidence, though the nature of the connection, if any, remains unknown.

Alvin's death also magnified the religious anxieties and divisions within the family. Joseph's younger brother William remembered that a Presbyterian minister preached at Alvin's funeral and "intimated very strongly that he had gone to hell, for Alvin was not a church member." The suggestion angered Joseph Sr. For her part, Lucy was troubled by fear of damnation. She had heard many ministers warn that individuals should make haste to secure their salvation. "Forgiveness must be obtained in the present world or it can never be obtained," declared Jesse Townsend, pastor of Palmyra's Western Presbyterian Church in the late 1810s. Townsend taught that those who did not repent would bear their guilt forever and endure everlasting misery. After Alvin's death, Lucy started attending meetings again, and she and three of her children—Hyrum, Sophronia, and Samuel—became members of Western Presbyterian. Joseph Sr. apparently accompanied her to a meeting once but would not join the church.[36]

Joseph Jr. refused to go even one time. "I will take my Bible and go out into the woods and learn more in two hours than you could if you were to go to meeting two years," he explained. Like his parents before him, the young seer had little patience with doctors, teachers, or ministers.[37]

The Smiths faced earthly reckonings in 1825. They lacked the money to settle the debts for their home's construction. Russell Stoddard, the chief builder and carpenter on the project, sued Joseph Sr. and won a judgment of $66.59. Even worse, the Evertson heirs now had a new agent, John Greenwood, who demanded the remaining money due for the land. He gave them a deadline of Christmas Day, 1825. There was no obvious way the family could clear its debts and make the final payments. They would lose everything, house and land.[38]

What had gone wrong? Lucy heard talk that "we stopped our labor and went at trying to win the faculty of Abrac, drawing magic circles, or sooth saying to the neglect of all kinds of business." She maintained that they never "suffered one important interest to swallow up every other obligation." Lucy is probably correct that digging for stones and treasure needn't have interfered with the more mundane labor that would have helped the family meet its obligation. The basic problem was that none of the remaining men in the family possessed much economic drive.[39]

In October 1825, workers completed the Erie Canal. Palmyra's future and that of the surrounding region seemed boundless. By contrast, the Smith family's far more limited ambitions had collided with stark financial realities. After a decade in Palmyra, the Smiths had as much wealth as they had brought from Vermont: nothing.

Joseph Jr., who turned twenty in December 1825, now took center stage in the family. He didn't have Alvin's more ordinary industry, but Joseph's unusual talents shaped a more extraordinary path.

CHAPTER THREE

Plates (1825–1827)

I N THE MIDST OF his family's financial crisis, Joseph landed a job as a treasure hunter. Josiah Stowell, a prosperous Chenango County farmer, was trying to find a long-lost Spanish silver mine just south of the New York–Pennsylvania border. The odds were long, as there had never been a Spanish silver mine in the region. Stowell wasn't alone in his fervor, though. Other men in the area had employed a "peeper," a seeress named Odle, who hadn't found the mine. That didn't discourage Stowell. Rather than abandon the quest, he sought a better peeper.[1]

Through a son who lived in Manchester, New York, Stowell heard that Joseph Smith Jr. had the "skill of telling where hidden treasures in the earth were by means of looking through a certain stone." During a visit to the area, Stowell met Joseph, who demonstrated his talent. In later courtroom testimony, Joseph stated that by looking into his stone, he could tell "where coined money was buried in Pennsylvania." Joseph was able to describe Stowell's house as well as other features of his property, a place he had never visited. Stowell was convinced of Joseph's gift and urged the young man to return to Chenango County with him. The pay was not princely. Joseph later commented that he received $14 a month as a "money digger," but Stowell also offered Joseph and his father shares in any potential quarry.[2]

Becoming a peeper-for-hire, or "glass-looker," carried risks. A 1788 New York State law classified "persons pretending to have skill . . . to discover where lost goods may be found" as "disorderly persons," alongside beggars, palm readers, and prostitutes. Violators faced the possibility of imprisonment. The legislators who enacted such laws believed that it was impossible for persons to tell fortunes, cast enchantments, or find buried treasures by peering into stones. Such practices were fraudulent and dangerous. "Magic was bad behavior," explains the historian Adam Jortner. "It ruined morals, encouraged mobs, and promoted panic." The Smiths may or may not have known about the law. Regardless, they needed money—the deadline for the remaining land payments was drawing close. Joseph took the job.[3]

In late October 1825, Joseph and his father headed southeast in Stowell's employ. They boarded with Isaac Hale, who lived near the site of the dig in Harmony, Pennsylvania. Hale and his wife Elizabeth had moved to the Susquehanna Valley from Vermont in the late 1780s. Isaac Hale was renowned as a hunter; he and his sons shot deer, elk, and other game, salted the meat, and sent it down the river to Philadelphia. They also cleared land and built houses for the wealthiest settlers in the region. Around 1810, the Hales moved into a frame house that Lucy Mack Smith described as a "mansion." The Hales probably boarded the treasure seekers in an older log house on their property. Joseph and his father, on the verge of losing their own home and land, were impressed with the Hales, who had achieved the prosperity that had eluded the Smiths.[4]

Isaac Hale signed his name as a witness to articles of agreement that laid out the terms of the money-digging operation. The three major shareholders were Josiah Stowell; his brother, Calvin Stowell; and William Hale, a relative of Isaac Hale. They would reap the greatest rewards should the quest succeed. Joseph Jr. and Joseph Sr. also signed the document, which promised them two-elevenths of any spoils.[5]

Josiah Stowell's sons recalled that Joseph used both of his seer stones as he tried to find the Spanish silver. Sometimes he held his white stone up to a candle or to the sunlight. On other occasions, following a method employed by some treasure hunters, he placed one of his stones in his hat, blocked out the light, and peered into it. Isaac Hale remembered that Joseph took them "near the place where he had stated an immense treasure would be found," but then faltered. "He said the enchantment was so powerful that he could not see," Hale explained. The company gave up after two or three weeks. Joseph and his father relocated to Stowell's farm in nearby Bainbridge, New York, where they worked for their board. It was a modest wage rather than the windfall the family needed.[6]

While Joseph and his father were away from Manchester, the man who had built their house bought their land. Back in February 1825, Russell

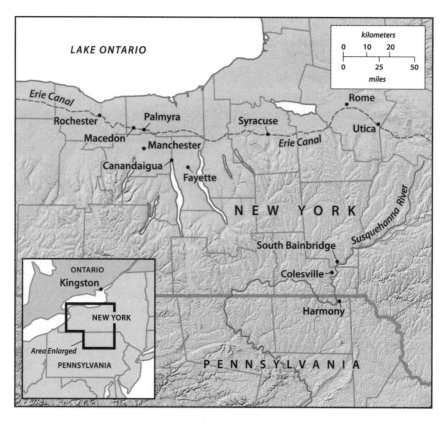

Joseph Smith's activities in New York and Pennsylvania.
(Map by John Hamer)

Stoddard had sued Joseph Smith Sr. for payment for the work he had
done for them. The elder Smith acknowledged the debt, but he lacked
the means to pay it. Stoddard offered to buy the house, but the Smiths
refused. With the deadline approaching and the Smiths more than a
hundred miles away, Stoddard devised a scheme to settle the debt and
enrich himself at the family's expense. Per Lucy Mack Smith, Stoddard
informed John Greenwood, the agent, that Joseph Smith Sr. and his son
had "run away" and alleged that Hyrum was destroying the farm's or-
chard and fences. Presuming that he would never get the promised payment from the Smiths, Greenwood sold the land to Stoddard, whose
men told the family to clear out immediately. "Damn you, help yourselves if you can," they sneered at the Smiths. It isn't clear whether Stoddard's purchase came before or after the Christmas Day deadline, but it

doesn't seem that the family had any immediate prospect of making the payments. It is odd that the two Josephs remained in Bainbridge for so long instead of returning home to face the crisis. Perhaps they could have persuaded Greenwood to grant them an extension.[7]

Lucy and Hyrum scrambled to save their farm. With the support of Gain Robinson, a Palmyra physician and friend of the family, they obtained testimonials to their good character. Hyrum then went to Canandaigua and complained to Greenwood about the injustice of Stoddard's actions. Greenwood summoned Stoddard and urged him to relinquish the deed. He agreed to do so only if the Smiths raised $1,000 within two days. "I now felt that all must go at one fell swoop if this last resort failed," wrote Lucy Mack Smith. She and her husband would be destitute in their old age.[8]

Joseph Jr. and his father finally returned to Manchester precisely during this two-day window. The Smiths now cast about for a financial savior. Joseph Sr. showed the farm to Lemuel Durfee Sr., an early Palmyra settler and a Quaker. He agreed to purchase the land and to allow the Smiths to remain on the property for a year. In return, Samuel Smith—Joseph's younger brother—would work for Durfee for six months. The Smiths again would be tenants rather than landowners, but they would keep what they had built, and perhaps Durfee would extend the arrangement beyond the first year. Joseph Sr. and Durfee reached Greenwood half an hour before his offer expired.

Secure in the knowledge that his parents and siblings could stay in their home, Joseph Jr. returned to Bainbridge. He spent most of the winter working on Josiah Stowell's farm, also continuing, with several local men, to dig for treasure. One of those men, Jonathan Thompson, testified that he accompanied Joseph on one such nighttime errand. Joseph looked into his stone and discerned the location of a buried chest. The party started to dig and then "struck upon something sounding like a board or plank." Joseph explained that two Indians had quarreled while burying the trunk. One had killed the other, who had then been buried as the chest's guardian. "On account of an enchantment," Thompson explained, "the trunk kept settling away from under them while digging." No matter how furiously they dug, the treasure remained out of reach.[9]

According to Thompson, Joseph at this point proposed a way to break the charm. Stowell went to his farm and returned with a fine lamb. The group slaughtered it, and Joseph walked in a circle around the dig site, sprinkling its blood "upon the ground, as a propitiation to the spirit." The sacrifice was in vain, as the men still couldn't recover the chest. Thompson may have embellished or made up the story in order to besmirch Joseph's reputation, though a Palmyra resident told a similar tale about another Joseph-directed treasure dig. For some Americans, the treasure quest and the practices associated with it smacked of witchcraft.[10]

Josiah Stowell's family members had grown alarmed that he was "squandering his property in the fruitless search for hidden treasures." Upon the complaint of Peter Bridgeman, Stowell's nephew, Joseph was brought before Justice of the Peace Albert Neely and charged with being "a disorderly person and an imposter." Justice Neely heard from several witnesses, including the defendant, whom he identified as "Joseph Smith the glass looker." Two of Stowell's sons complained about what they regarded as rank deception, but their father professed "the most implicit faith in the prisoner's skill." According to William D. Purple, a Bainbridge resident who took notes at the trial, Joseph exhibited his dark, egg-shaped stone. The verdict in the hearing remains unknown. One local man claimed that Joseph was "designedly allowed to escape" on account of his youth.[11]

Despite the trial, the months along the Susquehanna were fruitful for Joseph. Josiah Stowell believed in his gift, as did Joseph Knight Sr., a friend of Stowell with a farm in nearby Colesville, New York. Stowell and Knight would prove important supporters in the years ahead. Also, Joseph became acquainted with Emma Hale, the seventh of Isaac Hale's nine children. Eighteen months older than Joseph, Emma was tall, with black hair that she parted in the middle. Her life had been free from the grinding poverty that afflicted the Smiths, but she was accustomed to hard work. Emma could pilot a canoe on the Susquehanna, cure sausages, and make candles from tallow. Baptized in a Congregational church, she was now active in the Methodist "class" that met in local homes. Joseph and Emma quickly became smitten with each other.[12]

Isaac Hale was alarmed by his daughter's growing affection for Joseph. Hale had not opposed the treasure quest at first, but he certainly felt Emma deserved better than a failed "glass-looker" as her husband. When Joseph left the area after the trial, Hale hoped he had seen the last of him.

By the fall of 1826, however, Joseph was back, working on Joseph Knight's farm. He resumed his attentions to Emma, and the courtship quickly advanced to discussions about marriage. When Joseph asked

Isaac Hale for his consent, he was flatly refused. Emma's father regarded Joseph as "a stranger," and he disapproved of Joseph's "business."[13]

Joseph wasn't deterred. In mid-January 1827, Knight loaned Joseph a horse and a sleigh, and Emma went with her suitor to Josiah Stowell's property. "While I was absent from home," Isaac Hale complained, "[Joseph] carried off my daughter." Emma later stated that when she left her parents' home, she hadn't decided to marry Joseph. She simply wanted to see him. But Joseph "importuned" her to marry him, and Stowell urged her to agree. Emma never reflected at length on the unusual courtship or elopement, only that she had "preferr[ed] to marry him to any other man I knew." Why would Emma consider marriage to a man in trouble with the law? Stowell and Knight were respectable, and they believed in Joseph's treasure-seeking talent. So had Isaac Hale before his disillusionment. And so did Emma. On January 18, 1827, the couple was married by a Chenango County justice of the peace.[14]

Shortly after the marriage, Joseph and Emma returned to his parents' home. Emma gave her father six months to cool down, then wrote and asked to retrieve her belongings. The couple traveled to Harmony. According to Isaac Hale, Joseph stated that he had given up "glass-looking" and resolved to "work hard for a living." Willing to set aside their past differences, and willing to excuse the circumstances of the marriage, Hale encouraged the couple to live on his property. Instead of bringing Emma's things to Manchester, they went back to fetch Joseph's possessions.[15]

The past several years had been a rocky transition to adulthood for Joseph. He had not become an economic provider for the family in the wake of Alvin's death. Then his employment as a treasure-seeking seer under Josiah Stowell had ended in failure and arrest. Now, at the age of twenty-one, how would Joseph provide for Emma and their future children?

Regardless of what he had promised Isaac Hale, Joseph had no intention of becoming a humble farmer. He had seen his parents struggle for years. They had chopped down trees, planted crops, boiled maple sugar, and sold oil cloths. Their hard work had not paid off. Joseph believed that he had a gift. He could see things in his stone. He had not found any treasures, but he was not backing down from his claims. Instead, as would be customary for the rest of his life, he grew more audacious in the wake of failure.

The Hill Cumorah, 1907. (Photograph by George Edward Anderson.
Courtesy of Church History Library)

It had been almost four years since Joseph's initial vision of Moroni
and his trip to the hill. Joseph's excitement about the encounter and the
plates had been palpable at first. Lucy remembered that as the family sat
together at night, "Joseph would give us some of the most amusing recitals which could be imagined. He would describe the ancient inhabitants
of this continent, their dress, their manner of travelling . . . their religious
worship—as particularly as though he had spent his life with them." Yet
it is not clear how much the angel and the plates had occupied Joseph's
attention and imagination in the intervening years. When looking
back on his first encounter with Joseph, Josiah Stowell did not mention
the plates, and they do not seem to have been a key part of Joseph's reputation as a seer.[16]

Each September, though, Joseph had gone to the hill. In 1824, he went
by himself because of Alvin's death. According to Willard Chase, the angel
told Joseph to bring someone with him the next year. Joseph decided to
take Samuel T. Lawrence, another local seer and treasure hunter. In Lawrence's company, Joseph looked into his stone and saw a "pair of spectacles"
with the plates. Again, though, he couldn't obtain the plates. Joseph decided that Lawrence "was not the right man," though they remained
friends and partners. Lawrence even covered the cost of one of Joseph's
trips to Pennsylvania.[17]

By the time Joseph and Emma returned from Harmony in late summer 1827, Joseph's focus had shifted definitively from the Susquehanna

silver mine to the Manchester hillside. He had told Josiah Stowell and Joseph Knight Sr. about the golden plates. Catching Joseph's excitement, the two men made plans to visit the Smiths.

One evening that September, Joseph came home several hours late from an errand to Manchester village. It was well after dark. Joseph Sr. asked his son for an explanation. "I have had the severest chastisement that I ever had in my life," he replied. The elder Joseph was upset that someone had detained and upbraided his son, but Joseph Jr. was just working some suspense and mystery into his story. The chastisement had come from Moroni, who told Joseph that he had been "negligent." It was time for him to do what God had commanded. "I know what course I am to pursue and all will be well," Joseph reassured his father. As the annual angelic appointment drew near, could he finally bring a treasure out of the earth?[18]

On September 20, Stowell and Knight arrived. Other men in the area were also attuned to Joseph's activities. Samuel Lawrence and Willard Chase saw themselves as Joseph's partners, entitled to a share of whatever he found. Joseph feared that they and other local treasure hunters would attempt to steal the plates from him. On the evening of September 21, Joseph sent his father to conduct surveillance at Sam Lawrence's house. If there were any signs that Lawrence intended to make trouble, Joseph Sr. should deliver a warning. Joseph Jr. would "thrash the stumps with [Lawrence]" if he found him at the hill. Joseph Sr. returned with a report that all was quiet.[19]

At midnight, Joseph and Emma took Joseph Knight's carriage and rode to the hillside. Joseph never said very much about what transpired, other than that he obtained what he had long sought. "[The] heavenly messenger delivered them up to me," Joseph recounted, and the angel warned him to guard them carefully. Along with the plates, Joseph reported finding "two stones in silver bows and these stones fastened to a breastplate." He at first called them "spectacles" and later "Urim and Thummim." The latter phrase comes from the Bible. The Urim and Thummim were objects placed in Aaron's breastplate, later used as a means to determine an individual's guilt or innocence. According to Lucy, Joseph hid the plates in a decaying birch log several miles from the Smith farm. He kept the "spectacles" with him.[20]

Joseph and Emma returned after sunrise the next morning and came into the house for breakfast. "Joseph called me into the other room," Joseph

Knight recalled. "He set his foot on the bed and leaned his head on his hand and says, 'Well I am disappointed.' " Joseph was playing games again. Knight presumed that the quest had failed and began to console his young friend.

Then the seer sprang his surprise. "It is ten times better than I expected," Joseph announced. He told Knight that the plates "appear to be gold." The spectacles, however, produced the most excitement at first. Joseph invited his mother to examine them, having covered them with a silk handkerchief. Lucy described what she felt as "two smooth three-cornered diamonds ... set in silver bows." The white stone from the Chase well had exceeded the power of Joseph's first seer stone. Now, Joseph reported that these stones far surpassed the white stone. "I can see anything," Joseph asserted. "They are marvelous."[21]

As rumors of Joseph's success spread, he and his family worried about would-be thieves. Either sometime before or shortly after his trip to the hillside, he went to Willard Chase, a cabinetmaker, and asked him to build a chest. Accounts are conflicting, but Lucy recalled that Chase accepted as payment "half money and half produce." The family, as usual, had no money. Joseph learned that a widow in nearby Macedon needed a hired hand to work on a well. It was a mundane job amid the recent excitement, but Joseph left to try to earn the money he needed for the chest.[22]

While Joseph was away, neighbors stopped by the Smith house asking to see the plates. Joseph's parents learned that Chase and Lawrence had recruited a "conjurer" from sixty miles away to "divine the place where the record was deposited by magic art." The conjurer was Luman Walters, an out-of-town seer, "magician," and "fortune teller" who had participated in several Palmyra-area digs. Joseph Sr. went back to spy at Lawrence's house and overheard the group. "We will have the plates in spite of Joe Smith or all the devils in hell," Walters shouted.[23]

An alarmed Joseph Sr. persuaded Emma that his son needed to return immediately to protect the plates, which were still hidden in the woods. Soon Emma was off to Macedon, riding a stray horse that had wandered onto the Smith farm. The widow who had hired Joseph loaned him a mount, and the couple sped back home.

Next came what Joseph's family and friends described as a harrowing errand. Joseph went to the hiding place on foot and wrapped the plates in a linen shirt. Fearing that his rivals were lying in wait to ambush him, Joseph decided it would be safer to return to the house through the woods rather than along the road. His enemies had spotted him, however. According to Lucy's account, three men attacked him on the way, each striking him with a gun. Joseph escaped by returning their blows with his fists. The third attack left him with a dislocated thumb.

Out of breath and in pain, Joseph reached the house and passed the plates through a window to Josiah Stowell and his mother. Joseph then put them in a box and nailed it shut. The Smiths removed a portion of their hearth, buried the plates, and relaid it.

The struggle was only beginning. Joseph Knight recounted that a "great rodsman" who came to the house "took out his rods and held them up and they pointed down to the hearth." After he left, the Smiths decided that Joseph Sr.'s cooper shop would be a better hiding place. They removed the plates from the box, wrapped them in cloths, and hid them amid flax in the shop's loft. Thinking to deceive their enemies, they also nailed the empty box shut again and buried it in the floor. According to Lucy, Sally Chase—Willard Chase's sister— divined the rough location of the plates by looking into her "green glass." On her advice men ransacked the shop, found the box, and split it to pieces—but they didn't look in the loft. Joseph and his family kept one step ahead.[24]

What was Joseph hiding in boxes, hearths, and lofts? When he later prepared a history of his life, Joseph described what he had obtained as "plates which had the appearance of gold." "Not quite so thick as common tin," they were "bound together in a volume, as the leaves of a book with three rings running through the whole." The entirety was close to six inches thick, and "a part . . . was sealed," unable to be examined. Joseph stated elsewhere that characters engraved on the plates were to be read from right to left, in the manner of Hebrew.[25]

Emma claimed to have felt the plates and seen their outline through a tablecloth. "They seemed to be pliable like thick paper," she explained half a century later, "and would rustle with a metallic sound when the edges were moved by the thumb." Josiah Stowell testified in court that he had seen a "corner" of the plates, which "resembled a stone of greenish caste." Other men stated that they experienced visions of the plates, but Joseph never let anyone examine them in an ordinary way.[26]

From the start, Joseph's claims generated fervent belief from those closest to him and skepticism from nearly everyone else. "Either something fishy was going on," observes Richard Bushman, "or Joseph did have a visitor from heaven."[27] Did Joseph actually have golden plates?

Did he at least have something that he considered to be an ancient record? Or did Joseph deceive his family and friends? In short, was Joseph Smith a prophet or a pretender?

The people closest to Joseph Smith—his wife, his parents, his siblings, and a few friends—all believed him. At the same time, because he did not show his family and friends the plates, there aren't witnesses in the ordinary sense of the term. But if Joseph didn't have golden plates, what did he have? Joseph's detractors, as well as recent scholars, have proposed alternative explanations. Sand and rocks or bricks? Printing plates?[28] Tin plates that Joseph fashioned himself?[29] There isn't sufficient evidence to support any of these speculations, but the absence of such evidence does not buttress Joseph's own assertions.

Along with an acknowledgment of the scanty evidence for this critical episode in Joseph Smith's life, readers deserve an author's best sense of what transpired. In this case, it is that Joseph did not have golden plates. When someone refuses to show a hidden, valuable object to others, the simplest explanation is that he does not possess it. There are other factors that point to this conclusion as well. As indicated in his conversations about the plates with his father and Joseph Knight, Joseph Smith was a playful young man who enjoyed jesting with others. He and his family were desperate for money, and Joseph was eager to prove his bona fides as a treasure hunter after repeated disappointments. He had sufficient motivation to engage in a bit of subterfuge.

Then there is the published Book of Mormon, which Joseph claimed was a translation of the engravings on the plates. Archaeology, DNA analysis of Indigenous Americans, and the relationship between the Book of Mormon and the Bible all point to the Book of Mormon as a nineteenth-century creation.

Whether Joseph fashioned plates or put some other object in the box, the act was more audacious than mendacious. It wasn't just an angelic vision. It wasn't even just engravings on a buried stone or on a scrap of metal. Joseph staked his reputation on a physical object, on a treasure even more remarkable than a lost Spanish silver mine. It was a remarkably bold gambit.[30]

And it worked. What Joseph related convinced a wide array of individuals, including family, friends, and hostile competitors. The plates were real to them.[31] The young seer knew he now had to produce something tangible. He insisted that the plates would be valuable not for their precious metal, but for their precious message.

CHAPTER FOUR

Lost in Translation (1827–1828)

A s of mid-october 1827, Joseph claimed to possess an astounding treasure. At the same time, he was as poor as ever. That month, he went to work for Peter Ingersoll, whose land lay to the north of the Smith farm, in return for some flour. The Smiths were still just scraping by. After the initial furor surrounding the plates had subsided, Joseph Knight recalled, Joseph "now began to be anxious to get them translated." For that task, Joseph sought a benefactor, someone whose support would give him the time and resources he needed to publish the record.[1]

He found one in Martin Harris, a prosperous Palmyra farmer. For many years, Harris had worked long days, had increased his landholdings, and had held a variety of local offices. His wealth separated him from the Smiths, but when it came to religion, Harris was a kindred spirit. "He was a religious monomaniac," commented Pomeroy Tucker, the local newspaperman, "reading the Scriptures intently, and could probably repeat from memory nearly every text of the Bible." Like several of the Smiths, Harris was a seeker without a church. And a visionary. According to Palmyra resident Lorenzo Saunders, Harris was "a great man for seeing spooks." Such religious quirks weren't unusual in the region, and Harris's neighbors regarded him as an honest and industrious man.[2]

Behind Martin Harris's outward probity, his household was fractured. Twenty years earlier, Harris had married his first cousin, Lucy Harris. Lorenzo Saunders described Lucy Harris as combative and "high

41

Martin Harris, ca. 1870. (Courtesy of Church History Library)

on self-esteem . . . a hard piece to live with." Martin Harris was an even harder piece. Saunders and other neighbors confirmed Lucy Harris's allegation that her husband beat her. She recalled that after one vicious assault, "the marks of his beating me . . . remained more than two weeks." For his part, Martin Harris wanted to escape the tumult. He had granted his wife a certain amount of financial independence by deeding her a piece of property and by giving her a "private purse," and he was preparing to leave his farm in the care of a hired hand and spend a year traveling. Before Martin Harris departed, however, he heard rumors of Joseph Smith's "golden Bible."[3]

Martin Harris had been acquainted with the Smiths for several years. Joseph had worked on Harris's farm, hoeing corn for 50 cents a day. It wasn't all work. Even though Harris was more than twenty years older than Joseph, the two men wrestled together for sport. Joseph also demonstrated his gift of spiritual sight. On one visit to the Smith house, Harris lost a pin with which he had been picking his teeth. No one could find it. "Take your stone," Harris requested. Joseph took one of his seer stones, placed it in his "old white hat—and placed his face in the hat." Then, without looking, Joseph reached out his hand and found the missing pin.[4]

In the fall of 1827, Joseph grasped that Martin Harris was almost singularly well positioned to support his translation project. Harris had money, was ready for a new direction, and already believed in Joseph's seeric gifts. When it came to visions and buried treasures, Lucy Harris was more skeptical than her husband, but not closed to the possibility. They decided to call on the Smiths but, in keeping with the state of their marriage, they went separately.

By the time of their visits, Joseph was keeping the supposed plates in what Martin Harris termed an "old Ontario glass-box," typically used to hold small windowpanes. When Lucy Harris arrived, she told Joseph that if he could show her that he really had gold plates, she would give him the money he needed to translate them. Joseph responded that God had instructed him not to reveal the plates to anyone, and he added that he preferred to deal "with men rather than their wives." She was offended, but, upon her request, Joseph looked into her eyes and assured her that he had indeed found an ancient record. He allowed her to lift the box. According to Lucy Mack Smith, that night Lucy Harris encountered a "personage" in a dream who showed her the plates. She gave Joseph $28.[5]

Martin Harris was next. Joseph told him that he had found the plates by "looking in the stone found in the well of Mason Chase," brother of Willard Chase. He also shared that the angel had told him that if he looked in the "spectacles," he would "show him the man that would assist him." He had seen Harris. Joseph's visitor was flattered but, like his wife, asked for proof. Joseph invited Martin to "heft" the box. Even without looking inside, Harris concluded that it contained more metal of any sort than Joseph could have afforded. He too went home seeking spiritual confirmation. He prayed and "covenanted" to support the work if God would reveal its truth. "He showed this to me," Harris stated, "by the still small voice spoken in the soul." Harris soon gave Joseph a bag of silver worth $50. The seer had his benefactor.[6]

After their reconciliation with Isaac Hale, Joseph and Emma had been planning to move back to Harmony, Pennsylvania. If they stayed in the area around Manchester and Palmyra, they could live with Joseph's parents, but odd jobs would never earn Joseph enough to establish his own household. Isaac Hale had offered to settle them in a home and farm near his own residence. Emma was pregnant with their first child, feeling "unwell," and she wanted to be with her parents. Given the conflicts with Willard Chase and Samuel Lawrence, it also was safer for Joseph to pursue his translation project elsewhere. At the end of October, Emma's brother Alva arrived in Manchester with a horse-drawn wagon to move the couple back to the Susquehanna.[7]

Joseph feared that enemies would ambush him as he left Manchester, so he took precautions. He spread rumors of his planned departure date, then left at night two days earlier. As for the plates, the box was stashed in a barrel, which was then filled with beans and nailed shut.[8]

Joseph, Emma, and her brother trudged east and south on wet and muddy roads, reaching Harmony in early December.[9] The joy her parents felt at Emma's return was dissipated by what her husband had stashed among the beans. Joseph had promised Isaac Hale that he had abandoned "glass-looking." Now he showed up with what he claimed were golden plates and stones through which he could see anything.

Even worse, Joseph refused his father-in-law's request to see the plates, though he encouraged him to pick up the box and feel its weight. Hale was underwhelmed. "[I] informed him," Hale stated a few years later, "that if there was anything in my house ... which I could not be allowed to see, he must take it away." Joseph hid his secret objects in the woods.[10]

The house Hale intended for Joseph and Emma was occupied by other members of her family, so they and Emma's parents lived under the same roof for a few months. Earning somewhere between 25 and 50 cents for a day's work, Joseph hauled hay and wood, plowed fields, chopped wheat, and husked corn. He and Emma then moved into a small frame house on thirteen acres of land that Isaac Hale offered to sell them on favorable terms. Over the summer and into the fall, Joseph planted and harvested buckwheat, dug a well, and tended to the cows, pigs, and oxen.[11]

Despite his father-in-law's hopes, Joseph still had no aspirations to become a respectable farmer. He had come to Harmony to produce his translation, and he got started as time permitted. As a first step, Joseph made drawings or rubbings of some of the characters, including what he identified as an "Egyptian alphabet." (The Book of Mormon identifies the language on the plates as "reformed Egyptian.") Emma then made additional copies from Joseph's drawings. Some of these copies survive; the characters on them do not closely resemble any known ancient language.[12]

In February 1828, Martin arrived in Harmony for a visit. "The Lord had shown him [Harris]," wrote Joseph in his earliest history, "that he must go to New York City with some of the characters."[13] While Joseph may have hoped that a learned man would confirm his gift, Harris had a clear motivation for this mission. He was considering financing the translation's publication. He wanted an impartial authority to confirm what the "still small voice" had told him.

Harris took a copy of the characters and set off to find someone who could identify them. He met with Samuel Mitchill, vice president of Rutgers Medical College in New York. Through a storied career as a diplomat and politician, Mitchill had developed a keen interest in questions surrounding the origins and languages of the Native peoples of the Americas. In addition to classical Greek and Latin, he had studied Hebrew and dabbled with Chinese. Like many Americans, Mitchill was thrilled that Jean-François Champollion had used the Rosetta Stone to begin deciphering Egyptian characters. At the time, though, neither Mitchill nor any other American could read Egyptian hieroglyphics. James Arlington Bennet, a New York City writer and editor, reported that Mitchill compared the engravings "with the hieroglyphics discovered by Champollion in Europe, and set them down as a language of a people formerly in existence in the East, but now no more." If Bennet's report is accurate, Harris must have been thrilled with Mitchill's speculation.[14]

Mitchill referred Harris to Charles Anthon, a promising young classicist at Columbia College. The physically imposing Anthon was a strict disciplinarian who did not suffer fools in his students. "Short visits make long friends," read an inscription above the mantelpiece in Anthon's study.[15]

Harris's visit was short but did not produce a friendship. The two men later provided diametrically opposed accounts of their meeting. According to Harris, Anthon provided a certificate that the characters were "Egyptian, Chaldean, Assyrian, and Arabic." After Harris explained that the characters were from golden plates that a young man had received from an angel, an angry Anthon took the certificate back and ripped it in pieces. He offered to translate the plates if Harris would bring them.

Book of Mormon "Caractors," transcribed by John Whitmer, ca. 1829–1831.
(Courtesy of Church History Library)

When Harris said he could not and that a portion of the plates was "sealed," Anthon dismissed him, saying "I cannot read a sealed book."[16]

Joseph understood Anthon's response as the fulfillment of a passage in the biblical Book of Isaiah, in which a "learned" man states that he cannot read a "sealed" book. God then delivers the book to an unlearned man and declares that he will perform "a marvelous work and a wonder." Joseph concluded that he was the unlearned man who could read through divinely prepared "spectacles" what "wise men" like Charles Anthon could not decipher.[17]

Anthon told a very different story about his interaction with Martin Harris. When Harris first appeared with his scrap of paper, Anthon presumed that it was a hoax, that Harris was attempting to embarrass him by asking him to identify and translate gibberish. Anthon looked at Harris's paper, which contained "Greek and Hebrew letters, crosses and flourishes, Roman letters inverted or placed sideways." It ended with a decorated circle "evidently copied after the Mexican calendar given by [Alexander von] Humboldt." Then Harris told Anthon about the golden plates and the spectacles and explained that he had come as a "last precautionary step" before financing the publication of Joseph's translation. Anthon warned Harris to "beware of rogues," but he refused to provide an opinion in writing.[18]

Regardless of the exact exchange between Anthon and Harris, the latter returned to Palmyra with strengthened faith. Martin Harris also returned to a livid Lucy Harris. He had left Palmyra without informing his wife about his plans, and now he was ready to give his resources—

their resources—to someone she increasingly viewed as a charlatan. According to Lucy Mack Smith, Lucy Harris refused to share a bedroom with her husband. She also asked her daughter's suitor to purloin Martin Harris's copy of the characters and make a transcription, which she showed to neighbors as evidence of Joseph Smith's imposture and her husband's credulity.[19]

Lucy Harris insisted on accompanying her husband on what was expected to be an extended stay with Joseph. The couple endured each other's company on the way to Harmony, and then an awkward, rancorous visit ensued. Lucy Harris announced that she would not leave until Joseph showed her the plates. According to Lucy Mack Smith's secondhand report, she then ransacked the house and searched its perimeter. Her resolve faltered when she encountered a "tremendous great black snake," perhaps understood as a guardian spirit or as a manifestation of Satan. Shaken, she took lodgings elsewhere and spent the next two weeks telling anyone who would listen that Joseph was a "grand imposter" who intended to defraud her husband. Martin Harris accompanied his wife to Palmyra, then traveled back to Harmony.[20]

Joseph was ready to begin the translation in earnest. He already had been dictating some text to Emma, and Harris now became his scribe. Although accounts differ in details, they agree that Joseph's basic method was the same he had used when in Josiah Stowell's employ. Emma recounted that Joseph sat "with his face buried in the hat, with the stone in it." Some sources emphasize the "spectacles" and refer to them as "Urim and Thummim," but Joseph at least mostly used the white seer stone he had found with Willard Chase. The Book of Mormon refers to "a stone, which shall shine forth in darkness unto light." The passage identifies "Gazelem" as the name of the stone, or perhaps of the servant who would use it. Later generations of Mormons used the name Gazelem both for Joseph's white stone and for Joseph himself.[21]

When he looked into his stone, Joseph now saw words rather than lost objects or buried treasures. "By the aid of the seer stone," Harris explained, "sentences would appear and were read by the prophet." Harris wrote the words down and then read them back to Joseph. If Joseph was not satisfied, they would make a second attempt. If Harris had gotten it correct, Joseph would say, "Written," and then a new sentence would appear.[22]

What about the plates? Emma later recounted that they "often lay on the table" covered only by a linen tablecloth.[23] The mysterious plates, though, were not integral to the translation. They at most served as an object of inspiration. What Joseph produced was not a "translation" in any ordinary sense of the word. He did not render writing from one language into another. It was a revelatory rather than a scholarly effort.

Joseph was reticent about the translation process. When his brother Hyrum asked him to relate the story to an audience, Joseph answered that God did not intend for him "to tell the world all the particulars of the coming forth of the Book of Mormon." When the book was published, Joseph announced sparsely that he had "translated, by the gift and power of God."[24]

As the spring of 1828 progressed, Joseph kept dictating, and Harris kept writing. By June, Harris had recorded 116 pages of what Joseph termed the "Book of Lehi." Harris wanted to show and read it to his family and friends in Palmyra in order to "convince them of the truth." Joseph wavered. The manuscript represented two months' work, and there was no copy. On the other hand, Harris was Joseph's potential source of funding for the book's publication. Joseph "inquired of the Lord," probably by using his seer stone. The answer was no. Harris asked again. On the third such inquiry, Harris received permission but had to promise to show the manuscript to only a few close family members.[25]

Harris's departure with the pages ushered in a dark season. On June 15, Emma gave birth to a son who died soon after the delivery. Sophia Lewis, cousin by marriage to Emma, stated a few years later that she had been present at the birth and that the baby was "very much deformed." Lewis probably made her statement out of malice, as it appeared in a collection of affidavits critical of Joseph Smith. As they had for centuries, birth defects in early nineteenth-century America evoked the possibility that God was punishing parents for their transgressions. Lewis also remembered that Joseph had expected his first child to be a boy and to play a special role in his work with the golden plates. A family Bible records the infant's name as Alvin, though the child's gravestone was nameless. Joseph may well have planned to name his first son after his beloved late brother, and he may have hoped that his son could assume the role Alvin would have played had illness not cut short his life.[26] Joseph buried the baby in a graveyard within sight of the couple's cabin. Emma was weak after the birth, and the family worried that she might follow her baby to the grave.

Joseph, meanwhile, became more and more anxious about the manuscript Martin Harris had taken to Palmyra. After two weeks, Emma had

Gravestone of "an infant son of Joseph and Emma Smith," June 15, 1829.
(Courtesy of Church History Library)

regained some strength, so he left her in the care of her parents and traveled to his parents' home. Joseph struggled to sleep during the journey.
He was still reeling from his infant son's death, and he worried about
both Emma's health and his translation. By the time Joseph approached
Manchester, he was so exhausted that he could not walk the last several
miles without the assistance of a stranger.

His anxiety about the manuscript was warranted. According to Lucy
Mack Smith, Martin Harris had shown the manuscript to his wife, who,

surprisingly, seemed pleased with it. They kept it locked in her bureau. Then, after he showed it to the several individuals included in the promises he had made to Joseph, the couple set off to visit one of her relatives. Lucy Harris remained with her family when Martin returned to Palmyra. Left to his own devices, Martin Harris set caution aside. A visitor wished to see the manuscript, and he obliged. Harris picked the lock, damaging his wife's bureau in the process. Thereafter, Harris kept the manuscript in his own set of drawers and showed it to anyone who wished to see it. Lucy Harris was irate upon her return when she discovered her mangled bureau.[27]

When Joseph reached the Smith farm, he immediately sent for his scribe. It was only then that Martin Harris realized that the manuscript was missing. "It is gone," he told Joseph, "and I know not where." The news crushed Joseph, and he feared that it would kill Emma. "All is lost," Joseph cried. "What shall I do? I have sinned." Lucy Mack Smith remembered her son pacing while "weeping and grieving like a tender infant." Joseph refused to eat all day until sunset, and he left for Harmony the next morning.[28]

A number of sources suggest that Lucy Harris either burned the manuscript or stole it, perhaps with the intention of exposing Joseph as a fraud if he failed to dictate the same material verbatim. At first, Martin Harris was sure of her guilt. According to one local informant, he beat her "with a rod." Lucy Harris continued to profess her innocence, and in later years, Martin Harris claimed to believe her, suggesting that an angel, perhaps the one who had given the plates to Joseph, had taken the pages.[29]

Regardless of who lost it, took it, or burned it, Joseph returned to his Harmony home consumed by a sense of failure. In fact, Joseph recalled that prior to his trip to Palmyra, the spectacles had been taken from him because he had "wearied the Lord" with his repeated intercessions on behalf of Martin Harris. According to Lucy Mack Smith, the angel did take the plates, but suggested that if Joseph repented, he might receive them back on the anniversary date of September 22.[30]

Meanwhile, in the midst of his despair, Joseph produced the first of many texts that he and his followers came to call "commandments" or "revelations." The text contained a mixture of chastisement, warning, and instruction, and it provides a window into Joseph's self-understanding. "Thou art Joseph," it reminded him. "And thou wast chosen to do the work of the Lord." He had sinned by ignoring the "counsel" of his "directors," probably a reference to the spectacles or seer stones. If he continued to transgress, he would "be delivered up and become as other men and have no more gift." But if he repented, he would "again be called to the work." That work was to bring forth knowledge of ancient peoples with what sounded like Old Testament names: Nephites, Jacobites, Josephites, Ishmaelites, and Lamanites. The last people, the Lamanites, had "been suffered to destroy their brethren." The purpose of the history was to convert the descendants of the Lamanites—the Native peoples of the Americas—"to the knowledge of their fathers ... that they may believe the Gospel and rely upon the merits of Jesus Christ." The Indians would become Christians, as their ancestors had been.[31]

The speaker in the text refers to "my people the Nephites," seemingly identifying himself as one of them. So the revelation may have resulted from yet another encounter with Moroni. The temporary loss of the plates was akin to Joseph's initial failure to obtain them, as was the promise that they would be delivered to him again. As his confidence in his ability to bring forth his message waned and waxed, plates and spectacles disappeared and reappeared. Joseph was still finding his way.[32]

As Joseph Knight recalled, Joseph was "poor and [had] not means to live but work." Joseph slaughtered pigs to prepare meat for the winter, and he brought in a small harvest of buckwheat and corn. He also hired out, chopping wood for other men and plowing their fields.[33]

Despite these exertions, Joseph ended 1828 in debt and in need, and he and Emma received no succor from the Hales or Lewises. He visited Joseph Knight and asked for help. Against the wishes of his own wife, Knight gave Joseph $3, some food and other supplies, and a pair of shoes. It was a bleak winter.[34]

A stretch of melancholy was not uncommon in Joseph's life. He had passed through similar seasons after the intensity of his earlier visions and after his brother Alvin's death. Joseph always emerged from these periods of doubt with renewed audacity. The manuscript's loss had knocked him on his heels, but as the months passed, he readied himself for another attempt.

CHAPTER FIVE

Witnesses (1829)

A s OF EARLY 1829, Joseph Smith was a decidedly unsuccessful glass-looker and seer. He claimed to have found one treasure, which he refused to show anyone. His most fervent follower had lost his book manuscript. Moreover, his earthly affairs were a mess. Joseph was in debt, and his wife's father despised him. Isaac Hale demanded that Joseph pay him for the land and house he had provided. Otherwise, Hale threatened, Joseph and Emma could clear out.[1]

Several men buoyed Joseph's spirits and finances through the winter. Joseph's father and his brother Samuel came to visit in January. On their way to Harmony, they stopped at the Colesville, New York, home of Joseph Knight Sr., who gave Joseph Sr. a little money so that Joseph Jr. could "buy paper to translate." The gift helped Joseph resume translating on a limited basis, with Emma and Samuel Smith serving as scribes.[2]

During his family's stay in Harmony, Joseph presented his father with a revelation. Quoting biblical passages, it declared that "a marvelous work is about to come among the children of men," and it informed Joseph Sr. that he was "called to the work." For many years, the Smith family had been fractured by religion. While Lucy Mack Smith had attended Methodist meetings and then joined Palmyra's Presbyterians, Joseph Sr. had stood aloof. By 1828, Lucy had stopped attending Presbyterian worship. Joseph Jr.'s parents and siblings increasingly accepted his religious leadership.[3]

Joseph produced another revelation during a March 1829 visit by Martin Harris, whose faith was bent but not broken. Harris had held

Joseph's box. When he had asked God whether Joseph was telling the truth, he had received a positive answer. Then he had spent money and months assisting Joseph in the spring of 1828, but that partnership had ended in the manuscript debacle. Couldn't Joseph finally show him the plates and resolve his doubts?

"I the Lord am God," began the revelation. Joseph dictated the text in the voice of Jesus Christ, who suggested that he would permit "three witnesses" to see the plates so that they would "know of a surety." If Harris humbled himself and confessed his past mistakes, he would become one of those favored three. If not, he would be "condemned." As for Joseph, he had been given "a gift to translate the book," but after translating a few more pages, he should "stop and stand still" until the Savior provided the "means" for him to accomplish the work. If Joseph ignored this directive, he would "have no more gift" and lose everything that God had given him. Harris returned to Palmyra without seeing the plates, but the promise satisfied him for the time being.[4]

The early 1829 revelations, especially the message to Martin Harris, signaled a shift in Joseph's authority. Prior to this point, Joseph's actions and leadership had been rooted in his visions. Heavenly beings visited him and revealed things to him. As had been the case throughout most of Christian history, it was controversial for a man to claim that God, Jesus, or angels spoke to him. Now, though, Joseph went a step further. He claimed that Jesus Christ spoke *through* him. He was Christ's oracle. For many of Joseph's future followers, the fact that Joseph brought forth the word of the Lord, that he could inquire of the Lord and receive an answer, was part and parcel of what it meant for him to be a prophet.

The "means" to continue the translation arrived in the form of Oliver Cowdery. The slender, angular, dark-haired Cowdery was one year younger than Joseph. Like the Smiths, the Cowdery family had emigrated from Vermont to western New York, where, in the fall of 1828, Oliver Cowdery had secured a teaching position in Manchester. He boarded with the Smiths, with whom he quickly formed a close bond. Their talk about the golden plates piqued his curiosity.

Cowdery was inclined toward belief in the miraculous. He was a rodsman, like Joseph Smith Sr. It isn't clear whether Cowdery used his gift for digging wells or searching for buried treasure, but he also understood his rod as a conduit for revelation. Through it, God would answer questions and reveal mysteries.

Oliver Cowdery, late 1840s. (Courtesy of Church History Library)

When Cowdery heard about Joseph's fitful attempts at translation, he concluded that he should become his scribe. Indeed, he grew consumed with the idea, saying that it was "working in my very bones insomuch that I cannot for a moment get rid of it." As Martin Harris had done, Cowdery prayed about it, and he saw "the plates in a vision." Once the school year ended, Cowdery hastened to Harmony.[5]

Cowdery's departure came at a difficult time for the Smith family. For three years, Lemuel Durfee had allowed the Smiths to remain in their home, but he now wanted the property for his daughter and her husband. His decision meant the Smiths had to leave their frame house and move back into the log cabin, which had become the home of Hyrum Smith after his 1826 marriage to Jerusha Barden. Lucy Mack Smith found it deeply sorrowful to leave a home connected with her late son Alvin, and she blamed Durfee for depriving her and Joseph Sr. of their comfort. There were now nearly a dozen Smiths jammed into the old cabin, so Lucy Mack Smith encouraged Cowdery to find somewhere else to board. That he wanted to serve as her son's scribe was ideal.[6]

The schoolteacher was a godsend for Joseph Jr. On April 5, the day of Cowdery's arrival, the two conversed late into the night. Cowdery then helped Joseph get his financial affairs in order. He drafted an agreement in which Isaac Hale sold to Joseph the land and house that he and Emma had occupied for the past year. Cowdery had just received his teacher's salary and used it for the initial payment on the house. A decade later, he stated that he gave "the last cent of my honest earnings to save him from being turned into the streets."[7]

The two men began working on the translation, beginning several months of what Cowdery termed "days never to be forgotten." Cowdery later told a prospective convert that Joseph "put his face into a hat and the interpretation then flowed into his mind." Cowdery wrote down the words as Joseph spoke. One thing had changed since the earlier translation efforts, however. At least some of the time during the previous year, Joseph had kept the plates nearby while he dictated. Now the plates were entirely immaterial to the process.[8]

The partnership raised a key question in Cowdery's mind. Why couldn't he do the same thing Joseph did? After all, as one of Joseph's revelations reminded him, Cowdery had the "spirit of revelation" and "the gift of working with the sprout," or rod. "Therefore," Jesus Christ told him through Joseph, "whatsoever ye shall ask [God] to tell you by that means that will he grant unto you." At first, Joseph encouraged his new scribe. "I grant unto you a gift if you desire of me," Jesus announced, "to translate even as my servant Joseph." The Christian Savior added that there were many "ancient records which have been hid up," not only the plates that Joseph had received from the angel.[9]

Cowdery gave it a try, presumably with his rod as a conduit. It is unclear whether he attempted to produce a portion of the Book of Mormon, or whether he sought to bring forth another text. Regardless, Cowdery faltered. In response, Joseph dictated another revelation that both chastised and consoled his scribe. Cowdery's approach had been wrong. He had expected God to simply reveal the words to him. Instead, the right method was to "study it out in your mind" and then ask God for spiritual confirmation. In the revelation, Christ told Cowdery to forget about translating for the time being.[10]

Joseph wanted others to share in the spiritual gifts he enjoyed. They should have visions and revelations of their own—as long as they didn't supersede his. His role was preeminent. Joseph was the seer and translator. Cowdery was his scribe.

The resumption of the translation forced Joseph to confront a thorny question. If someone, such as Lucy Harris, had the missing manuscript, it could be compared with his second effort. If he didn't produce the same text twice, it would sow doubts about his prophetic gifts and the existence of the plates. The matter caused Joseph considerable anxiety. When he and Cowdery had begun working together, Joseph had sidestepped the problem by picking up where he had left off with Harris. They had worked rapidly, and Joseph now wondered what he should do about the earlier material.

Yet another revelation provided a solution. In it, Jesus Christ declared that Joseph should not try to replicate what he had previously translated. The good news, the Lord continued, was that the plates contained a different version of the same history. Joseph described an increasingly complex record. There were multiple and overlapping histories, an array of authors and editors, and several sets of plates, some large and some small, some available and some sealed. Instead of reproducing the "Book of Lehi," Joseph would translate from "a more particular account." If the Harris manuscript surfaced, Joseph would have an answer for why his second translation diverged from the first.[11]

Since Cowdery's arrival, Joseph had focused on the translation to the exclusion of other responsibilities. He hadn't been hiring out, at least not often, and he probably didn't plant crops that spring. Joseph soon ran out of paper, and he and Emma were short on food. Once again, Joseph sought help from Joseph Knight, who arrived with grain, potatoes, a barrel of mackerel, a pound of tea, and more paper. The seer and the rodsman kept working at a feverish pace.[12]

What did Joseph envision after the translation's publication? His spring 1829 revelations provided hints. "I will establish my church," proclaimed Jesus Christ in one text, "yea even the church which was taught by my disciples." The Lord would eliminate errors that had crept into churches through the wiles of "priestcraft" and restore "the true points of [his] doctrine" that had been lost. Joseph intended to bring about the reestablishment of ancient Christianity in its original purity.[13]

How would this work of restoration unfold? The translation stressed the necessity of baptism. For instance, one passage instructed men and women to show their willingness to repent of their sins and keep God's commandments by "going into the waters of baptism." American Protestants were divided—sometimes bitterly—about the when and how of baptism. Most denominations baptized infants (and previously unbaptized adult converts) by sprinkling or pouring water on their heads. Baptists, by contrast, baptized by immersion, and only those individuals mature enough to profess their own faith.

Susquehanna River, near where Joseph Smith and Oliver Cowdery
baptized each other. (Photograph by George Edward Anderson;
courtesy of Church History Library)

Unlike those in his family who had joined the Congregationalists or
Presbyterians, Joseph had never been baptized, either as an infant or as
an adult. On May 15, 1829, Joseph and Oliver Cowdery went down to
the banks of the Susquehanna River, waded into its cold waters, and baptized each other by immersion. They probably used words from Joseph's
translation, words that echoed New Testament formulations: "Having
authority given me of Jesus Christ I baptize you in the name of the Father and of the Son and of the Holy Ghost."[14]

Where did that authority come from? Several years later, Joseph referred to "the reception of the holy priesthood by the ministering of angels." By the mid-1830s, Joseph and Cowdery narrated that John the
Baptist had visited them as an angel and had ordained them "unto the
lesser or Aaronic priesthood." Granted authority by the very figure
who had baptized Jesus Christ, they then baptized each other. While earlier documents do not mention John the Baptist or priesthood, Joseph

understood the baptisms as obedience to Christ's command and also as
a precondition for the eventual formation of a church. Shortly after the
first baptisms, Joseph's brother Samuel arrived in Harmony for another
visit. Cowdery soon baptized Samuel.[15]

Oliver Cowdery's arrival in Harmony had catalyzed Joseph's progress on
the translation. Other new supporters helped him finish it. Peter Whitmer Sr. and his family were of German descent and had moved from
Pennsylvania to what became the township of Fayette, New York, about
twenty-five miles southeast of Palmyra. Peter Whitmer was a respectable
farmer who owned land, held minor civic offices, and belonged to a German Protestant congregation. He, his wife Mary, and several of their
adult children lived together in a log home.[16]

David Whitmer, Peter Whitmer's twenty-four-year-old son, became
acquainted with Oliver Cowdery and the Smith family. Like Cowdery, he
was intrigued by what he heard about the golden plates, and he asked
Cowdery to confirm the story's truth. Cowdery sent word to David Whitmer that Joseph indeed possessed an ancient record. He also had some
surprising news. God had commanded Whitmer to bring Joseph and
Cowdery to the Whitmer home in Fayette. The pair needed provisions
while they completed the translation, and they wanted a respite from what
Joseph described as mounting opposition to him in Harmony.[17]

Whitmer did as he was commanded. Around the first of June 1829,
Joseph and Cowdery loaded a few things into Whitmer's wagon and left
behind the house, farm, and Emma. And the plates. Unlike in the fall of
1827, Joseph did not stash the plates in a box or barrel for the journey.
Although legends developed about the miraculous appearance of the
plates in Fayette, Joseph gave every indication that he did not need their
physical presence for the translation.

Soon after Joseph moved into the home of Peter Whitmer Sr., he
went to Seneca Lake and baptized David Whitmer and Peter Whitmer
Jr. Cowdery baptized Hyrum Smith, Joseph's older brother. What had
begun as a quixotic literary project was becoming a fledgling movement.

That same month Joseph and Cowdery had a joint visionary experience, in which they heard "the voice of God in the chamber of old Father Whitmer's." As Joseph later narrated, God had promised them a
higher priesthood, which would include the authority to give "the gift of
the Holy Ghost" by the laying on of hands. According to Joseph, while
they were in Whitmer's room, God also told them that he and Cowdery

should ordain each other as elders, but that they should wait to do so until the growing number of baptized individuals could assemble together for the occasion.[18]

As the translation neared its conclusion, Joseph dictated a passage prophesying that "three witnesses" would see the hidden book. Joseph's revelations had already suggested that Harris, Cowdery, and David Whitmer would have this privilege. As he contemplated financing the book's publication, Harris remained desperate to see the plates.

Joseph and the chosen three prayed in a "remote field" near the Whitmer home.[19] They knelt and, one at a time, each man beseeched God to reveal the plates. Nothing. They each prayed a second time. Still nothing. Martin Harris speculated that his presence was an obstacle. He withdrew from the others, who resumed praying.

Harris's departure did the trick. An angel appeared, holding the plates. "He turned over the leaves one by one," Joseph later recalled, "so that we could see them, and discern the engravings." David Whitmer's recollection was even more fantastic. There was a table, upon which lay not only the plates but also the spectacles, the breastplate, and other objects described in the Book of Mormon.[20]

Joseph went to find Harris. He was still at prayer and still frustrated. Harris and Joseph now prayed together and saw "the same vision." Harris was ecstatic. "Mine eyes have beheld," he cried out. He jumped up and shouted, "Hosanna." The three men—Harris, Cowdery, and David Whitmer—signed a statement, probably composed by Cowdery, stating that an angel had shown them the plates and the engravings on them. They knew that the "work is true." They would bear witness.[21]

The number of witnesses soon grew. Joseph took five members of the Whitmer family to the old Smith log cabin on the Palmyra-Manchester line. With them, his father, and his brothers Hyrum and Samuel, Joseph went to a grove of trees the family had used as a place for "secret prayers." According to Lucy Mack Smith, Joseph "had been instructed that the plates would be carried there by one of the ancient Nephites." When they emerged from the woods, eight men put their names to a remarkable statement. "Joseph Smith Jr.," they testified, "has shown unto us the plates which hath been spoken, which have the appearance of gold . . . we did handle with our hands."[22]

The physicality of these claims is striking. The first set of witnesses asserted that, while in Joseph's company, an angel had shown the plates to them. They described their experience as visionary. The eight witnesses, by contrast, asserted that Joseph had handed metal plates to them. They had not only seen them but also had held them.

The experiences of the witnesses point to the power of Joseph's spiritual leadership. Many Americans claimed to have visions. Joseph Smith had the much rarer ability of enabling others to share those visions. In this case, moreover, he made a mysterious hidden object present for other people. The immaterial became real. As one of Joseph's revelations stated, they had "seen them even as my servant Joseph Smith Jr. has seen them," perhaps a tacit acknowledgment that he too had seen the plates only through visions rather than in an ordinary physical sense.[23]

Joseph and Oliver prepared the witnesses' statements as part of their preparations to publish the Book of Mormon. For those open to Joseph's claims, the two testimonies corroborated the miraculous provenance of the record. For skeptics, statements signed by Joseph's chief scribe (Cowdery), Joseph's financial backer (Harris), Joseph's father and two brothers (Hyrum and Samuel), and an array of Whitmers (five brothers and their brother-in-law) amounted to thin evidence. "I could not feel more satisfied and at rest," Mark Twain later jabbed, "if the entire Whitmer family had testified." Still, Joseph was relieved that other men had staked their reputations to the plates.[24]

Either just before or after the experiences of the witnesses, Joseph and his scribe completed the translation. What happened to the plates? Joseph said only that once he was finished, he "delivered them up" to the messenger from whom he had received them. Legends developed in later years. Joseph had gone back to the hill, perhaps in the company of Cowdery. The entrance to a vast cave appeared in the hillside. They entered it and laid the plates on a table. Looking around, they saw "wagon loads" of plates as well as the breastplate, a sword, and a host of other treasures.[25]

By the end of June 1829 Joseph had a hefty manuscript, about six hundred pages. Now it was time to arrange for the book's publication. Joseph found someone to print the title page and took steps to secure copyright for *The Book of Mormon.* Next, Harris, possibly with Joseph, Cowdery, and Hyrum Smith, visited E. B. Grandin, the new editor of Palmyra's *Wayne Sentinel.* They surprised Grandin with their request that he print five thousand copies of the book.

Grandin said no. He thought the book's prospects were dim, and he advised Harris not to finance its publication. Grandin underestimated

Joseph Smith's persistence. Joseph and his supporters talked with other publishers and found one in Rochester, Elihu Marshall, willing to take on the project. Harris then returned to Grandin and told him that the book would be published with or without him. It would be more convenient for them if the job was done in Palmyra, and why shouldn't Grandin profit from it? The Palmyra printer reluctantly assented, but his price was a steep $3,000. He didn't demand all of the money up front, but he wanted the agreement backed by tangible assets, such as Harris's land.[26]

According to Lucy Mack Smith, the initial plan was for Harris to provide half of the funds and for Joseph and his brother Hyrum to pay the remainder. The Smith brothers had no way of raising $1,500, though, and Joseph pressured Harris to sell land in order to meet Grandin's terms. Joseph produced a revelation. "I command you," Jesus Christ instructed Harris, "that thou shalt not covet thine own property, but impart it freely to the printing of the Book of Mormon." The command was sobering. Harris should give "all save the support of thy family." Indeed, Grandin's asking price was more or less the value of Harris's land. The Lord reminded Harris of his past transgressions and warned him that he would suffer punishment if he failed to repent now. God would smite him. "How sore you know not!" Christ admonished. Should he prove faithful, however, Christ would pour out his spirit upon Harris, a blessing more valuable than any earthly treasure.[27]

Harris was wobbly. While Joseph prodded him to sell his land, Lucy Harris pressured him to keep it. She importuned their neighbors and friends to talk sense into her husband. In the end, Martin Harris heeded Joseph rather than his wife. He did not sell his farm, but in August 1829 he guaranteed Grandin's payment by mortgaging his property. If he did not pay the $3,000 within eighteen months, Grandin would assume ownership of his land. Lucy Harris found some comfort in the fact that she retained one parcel of their land in her own name.[28]

As the work of printing began, Joseph returned to his home in Harmony and was reunited with Emma. Presumably Josiah Stowell, Joseph Knight, or Isaac Hale had helped put food on Emma's table during her husband's extended absences. The couple's circumstances remained humble, but Joseph brimmed with newfound confidence about their future. A year that had started out bleakly ended with promise. Against considerable odds and after prior false starts, a book that bore his name as "author and proprietor" would be published.

The book's publication heralded the restoration of Christ's pure church, and, if it sold well, it could enable Joseph to avoid his family's pattern of tenant poverty. "There begins to be a great call for our books in this country," he reported to Cowdery in October. It turned out that Joseph was wildly optimistic about the book's commercial potential, but the Book of Mormon marked a dramatic change in the trajectory of Joseph's life.[29]

CHAPTER SIX

A Choice Seer (1829)

"A VILER IMPOSITION WAS never practiced," the *Rochester Daily Advertiser and Telegraph* proclaimed within days of the Book of Mormon's publication. "It is an evidence of fraud, blasphemy and credulity."[1] Now that Joseph Smith's book was a matter of printed and bound pages rather than secret metal plates, anyone could assess it. Indeed, the Book of Mormon itself invites scrutiny, perhaps a tacit acknowledgment that most readers would approach it with suspicion and skepticism. "I would exhort you," its final chapter pleads, "that ye would ask God the Eternal Father, in the name of Christ, if these things are not true." Those who asked the question with "a sincere heart, with real intent, having faith in Christ," would receive confirmation from the Holy Ghost.

There are other ways to interrogate the book besides prayer. Does archaeology confirm the history the Book of Mormon narrates? Do DNA studies link modern Indigenous Americans to Book of Mormon peoples? What about the text itself? Do its names, words, and poetry suggest an ancient Semitic source? Or is there evidence for its composition in the early nineteenth century? Did Joseph Smith borrow or adapt ideas from other books and from his cultural milieu? And if the Book of Mormon is not an ancient record, and if Joseph never had golden plates, does that make him a fraud?

Those questions matter, but so do other lines of inquiry. The Book of Mormon received devastating early reviews in American newspapers, and it has never gained respect from literary critics. From the start, though, select readers accepted the Book of Mormon as scripture and reoriented their lives accordingly. What was so powerful about the Book of Mormon and its message? And what does the text reveal about Joseph Smith?

Before answering these questions, it is best to begin with content of the Book of Mormon, an epic story about peoples and plates that unfolds over a millennium.

A man named Lehi and his sons Laman, Lemuel, Sam, and Nephi live in Jerusalem during the reign of King Zedekiah (c. 597–587 B.C.E.). Nephi narrates his family's story. Lehi has a vision of Jesus Christ descending from heaven. As Joseph Smith would narrate about his earliest vision, Christ's "luster was above that of the sun at noonday." Jesus gives Lehi a book that contains a warning that Jerusalem and its inhabitants will soon be destroyed. Lehi and his family leave their home and flee south to the shores of the Red Sea.

The story quickly gets spicy. Lehi has a dream that his sons should return to Jerusalem and retrieve "plates of brass" from a wicked man named Laban. They obey, but Laban will not give them the plates. Laman and Lemuel are so frustrated that they beat their younger brothers. Eventually, Nephi sneaks into Laban's house and finds him drunk. He also finds a sword, and the "voice of the Spirit" commands him to kill Laban. Nephi hesitates, but eventually decapitates Laban and finds the plates, which contain the "five books of Moses," the subsequent history of the Jews, and "the prophecies of the holy prophets."

The family travels further into Arabia, where Lehi and his wife have two more sons, Jacob and Joseph. Then they build a ship and, with the help of a mystical compass known as Liahona, cross the ocean to the Americas.

As his death approaches, Lehi gathers his sons for final words of instruction and blessing. He reminds his youngest son, Joseph, that they are descendants of the biblical Joseph, who was sold into slavery and then became Pharaoh's right-hand man. Lehi then narrates a prophecy attributed to that illustrious ancestor. Joseph—the biblical Joseph—foretells the coming of two great leaders. One of them is Moses, who will deliver God's people out of bondage and write God's law. The other will be a "choice seer." This "mighty" seer will bring forth long-hidden words, writings that persuade another people to repent of their sins and return to their ancient covenants with God.

Who is the choice seer? The Book of Mormon provides a clear answer. "His name shall be called after me," states the biblical Joseph, "and it shall be after the name of his father. And he shall be like unto me." Here is a window into how Joseph Smith understood himself. He would have visions like Lehi. He would write like Moses. He would wield power like Joseph.

Lehi's descendants divide into two warring peoples, named for his sons Nephi and Laman. The Book of Mormon at times becomes a history of bloody battles between mostly good Nephites and mostly wicked Lamanites, but it is also a story of record keeping. The Nephites retain the plates of brass, record their own history on other plates, and gain custody of still other plates.

One set of plates acquired by the Nephites narrates an even more ancient history connected to another biblical narrative. Humans have attempted to build a "great tower" (the Tower of Babel) that would reach the heavens, and their hubris prompts God to create separate languages and scatter people across the earth. A man identified only as "the brother of Jared" begs the Lord to spare his people from this punishment. The Lord grants the request, and he instructs them to head into the wilderness, build enclosed barges, and travel to a "land of promise" across the ocean.

As these people sojourn on the coast in preparation for their voyage, the brother of Jared "molten[s] out of a rock" sixteen small, clear stones. He asks the Lord to touch the stones, so that they will shine and provide light during the ocean crossing. Again, the Lord grants his request. Jared's brother sees "the finger of the Lord" touch the stones one by one, and he falls to the earth when he realizes that the Lord's finger is "as the finger of a man, like unto flesh and blood." He asks the Lord to reveal the rest of himself. Once again, the Lord grants his wish. "Behold," he announces. "I am Jesus Christ. I am the Father and the Son." Thousands of years before Jesus is born in Bethlehem, he has revealed his divinity and his body.

Back to stones and ships. Jesus Christ instructs the brother of Jared to write a record of what he has seen in a language incomprehensible without the use of two other stones called "interpreters." The brother of Jared complies, writes his record, and seals it up along with the interpreters. Meanwhile, after he places two of the luminous stones in each vessel, the people float in their barges to the promised land. Their descendants suffer from strife, rebellion, and the machinations of secret societies.

Their enemies wipe them out, but a prophet named Ether completes his people's history, inscribed on twenty-four plates of pure gold. Ether buries this record.

Several centuries later, the Nephites discover these Jaredite plates and the interpreters. A king named Mosiah translates them "by the means of those two stones which were fastened into the two rims of a bow." Book of Mormon readers learn that "whosoever has these things is called seer." Mosiah mourns when he learns about the destruction of the Jaredites, but he makes sure that their history and the interpreters are preserved.

Meanwhile, as the Nephites fight with their enemies, prophets appear who make detailed predictions about a coming Messiah, Jesus Christ, who will be born of a virgin, be crucified, and rise from the dead. Following events in Jerusalem, Christ appears to the Nephites and ushers in a golden age of peace and piety. The good times end after two centuries. False churches arise. The "true believers in Christ" become known as Nephites, and those who reject the truth become known as Lamanites.

The Nephites, like the Jaredites before them, suffer crushing defeats. Among the last survivors are Mormon and his son, Moroni. Mormon is the primary editor of the above history, which therefore bears his name. Moroni continues his father's work, includes an abridgment of the Jaredite plates, and then buries all of these records.

Buried plates again await future discovery and translation, this time by Joseph Smith, another seer with stones. When Joseph Smith compiled a history of his life, he claimed to have received "two stones in silver bows" and stated that "the possession and use of these stones was what constituted seers in ancient or former times." In other words, Joseph was a seer like Mosiah. God had chosen him to restore long-lost histories and to restore Christ's church to its original unity.[2]

There is a fundamental difference between the Book of Mormon and scriptures such as the Tanakh, the New Testament, or the Qur'an. There are long-running debates about the precise combination of myth and history in the biblical accounts, or the extent to which the Qur'an accurately represents the early seventh-century emergence of Islam. Nevertheless, Jewish, Christian, and Muslim scriptures are indisputably ancient. They are the products of long-ago civilizations and communities. No one debates whether the peoples of Israel and Judah existed. There is no serious question about the existence of Jesus, Paul, or the Prophet Muhammad. By contrast, there is a lack of evidence for Jaredites, Nephites, and Lamanites in the Americas. Few if any non–Latter-day Saints accept that Lehi, Mormon, and Moroni were historical figures.

Archaeologists have not discovered sites or inscriptions that closely match the Book of Mormon narrative.[3] The DNA of Indigenous Americans does not reveal Hebraic ancestry.[4] Linguistic elements of the Book of Mormon that resemble Hebrew could reflect the influence of the Bible, not original elements of Jaredite or Nephite culture. There are also a host of anachronisms in the text, from the presence of horses in ancient American civilizations to the incorporation of New Testament material in portions that predate those texts.[5] Indeed, some scholars conclude that the anachronisms are so "ostentatious" as to suggest that the Book of Mormon "arguably never portrays itself as an ancient text."[6] The consensus of non–Latter-day Saint experts is that the Book of Mormon's narratives are fictional rather than historical.[7]

Fiction, but not good fiction. Mark Twain lampooned the Book of Mormon as "chloroform in print." Given its repetitious and sometimes labored language, Twain posited that the true miracle was Joseph's ability to stay awake while composing or translating it.[8] More recent critics have been similarly dismissive. The literary critic Harold Bloom regarded the Book of Mormon, along with Joseph's other scriptural productions, as "stunted stepchildren of the Bible." Bloom, who lauded other aspects of Joseph's vision as religious genius, didn't consider the Book of Mormon worth reading.[9]

Curiously, even as critics have disparaged the Book of Mormon, many of them have doubted that a man in his early twenties with little formal education could have written it. Within a few years of the Book of Mormon's publication, detractors alleged that Joseph, perhaps with the help of one of his associates, had reworked someone else's manuscript, or had taken inspiration from another book. The idea that American Indians were the descendants of Jews was common during Joseph Smith's lifetime, but the Book of Mormon does not closely resemble any known text in either its narrative or its argument.[10]

Joseph did make use of one obvious source, though. One early detractor described the Book of Mormon as "a most foul plagiarism from the Old and New Testaments."[11] Despite Emma Smith's insistence that her husband used no "manuscript" or "book," Joseph consulted the King James Bible during the translation.[12] He would have needed a copy at hand for the incorporation of long passages from Isaiah and the Sermon on the Mount. From start to finish, moreover, the Book of Mormon drips with biblical quotation and allusion. Plagiarism is an overly blunt conclusion, however. For the most part, Joseph took inspiration from the Bible rather than simply copying it.

In the absence of evidence that anyone helped him compose the manuscript, the simplest conclusion is that Joseph Smith authored the Book of Mormon. One corollary of that conclusion is that at least on some level, Joseph deceived his family, friends, supporters, and readers. He pretended to have golden plates, or pretended that engravings on metal plates were the basis for a translation. Joseph then asked Martin Harris to risk his property to publish the Book of Mormon.

Another possible corollary is that Joseph Smith was both bold and brilliant. He convinced a key set of followers—his family, Martin Harris, Oliver Cowdery, the Whitmers—that he had found an ancient record and could translate it. Then, after producing a lengthy and complex text, he convinced Harris to pay for its publication, partly through the dictation of divine commandments. It was an incredibly unlikely achievement. The Book of Mormon project from start to finish was a stunning display of American audacity. Such chutzpah, if displayed by a political or business leader rather than a religious figure, would almost certainly elicit more respect than ridicule or condemnation.[13]

Only if we understand Joseph Smith as the book's author can we credit him for the native genius necessary to produce a complex set of interlocking narratives. And the Book of Mormon is more than purportedly ancient stories. In its pages, Joseph delivered religious broadsides. He shared an apocalyptic vision of the future. He howled in social protest. And, most of all, he painted a portrait of Jesus Christ that was at once familiar and compellingly original.

The Book of Mormon contains grand theological arguments. For instance, Lehi teaches his sons that the disobedience of Adam and Eve, although a transgression, was a necessary step for human progress. Had they not partaken of the forbidden fruit, they would have remained in the Garden of Eden, childless, lacking in knowledge, and therefore devoid of true happiness. "Adam fell that men might be," Lehi interprets, "and men are, that they might have joy." They did not fall because God or even the devil made them do it. They were free to choose, just like their descendants. "The Messiah cometh in the fulness of time," Lehi continues, "that he may redeem the children of men from the fall." Through the Messiah, identified in other passages as Jesus Christ, humans can "choose liberty and eternal life" or, if they wish to follow Satan in his misery, "captivity and death." Like the Methodists, Joseph rejected Calvinism and its doctrine of predestination. He celebrated human liberty and agency.

Joseph also weighed in on a host of topics controversial among American Protestants of his day. The Book of Mormon commands baptism by immersion, labels the baptism of infants an abomination, and teaches that all infants and young children will be saved. Joseph also rejected his father and paternal grandfather's belief in universal salvation. In one Book of Mormon narrative, a false prophet named Nehor teaches that "all men should have eternal life," thereby tempting people away from the church of Christ.

Some of the Book of Mormon's most arresting ideas lay well beyond the intra-Protestant debates of the early nineteenth century, however. "And it shall come to pass," Nephi declares, "that the Lord God shall commence his work among all nations, kindreds, tongues, and people, to bring about the restoration of his people upon the earth." This restoration would commence with Indigenous Americans, the descendants of the Lamanites, who would return to the faith of their ancestors. When they had fallen into wickedness, God had cursed them with a "skin of blackness" so that the Nephites would find them unattractive and not reproduce with them. When restored to their ancient faith, however, the Lamanites would become a "white and a delightsome people."

This message was intended as good news for Native peoples, but as a warning to other Americans. Joseph anticipated an imminent apocalypse and the return of Jesus Christ to the earth. So did many American Protestants. Joseph, though, had a very different future in mind, one in which God was preparing to judge most Christians. As God's chosen people, redeemed Lamanites—Native Americans—would build the millennial New Jerusalem, and they would be God's agents of judgment against those Gentiles—Euro-Americans—who reject Christ's true church.[14]

The Book of Mormon identifies a number of reasons for God's wrath. In a prophecy about the "last days," Lehi's son Nephi condemns "false teachers" who are prideful and corrupt. "They rob the poor because of their fine sanctuaries . . . [and] their fine clothing," he thunders. "They wear stiff necks and high heads." Joseph had a warning for such "puffed-up" individuals: "they shall be thrust down to hell!" What was the source of Joseph's righteous anger? The religious elites in Palmyra had sneered at the Smiths because of their ragged clothes and lack of sophistication. Such passages may contain echoes of Joseph's own slights, but the Book of Mormon's social protest flows out of the Bible as well. Joseph included passages from Isaiah and Malachi that make similar critiques of religious hypocrites.[15]

It was not just that the Methodist and Presbyterian ministers enriched themselves at the expense of the poor. Their churches also lacked true godliness and power because they denied the gifts of the Holy Spirit as outlined in the New Testament. "If there were miracles wrought then," Moroni wonders, "why had God ceased to be a God of miracles?" In its closing pages, the Book of Mormon promises that Christ's true followers will speak in tongues, heal the sick, and prophesy. Joseph grew up in a world replete with visions, dreams, seer stones, divining rods, and divine healings. It had stung when a Methodist minister had rejected his vision, telling him that visions and revelations had "ceased with the apostles." Now Joseph rebuked those who thought that true Christianity—as Joseph understood it—was a thing of the ancient past.[16]

The Book of Mormon's title page, which Joseph stated was included on the plates, announces that its purpose is "the convincing of the Jew and Gentile that JESUS is the CHRIST, the ETERNAL GOD, manifesting himself unto all nations." Lehi's story begins with a vision of the Messiah, and Moroni ends by calling on his future readers to "come unto Christ, and be perfected in him." The basic message was familiar. Jesus Christ is the Messiah, the divine Son of God, the Savior of all nations.

After Jesus appears to the Nephites in the Book of Mormon, he gives sermons that resemble those found in the New Testament, then tells the people that he will leave them and return to his Father. The people beg him to stay. "Behold," Jesus replies, "my bowels are filled with compassion towards you." He tells the people to bring the sick, the lame, and the otherwise afflicted to him. Jesus heals them. He overflows with compassion for the downtrodden.

After Jesus establishes his New World church, there is the long stretch of unity and peace. "Neither were there Lamanites, nor no manner of Ites," a Book of Mormon prophet records, "but they were in one, the children of Christ, and heirs to the kingdom of God." Here is a departure from the New Testament, whose epistles narrate intense disagreements among the early followers of Jesus.

Joseph hated religious disunity. His own family divided over the issue of which church to join, if any, and Joseph later recalled the confusion and uncertainty he felt because of denominational rancor. Here was the solution, both to his father's skepticism and his mother's Presbyterianism, and to the disunity he saw exhibited by the Christians around him. Through the Book of Mormon, Joseph proclaimed that Christ was about to restore his one true church. Joseph's immediate family had already accepted his religious authority and message. The Book of Mormon was the first step in spreading that message of restoration to the wider world.

Joseph Smith was not the only early nineteenth-century American prophet. Other men and women had visions, dictated or wrote revelations, and produced texts that they and their followers regarded as divinely inspired and authoritative. Nat Turner, an enslaved Virginian and Joseph's rough contemporary, interpreted "hieroglyphic characters" he saw on stars and leaves as prophecies of Christ's imminent Second Coming. Ellen White, one of the founders of Seventh-day Adventism, experienced visions in a trance-like state and then wrote out their content for her followers. Later in the century, Mary Baker Eddy's *Science and Health* became an authoritative text for Christian Scientists.[17]

Joseph Smith, though, is the most successful creator of scripture in American history by a wide margin. Most of his contemporaries rejected the Book of Mormon. Most people who encounter it today do so as well. But a small community around Joseph accepted it from the start, and millions of people around the world have done so over the past two hundred years. When they accepted Joseph's book as scripture, they fulfilled its prophecy that he would become a choice seer.[18]

CHAPTER SEVEN

Moses (1830)

JOSEPH SR. ARRIVED IN Harmony in January 1830 with alarming news. Abner Cole was printing excerpts of the Book of Mormon in his recently established Palmyra newspaper. Cole published the *Reflector* under the pseudonym Obadiah Dogberry, from the Old Testament prophet and a character in Shakespeare's *As You Like It.* A free-thinking skeptic, Cole skewered those he saw as hypocrites or frauds. The editor praised himself as someone who "flogs *fop* or *fool* where'er they'r found / And single-handed stands his ground."[1] Cole loathed Protestant ministers who demanded tithes from their congregants and in return sought to deprive them of whiskey and the Sunday transport of mail. But he also hated upstart sectarians who, in his view, hoodwinked the credulous.

Cole used E. B. Grandin's press at night and on Sundays to produce the *Reflector,* and he found the pages of the Book of Mormon hanging in the print shop irresistible. The first 1830 issue of the *Reflector* contained the story of Lehi's vision and his decision to leave Jerusalem. Hyrum Smith and Oliver Cowdery confronted Cole and reminded him that they had secured a copyright. "I don't care a damn," Cole responded. "That damned Gold Bible is going into my paper." Cole printed two more excerpts.[2]

Father and son raced back to Palmyra to confront Cole. If individuals could satisfy their curiosity through the *Reflector,* they might not buy the Book of Mormon. When he reached Palmyra, Joseph Jr. went to the print shop, greeted Cole cordially, and told him to desist. Cole, who was twice Joseph's age, took off his coat, rolled up his sleeves, and dared Joseph to fight. Joseph didn't take the bait. He simply threatened to sue. Cole calmed down and acquiesced, though he continued to dog Joseph in print. The next summer he published a satirical "Book of Pukei."[3]

Joseph had parried Cole's threat, but the *Reflector* extracts served as a reminder of the project's fragility. Martin Harris was also nervous. He stood to lose his land unless enough books sold to cover Grandin's $3,000 price. It seems that Joseph and Harris had not worked out who would benefit from the prospective sales. For instance, if Josiah Stowell bought $500 worth of books from Joseph, would that money go toward Harris's debt to Grandin, or to Joseph for other purposes? Harris seems to have made it clear that he did not intend his guarantee to Grandin to be a gift. Grudgingly, Joseph signed an agreement with Harris stating that the latter had "an equal privilege" in selling the Book of Mormon "until enough of them shall be sold to pay for the printing." The agreement gave Harris a possible way of saving his farm, though it precluded him from turning a profit. The discussion and agreement annoyed Joseph, who by revelation had urged Harris to "impart" his property "freely."[4]

Meanwhile, Hyrum Smith received advice that his brother could sell the Book of Mormon's Canadian copyright.[5] The sale would provide needed funds and discourage its unauthorized reprinting over the border. When presented with the suggestion, Joseph placed his seer stone in his hat, looked into it, and dictated a revelation. God instructed Oliver Cowdery, Hiram Page (one of the group of eight Book of Mormon witnesses), Josiah Stowell, and Joseph Knight to travel to Kingston in Upper Canada. They were to sell the Book of Mormon's copyright within that jurisdiction. These four men had pleased God with their faithfulness. Therefore, they would receive "the temporal blessing as well as the spiritual." Indeed, the Lord added, all of Joseph's supporters had pleased God, "save Martin only." Harris was too concerned with the state of his own finances. The exclusion of Harris seems decidedly uncharitable given how much he had risked to enable the Book of Mormon's publication.[6]

According to an 1848 letter written by Hiram Page, the group prepared for the Canadian trip "in a sly manner so as to keep Martin Harris from drawing a share of the money." At least Cowdery and Page, and possibly Stowell and Knight, went to Kingston. It had been a cold enough winter that they could walk across the frozen eastern end of Lake Ontario. It turned out that Joseph and his friends were poorly informed about British copyright law. They would have had to register a copyright in London, and it would have been impossible to enforce in the Canadian provinces. When the men returned home, they asked Joseph why they had not succeeded. David Whitmer recalled that Joseph inquired of the Lord and received another message: "Some revelations are of God, some revelations are of man, and some revelations are of the devil." Page concluded that Joseph had confused God's will with his own "carnal desires." At the time, though, the failure did not shake their faith in Joseph's leadership.[7]

Joseph returned to Harmony after his confrontation with Abner Cole, the agreement with Martin Harris, and the Canadian copyright revelation. Then, in mid-March 1830, Joseph Knight Sr. came with a wagon and team to transport the seer back to Manchester. Grandin's typesetter had printed the final pages of the Book of Mormon. The stacks of paper were bound. The book was for sale, the price set at $1.75.

As the two Josephs approached Manchester, they saw a man crossing the road ahead of them, carrying something in his arms. It was a disconsolate Martin Harris with a pile of books. "Nobody wants them," he lamented. Harris felt the sting of failure and foresaw the loss of his property. "I think they will sell well," Joseph reassured him. Neither man was exactly correct. The church printed several more editions during Joseph's lifetime to meet demand for the Book of Mormon. At least at first, however, most people didn't want to pay for a copy, so the anticipated profits didn't arrive.[8]

The book's publication signaled to Joseph that it was time to organize a church. On April 6, several dozen individuals gathered at Peter Whitmer Sr.'s home in Fayette. They probably stood and sat outside instead of cramming into the house. At this meeting, Joseph and his followers established what they called the Church of Christ, using the simple name given by Jesus Christ in the Book of Mormon.[9]

The occasion combined ritual formality and spiritual ecstasy. After opening prayers, Joseph and Oliver Cowdery ordained each other as the church's first and second elders, signifying their presiding authority. They celebrated the Lord's Supper, blessing and distributing the bread and wine. The pair next laid their hands on each member and asked God to give them the "gift of the Holy Ghost." Many of those present felt divine power course through their bodies. Some people prophesied and spoke "with new tongues." As at Protestant revivals, a number of men and women were so overcome that they collapsed and had to be laid on beds. When they recovered, they declared that the heavens had opened and that they had seen Jesus Christ and God the Father.[10]

On the day of the church's organization, Joseph dictated a revelation in which Jesus Christ proclaimed that he should be called "a seer and translator and prophet." The Lord would speak through him. "His word," Christ explained, "ye shall receive as if from mine own mouth." Joseph expected other church members to exercise a wide variety of spiritual gifts, but he consolidated authority in his own person.[11]

Soon after the church's establishment, Joseph went to the Smith residence along the Manchester-Palmyra line. Joseph Sr., Oliver Cowdery, Joseph Knight Sr., and Martin Harris accompanied him to a stream that flowed just west of the family's log home. It was after dark. Joseph Sr. and Harris waded into the frigid water, and Cowdery baptized them. When he saw his father and his benefactor come out of the water, Joseph burst into tears. According to Knight, Joseph "would sob and cry and seemed to be so full that he could not live." The prophet fled into the woods to weep alone. Cowdery and Knight went to his side and eventually brought him into the house.[12]

Joseph's mother was baptized soon afterwards, as were his brothers William and Don Carlos and his sisters Sophronia and Lucy. Then, in late June 1830, Emma Smith was baptized in a stream on the Knight farm in Colesville, New York. The family's newfound spiritual unity was deeply gratifying to Joseph.

Joseph traveled relentlessly to preside over meetings, preach and teach, and bring new members into the church. Between Manchester, Fayette, Harmony, and Colesville, he met friends and dodged opponents. Joseph was a physically vigorous young man, not yet twenty-five years of age. In many ways he was like a young Methodist itinerant, always on the move and comfortable sleeping rough.

In Colesville, Joseph had a series of conversations with Newel Knight, son of Joseph Knight Sr. The younger Knight attended prayer meetings with Joseph, but he hesitated to pray out loud in front of others. Joseph encouraged him, but Knight held back, at one point retreating into the woods to pray by himself. When he returned, he felt guilty for his lack of courage, then descended into a state of spiritual anguish, "his visage and limbs distorted and twisted into every possible shape and appearance." It got worse. Knight was "caught up off the floor of the apartment and tossed about most fearfully." Joseph watched in horror and eventually managed to grab hold of Knight's hand. The afflicted man begged Joseph to cast the devil out of him, screaming that his flesh was "about to cleave from my bones." Joseph rebuked the devil and commanded him "in the name of Jesus Christ to depart." Knight cried out that he saw the devil leave.

Knight was now filled with spiritual ecstasy and light. He saw the heavens open. Then he rose in the air. "I found that the Spirit of the Lord had actually lifted me off the floor," he later recounted, "and that my shoulder and head were pressing against the beams." When he came out of the trance, he was weak, and his friends laid him on his bed. Knight soon was baptized into the church.

"The age of miracles has *again* arrived," sneered Abner Cole in the *Reflector* when he got wind of the developments in Colesville. Mocking aside, Cole had put his finger on a key characteristic of Joseph's movement. As the Book of Mormon taught, Joseph believed that men and women should exercise the spiritual gifts enjoyed by Jesus's ancient followers. They should speak in tongues. They should prophesy. And they should call on God in the name of Jesus to heal diseases and cast out demons. Americans at this time were sharply divided over the validity of such experiences, some seeing them as the power of God and others as delusion, the work of the devil, or as too similar to Catholic "superstition." The Church of Christ at its founding fell on the robustly supernatural side of this divide.[13]

The recent baptisms had alarmed some locals, who were upset at conversions within their families. On the evening of Emma's baptism, a constable came to the Knight home and arrested Joseph. Four years ago, he had stood trial as a "disorderly person" for "pretending . . . to discover where lost goods may be found." The authorities let him off that time. As far as Joseph's detractors were concerned, he was up to his old tricks, still looking into a stone and still fleecing the gullible.

In the resulting trial, Oliver Cowdery testified that Joseph had translated the Book of Mormon by looking into "two transparent stones." Josiah Stowell again reaffirmed his faith in Joseph's gift. None of the witnesses, however, provided evidence that Joseph had engaged in glasslooking or other disorderly activities in Chenango County since 1826. Because the statute of limitations had lapsed, the case was dismissed.[14]

Immediately following his release, Joseph was arrested again on the same charge, this time by a constable from neighboring Broome County. At the ensuing second trial, before Justice of the Peace Joel K. Noble,

Newel Knight testified that Joseph "could see in a stone" but that he did so with honorable motives. "Formerly he looked for money," Knight explained, "but latterly he had become holy." As evidence of Joseph's righteousness, Knight related that the defendant had cast a devil out of him. He had seen "the devil *as he departed*" and knew that "Smith did it by the *power* of God."[15] Knight's testimony did not convince Noble of Joseph's holiness. The justice later commented that he considered Joseph a "vagrant idler," "liar," "deceiver," and a "nuisance to good society." But there was no proof he had used his stone to seek treasure in Broome County anytime recently, so Noble also dismissed the charges.[16]

In June 1830, just before the twin arrests and trials, Joseph dictated a different sort of revelation, one whose narrative style resembled that of the Book of Mormon. In it, the biblical Moses—sometime after the burning bush but before the exodus—is whisked onto "an exceeding high mountain" and sees God face-to-face. Moses later beholds the world and its multitude of inhabitants. How did you make all of this? Moses asks God. The divine response connects the Book of Genesis—the first book in the Jewish Torah and Christian Old Testament—to the New Testament Gospel of John. "By the word of my power have I created them," God declares, "which is mine only begotten Son, full of grace and truth." As does the Gospel of John, Joseph's revelation identifies Jesus Christ as God's agent of creation. Moses also learns that God has created "numberless" worlds, all for the purpose of bringing about "the immortality and the eternal life of man."

By the early nineteenth century, some scholars were questioning the traditional Jewish and Christian belief that Moses had authored the Torah. How could he have written about events before and after his death? Joseph's June 1830 revelation settled the question. "Write the things which I shall speak," God instructs Moses. There was also a warning and a promise. Wicked individuals would remove many words from the Bible, but God would raise up someone comparable to Moses to restore the lost portions. When they read or heard these lines, early members of the Church of Christ knew whom God had chosen for this work of biblical restoration.[17]

Joseph lived in a "Bible-drenched" culture. Even northeasterners who did not affiliate with a church knew the characters and cadence of the King James Bible. Cheaper methods of printing and indefatigable Bible salesmen and missionaries made its presence pervasive. As of 1830, the American Bible Society was in the midst of a multiyear campaign to bring a Bible to every American home, even in the backwoods and on the frontier. Regardless of denominational affiliation, and regardless of how often they read it or how they interpreted it, most Americans approached the Bible with reverence. It was the word of God, a credible history, and a treasury of ethics and wisdom.[18]

At the same time, even some pious Americans found fault with the King James Bible. Its language was archaic and, like any translation, it was imperfect. The Baptist reformer Alexander Campbell considered the King James Bible both obsolete and inaccurate. "A living language is continually changing," Campbell reasoned. The Bible had to change with it, or it would lose its vitality and power. Accordingly, in 1826 Campbell published a new edition of the New Testament, known among his followers as the "Living Oracles." He replaced outdated words and phrases with more contemporary language and more precise translations.[19]

Other Americans had stronger objections to the Bible as it was. Josiah Priestley, an English theologian and scientist, moved to the United States in 1794. Priestley was a thorough-going rationalist. He believed that subsequent generations of Christians had layered onto the moral teachings of Jesus absurdities such as the virgin birth and the resurrection.

Thomas Jefferson found inspiration in Priestley's books, including his massive *History of the Corruptions of Christianity*. Like Joseph Smith, Jefferson kept aloof from the churches of his day, but he admired Jesus and referred to his teachings as "a system of the most sublime morality which has ever fallen from the lips of man." The former president used a razor and scissors to extract Jesus's ethical teachings from the miraculous legends Christians allegedly had appended to them. The result was the *Life and Morals of Jesus of Nazareth*, which Jefferson chose not to publish during his lifetime. Jefferson's Jesus doesn't turn water into wine or walk on water, and his corpse stays in the tomb.[20]

What Joseph Smith attempted was more audacious than Jefferson's razor-and-scissors hatchet job on the gospels. When Joseph read the Bible, he pondered its mysteries, the apparent gaps in its narratives, the theological questions it posed. In the Book of Mormon, Joseph asserted that "plain and precious things" from the Bible had been lost. The diagnosis was provocative, but Joseph's proposed solution was even bolder. He could restore the missing portions through revelation.

In the summer and fall of 1830 Joseph dictated a revised, expanded, and Christianized version of the early chapters of Genesis. He called it his "translation of the scriptures." Joseph tidied up some of the Bible's apparent contradictions. Why, for instance, does Genesis include two accounts of the world's creation? In the first chapter, God creates the earth and everything on it, including a man and a woman. Then, in the second chapter of Genesis, God does it all again, in a somewhat different order and manner. In Joseph's redaction, God first creates everything in heaven "spiritually" before anything was "naturally" on the earth. This two-step creation included human beings. "In heaven created I them," God tells Moses, "and there was not yet flesh upon the earth." Joseph both solved a perceived problem in the text and introduced the idea that a spiritual creation in heaven preceded the mortal life of men and women on earth.[21]

The fourth chapter of Genesis features another well-known but confusing story. Cain and Abel, sons of Adam and Eve, both make sacrifices to the Lord. Cain brings part of his harvest; Abel sacrifices some of the young animals in his flock. God likes Abel's sacrifice but rejects Cain's. Why? The text doesn't say, but, miffed by God's rejection, Cain murders his brother.

The Book of Mormon touches on this biblical passage. It refers to a Satanic plot involving Cain, whom it depicts as the progenitor of secret oaths that wicked men use to gain power and plunder. "Secret combinations" are a recurrent evil that contribute to the destruction of the Jaredites and Nephites.

This Book of Mormon theme intersected with developments in American culture. In the early decades of the American republic, Freemasonry grew rapidly. The fraternity traced its origins to medieval craft guilds but now appealed to affluent and upwardly mobile men seeking social and economic advantage.

Freemasonry also granted access to a world of ancient myths and rituals that blended biblical content with more esoteric material. Initiates swore not to reveal these ceremonies on pain of a gruesome death. In 1826, William Morgan, a western New York member of the fraternity, announced that he would publish an exposé and critique of the order. Other Masons had divulged many details, but Morgan's publication plans nevertheless cost him his life. Jailed for the failure to pay a small debt, he was seized from a Canandaigua, New York, jail, only ten miles from the Smith farm. Morgan's presumed murder by his Masonic enemies temporarily discredited the fraternity and led to the rise of a short-lived but politically potent Anti-Masonic Party. Although Joseph's brother Hyrum had joined Palmyra's Masonic lodge sometime in the 1820s, the new scripture's critique of secret societies was so blatant that an Ohio news-paper asserted that "the Mormon Bible is Antimasonic."[22]

In Joseph's Bible revision, a Satanic conspiracy becomes central to the Cain and Abel narrative. Cain "loved Satan more than God" and was envious of his brother's flock. After God's rejection of his sacrifice, Satan promises Cain that he will deliver Abel into his hands, and he inducts Cain into a secret society. "Swear unto me by thy throat," Satan instructs Cain, "and if thou tell it thou shalt die." Cain agrees. He became "Master Mahon [later Mahan]," using secrecy to "murder and get gain." Cain then passes down the "secret combination" to his descendants, who also serve Satan. It is possible that "Master Mahon" was a clumsy code for "Master Mason," a degree within Freemasonry.[23]

As he worked his way through the early chapters of Genesis, Joseph Christianized Old Testament passages and harmonized the Bible's con-tent with that of the Book of Mormon. For instance, after his expulsion from Eden, Adam learns that his fall was part of a divine plan to bring about his eternal life and glory. And that plan hinges on Jesus Christ, who created the world and whose sacrificial death redeems human be-ings. "This is the plan of salvation unto all men," God teaches Adam, "through the blood of mine Only Begotten." Joseph intended to bring everything together in "one eternal round" connecting the world's cre-ation, those who had been baptized into the new Church of Christ, and everything in between. There was one Savior and one plan of salvation. God raised up prophets to point human beings toward that plan. In an-cient times, there was Moses. There were Christ's disciples in Jerusalem and among the Nephites. And now there was "Joseph the Seer."[24]

Joseph was intellectually precocious and curious, but he would never be-come a scholar like Jonathan Edwards, the Great Awakening minister who still towered over much of American theology. Edwards was a loner. He hated small talk and spent more than a dozen hours a day in his study, sometimes skipping dinner to continue his reading and writing.[25] Joseph would have loathed that life. He could work intensely on a proj-ect for a few weeks or a couple of months, but for the most part, his ideas took shape not through sustained study or composition, but through contemplation and conversation. He loved the company of family, friends, and strangers, and he preferred to work in collaboration with someone like Oliver Cowdery. Full of mirth, quick to laugh, Joseph was also happy to put work aside for a hearty meal or a wrestling match.

The seer, translator, and prophet rarely found time to devote himself to any one subject for very long. The revision of Genesis proceeded amid an ongoing flurry of activity and movement. In addition to repeated trips to Colesville and correspondence with those in Manchester and Fayette, Joseph dictated a series of revelations, including the first known divine message addressed to Emma.

For much of the last two years, Joseph had been on the move, and Emma had stayed behind in Harmony. Although she had been Joseph's scribe for a small portion of the Book of Mormon translation, Joseph clearly preferred to work with Cowdery. Moreover, eleven men had received a vision of the plates. Why hadn't Emma? She had only seen the plates under a cloth. What role, if any, would she play in the church?

Joseph provided answers to these questions in the words of Jesus Christ. "Thou art an elect lady," Joseph dictated, using a New Testament phrase. "Murmur not because of the things thou hast not seen." As for her role, she would be a scribe when Cowdery traveled, and she would make the selections for the church's hymnal. Also, under Joseph's leadership, she would "expound the scriptures and exhort the church." Her most important task, however, was to comfort and console Joseph. "Beware of pride," the Savior instructed Emma. "Let thy soul delight in thy husband and the glory which shall come upon him." If she found her glory in Joseph and kept God's commandments, one day she would come into Christ's presence.

The revelation also addressed this-worldly concerns. Joseph had not planted his fields in the spring, and now, at the height of summer, he labored to make up for lost time. Emma accepted her husband as a seer and prophet, but she worried about his ability to put food on their table. "Thou needest not fear," the revelation told Emma, "for thy husband shall support thee from the church." That was Joseph's "calling," not planting, harvesting, slaughtering, and tapping maple trees.[26]

Joseph soon abandoned his belated efforts to sow a harvest for the fall. He decided to leave Harmony. Emma's relatives despised him for his apparent indolence, and the lawsuits and other forms of opposition disrupted church activities. In August, Joseph borrowed money from a Harmony merchant and used it to make the remaining payments on the farm that he owed to Emma's father. Then, after a final visit to the church in Colesville, Emma and Joseph left her family and their home behind and headed northwest toward Fayette. Emma was pregnant for the second time. They were together. It was another new beginning.

CHAPTER EIGHT

Enoch (1830–1831)

JOSEPH RETURNED TO THE Fayette, New York, home of Peter Whitmer Sr. in September 1830. He was safe from the mobs and legal harassments he had endured in Chenango and Broome Counties, but other challenges confronted the budding prophet. Hiram Page, one of the eight witnesses who claimed to have seen and held the Book of Mormon plates, was writing his own revelations. He had dug a black stone out of the earth. When he gazed into it, a sentence would appear. After he wrote it down, another sentence would replace it. Minus the hat, it was Joseph's old method. As a then former member of the church commented a year later, Page's dictation "bore most striking marks of a Mormonite revelation." Soon Page had a sheaf of revelations. It isn't clear what they contained, but they apparently clashed with some of Joseph's commandments. Even worse, Oliver Cowdery and members of the Whitmer family—Page was married to Catherine Whitmer, daughter of Peter Whitmer Sr.—gave credence to the new revelations.[1]

Joseph had stopped using his seer stone as a conduit for his revelations. He now dictated the words of the Lord in a trance-like state without the stone, hat, or any other device. William McLellin, who joined the church the next fall, wrote an account of the process. First, the "prophet and revelator enquires of God." Then, he "spiritually sees, hears and feels, and then speaks as he is moved upon by the Holy Ghost." A scribe read the dictation back to Joseph sentence by sentence for his approval. The change in method raised questions. Had Joseph's revelations come because he was God's chosen seer? Or did he simply happen to have a special stone? If he didn't use his stone, could church members trust his commandments? And if Page had a seer stone, could he now deliver the words of the Lord?[2]

Oliver Cowdery, meanwhile, contended against Joseph on other fronts. He objected to a statement in the church's recently adopted "Articles and Covenants." That document stated that prior to their baptism, believers needed to demonstrate through their "works" that they had "received of the spirit of Christ." It was a theological point Protestants had debated for centuries. Did individuals seeking church membership have to demonstrate external signs of internal faith? Cowdery denounced the requirement as "priestcraft" and, according to Joseph's later history, "commanded [Joseph] in the name of God" to strike it out.[3]

Joseph met these challenges firmly. He addressed a revelation to Cowdery. In it, Jesus Christ declared that "no one shall be appointed to receive commandments and revelations in this church excepting my servant Joseph, for he receiveth them even as Moses." Cowdery was like Aaron, Moses's brother. His job was to proclaim the revelations that Joseph received, not to question them or produce his own. The revelation also clarified that Joseph's authority came from God, not a stone. "I have given him [Joseph] the keys of the mysteries of the revelations," the Savior explained. As for Hiram Page, Cowdery was instructed to take him aside for a private chat and tell him that he had been deceived by Satan.[4]

In September 1830, the church—now with around sixty members—held another conference. Page and Cowdery fell into line. Page renounced his stone, and the elders affirmed that Joseph was the sole receiver of revelations authoritative for the church. According to Emer Harris, Martin Harris's brother, Page's stone "was broke to powder and the writings burnt." Cowdery signaled his obeisance by reading the Articles and Covenants aloud.[5]

Joseph still used his seer stones on occasion, but told his followers that he no longer needed them. Orson Pratt, who joined the church later that fall, recalled that Joseph "was so thoroughly endowed with ... the spirit of revelation that he oftener received them without any instrument, or other means than the operation of the spirit upon his mind." It was Joseph who was Christ's oracle, not anyone who chanced upon a seer stone.[6]

The conflicts with Page and Cowdery pointed to a fundamental instability within the movement. Was the Church of Christ led by a

Moses-like prophet, or was it a church of many prophets and revelators? Joseph wanted it both ways. "Joseph Smith was the Henry Ford of revelation," the scholar Kathleen Flake explains. "He wanted every home to have one, and the revelation he had in mind was the revelation he'd had."[7] Joseph had a knack for helping other men and women to have visions of the divine, but he also attracted an array of headstrong and independent-minded followers who brought forth their own prophetic claims, challenging his authority in much the way that he had challenged that of other churches and ministers. Making space for the broad exercise of spiritual gifts while maintaining his prophetic authority took firmness, patience, and a certain amount of finesse.[8]

American Protestants who attended a Church of Christ meeting would have found much that was recognizable. Joseph and his followers preached. They baptized. They celebrated the Lord's Supper. Like the Methodists, they held frequent conferences. The powerful expressions of the Holy Spirit resembled what took place at Protestant revivals. To be sure, Protestant sects didn't have a "seer and translator and prophet" at their head or a new volume of scripture, but the basic contours of religious activity were familiar.

Joseph, however, was working toward the realization of a much more radical vision. In the Book of Mormon, the prophet Ether foretells that God will gather "the remnant of the seed of Joseph"—the Indians, the descendants of the Lamanites—into a "New Jerusalem," a second Zion. Joseph clarified in a September 1830 revelation that not only converted Indians would be gathered, but also the members of the Church of Christ. "Ye are called to bring to pass the gathering of mine elect," he dictated. "They shall be gathered in unto one place." There was no time to waste, as Christ soon would return and reign with his church on earth for a thousand years. That triumph would be preceded by tribulations: darkened sun, a blood-colored moon, falling stars, and hailstorms. Flies would eat human flesh, which would become infested with maggots. Much of this was standard biblical fare, straight out of the Book of Revelation. The gathering would shelter Christ's true followers from this coming storm.[9]

Jesus's earliest followers expected his imminent return, and the idea has waxed and waned over the history of Christianity. In the early 1830s, American Protestants were transfixed by the expectation of Christ's millennial reign, though they disagreed about its timing. The famed Presbyterian evangelist Charles Finney, holding a revival in Rochester in the fall of 1830, told a congregation that if Christians "were united all over the world the millennium might be brought about in three months." Christians had it within their power to commence a thousand-year period of peace and justice, to be followed by Christ's return.[10]

William Miller, a Baptist minister in Vermont, also believed the millennium was nigh, but that its advent would be cataclysmic. Based on his own reading of biblical prophecies, Miller became convinced that Christ would return to earth no later than 1843. Christians would rise into the air to meet their coming Lord, while the world and the wicked would burn. Then Christ would descend to a purified earth and reign with the righteous for a thousand years.[11]

Joseph Smith's views were closer to Miller's than Finney's, but he gave these ideas his own twist. For the Mormon prophet, the Second Coming was more about a particular place than a prophesied time. Joseph expected his followers to build a literal city, not simply to reform the societies in which they lived. The city of New Jerusalem would include a temple. Furthermore, one of Joseph's revelations stated that the city—the place of gathering—would be "among the Lamanites," thus presumably somewhere on the western frontier. The idea that Christians should settle among the Natives in the West to meet their returning Savior was singular in the history of American Christianity.[12]

Joseph fleshed out this vision of Zion as he proceeded with his Bible revision. In its genealogy of Adam's descendants, the Book of Genesis includes Enoch, who "walked with God: and he *was* not; for God took him." Where did God take him? Why? Legends about Enoch provided answers. A book of Enoch (what many scholars now call I Enoch), written around the third century B.C.E., describes Enoch's receipt of heavenly mysteries and—expanding on another passage in Genesis—narrates that angels ("the sons of God") mated with human women and brought forth a race of giants. Early Christians also took an interest in the figure of Enoch. The New Testament Epistle to the Hebrews explains that because Enoch's faith pleased God, he was spared the agony of death and instead was immediately "translated" into God's presence.

The figure of Enoch still resonated in the early nineteenth century, and not just because of the passages in Genesis and Hebrews. Richard Laurence, an Anglican minister and Oxford don, published an English translation of I Enoch in 1821, but Enoch material circulated on a more popular level as well. In the rites of Royal Arch Masonry, Enoch seeks the name of God in order that he may be restored to Edenic perfection.

God appears to him in a vision, sends him to the top of a mountain, and reveals to him a triangular plate of gold. The plate contains characters, which God warns him never to pronounce. Enoch then builds an underground temple that hides the plate, which Solomon's architects eventually discover.[13]

Regardless of what precipitated his interest in Enoch, Joseph transformed the brief Genesis passage into a grand story. At a time of human wickedness, God raises up a "seer," choosing Enoch, a young lad who is "slow of speech" but faithful. God bestows upon him "power of . . . language," and Enoch becomes a traveling preacher, urging people to repent and be baptized. When enemies come to do battle against God's people, Enoch's words bring forth earthquakes and floods to protect them. Even the "giants of the land st[and] far off." Enoch gathers his people into a city. They are "of one heart and of one mind." No one is poor. God calls the people and their city "Zion."

Enoch, like Moses, walks with God and even talks with him "face to face." After a vision in which God shows Enoch all of the inhabitants of the earth and their wickedness, God takes the entire city of Zion up into heaven, looks upon the "residue" of humanity, and weeps. God tells Enoch that "in the last days" he will judge the wicked but preserve his "elect." There will be a New Jerusalem, and the city of Enoch will unite with it and enjoy God's millennial reign.[14]

Joseph taught church members that they would fulfill these prophecies. They were the "Gentiles" who would join with the "remnant of Jacob," the Natives. Gathered to a New Jerusalem, a second Zion, they would be of one heart and mind. Joseph would be a second Enoch.

Given the context of the United States in 1830, it was an utterly preposterous vision. Just a few months earlier, President Andrew Jackson had signed the Indian Removal Act, which forced Native peoples living east of the Mississippi River to resettle to its west. The policy had some white critics, but, on balance, white Americans didn't want to live with or near Indians. They wanted to clear Native lands for white settlements.

The young church's hope for Native converts was somewhat less farfetched. In the first several decades of the nineteenth century, many Cherokee had embraced various forms of Christianity, and prominent Cherokee leaders appealed to shared Christian principles in their arguments against dispossession and removal. Joseph's first known revelation had explained that the Book of Mormon plates had been prepared "that the Lamanites might come to the knowledge of the Fathers and . . . believe the Gospel." Now, in September 1830, Joseph's revelations called Oliver Cowdery, Peter Whitmer Jr., Ziba Peterson, and just-baptized Parley P. Pratt as missionaries to the Lamanites.[15]

The twenty-three-year-old Pratt was well suited for missionary work. Raised in central and eastern New York State, Pratt had made his own way to the Ohio frontier. When he was only nineteen, he had spent a winter living in a log hut thirty miles west of Cleveland. Pratt's religious life had already taken a series of twists and turns. While still in New York State, he had joined a Baptist church. Then, in 1829, he met a minister named Sidney Rigdon, who belonged to a movement loosely organized by Alexander Campbell and Walter Scott. They were bent on "a restoration of the ancient order of things," the recovery of early Christianity as described in the New Testament.[16]

The idea of restoring ancient primitive Christianity appealed to many Americans in the early nineteenth century. There was an obvious chasm between what Americans read about in the New Testament and what most experienced in their churches. Early Christians had spoken in unknown spiritual tongues. They had witnessed miraculous healings. At least in Jerusalem, the earliest Christians had sold their possessions and held the proceeds in common. These practices had vanished, at least in most contexts, and nonbiblical customs had crept in: creeds, denominations, ministerial salaries and educational requirements. Many Campbellite reformers still belonged to Baptist associations, but they increasingly referred to themselves as simply "Christians" or "Disciples."[17]

Sidney Rigdon became a leading light among the Campbellites in northeastern Ohio. He pastored a congregation in the town of Mentor but traveled to speak to churches and families across the region. Physically, Rigdon was unprepossessing, and he spoke without the histrionics of some revivalists. As a preacher, however, Rigdon was a "masterpiece" and could seal the spiritual deal. "He was just the man for an awakening," observed a Disciples historian.[18]

Baptism for Rigdon was not a symbolic act that accompanied conversion. Rather, a believer obtained forgiveness for sins through the act of baptism. The ritual was thus essential for human salvation. Rigdon baptized scores of individuals and established a string of "reformed Baptist" congregations in the region.

Rigdon and some of his followers became convinced that Christians should hold their property in common. On the outskirts of Kirtland, Ohio, a number of households—led by Isaac Morley and Lyman

Sidney Rigdon, 1873. (Courtesy of Church History Library)

Wight—covenanted with each other to share their possessions. Around five dozen individuals lived on the Morley farm, calling themselves the "Big Family," or simply the "Family."[19]

Parley Pratt was not part of Morley's Family, but he was among the scores of men and women in northeastern Ohio convinced by the teachings of Sidney Rigdon. Fired with zeal, and possibly also escaping creditors in Ohio, Pratt headed back to New York to preach to friends and family. He made his evangelistic start not far from Palmyra and soon heard about "a VERY STRANGE BOOK!" When he got his hands on a copy of the Book of Mormon, Pratt read it all day and all night, not even stopping to eat. He rushed to meet Joseph. The prophet was still in Harmony, but Hyrum Smith convinced Pratt that he had found the restoration of Christ's true church. Cowdery baptized Pratt, who within days was baptizing others. When Joseph moved to Fayette, he immediately sized up Pratt as a willing and able missionary.[20]

On their way to present-day eastern Kansas, the missionaries to the Lamanites stopped in Kirtland. Pratt's contacts with the Rigdonites in the area made it easy for him and his companions to find opportunities to preach. Pratt baptized Isaac Morley, and many other members of the "Family" also converted. Frederick G. Williams, a physician and former member of Rigdon's congregation, joined the missionaries as they resumed their westward trek. Sidney Rigdon himself was baptized in November, and his conversion inspired many others in the area to follow his example.

In December 1830, Rigdon visited Fayette, eager to meet the man who had brought forth the Book of Mormon. He could not have received a warmer welcome from the prophet. At the time, Joseph was still a few weeks shy of his twenty-fifth birthday. Rigdon was twelve years his senior, an experienced and successful preacher. His conversion lent a decided gravitas to the fledgling church. Joseph took quickly to talented newcomers. He had done so when Oliver Cowdery showed up in Harmony, and now, in Cowdery's absence, he did so again. A few days after meeting Rigdon, Joseph dictated a revelation in which Jesus Christ compared Rigdon to John the Baptist. Through his reformed Baptist principles and preaching, Rigdon had prepared the way for scores of people to join the Church of Christ. He became Joseph's new right-hand man.[21]

The Ohio conversions and Rigdon's arrival prodded Joseph toward a decision he had been contemplating for several months. Joseph did not yet know where the New Jerusalem would be built, but he knew western New York wasn't Zion. Church members were scattered: some in Colesville, others in western New York, and now many more in northeastern Ohio. According to Lucy Mack Smith, individuals opposed to her family's religious activities were determined to harass them by pressing for payment on outstanding debts. Joseph's father spent weeks that fall in a Canandaigua jail for his failure to settle a small obligation. Meanwhile, Emma's second pregnancy proved a struggle. Sometime after the missionaries to the Lamanites departed in October, her strength gave out, and she endured "a heavy fit of sickness" for four weeks. She and Joseph divided their time between the Whitmer residence in Fayette, the family home on the Palmyra-Manchester line, and the Macedon, New York, home of Joseph's sister, Sophronia.[22]

It is no wonder Joseph was thinking about gathering his family and church to a place where they could be together and clear of their enemies. The conversions in northeastern Ohio pointed the way. The church was growing rapidly there. Land was cheap, and creditors would be unlikely to pursue them at such a distance.

A December revelation instructed church members to "assemble together at the Ohio . . . because of the enemy and for your sakes."[23] When
Joseph announced the plan at a conference held in Fayette on January 2,
1831, church members were stunned. When they joined the Church of
Christ, men and women understood it as a seminal moment, but their
outward lives did not necessarily change. Some men undertook missions,
but most families stayed in their homes.

Now Joseph was asking church members to uproot themselves and
move to Ohio. Those with property were particularly hesitant to obey
the command. Some suspected that "Joseph had invented it himself to
deceive the people that in the end he might get gain." Others worried
that if word spread of the planned migration, they would not get fair
prices for their land.[24]

Joseph responded to the grumbling and questions with a revelation.
"I am the same which hath taken the Zion of Enoch into mine own
bosom," Jesus Christ told church members. Apocalyptic judgment was
nigh. "The angels are waiting the great command to reap down the earth
to gather the tares that they may be burned," he warned them. There
were promises of rich blessings for obedient church members, however.
Christ encouraged them that if they responded faithfully and gathered to
Ohio, they would receive land for the "inheritance" of their children
"forever." They would live under the laws of Christ as a "free people."
Like the early Christians on Pentecost, they would be "endowed with
power from on high" and be ready to take the gospel to the world. Property should not stand in the way. Those who could not sell now could retain and lease their farms. According to one local report, after a long
night of fasting and prayer, church members assented. The various
branches of the church made plans to move in the spring.[25]

Joseph and Emma departed for Ohio in late January 1831. It was the
dead of winter; they traveled through the snow on Joseph Knight's
sleigh. Emma was entering the final few months of her pregnancy. Joseph was leaving the woods, hillside, and home that had launched his
prophetic career. Now he was bound for the region where the greatest
number of church members lived. It was a step toward Zion and the millennium. Joseph would find, however, that peace and unity were a long
way off.

CHAPTER NINE

Flying High (1831)

J OSEPH SMITH KNEW HOW to make an entrance. On February 4, 1831, he and Emma rode into Kirtland. They pulled up to Newel K. Whitney's White Store, and Joseph bounded inside. He reached his hand out and greeted Whitney by name. The storekeeper wondered who the tall, thin stranger was. "I am Joseph the Prophet," was the response. "You have prayed me here, now what do you want of me?"[1]

Newel Whitney, or N.K., as he was often known, was ten years older than Joseph and many times more prosperous, thanks to the store he owned in partnership with Sidney Gilbert. The Whitneys, like Sidney Rigdon, were former Campbellites who had been baptized into the Church of Christ. Gilbert and his wife, Elizabeth, followed suit in the spring of 1831.[2]

Once acquainted with the brash newcomer, Whitney took the prophet to meet other Kirtland church members. While Joseph was visiting in Sidney Gilbert's house, he heard a crash and screams outside. The wagon carrying Joseph and Emma's goods had careened down a slippery hill. No one was hurt, but the accident illustrated the difficulty of being constantly on the move. Joseph continued his peripatetic ways, but Kirtland was the hub of his activities for the next seven years. Whitney and his wife, Elizabeth Ann (she went by her middle name), welcomed Joseph and Emma and gave them a bedroom in their home. Newel, Ann, and their three children relocated upstairs.[3]

Joseph Smith's activities in northeastern Ohio. (Map by John Hamer)

Kirtland was an agrarian town situated on the Chagrin River, about five miles southeast of Lake Erie. The town claimed a thousand persons in the 1830 census, and a sizeable minority of them, as many as a third, had accepted the message brought by Oliver Cowdery, Parley Pratt, and the other missionaries to the Lamanites. There were scores of additional converts in neighboring towns, such as Mentor, the site of Rigdon's former congregation. A church that had counted only sixty members at its September 1830 conference in Fayette, New York, suddenly had hundreds of adherents in Ohio.[4]

The "Mormonites" (as Eber D. Howe, editor of the nearby *Painesville Telegraph*, called them) became known for their dynamic, even outlandish spirituality. Some men and women had dreams and visions in which they saw Jesus Christ and conversed with angels. Others spoke or even sang in spiritual tongues. Especially among the movement's younger converts, the physical manifestations of the Spirit were powerful. Fourteen-year-old Lucy Stanton and other young women would "scream hello 'Glory!' and clap their hands, and finally apparently become unconscious." Burr Riggs, a nineteen-year-old, would "jump up from the floor, strike his hand against the joist . . . and swing some minutes, then fall like he was dead." Riggs then would come to and talk about what he had seen.[5]

When Kirtland church members spoke in tongues, some understood it as "talking Injun." Men and women acted out elaborate performances in which they preached to imagined Lamanite audiences. "Playing Indian" was a long-established white American form of entertainment, and in Kirtland it took specifically Mormon forms. "Some would act like an Indian in the act of scalping," John Whitmer recounted. "Some would slide or scoot . . . on the floor, with the rapidity of a serpent, which they termed sailing in the boat to the Lamanites." The combination of pantomime and spiritual power entertained and sometimes horrified those who witnessed it. When Joseph arrived in Kirtland, he wasn't sure what to make of such behavior.[6]

Joseph also learned that he wasn't the only revelator in town. As had some Shakers and Methodists, the Ohio Mormons took inspiration from the Book of Revelation, in which John of Patmos receives a book from an angel. Sixteen-year-old Heman Bassett, part of the fall 1830 wave of baptisms into the Church of Christ, read aloud from a revelation he claimed to have received "from the hand of an angel." Another Kirtland revelator was an African American man known only by his first name, Peter, who had been born into slavery around 1775. "Black Pete got sight of one of those revelations carried by a black angel," stated George A. Smith, Joseph's young cousin. According to George A., Peter jumped off a riverbank in an attempt to catch the heavenly message and crashed into the treetops below. "He sometimes fancies he can fly," sneered a local newspaper.[7]

There was also a prophetess named Laura or Louisa Hubble. Joseph later noted that "a woman came with great pretensions to revealing commandments." Joseph drew a distinction between the gift of prophecy and the prerogative to command others by revelation. For instance, that winter a fourteen-year-old girl "prophesied . . . of the destruction of many notable cities," specifically in China. Her words did not pose a challenge to Joseph's leadership, but Black Pete, Hubble, and other revelators

threatened to splinter the Church of Christ in northeastern Ohio because they presented rival sources of charismatic religious authority.[8]

In other respects, moreover, there was a complete lack of order
among the Kirtland converts. Shortly after Levi Hancock was baptized,
he paid a visit to Isaac Morley and his Family. While there, Heman Bassett took Hancock's pocket watch and walked off with it. Hancock confronted Bassett after learning that the young revelator had sold it. "I
thought it was all in the family," Bassett responded wryly. In nearby
Chardon, many church members shared a single home. A newspaper reported that it lacked any chairs and that when food was placed on the
table, "every inmate takes a piece of meat and potato in his hand, and de-
vours them as he walks about the room." Residents allegedly wore any
clothes they could find on the premises. Joseph needed to impose some
order on Kirtland's spiritual chaos. Otherwise, the Church of Christ in
Ohio would collapse as quickly as it had grown.[9]

The prophet wasted no time taking charge. "Hearken and hear, O my people," began a revelation Joseph dictated on the night of his arrival. As was
customary, the words in the revelation were those of Jesus Christ. "I will be
your ruler," the Lord told church members. Joseph made it clear that he
and he alone was Christ's chosen prophet. It was the same message he had
delivered in Fayette after Hiram Page had produced his sheaf of revelations. Hubbell and "Black Pete" quickly drifted away from the movement.[10]

Joseph's first Kirtland revelation also addressed practical matters.
The prophet couldn't remain in the Whitney residence for long. The
Lord declared that "Joseph should have a house built in which to live and
translate." When he joined the Church of Christ, Sidney Rigdon had lost
the home his former congregation had provided for him. He wouldn't
get a new house, but should be given "a comfortable room." The revelation also called Edward Partridge to be the church's bishop, a new office.
Partridge owned a hattery in nearby Painesville. He was told to leave his
business behind and devote all of his time to the church. As bishop, he
would play a key role in the church's financial affairs and in its provision
of land and sustenance for new arrivals.[11]

A few days later, Joseph assembled a group of the church's elders for
what became a revelatory question-and-answer session. The elders posed
questions; Joseph dictated responses from Jesus Christ. Some of the
more pressing questions concerned the financial arrangements of the
church and its members. "Thou shalt consecrate all thy properties . . .

unto me with a covenant and deed which cannot be broken," Jesus Christ commanded. Bishop Partridge would then allocate back to each man whatever he needed for himself and his family. The church would retain the "residue," using those funds to assist the poor and for land purchases. There was also a warning: those who apostatized would not receive back that which they had consecrated.[12]

The law of consecration, however, did not mean holding all things in common. Church members should not snatch each other's watches and shirts. "Thou shalt not take thy brother's garment," the Lord commanded. Joseph didn't want a church of loafers and freeloaders. And when church members arrived from New York or elsewhere, each family would have a place to live "by themselves." The church would form tight-knit communities of families, not a Morley-style Family.[13]

Then there was the issue of spiritual gifts. Joseph was concerned about the behavior at some church gatherings, but he did not want to extinguish the power that coursed through his movement. On March 4, 1831, church members rousted Joseph while it was still dark. He rushed to the side of a woman who was suffering from a demon. "I went and had an awful struggle with Satan," Joseph wrote his brother Hyrum, "but being armed with the power of God he was cast out and the woman is clothed in her right mind." The exorcism, he added, was evidence that "the Lord worketh wonders in this land." Joseph also presided over miraculous healings. Jared Carter, who had joined the church in Colesville and had moved to Kirtland, recorded that Joseph came to his house when his youngest child was "distressingly sick." Carter feared his son would die. After Joseph called on the Lord, "the child was healed immediately." Reports of miracles circulated throughout the region.[14]

In meetings and private gatherings, wild spiritual scenes continued despite the unease of some church members. Men and women swooned, made bizarre gestures, became "disfigured in their countenances," and fell "into ecstasies." Some church leaders pressed the prophet to provide some guidance and clarity. Joseph's revelations insisted that visions, prophecies, and tongues were valid spiritual gifts, but he was less certain how to regulate these physical manifestations of the Spirit. He merely instructed church leaders to ask God whether the spirits and gifts they encountered were from God or from the devil. It wasn't always easy to know.[15]

After several weeks of living with the Whitneys, Joseph and Emma moved into Isaac Morley's home. Later in the spring, in keeping with

Joseph's first Kirtland revelation, a frame house was built for the prophet and his family on the Morley farm. Joseph's father and brother Hyrum came to Kirtland in early April, and his mother and other family members were on the way.

Meanwhile, the missionaries to the Lamanites reached Jackson County in far western Missouri. It had been an arduous journey through what settlers in the region remembered as the "winter of the deep snow." Peter Whitmer Jr. and Ziba Peterson stayed and worked in the frontier town of Independence, while Oliver Cowdery, Parley Pratt, and Frederick Williams headed farther west. They spent a night with the Shawnee, then crossed the frozen Kansas River and met with William Anderson (Kikthawenund), a Delaware (Lenape) chief, and his people.[16]

The aged Anderson, born in 1757 in southeastern Pennsylvania, had spent much of his life being pushed west. White soldiers and politicians had forced a string of removals: to the White River in Indiana and then to Missouri. In 1829, under pressure from white settlers who had arrived from Mississippi, Anderson agreed to abandon his people's right to their Missouri land in exchange for a tract north of the Kansas River.[17]

Anderson already had listened to and rejected Moravian, Baptist, and Methodist preachers. He wasn't excited to see another delegation. The newcomers claimed to possess a book about his people's ancestors, and they predicted a glorious future for the Delaware. As the missionaries had traveled through Ohio, newspapers had reported their expectation that the conversion of Natives would "make them a *white* and delightsome people, and be reinstated in the possession of their lands of which they have been despoiled by the whites." According to Parley Pratt's later account, he promised the Lenape that they would be "restored to all their rights and privileges." It was a striking and potentially incendiary message.[18]

Cowdery wrote to Kirtland that Anderson and his people had received their preaching with gratitude and that many Shawnee also believed. The report was wildly optimistic. Anderson was used to parrying offers of education and evangelism from Christian missionaries. He wasn't interested, in part because he knew that white settlers always followed in the wake of white missionaries.[19]

The mission to the Lamanites ended abruptly. Richard Cummins, federal Indian agent for the territory, told Cowdery and his companions that he would imprison them if they continued to preach without a permit. They weren't likely to get one. Cummins informed Superintendent of Indian Affairs William Clark—of Lewis and Clark fame—that the missionaries "act very strange." After just a few days with the Delaware, the missionaries retreated back to Kaw Township in Jackson County.[20]

News from Missouri focused Joseph's mind on biblical prophecy. On March 7, 1831, Joseph dictated a long revelation in which Jesus Christ spoke at length about the coming tribulations and the establishment of Zion. The revelation also engaged a confusing New Testament passage. In the Gospel of Matthew, Jesus predicts that in the wake of war and famine and the desecration of the Jerusalem Temple, he will return in clouds of power and glory. "This generation shall not pass," Jesus concludes, "till all these things be fulfilled." But the Romans had destroyed the temple, and Jesus had not returned. Was Jesus's prophecy incorrect? Or had his followers misunderstood it?

Joseph Smith didn't like loose ends in the Bible. His March 1831 revelation clarified the vexing passage in Matthew. According to the revelation, Jesus meant that those who had heard his prophecy would not pass away prior to the temple's destruction. But his other predictions were not about the first century. They were about members of Christ's true church in the early 1830s. In other words, there were men and women in the Church of Christ who would live to witness Christ's return. While the world suffered from blood, fire, and smoke, God's saints would take refuge in Zion and greet their Lord.

The same revelation included some immediate instruction for both Joseph and the church. Once settled in Kirtland, Joseph had resumed his Bible revision project and had dictated through, roughly, the midpoint of the Book of Genesis. At this rate, it would be a very long time before Joseph reached the passage in Matthew he had just clarified through revelation. With that in mind, Jesus told Joseph to set aside his Genesis revision and instead translate the New Testament, "that ye may be prepared for the things to come."[21]

Joseph began on the New Testament the very next day. For the most part, he edited with a much lighter touch than he had applied to Genesis. That changed when he reached the twenty-fourth chapter of Matthew, which he brought into alignment with his recent revelation. The revision repeated that a first tribulation had befallen "the Jews" shortly after Jesus's lifetime. A second tribulation would come later, at a time when faithful disciples preached the gospel to all nations. "Then shall the end come," the revision explained. Jesus hadn't made a false prophecy.

Instead, the biblical text had become corrupted. Now Joseph had restored it.[22]

At the end of April, Emma gave birth to twins who lived for at most a few hours. Three years before, Emma and Joseph had endured the still-birth of a deformed son. Now they experienced a double dose of sadness. According to a local newspaper report, Emma only survived because of the late intervention of a physician. She didn't name the twins she and Joseph surrendered to the grave. The couple wondered whether future pregnancies would end with the same sorrow.[23]

The very day of Emma's delivery, Julia Murdock—who with her husband, John, had been baptized the previous fall—gave birth to twins of her own. The Murdock twins were healthy, but the placenta didn't expel following the birth. Six hours later, Julia called John to her side, reached out her hand, bid him farewell, folded her hands across her stomach, and died. "The anguish of soul that I felt at this time you may try to imagine," John Murdock recalled. The widowed Murdock had three other children as well. He could have asked his wife's family to raise them, but they were not church members.

Joseph sent word to Murdock that he and Emma would raise the twins. As Lucy Mack Smith put it, "These children were taken to supply the places of a pair of twins which [Emma] had lost." Given Murdock's concern about his children's religious upbringing and salvation, the adoption was a ready solution. Murdock, however, resented Emma's request that he never reveal himself to the children as their father. The Murdock twins received the names Julia and Joseph, named for their birth mother and adoptive father.[24]

Soon after the twins joined the household, Joseph traveled to Fairport, a village on the shores of Lake Erie. There he met his mother, several siblings, and around eighty church members from Fayette, Waterloo, and other Finger Lakes towns. Joseph Knight Sr., Martin Harris, and dozens of other church members followed. Not everyone came. Josiah Stowell, one of Joseph's most stalwart supporters over the past five years, remained in Bainbridge. Still, the church was gathering, and Joseph's family was reunited.[25]

By the time he moved to Kirtland, Martin Harris had lost the land he had mortgaged to pay for the Book of Mormon's printing. Harris still had hundreds of copies of the book, which Joseph instructed him not to sell for less than $1.25, a discount from the original price, but still high.

Julia Murdock Smith, ca. 1850s.
(Courtesy of Community of Christ Archives)

As John H. Gilbert, Grandin's typesetter, commented, Harris was "cleaned out financially." Harris lamented that the books wouldn't sell but, at least in later years, he harbored no bitterness. "I never lost one cent," he stated. "Mr. Smith paid me all that I advanced, and more too." Perhaps Harris meant that he had been repaid spiritually, as it is unlikely that Joseph could have repaid him the money. Harris's case was extreme, but the Whitmers, the Knights, and many other families also sacrificed a great deal by uprooting themselves from their New York homes and by more firmly attaching their fortunes to Joseph Smith.[26]

In early June 1831, around sixty men attended a church conference held in a schoolhouse near Isaac Morley's house. Joseph opened the conference with preaching and prayer. "He is not naturally talented for a speaker," observed Jared Carter during the conference, "yet he was filled with the power of the Holy Ghost so that he spoke as I never heard man speak." Those in attendance anticipated an outpouring of miracles, and they weren't disappointed.[27]

The conference's main business was the ordination of around two dozen men to the "high priesthood." Joseph reminded the congregation that Jesus had compared the kingdom of God to a grain of mustard seed. It would grow into an enormous tree, "and the angels of heaven would some day come like birds to its branches." The prophet told his listeners that some of them would live to see it. Others of them "must die for the testimony of this work." He then looked intently at Lyman Wight, one of the many converts from the Morley Family, and among the first to be ordained as a high priest. Joseph told Wight he wouldn't have to wait to see his Savior. He would meet the Lord "near the corner of the house." Joseph then laid his hands upon Wight and blessed him. Wight stepped toward the congregation. "I now see God and Jesus Christ at his right hand," he announced. "Let them kill me. I should not feel death."[28]

Not everyone responded so positively. Harvey Whitlock "turned as black as Lyman was white," recalled Levi Hancock. "His fingers were set like claws." Whitlock's whole body contorted, and he couldn't speak as he staggered around the room. According to Ezra Booth, a recent convert who left the church a few months later, Joseph wasn't sure how to proceed at first but soon "learnt by the spirit, that Harvey was under a diabolical influence, and that Satan had bound him." Joseph set him free. He laid his hands on Whitlock's head and ordered Satan to depart from him. Whitlock's muscles relaxed. Other men were similarly afflicted and received the same prophetic exorcism.[29]

Joseph had introduced and ordained men into the "high priesthood." What was it? Priesthood for Joseph was not just about ecclesiastical office. It granted access to spiritual authority and power. One of Joseph's revelations had promised that in Ohio the church's elders would be "endowed with power from on high," preparing them for successful missions. Joseph explained that "the order of the high priesthood is that they have power given them to seal up the Saints unto eternal life." Their words, and the rituals of baptism and confirmation over which they presided, would bring about human salvation. Church members also associated the high priesthood with the power to heal physical infirmities. In the months and years ahead, Joseph came to use "high priesthood" interchangeably with "Melchizedek priesthood." In the Book of Genesis, Melchizedek is king of Salem and "priest of the most high God." He brings bread and wine to Abraham. The New Testament Epistle to the

Hebrews identifies Jesus Christ as a high priest "after the order of Melchizedek."[30]

Joseph also used the conference as an opportunity to take a strong stand against the extreme spiritual ecstasy that had stirred division in Kirtland. He made it clear that certain behaviors were beyond the pale. No screaming. No collapsing. No running. "Heman Bassett," Joseph commanded one of the more unruly church members. "You sit still. The devil wants to sift you."[31] Church leaders still encouraged prophecy and visions and healing, but with less spiritual chaos. Speaking in tongues became less common, as did the wild physical manifestations of the Spirit. Bassett left the church.

On the conference's final day, the prophet dictated a revelation to the church's elders. In it, Jesus Christ announced that the church's next conference would be in Missouri. That would be the place where the "remnant of Jacob"—converted Indians—and church members would build their new Zion. "Assemble yourselves together to rejoice upon the land of your inheritance," Christ commanded. Joseph and Sidney Rigdon would attend the Missouri conference. The revelation also called by name those elders—most of whom had been ordained as high priests—who would journey west, preaching and baptizing on the way.[32]

It was another instance of a revelation asking individuals to make great sacrifices. Most of the men had little money to provide for their families in their absence. Parley Pratt had just returned to his wife from the mission to the Lamanites, and now he left again. All of Bishop Edward Partridge's children were gravely ill with measles when he said goodbye to his family. Levi Hancock didn't want to go because he would leave behind a "young lady" he wished to marry. It was hard to say no, however. The conference had made plain the power of both Satan and Jesus Christ. "When I would think of the old Jack and the man of sin [both nicknames for Satan] who had been revealed before us all," recalled Hancock, "I found myself harnessed and I said let all other things go I will do as I am told." With faith in God, afraid of the devil, and obedient to Joseph's revelations, he and the others departed almost immediately.[33]

Joseph left Ohio buoyed by what he had accomplished in the last four months. It was a little more than a year after the founding of the Church of Christ. He had arrived in Ohio among church members who didn't know him and had introduced himself as their prophet and revelator. There were plenty of fresh converts with more zeal than constancy, and thorny issues such as communal sharing could have sundered the fledgling church's unity. Joseph had shown church members his spiritual fire, but he also had exhibited patience with certain issues and personalities. The move to northeastern Ohio had been a resounding success. Now he would strike out for the frontier.

CHAPTER TEN

Land of Joseph (1831)

O N JULY 14, 1831, Joseph Smith, Martin Harris, and Edward Partridge walked through the small frontier settlement of Independence in Jackson County, Missouri. They had left Kirtland on June 19, traveled by steamer from Cincinnati to Louisville and from there to St. Louis, and then traversed the remaining 250 miles on foot. Joseph's intention was to lay the cornerstone for a future temple, hold a church conference, and then return home to Kirtland and his family.

Jackson County had long been a crossroads of peoples and goods. European and then American explorers and trappers traded with the Osage who lived along the banks of the Kansas and Missouri Rivers. White settlement led to a number of involuntary migrations. In 1808, the Osage signed a treaty with the United States that ceded their Missouri land, and the creation of the Shawnee and Delaware reservations to the west brought U.S. Indian agents to the region. Meanwhile, Missouri joined the Union as a slave state in 1821. Out of a total population of nearly three thousand in 1830, there were about two hundred slaves in Jackson County, and the number of enslaved persons grew rapidly over the next decade. The western Missouri frontier, with its growing population of slaveholders and slaves living adjacent to Native peoples coerced to move west, bore little resemblance to the unity and peace Joseph envisioned for his American Zion.

Independence, incorporated in 1827, was the Jackson County seat. Ezra Booth, one of the many elders who made the journey that summer, described it as a "new town, containing a courthouse, built of brick, two or three merchant stores, and fifteen or twenty dwelling houses, built mostly of logs hewed on both sides." When the writer Washington Irving passed through Independence the next year, he noted that the fertile soil was "like that of a garden" but that he found "rougher and rougher life" the closer he got to town. Church members and non-Mormon settlers didn't like the looks of each other. William W. Phelps, who came in Joseph's group, commented that he and the other northerners felt distinctly unwelcome among their slaveholding neighbors. "They hate Yankees worse than snakes," Phelps wrote.[1]

Independence's roughness did not discourage Joseph. A week after his arrival, he dictated a revelation affirming that this part of Missouri was "consecrated for the gathering of the Saints." (Church members increasingly referred to themselves as Saints, using a New Testament term for the faithful followers of Jesus Christ.) And with the prophet on the ground, there was no longer any need to be vague. This would be the New Jerusalem, the new Zion. Joseph's revelation specified that "the spot of the temple is lying westward upon a lot which is not far from the courthouse." In order to turn prophecy into reality, church members needed to buy land, starting with the temple lot but also other parcels between Independence and the county's western border. The revelation coupled grand plans with individual mandates, appointing individuals to purchase land (Sidney Gilbert), allocate properties (Edward Partridge), establish a store (Gilbert), and start a printing operation (Phelps).[2]

It was a typically bold plan for Joseph, who had never set foot anywhere west of northeastern Ohio. Now he intended to build a millennial city on the western frontier, an endeavor that required not only conversions to the church but the financial acumen needed to run mercantile, printing, and real estate operations. Joseph was still only twenty-five. He lacked experience but he had confidence in himself, in the men who were with him, and in God.

Not everyone shared the prophet's confidence. The elders had departed Kirtland expecting to greet large numbers of Native and white converts in Jackson County and the territory to its west. But despite Oliver Cowdery's sunny initial reports, the mission to the Lamanites had failed. There weren't any baptisms among the Delaware or the Shawnee, and there were only a handful of white converts.

The lack of conversions led some members to question Joseph's prophetic leadership. Ezra Booth was among the disaffected. He recalled that back in Kirtland, Joseph had reported a vision "that Oliver [Cowdery] had raised up a large church in Missouri." The reality crushed Booth's exalted expectations.[3]

Even more stalwart church members, such as Bishop Partridge, wondered how in the world they would build Zion in this remote and inhospitable place. "We have to suffer," Partridge wrote his wife Lydia in August, "and shall for some time many privations here which you and I have not been much used to for years." Partridge was also suffering because of a breach with Joseph. The two men quarreled over the prophet's selection of land to purchase, which Partridge regarded as "inferior" to adjacent lots. Partridge also intimated that Joseph's prophecies about Missouri had proven false. The nub of the dispute, though, was that Joseph asked Partridge to remain in Missouri. The bishop had expected to be back in Ohio with Lydia and their four daughters by summer's end. When Partridge made his displeasure known, Joseph interpreted it as disloyalty. He chastised the bishop with a revelation in which the Lord warned him to repent of his "unbelief and blindness of heart." The relationship between the two men remained strained for months.[4]

Joseph made attempts to revive the Lamanite mission. Soon after his arrival in Jackson County, he and a group of elders went over the border on a Sunday. Joseph withdrew to pray alone, then returned and uttered a revelation. In it, the Lord selected William Phelps as that day's preacher. He spoke to a mixed group of whites, Natives, and African Americans. It was a good start, but further evangelistic incursions would have risked the interference of U.S. Indian agents.[5]

The same revelation also suggested a creative way to circumvent the restrictions on missionary work. According to both Ezra Booth and William Phelps, the prophet announced that the elders should marry Native women. Joseph particularly encouraged Martin Harris, who was separated from his wife, Lucy. The idea of a "matrimonial alliance" was probably a passing thought to Joseph, but it lodged in Phelps's mind. In 1861, he recalled that he had discussed the matter with Joseph. Most of the elders were already married. How could they obey the revelation? Joseph answered that they would follow the example of the biblical patriarchs Abraham and Jacob, who married multiple women. One should be cautious with Phelps's late reminiscence, however. Had Joseph even hinted at polygamy, Booth would have divulged it after his break from the church. Regardless, neither Harris nor any of the other elders acted on Joseph's suggestion.[6]

Joseph quickly turned his attention to his other objectives. He laid—quite literally—a foundation for what he predicted would unfold over the next several years. On August 3, Joseph and a group of elders dedicated the temple site, which Partridge purchased several months later. The prophet placed a stone at what was intended to be the temple's northeast corner. The next day Joseph presided over the church's first conference in Zion. About forty-five members were present at the home of Joshua and Margaret Lewis, Missouri converts who lived in Kaws Township, twelve miles west of Independence.[7]

On August 9, less than a month after he had reached Independence, Joseph and a group of about ten men—including Sidney Rigdon and Oliver Cowdery—headed back east, traveling down the Missouri River by canoe. As Phelps commented, the river was "always rily and bubbly," and so were the moods of the Ohio-bound Saints. The actions of some in the group irritated Cowdery, who declared that they would suffer an accident if they did not improve their behavior. Even experienced paddlers and ship captains found the Missouri challenging and were often caught in its snares. A day or two into the trip, the canoe carrying Joseph and Rigdon nearly capsized when it struck a submerged tree.[8]

Joseph ordered the party to make camp. Once on shore, Phelps had a vision in which he saw "the Destroyer, in his most horrible power, ride upon the face of the waters." Church members renamed the Missouri "the river of destruction." No one wanted to get back in the canoes.[9]

Joseph dictated a revelation in which Jesus Christ ordered the company to abandon river travel and instead proceed by land until they reached canal routes. The revelation also told Joseph, Rigdon, and Cowdery to head with all possible speed for Cincinnati, whereas the others should preach along the way. The next day, on the northern banks of the Missouri at Chariton, Joseph met his brother Hyrum, John Murdock (the father of his adopted twins), John Whitmer, and Harvey Whitlock. After the joyful reunion, the threesome continued. It grated on Ezra Booth that the prophet and his scribes traveled by stagecoach at considerable expense, while the other men walked. Before the end of the month, Joseph had reached Kirtland and reunited with Emma, Julia, and young Joseph.

Joseph never hesitated to ask his followers to make great sacrifices. Sell land. Move to Ohio. Keep going to Missouri. Leave your family behind. Bring your family to the frontier. Buy land. Build a New Jerusalem.

Not surprisingly, some of Joseph's followers felt as if they were careening down a raging river and made for the safety of shore. Or they resented it when the prophet didn't appear to share in the sacrifices he required of them. Ezra Booth left the church and published scathing criticisms of Joseph's behavior on the trip.

Other men and women lived through the same events and found their faith in Joseph and the Church of Christ strengthened. "[I] beheld great and marvelous things such as my eyes once never even contemplated of seeing in this world," wrote Reynolds Cahoon of his brief stay in Missouri. In his diary, Cahoon didn't mention any contention among the brethren in Jackson County but did record attending a "glorious meeting" on the Sabbath. While Cahoon noted that Joseph, Rigdon, and Cowdery traveled by stage, it didn't bother him in the least.[10]

Joseph himself was more chastened than he let on at first. One of his Missouri revelations instructed church members to "let the work of the gathering be not in haste nor by flight." The revelation reminded the Saints that Jesus Christ would return soon, but first the elders needed to go forth and preach the gospel "unto the uttermost parts of the earth." If the time wasn't quite ripe for the conversion of Native peoples, that could wait. Building Zion in Jackson County would require patience. Once back in Ohio, a revelation announced that the Lord would "retain a strong hold in the land of Kirtland for the space of five years."[11]

Still, Joseph's trip to Missouri had set things in motion. Several hundred church members had reached Jackson County by the fall of 1831. A church newspaper referred to the area as "the land of Zion which is the land of Joseph." In other words, Jackson County and the land to its west were for the Indians, the descendants of the biblical Joseph. And for the Saints of God, who would gather to Zion under the leadership of Joseph Smith. The prophet would be back.[12]

CHAPTER ELEVEN

Pure Language (1831–1832)

THE TRIP TO INDEPENDENCE was the farthest Joseph had ever traveled, almost a thousand miles in each direction. When he returned to Kirtland in late August 1831, Joseph was reunited with Emma and their adopted twins, Joseph and Julia. Emma had remained in the home on the Morley farm during her husband's absence, but Isaac Morley sold his land that fall. The Smiths had to move yet again. John and Elsa Johnson invited the Smiths to their home in Hiram, a small village twenty-five miles southeast of Kirtland.

The Johnsons had compelling reasons to extend the offer. For the previous several years, Elsa Johnson had been suffering from painful rheumatism. She couldn't raise one of her arms above her head. The Johnsons had a thriving dairy business that depended on Elsa's labor as well as that of John and their many children. Women typically churned the butter and oversaw the curing of the cheeses. Elsa Johnson now struggled to do the work.[1]

In February 1831, the Johnsons' son Lyman was baptized into the Church of Christ. A month or two later, the couple went to visit Joseph Smith. The prophet took Elsa Johnson's hand, prayed silently, and "pronounced her arm whole, in the name of Jesus Christ." Joseph then left the room. Elsa Johnson surprised everyone by stretching out her arm, finding that it was "as good as the other." The next day, she could do her chores without pain. Even individuals who became fierce critics of

Joseph conceded that she had been healed. The Johnsons and several of their other children soon were baptized.[2]

The cluster of believers in and around Hiram made it a good base for Joseph after his return from Missouri. The four Smiths occupied a back room, and the Johnsons, seven of their children, and some of John Johnson's brothers lived in the rest of the elegant house. John Johnson improved a log cabin across the street for the use of Sidney Rigdon and his family. At the end of October, the Johnsons had the upper room of their house divided to create a work space for the prophet. Featuring views over the Ohio countryside, it was an ideal setting for Joseph to resume work on his Bible translation.[3]

Church affairs were less bucolic. Joseph faced defections and doubters. Ezra Booth, just back from Missouri himself, had a series of contentious meetings with Joseph. Booth and Isaac Morley had disregarded Joseph's revelation that they should make their return slowly by preaching along the way. Morley quickly begged Joseph's forgiveness, but Booth refused to back down. Hadn't Joseph and his top associates done the same thing? A church conference in early September voted "that Ezra Booth be silenced from preaching as an elder in this church."[4]

Silencing Booth proved impossible. He aired his frustrations and grievances in a series of letters in the *Ohio Star*, published in nearby Ravenna. Booth denounced Joseph as a deceiver and an infidel. Joseph ruled through pretended revelations, stole his followers' property, and revised the Bible as it suited him. Those were the most serious allegations, but Booth also described a man who simply didn't act like a prophet, or at least didn't act the way Booth thought a prophet should. "Have you not often discovered in him," Booth asked in a published letter to Bishop Edward Partridge, "a spirit of lightness and levity, a temper of mind easily irritated, and a habitual proneness to jesting and joking?" This was on the mark. Joseph loved to joke and laugh, and, when stirred to anger, he lashed out. For many friends and followers, these traits were among the reasons they loved Joseph. He was approachable and sociable. Booth wanted more decorum.[5]

There were other defectors. Alexander Campbell, alarmed by the string of conversions from his movement, had spent several weeks in Ohio that summer preaching against Mormonism. "A good many of those bewitched by the false prophets," Campbell crowed, "had begun to recover their reason, and desert the ranks of the new Apostle [Joseph]." Symonds Ryder, a former Campbellite minister in Hiram, had been baptized in June 1831 but, like Booth, left the church in September. Some later accounts assert that Ryder grew disaffected when Joseph's revelations failed to spell his name correctly, but doubts over the law of consecration were more decisive. Regardless, Joseph now had a growing number of determined antagonists in northeastern Ohio. A stink bomb dispersed one church meeting in the town of Garrettsville.[6]

The efforts of Booth, Ryder, and Campbell blunted the church's previously meteoric growth, but converts from elsewhere trickled into the area. William McLellin was a young, recently widowed schoolteacher in eastern Illinois. He heard two missionaries testify to the Book of Mormon in the summer of 1831. He bought a copy of the book, read it, and rushed to Jackson County. McLellin arrived after Joseph had left to return to Ohio, but he continued discussing the Book of Mormon with Hyrum Smith, who soon baptized him. Still wanting to meet Joseph, he headed east.

On October 25, he finally found Joseph and attended a church conference in Orange, Ohio, at which Oliver Cowdery ordained him a high priest. The next day, he stumbled while stepping off a large log and badly hurt his ankle. That night, he asked Joseph if God could heal his ankle. The prophet flipped the question around. Did McLellin believe that God would heal him? The new convert answered yes. Joseph then laid his hands on McLellin's swollen and tender ankle, and it was healed. Joseph also produced a revelation in the words of Jesus Christ, given in response to several of McLellin's questions. The healing and the revelation confirmed McLellin's faith.[7]

Joseph dictated a torrent of revelations that fall and into the winter, and he decided to publish an edition of them. Ohio newspapers already had printed several, and Ezra Booth warned readers that Joseph's revelations—"concealed from the world"—demanded extravagant gifts from his gullible followers. Publication would help Joseph control and spread his message. The plan was to print ten thousand copies of the *Book of Commandments*, double the print run of the Book of Mormon.[8]

The decision to publish the revelations was controversial among the Saints, in part because it contradicted Joseph's earlier guidance. "Keep these things from going abroad unto the world," Jesus Christ had commanded in March 1831. David Whitmer recalled his fear that the edition would alarm non-Mormon settlers in Jackson County because they would learn that the Saints planned to move en masse to their New Jerusalem.

There were other reasons to hesitate. Most of the revelations presented themselves as divine words, most commonly that of Jesus Christ, but they took their form in the diction of Joseph and the spelling of his scribes. If left unrevised, infelicities of language could embarrass the church. On the other hand, if church leaders revised the messages, would that cast doubt on their divinity?[9]

It annoyed Joseph that some of the elders questioned the wisdom of his proposal. It annoyed him even more that they seemed underwhelmed with the revelations themselves. So the prophet laid down a challenge. Did the elders think they could do better? In yet another revelation, Jesus Christ dared anyone dissatisfied with Joseph's production to consider whichever they considered the least impressive. Could any of them do even that well? William McLellin gave it a shot, either because he still wanted to test Joseph or because he had agreed to prove the prophet's point. He failed and by failing bolstered the group's faith in Joseph's revelations.[10]

Joseph did not consider the language or even the substance of his revelations sacrosanct. Quite the contrary. A church conference resolved that Joseph, as guided by the Holy Spirit, should correct "errors or mistakes" he discovered in his revelations and Bible translation. With Joseph Smith, everything was always subject to revision. The prophet and his associates spent some time reviewing and correcting them in mid-November, and then Cowdery and Whitmer took the manuscript to Jackson County. The plan was for William Phelps to print it. A church that valued the Book of Mormon alongside the Bible would soon have a third volume of scripture, with the promise of more to come.[11]

A January 1832 revelation reminded the prophet to resume his New Testament revision, which became his focus for the remainder of the winter. It was a stretch of unusual repose for Joseph and Emma. He made a trip to the nearby town of Amherst, where the elders gathered at a church conference and ordained him as "President of the High Priesthood." Otherwise, Joseph spent much of his time in the upstairs room of John Johnson's house. Rigdon was often by his side, taking dictation for revelations and for the Bible translation.[12]

In mid-February, Joseph and Rigdon had reached the fifth chapter of John's gospel, where Jesus prophecies that at some point in the future, the dead "shall come forth; they that have done good, unto the resurrection of life; and they that have done evil, unto the resurrection of damnation."

Many Americans pointed to verses such as this to counter the arguments of Universalists, who taught that all people would be saved, perhaps after some sort of temporary punishment. For most Protestants, the afterlife was a binary, up-or-down affair, including eternal damnation for the wicked in a literal, very hot hell.[13]

Joseph gave conflicting signals on Universalism, which had appealed to his father and paternal grandfather. The Book of Mormon condemns the teaching that all will be saved, but one of Joseph's earliest revelations had explained that the Bible's rhetoric about "eternal damnation" was a scare tactic and a language trick. "Endless punishment" wasn't literally endless. It simply meant God's punishment. It seems that Joseph was uncomfortable with both "ultra" Universalism (not even a temporary punishment for unrepentant sinners after death) and traditional Protestant teachings about hell.[14]

The Bible revision led Joseph to reflect on his understanding of the afterlife. He revised "the resurrection of damnation" to "the resurrection of the unjust." The wicked were not necessarily headed for eternal damnation. That was just the starting point, though. As Joseph and Rigdon marveled and meditated on these words, they had a vision. They saw Jesus Christ at God's right hand and the "holy angels" worshiping the Father and the Son. Jesus spoke to them and told them to write down his words. It is a singular example of Joseph inviting someone else to participate fully in his revelatory process.[15]

The joint vision sketched out a radically different understanding of the afterlife. Only a small number of men, the "sons of perdition," would suffer everlasting fire-and-brimstone punishment. These were men who denied the truth after they received it. They would be the "only ones who shall not be redeemed." Joseph preserved hell but made it much less populous.

Everyone else would be saved, but not to the same degree of divine glory. Here the vision engaged another New Testament passage. In his first letter to the Corinthians, Paul writes that "there are also celestial bodies, and bodies terrestrial: but the glory of the celestial is one, and the glory of the terrestrial is another." The sun, the moon, and the stars differed in their glory. So would the eternal glory of men.

In order to attain "celestial" glory, men needed to believe in Jesus's name, be baptized by immersion, and receive the Holy Ghost by the laying on of hands. In other words, they needed to belong to Christ's one true church, the Church of Christ as founded by Joseph and his followers in 1830. As "priests and kings" after the order of Enoch, Melchizedek, and Jesus Christ, they would receive a fullness of God's glory and reign with Christ in the New Jerusalem. They would be "gods, even the sons of God." Other men would receive "terrestrial" or "telestial" glory, the former for good men deceived by false teachings or those who were not "valiant" in their faith, the latter for wicked individuals.

There were precedents for some of these ideas. Alexander Campbell, a formative influence on Sidney Rigdon's thought, wrote about kingdoms of Law, Favor, and Glory. The glory of Christ's favor, Campbell explained, differed from the law of Moses "as the sun excelled a star." Farther afield, the Swedish scientist and mystic Emanuel Swedenborg, whose ideas touched the lives of Americans such as John Chapman ("Johnny Appleseed"), outlined a heaven subdivided into celestial, spiritual, and natural realms. In Swedenborg's vision of the afterlife, men and women became angels, and they retained a capacity for progress. The inhabitants of the lower heavens could advance in spiritual awareness and progress toward paradise.[16]

Joseph, however, wasn't simply adopting the notions of Campbell, Swedenborg, or anyone else. Although Swedenborg's ideas had broad currency in the early nineteenth century, there is no evidence that Joseph had had any particular contact with them at this point in his life. What Joseph did was to catch hold of certain currents of thought and, through extended periods of contemplation, biblical study, and mystical experiences, mold them into his own distinctive teachings.[17]

As a young man, Joseph had pondered the state of his soul and had begged God to forgive his sins. He had wondered whether God would save all people. Now he longed for celestial power and glory, for himself and for the other members of Christ's true church.

How could humans find that power? One source was language. In the Book of Genesis, the world comes into being as God speaks. God speaks to the first man, Adam, who names the creatures of the earth. Joseph believed that there was power inherent in the original language spoken by God, Adam and Eve, and their immediate descendants.

Then, after humans attempt to build a great city—Babel—with a tower to heaven, God confounds their language and scatters them over the face of the earth. Many philosophers and theologians postulated that after Babel, words became disconnected from the nature of the things they signified, losing their clarity and potency.

Joseph felt the curse of Babel keenly. Language did not come easily to him. "I hope you will excuse . . . my inability in conveying my ideas in writing," he asked Emma. But it was not just a matter of his own limited attainments. In a letter to the much more educated and eloquent William Phelps, Joseph complained about the darkness that came from writing in a "crooked, broken, scattered, and imperfect language." He wished that they could read the "eternal wisdom engraven upon the heavens." Instead, heavenly mysteries remained imprisoned behind twisted bars of fallen words.[18]

The concept of an original heavenly language had fascinated Jews and Christians for many centuries. For instance, seventeenth-century Plymouth Colony governor William Bradford learned Hebrew because he thought God had spoken to the ancient patriarchs in that tongue. Other Protestants speculated that God would restore a single pure human language at the time of Christ's Second Coming.

If the full recovery of primordial language remained over the millennial horizon, what about a potent word or phrase for the here and now? This aspiration ran through many traditions, from Jewish Kabbalah to alchemy to the incantations and spells used by treasure seers. Freemasonry provides another example from Joseph's lifetime. The rites of Craft Masonry focus on the figure of Hiram Abiff, identified as the architect of Solomon's Temple and murdered when he refused to reveal the "Master's word" to three attackers. In the degrees of Royal Arch Masonry, initiates learn God's sacred name, whose power can shake heaven and earth, and they swear an oath not to divulge the name. Some Masons suggested that their codes, ciphers, and rites contained elements of the original universal, heavenly language of God.[19]

The Mormon prophet, not surprisingly, had his own ideas on this subject. In the Book of Mormon, the Jaredites escape the curse of Babel, and the "plates of Jared" are engraved in "pure language." Joseph returned to the motif in his revision of Genesis, in which the descendants of Seth keep a "book of remembrance . . . in the language of Adam," which was "undefiled." Joseph's followers could also access the primordial language in a more immediate way. When members of the Church of Christ spoke in unknown, spiritual tongues, many believed that their ecstatic speech was in the heavenly language spoken by Adam. Those who claimed the spiritual gift of interpreting tongues could then translate the words into English.[20]

Joseph asserted that he received bits of heavenly language directly from God. He developed the idea through his ongoing engagement with the Bible. As he neared the end of his New Testament revision, Joseph came to the abundantly symbolic Book of Revelation, in which Jesus Christ promises to "him that overcometh" that he will "write upon him the name of my God." Joseph dictated a revelation that his scribe labeled "a sample of pure language." The revelation took the form of a dialogue. "What is the name of God in pure language?" Joseph asked. The answer was "Awmen" (Ahman in later manuscripts), meaning the "being which made all things." Jesus Christ was "Son Awmen," and men were "Sons Awmen."[21]

The "Sample of Pure Language" hints at some of Joseph's more arresting theological proposals. If God was *Ahman*, Jesus was *Son Ahman*, and men were *Sons Ahman*, there was a family relationship among them. They were the same sort of being. Members of the Church of Christ were sons of God. They would reign with Christ as "priests and kings." They would build a New Jerusalem. They were the recipients of hidden mysteries and blessed with spiritual knowledge and power.

Joseph and his followers soon received a sober reminder of their earthly lack of power. Before dawn on March 25, 1832, a dozen intruders burst into Joseph's bedchamber and assaulted him.[22]

It was already an anxious time. The twins Joseph and Julia were sick with measles, and Emma in particular had been losing sleep caring for them.

The night of March 24, Emma went to bed with Julia, while her husband sat awake with young Joseph. She eventually encouraged him to lie down with the boy on the trundle bed. "*Murder!*" Emma's cry woke him. Joseph then found himself being carried out of the room. He offered fierce resistance, kicking one man in the face, but the mob got him outside. One attacker pulled out a handful of Joseph's hair, leaving a permanent bare spot. Some of the men grabbed him by the throat, and he passed out.[23]

When Joseph came to, he saw Sidney Rigdon motionless on the ground nearby. The vigilantes, "disguised with colored faces," debated Joseph's fate. The plan was to tar and feather the prophet and his top associate, but some men wanted to do more. Should they kill Joseph? Or castrate him? It was a chaotic scene. Finally, someone fetched a bucket full of warmed tar. They jammed a "tar paddle" into his mouth, knocking out one of his teeth. The men tore off Joseph's clothes, covered him with tar, and pressed feathers onto him. Richard Dennison, a physician and member of the mob, tried to pour a vial of aqua fortis—nitric acid—into Joseph's mouth. Joseph clenched his teeth, which broke the vial. He spat out the acid, some of which burned his face. When the mob finally left, Joseph was naked, dazed, and struggling for breath.[24]

Joseph pulled the tar away from his lips and staggered toward the Johnson house. Emma fainted when she saw her husband. Friends spent the night scraping off the tar and washing Joseph's raw flesh. Rigdon, who had also been tarred and feathered, was in even worse shape. The back of his head was lacerated, and he was delirious.

In a show of resilience and defiance, Joseph preached at a nearby schoolhouse the next morning, with his "flesh all scarified and defaced." Joseph baptized three individuals that afternoon.

There were about two dozen mobbers in all. Joseph identified Symonds Ryder as the ring leader; Ryder lived right next door to John and Elsa Johnson. And there were conspirators within the Johnson family itself, including Eli Johnson, John Johnson's brother. In the language of the recent vision, these were the sons of perdition, men who had committed the unpardonable sin of apostasy. Along with Dr. Dennison, there were also several upstanding members of the community involved, including a justice of the peace and a schoolteacher.

Why did these men perpetrate such a vicious attack on Joseph and Sidney Rigdon? Joseph attributed the violence to religious persecution, noting that the mobbers were mostly Campbellites, Methodists, and Baptists, upset that they had lost members to an upstart sect and its young prophet. Many decades later, a rumor emerged that Eli Johnson targeted Joseph because the prophet had been "too intimate" with Marinda Nancy Johnson, the then sixteen-year-old daughter of John Johnson. Fawn Brodie advanced the allegation in her biography of Joseph Smith. There is no evidence to support the charge, which would raise the question of why the mob also beat Sidney Rigdon to near death.[25]

As soon as Joseph had reported finding golden plates, he had faced opposition. He told stories of dodging assailants in forests and of mobs who harassed those who wished to be baptized. The March 1832 assault was on another level, however. In New York, church members had been scared, but no one had been seriously hurt. The Hiram mob, by contrast, left lasting marks. Those who met Joseph noticed the way his missing tooth marred his countenance, and until a dentist fashioned him a replacement, he spoke with a "whistle-like sound."[26]

Young Joseph's condition deteriorated in the days following the attack. He died. Joseph and Emma blamed his death on the mob. So did
John Murdock, the boy's birth father, who stated that when the attackers
seized the prophet, they left the child exposed to the cold.[27]

The previous summer, Ezra Booth and Edward Partridge had questioned whether Joseph demanded others to sacrifice while he dodged
hardships. They walked on foot while he traveled by stage. He returned
to his wife and children while keeping them separated from their families. Joseph did ask a great deal of his followers. Indeed, he called on
them to sacrifice everything they had. The mob attack, however, was a
reminder that Joseph also risked everything, and his fidelity to his prophetic calling cost him dearly.

Emma Smith's sacrifices often garnered less attention. Shortly after
their adopted son's death, Joseph left Ohio, traveling back to Missouri in
the company of Rigdon and Newel Whitney. Joseph had dictated a revelation that commanded him to proceed to Zion without delay. Emma
knew that she was pregnant again by the time her battered and bruised
husband departed. In 1828, Joseph had left just a few days after the still-
birth of their first child. Now, she was again without her husband in the
midst of grief. Afraid of additional violence, Joseph wrote and encouraged her to move to Kirtland. She took the advice, staying with a series
of families over the next several months.

Joseph had an almost preternatural resilience. He was not easily
daunted, and he moved on quickly from failures and setbacks. If abandoned by one friend or close associate, he would find another. He would
challenge the Saints with one bracing idea, such as the consecration of
property, and then introduce another proposition, such as a tripartite
heaven. Not everyone would stick with him—but, if others couldn't or
wouldn't keep up, Joseph kept moving.

CHAPTER TWELVE

Olive Leaves (1832–1833)

HOW COULD JOSEPH LEAD a still-fledgling church whose two centers were separated by a thousand miles? Letters back and forth took weeks, and distance bred suspicion and resentment. Church leaders in Zion bristled at Joseph's attempts to correct and direct them from afar. These associates were Joseph's friends, and he was hurt when conflicts arose.

Part of the challenge was a proliferation of councils, quorums, and offices. Church leadership was a bramble of changing names and titles. At the time of the church's initial organization in 1830, Joseph had been designated "First Elder" and Oliver Cowdery "Second Elder." Cowdery hadn't been formally demoted, but while he remained in Missouri, Sidney Rigdon had supplanted him as Joseph's primary assistant. Soon after Joseph was ordained as "President of the High Priesthood," he selected Rigdon as one of his two counselors. The prophet and his counselors together comprised "the presidency of the High Priesthood" (later the "First Presidency"). Cowdery's standing as "Second Elder" lost relevance.

The other counselor in the presidency was Jesse Gause, a former schoolteacher who was twenty years older than the prophet. Gause's religious past included a recent affiliation with the Shakers. Along with his wife, Minerva, he had moved to a Shaker community near Kirtland. Communal living among the Shakers would have required the Gauses to practice abstinence and to sleep in separate quarters. Perhaps Jesse

Gause was not keen on the arrangement. Either in late 1831 or early 1832, he was baptized into the Church of Christ. Minerva Gause did not follow his example. Like Rigdon before him, Jesse Gause made a strong impression on Joseph, who promptly elevated him to a high office.[1]

Joseph and Bishop Edward Partridge had clashed during the prophet's first trip to Zion, and the ill feelings remained unresolved. The previous fall, Sidney Rigdon had sent a letter to Missouri in which he accused Partridge of having "insulted the Lord's prophet . . . and assum[ing] authority over him." Rigdon also accused the bishop of withholding funds intended for his and Joseph's travel expenses. Partridge's associates in Missouri in turn accused Rigdon of obeying "hasty feelings" rather than the "spirit of Christ." Partridge let it be known, however, that he wanted to "bury the matter" and end the conflict.[2]

When the prophet reached Jackson County in late April 1832, both he and the Missouri leaders were determined to establish peace. A council of high priests and elders recognized Joseph as "President of the High Priesthood," and Bishop Partridge gave him "the right hand of fellowship." Rigdon was satisfied. "All differences settled," John Whitmer noted, "and the hearts of all run together in love."[3]

While in Zion, Joseph revamped the church's business operations by establishing what was called the "United Firm." This umbrella structure included a newly created Gilbert, Whitney, and Company store in Independence; the Whitney stores and ashery in Kirtland; the publishing operation of William W. Phelps in Missouri; and Bishop Partridge's landholdings for the Saints in Missouri. By revelation, the Lord ordered these leaders—Joseph, Edward Partridge, Newel K. Whitney (recently appointed as a second bishop within the church), Sidney Gilbert, Sidney Rigdon, John Whitmer, Oliver Cowdery, William Phelps, and Martin Harris—to be "bound together by a bond and covenant that cannot be broken." Revenue from the mercantile and literary establishments should provide for their personal necessities. Any profits should become the church's "common property." Profits were a distant hope. The church needed capital, especially for the purchase of additional lands in Missouri. The firm's members authorized Whitney to obtain a $15,000 loan.[4]

Joseph started back to Ohio on May 6, traveling by stagecoach in the company of Rigdon and Whitney. The prophet had stayed in Missouri for a fortnight, enough time to reconcile with Bishop Partridge and sketch business plans, but not long enough to build the actual cohesion and unity needed for the challenges ahead. The fragility of these relationships and plans weighed on Joseph's mind as he bumped and lurched along the road.

As they approached New Albany, Indiana, the horses became startled, and the coach hurtled toward a crash. When Whitney jumped out, his foot got caught in the wheel; his foot and leg broke in several places. Joseph and Rigdon escaped unscathed. Joseph stayed with Whitney as the bishop recuperated, while Rigdon proceeded to Kirtland.

The prophet and bishop lodged at a tavern in Greenville, Indiana. While there, Joseph wrote a letter to Emma. It is a rare letter in Joseph's own hand, and it reveals a deep loneliness and sorrow. When Martin Harris arrived with a letter from Elizabeth Ann Whitney, Joseph was hurt that Emma "did not take the trouble" to write. "My situation is a very unpleasant one," he informed her. The prophet also felt abandoned by the Saints in Missouri. He had written them about Whitney's accident and the interrupted journey home. Why hadn't they visited, or at least sent words of comfort? Joseph took it as a sign that the comity and unity they had enjoyed in Missouri were illusory. Whitney wet his pillow with tears when he contemplated the "conspiracy" against them.[5]

Joseph also contracted a dire case of food poisoning in Greenville. When rising from the dinner table, he walked to the door and vomited so forcefully that he dislocated his jaw while expelling copious amounts of blood and food. Joseph got his jaw back into alignment on his own, and then Whitney prayed over him. The sickness passed, but Joseph temporarily lost much of his hair.[6]

During these doleful days, Joseph frequently retreated into a grove on the outskirts of the small town, though the walks did not provide a respite from his dark mood. Joseph saw several fresh graves during one stroll. It was hard to escape the specter of death. Harris's letter brought news that Hyrum Smith's daughter, Mary, had died. Just short of her third birthday, she had expired in her father's arms. Joseph thought of his own four dead children and his adopted daughter. "I should like [to] see little Julia and once more take her on my knee," he wrote Emma.[7]

Joseph poured out his lamentations to God in his forested seclusion. He reflected on "all the past moments of my life" and regretted his many mistakes and sins. These stretches of solitary prayer stirred memories of a similar time in his youth, when in a vision Jesus Christ had assured him that his sins were forgiven. Once more, Joseph found consolation. "God is merciful," he informed Emma, "and has forgiven my sins." The future was uncertain. An accident could break a man's foot in an instant.

Death could snatch away one's child or spouse. Church members might apostatize, and friends might betray. "I will try to be contented with my lot," Joseph wrote, "knowing that God is my friend. In him I shall find comfort." Joseph resolved that with that comfort, he could face any earthly trial.[8]

By mid-June, Whitney's leg had healed enough to travel. He and Joseph went by steamboat up the Ohio River, then by stagecoach and wagon to Kirtland.

Joseph found Emma as disconsolate as he had been in Greenville. She had followed his advice to remove from Hiram to Kirtland, first seeking accommodation at the Whitney home. At the time, Ann Whitney was six months pregnant and sick. Her aunt, Sarah Smith (no relation to the prophet), believed that Joseph had made Newel and Ann Whitney the "dupes of priestcraft" and declared that there wasn't enough room in the house for both her and Emma. The prophet's wife was told to leave. She moved on, and kept moving, staying with Reynolds Cahoon, Lucy Mack Smith and Joseph Sr., and finally Frederick G. Williams. Emma was relieved that Joseph had returned but displeased that he had left her so adrift. He might have arranged a safe place for her to lodge in his absence. It is no wonder that she had not taken the time to write.[9]

Joseph and Emma—now about halfway through her third pregnancy—moved back into the Johnson home in Hiram. Joseph again resumed work on his Bible revision, reaching the end of the New Testament in July. Calmer patterns of life, however, did not shelter him from the ecclesiastical conflicts that had nagged at him since the beginning of the year. In late June, Sidney Gilbert arrived from Missouri with a letter from John Corrill, an assistant to Bishop Edward Partridge. Amid a list of complaints, it implied that Joseph was "seeking after monarchal power and authority." The next month, Joseph received what he considered a "cold and indifferent" letter from William Phelps.[10]

The prophet was furious. He had left his family "upon the mercy of mobs" to travel a thousand miles to set things right, and now his supposed friends were "raking up every fault." The Missouri leaders were meant to be laying the foundations for Zion, but they grumbled that too many Saints were coming west. Another group of around one hundred church members had arrived in Jackson County in June. They needed land. Joseph warned Bishop Partridge not to hold back any of his own means. Joseph's communications to the church's Missouri leaders betray a certain paranoia and prickliness. He suspected that Partridge, Phelps, and the others were not fully submissive to his authority.[11]

Closer to home, Sidney Rigdon was acting strangely. He appeared at an early July church meeting held in Joseph Smith Sr.'s barn and declared "that he had a revelation from the Lord . . . that the kingdom was taken from the church and left with him." According to Joseph's mother, Rigdon was upset that he had not been provided with a new house after the mob attack. Informed of Rigdon's statement by his brother Hyrum, Joseph rushed to Kirtland, assured church members that "the kingdom was ours and never should be taken from the faithful," and stripped his counselor of his priesthood license and offices. Rigdon then descended into a period of mental instability, marked by convulsions and what Lucy Mack Smith termed "astonishing encounters with the devil." Joseph blamed Rigdon's erratic behavior on the ill "feelings" of the Missouri Saints, but aftereffects from the assault were the more likely cause. By the end of the month, Rigdon had stabilized and repented, and Joseph ordained him to the high priesthood again. Bishop Whitney provided Rigdon and his family with a home.[12]

Rigdon's case was more pitiable than provocative, but Joseph never fully regained confidence in his counselor. The next year, he described Rigdon as "not capable of that pure and steadfast love" and as having "a selfish[ness] and independence of mind." Joseph had attracted talented associates, such as Cowdery, Rigdon, Phelps, and Partridge. He had not known any of these men for more than a few years, and many of them challenged his authority or proved mercurial. For instance, Jesse Gause, whom Joseph had elevated alongside Rigdon as his counselor in the presidency of the high priesthood, severed contact with the church for reasons that remain unclear. A church council formally excommunicated Gause in early December. As the head of a church barely two years old, Joseph had little choice but to place his confidence in unproven men.[13]

In mid-September 1832, Joseph, Emma, and Julia moved from Hiram back to Kirtland and took up residence in Newel Whitney's White Store. Whitney had remodeled the store's upper floor into three rooms. One became the Smith family's next temporary home. The prophet used the other two as a "council room" and "translating room," the latter a space in which he worked on the Bible revision and dictated revelations.[14]

A short while after moving into the Whitney store, Joseph produced a long revelation over the span of two days. Much of the wide-ranging text, presented as the words of Jesus Christ, expounded on the meaning of "priesthood." Joseph had introduced various offices, such as "priest," "elder," "teacher," "deacon," and "bishop." A more select number of men had been ordained as "high priests." What exactly was priesthood? And if there was a high priesthood, was there a lower priesthood?

In the Church of Christ, priesthood conveyed the right to hold certain offices and preside over church affairs, but it was more than a matter of church organization. Joseph taught that the "greater priesthood . . . holdeth the key of the mysteries of the kingdom, even the key of the knowledge of God." Through the priesthood and its ordinances, the power of God was made "manifest," plain to see. Through the authority of the priesthood men cast out demons, healed the sick and the lame, and sealed men and women unto salvation.

How did men obtain this authority? According to Joseph, priesthood on the earth began with Adam and proceeded through a patriarchal chain of transmission to figures such as Enoch, Melchizedek, and Moses. Because of the transgressions of the Hebrews in the wilderness, God had removed the greater priesthood from them. Jesus Christ had restored this priesthood, conveying it to his New Testament and Book of Mormon disciples. Joseph stated that he too had received this high priesthood.

Meanwhile, the descendants of Aaron, Moses's brother, had passed down a "lesser priesthood." Joseph clarified that the offices of elder and bishop belonged to the high priesthood; teachers and deacons held the lesser priesthood. The hierarchy and distinctions remained fuzzy for the time being. What mattered more was that both groups were promised access to divine power and glory. Those who received the priesthood and remained faithful—the latter-day sons of Aaron and Moses—would be "filled with the glory of the Lord upon Mount Zion in the Lord's house," the temple the church would build in Independence.

In the priesthood revelation, Jesus Christ ordered priesthood holders to undertake missions to preach the gospel and to care for the poor. The text singled out Bishop Whitney for a particularly important task. The Lord instructed him to go to Albany, New York City, and Boston and preach that the cities would become utterly desolate should their inhabitants reject the gospel.[15]

Joseph accompanied him. After what was probably a brief stop in Albany, the pair reached the biggest city Joseph had ever seen. The prophet marveled at the enormous buildings and the fashionably dressed people. He and Whitney stayed at the Pearl Street House and Ohio Hotel in Lower Manhattan. Joseph was unused to the circumstances, especially the "black and white and mulatto [waiters] running, bowing, and maneuvering" around the tables.

Bishop Whitney enjoyed seeing old acquaintances from past mercantile visits, and—despite the revelation's instructions—spent the days selecting goods for his United Firm store. Joseph, by contrast, was downcast. He was surrounded by multitudes but felt alone. God had threatened the city with destruction, and Joseph concluded that New York deserved it. It wasn't the fancy dress and big buildings. The problem, Joseph informed Emma by letter, was that people failed to give glory to God for them. Joseph compared New York to Nineveh, to which God had sent the reluctant Jonah. "My bowels are filled with compassion towards them," Joseph wrote, using a Book of Mormon phrase. "I am determined to lift up my voice in this city."

Joseph lifted up his voice rather softly. The Mormon prophet would have attracted notice in the city had he held public meetings or sought permission to preach in churches, but Joseph mostly hunkered down at the hotel. "I prefer reading and praying and holding communion with the Holy Spirit and writing to you than walking the streets," he told Emma. Joseph and Whitney visited Bishop Benjamin Onderdonk of the Episcopal Church's New York diocese.[16] No information exists about the substance of the meeting. Joseph also became acquainted with a young gentleman who had survived a recent bout with cholera, expressed interest in the church's teachings, but then did not continue the discussion the next day as planned. The prophet seems to have been intimidated by his surroundings.

Joseph missed his family. "Behold the thoughts of home of Emma and Julia rushes upon my mind like a flood," he wrote his wife. Joseph reminded Emma that he was her "one true and living friend on earth." He may have felt guilty about leaving her again, especially near the end of her pregnancy.[17]

The prophet and the bishop proceeded from New York to New England. Joseph preached in Boston. On November 6, the pair returned to Kirtland, one day after Emma gave birth to a son. She and her husband named him Joseph. This time the child lived. After the birth of his son, the outward circumstances of Joseph's life settled down. Uncharacteristically, he stayed put, not traveling beyond northeastern Ohio for the next year.

Shortly after Joseph III's birth, three men came to introduce themselves to the prophet: Heber Kimball and the brothers Joseph and Brigham Young. The visitors were among a group of Baptists and Methodists who had converted to Mormonism in the New York State town of Mendon, just outside of Rochester.

Like the vast majority of new church members, they were baptized without having met Joseph. Brigham Young had spent two years mulling over the Book of Mormon, then converted after he witnessed Pennsylvania church members speak in tongues and prophesy. "I had seen the power of God displayed," Brigham told his brother. As for Kimball, his clothes had barely dried from joining a Baptist church before he met Mormon missionaries who soon baptized him again.[18]

After Brigham's wife, Miriam Young, died in September 1832, the Young brothers and Kimball traveled to Kirtland to meet their church's prophet. On the way to Ohio, the party encountered a Methodist minister who "ridiculed the character of Joseph." Brigham found it difficult to defend someone on whom he had never laid eyes.[19]

When they reached Kirtland, the trio learned that Joseph was in the forest, chopping wood. He put down his axe and shook their hands. They offered to help. "So we chopped and loaded a little while," Brigham recalled, "and then [he] said, 'Let's go to the house.'" Brigham, a red-haired, barrel-chested furniture maker, was surprised but pleased to find a down-to-earth prophet, a man who spoke plainly and wasn't above simple labor.[20]

The fervor of the three newcomers impressed Joseph. Brigham Young spoke in tongues during a prayer meeting that night. Joseph had discouraged the practice in Kirtland, but it hadn't quite died out. After all, the last chapter of the Book of Mormon warned followers of Christ to "deny not the gifts of God," including "all kinds of tongues ... [and] the interpretation of languages." When Brigham spoke in tongues, those present looked to Joseph for his reaction. "He told them it was the pure Adamic language," Brigham later recalled. In other words, it was the heavenly language by which God spoke to Adam and Eve.[21]

Joseph now exercised the gift himself. "[I] came to Kirtland," church member Zebedee Coltrin wrote in mid-November 1832, "and heard him

[Joseph] speak with tongues and sing in tongues."²² Many others followed suit, speaking, singing, and interpreting tongues.

Joseph rarely made mention of national conflicts during these years. An exception was the nullification crisis that intensified soon after the 1832 presidential campaign. The controversy was years in the making. Congress had been steadily raising tariffs on imported goods in order to protect American manufacturing. Southern politicians opposed tariffs because they raised the price of goods and threatened to depress exports of cotton to Europe. When Congress in 1828 passed what southerners deemed the Tariff of Abominations, Charleston's ships lowered their flags to half-mast.²³

South Carolina's John C. Calhoun, vice president under both John Quincy Adams and Andrew Jackson, contended that a state could interpose its own sovereignty to nullify federal statutes it deemed unconstitutional. Calhoun himself wanted to avoid incendiary actions that could lead to the breaking apart of the country, but firebrands in his state were less cautious. Congress enacted a compromise measure in 1832 that reduced tariffs, but not enough to satisfy South Carolina politicians. Shortly after Jackson's fall reelection, a South Carolina convention declared federal tariffs null and void in the state. The delegates at the convention threatened that South Carolina would secede if the national government attempted to enforce the tariff. At the heart of the crisis was the question of whether the United States was a compact of sovereign states or a sovereign nation. President Jackson accused South Carolina of "disunion" and "treason," and he reinforced garrisons in Charleston's harbor.²⁴

Joseph understood the nullification crisis as a harbinger of the millennium. On Christmas Day, he dictated a prophecy that the "rebellion of South Carolina" would lead to a civil war between the North and the South. Beginning with Great Britain, the war would engulf the world, and divine wrath, in the form of famine, plague, and earthquakes, would make an end of all nations. "Wherefore," Joseph concluded, "stand ye in holy places and be not moved until the day of the Lord comes." When Joseph gazed into the future, he foresaw the destruction of latter-day Ninevehs like New York City. If the Saints stood firm in their Ohio and Missouri communities, they would withstand the looming "day of the Lord" and share in Jesus Christ's glorious reign.²⁵

The prophecy suggested that its predicted wars would "shortly come to pass." They did not, at least not shortly. While he affirmed the prerogative of the national government to use force to execute its laws, Jackson

offered an olive branch to South Carolina in the form of a bill that reduced tariffs over the subsequent ten years. Sectional tension receded for
the time being.

Joseph turned his attention back to the unresolved disunity within
the church. By the end of 1832, there were more than five hundred
Saints in Jackson County. But in Joseph's vision, Zion meant more than
migration and the physical building of New Jerusalem. It meant a people
of one heart and mind.

From Joseph's perspective, the problem was grumbling and complaining, a seeming lack of faith and submission. Kirtland leaders observed "low, dark, and blind insinuations" in a December letter from
Sidney Gilbert, and a letter from Phelps "betray[ed] a lightness of spirit"
incompatible with his responsibilities. The message from Kirtland was
clear. The Missouri leaders needed to repent of their rebellious spirit. If
they did not, they would be "cut off." Zion would be built without them.
For good measure, Joseph told Phelps that his newspaper was boring and
would fail if he didn't make it more interesting.[26]

There was only so much Joseph could do to correct matters in
Missouri. What he could do was foster the type of community he wanted
in Kirtland. In late December, he met with a conference of high priests
in the "translating room" above the Whitney store. Joseph arose and told
the men that if they wanted revelations and blessings from heaven they
needed to "become of one heart and one mind." The men bowed down
and prayed fervently. Then, one at a time, they stood up and expressed
their determination to keep God's commandments.[27]

Joseph began to dictate a revelation. It was nine o'clock in the evening. The divine voice poured out, a flood of words about the resurrection of the body, the celestial and other kingdoms, and the looming
apocalypse. Eventually, they retired for the night, and Joseph resumed
dictating at nine the next morning. "Call your solemn assembly," Jesus
Christ instructed the Kirtland high priests. They should assemble, organize themselves, and purify themselves. They were to establish a "house of
God," a space for prayer, fasting, faith, learning, glory, and order. Joseph
called it the "School of the Prophets." (Early American colleges such as
Harvard were sometimes known as "schools of the prophets" because they
trained ministers.) The prophet sent a copy of the revelation to Missouri.
He termed it "the olive leaf which we have plucked from the tree of paradise, the Lord's message of peace to us." Joseph hoped the Missouri Saints
would receive the revelation as an occasion to set grievances aside.[28]

Another revelation, dictated in early January 1833, contained further instructions for the school. The school's president or teacher should enter the room first and pray on his knees. When students came in, the teacher should arise, lift up his hands to heaven, and greet them with the following words: "Art thou a brother . . . I salute you in the name of the Lord Jesus Christ, in token of the everlasting covenant." The instructions reflected Joseph's desire to inculcate order, unity, and friendship.[29]

Before Joseph organized the school, he invited the church to the planned "solemn assembly." Men and women alike packed into the "council room" above the Whitney store. Spiritual fire burst into full flame. After Joseph prayed, he spoke "in an unknown tongue." Soon other men, and women also, followed suit. People sang and prayed in tongues late into the night.[30]

The conference continued the next morning with just the elders in attendance. Again, there was speaking, prayer, and singing in tongues. Then those present purified themselves. Each man washed his hands, face, and feet. Taking inspiration from Jesus's example, Joseph then "girded himself with a towel" and washed each man's feet. When he came to his father, Joseph paused. Before he would wash his father's feet, Joseph asked for a blessing. Joseph Sr. laid his hands on his son's head and pronounced that he would "continue in his priest's office until Christ comes." It was a tender moment. Frederick Williams then washed Joseph Jr.'s feet, bringing the ritual to an end.[31]

The men had been in the council room all day long. Finally, after they partook of the Lord's Supper, the meeting was dismissed. The men raised an uplifted hand to God as a symbol of their everlasting covenant, a reflection of their fellowship and "determination to share in each other's burdens whether in prosperity or adversity." They would stick to each other and to their prophet. This was the harmony and unity Joseph craved. A circle of devoted friends, with himself at the center.[32]

Meanwhile, the Missouri Saints accepted Joseph's "olive leaf." Bishop Partridge, Oliver Cowdery, and other leaders held similar "solemn assemblies" in several Mormon settlements in Jackson County. "We all then kneeled before the Lord," recorded John Whitmer, "and asked him to effect a perfect harmony between us and our brethren in Kirtland." The Missouri leaders sent a letter to Joseph expressing their contrition and newfound fidelity. The prophet was thrilled to get this news of reconciliation. Renewed hope for peace and unity allowed him to develop even grander plans for Zion and Kirtland. In both locations, however, Joseph's plans ran into fierce opposition. Enemies outside the church had no interest in olive leaves.[33]

CHAPTER THIRTEEN

Zion Is Fled (1833–1834)

A S OF EARLY 1833, Joseph boasted a long list of lofty titles: prophet, seer, translator, revelator, first elder, and president of the high priesthood. Still only twenty-seven years of age, he presided over church members numbered in the thousands, clustered in Missouri and Ohio but also scattered across the northern United States and into Canada.

Despite his astonishing success, Joseph felt a sting when critics mocked him for his limited education and lack of sophistication. In Palmyra, Abner Cole had dismissed him as the "*spindle shanked* ignoramus Jo Smith." The Baptist reformer Alexander Campbell termed Joseph "as ignorant and as impudent a knave as ever wrote a book." His followers called him "Brother Joseph" or "President Smith," but to his detractors he would always be "Joe Smith," a crude imposter who dictated his Golden Bible with his head in his hat, "completely closed up like a dog's head in a black yarn stocking."[1]

Joseph didn't need others to tell him about his lack of polish. He knew his limitations. He couldn't match Sidney Rigdon's oratory or write with William W. Phelps's poetic flair. "I am a rough stone," Joseph later declared. "I desire the learning and wisdom of heaven alone."[2]

That wasn't quite true. Joseph intended to smooth out some of his roughness. Joseph taught that only through the priesthood could men obtain the "key of the knowledge of God," but he also recognized value in more mundane forms of knowledge. "Seek learning even by study," another revelation instructed. Joseph wanted to become acquainted with the "best books" and with biblical languages. As the church grew in size and complexity, Joseph knew he needed every possible advantage for the challenges that lay ahead.[3]

The Kirtland School of the Prophets, which began after the January 1833 "solemn assembly," was the first of Joseph's quixotic attempts at remedial education. The elders met in a small upper room in Newel K. Whitney's store. They began with building blocks rather than the best books. "The science we engaged in for the winter was English grammar," Zebedee Coltrin stated, adding that they obtained "a general knowledge." Orson Hyde was the school's grammar teacher. In the late 1820s, after converting to the doctrines then preached by Sidney Rigdon, Hyde had decided to redress his educational deficiencies. Rigdon tutored him in the basics of English grammar. Now Hyde taught Joseph and a group of around twenty elders.[4]

It wasn't grammar all of the time. It was a school for prophets, after all. According to Coltrin's later recollection, the school assembled early in the morning, and participants fasted until they partook of the Lord's Supper later in the day. They each received a large chunk of warm bread and a glass of wine, and they frequently spoke and sang in tongues afterwards.[5]

The men didn't consume only bread and wine. They also were heavy tobacco users. According to Brigham Young's secondhand account, the men spat tobacco juice "all over the floor" and filled the room with dense smoke. Emma Smith, who oversaw its cleaning, made her distaste known to her husband. Hers was a common complaint about male behavior in Jacksonian America. A Methodist magazine compared the ubiquity of tobacco to the Egyptian plague of frogs. Spit and smoke polluted many indoor spaces.[6]

In late February, Joseph read a revelation to the school that addressed Emma's concern. The text introduced itself as a "word of wisdom" to the Saints. Reflecting contemporary medical advice and fads, its scope was much broader than a response to the tobacco mess and stench. Many physicians of the time blamed disease on "stimulants," a broad category including everything from distilled spirits to tobacco to caffeine to meat to mustard. Sylvester Graham, known for the cracker that still bears his name, gained fame and notoriety through his advocacy of vegetarianism and sexual restraint. Graham urged people to drink nothing but cold water. While most reformers were less extreme, temperance had growing appeal as a religious and social movement. The consumption of whiskey had soared during the first third of the nineteenth century. Male drunkenness was widespread. In Kirtland itself, a temperance society forced the shutdown of the town's distillery in early 1833.[7]

The Word of Wisdom counseled against the use of tobacco, wine, strong drinks such as whiskey, and hot drinks, later defined as coffee and tea. In the revelation, the Lord encouraged the consumption of herbs and fruit in season and told the Saints to eat meat only in times of winter and famine. According to Zebedee Coltrin's later recollection, when the members of the school heard Joseph's revelation, they immediately threw their tobacco and pipes into the fire. Adherence to the Word of Wisdom was sporadic, however. A decade later, Emma still served coffee and tea, and Joseph still drank wine.[8]

On March 18, the church's high priests assembled in the school-room. In keeping with another recent revelation, Joseph ordained Sidney Rigdon and Frederick Williams as "presidents of the high priesthood . . . equal in holding the keys of this last kingdom." Given his public chal-lenge to Joseph the previous summer, Rigdon must have been thrilled with this affirmation signaling that he was back in the prophet's good graces. Williams, who had accompanied Oliver Cowdery and Parley Pratt on the first mission to Missouri and Indian Territory, replaced the excommunicated Jesse Gause.[9]

Joseph spoke after the ordinations, promising that "the pure in heart . . . should see a heavenly vision." Then the men prayed quietly by themselves. According to the sparse minutes of the meeting, they had their "eyes . . . opened so as to behold many things." Joseph distributed bread and wine. "Many of the brethren," Williams recorded, "saw a heav-enly vision of the savior and concourses of angels." The evening was a culmination of two months of purification and instruction.[10]

It was now time to send the students out of the classroom. Joseph and other church leaders had agreed to buy several properties in Kirt-land, which a previous revelation—using language from the Book of Isa-iah—had defined as a "stake of Zion." The lands included a hundred-acre farm owned by Peter French, along with French's brickyard and tavern. The price for the French property was a steep $5,000, with a down pay-ment of $2,000. Zebedee Coltrin recalled that the purchase "made it necessary to call the elders out of school for the purpose of going again into the world and procuring means for paying for the farms." The prophet directed a dozen men to leave Kirtland, preach the gospel, and seek donations from church members.[11]

Joseph stayed in Kirtland, often working in the "translating room" on the second floor of the Whitney store. Over the first half of 1833, he brought his revision of the King James Bible to a conclusion, or at least to a pause. In early February, he finished reviewing his work on the New Testament. Joseph then sped through the remainder of the Old Testament, reaching the end in early July. A few excerpts were published, but the entirety never appeared in print during Joseph's lifetime. According to one of Joseph's later associates, John Bernhisel, the prophet "designed to go through it again" and never felt that it was ready for publication.[12]

One of the more striking revisions to the King James text came when Joseph corrected the prologue to the Gospel of John. "In the beginning was the word," the gospel text reads, "and the Word was with God, and the Word was God." The gospel teaches that this divine Word created all things and eventually became flesh and dwelt among human beings, bringing them grace and truth.

Joseph made significant changes. "In the beginning was the gospel preached through the son," he revised. "And the gospel was the word, and the word was with the Son, and the Son was with God, and the Son was of God." The starting point was the gospel. Moreover, *of* God departed from John's affirmation that the Word *was* God.[13]

The prophet returned to the same verses in a May 1833 revelation. At first, Jesus had not possessed the fullness of God's glory. Rather, he had "continued from grace to grace until he received a fulness" at the time of his baptism. The revelation added that Jesus "was called the son of God because he received not of the fulness at first." Joseph, thus, rejected the affirmation that Jesus *was* God but simultaneously rejected any diminution of Jesus's divinity. Jesus had grown into a fullness of divine glory.

There was much more. "Ye were also in the beginning with the Father," the revelation instructed. Humans had a premortal existence. As light and truth, as divine intelligence, as spirit, human beings were just as eternal as Jesus Christ. They also had the same divine potential. If they kept God's commandments, they could partake of the same glory. Just as Jesus Christ had become one with the Father, so too could humans. "The glory of God is intelligence," the text declared, "or in other words light and truth." If humans kept God's commandments, they would grow in that light and truth.[14]

The third-century theologian Origen believed in the premortal existence of human souls, and many early Christians believed that God had adopted Jesus as his son at the time of his baptism. In both ancient times and in Joseph's lifetime, some Christians had backed away from the notion that Jesus Christ was God or fully equal to God. Others had underscored the divine potential within human beings.[15]

Antecedents and parallels, again, do not detract from Joseph's creativity. His ideas thrilled some of his followers, perplexed others, and prompted still others to leave his church. Revelation was ongoing. Christ directed his church by specific commandments and, through Joseph, revealed doctrines that often startled and shocked. Humans were eternal. Like their Savior, they could share in the fullness of God's glory.

As Joseph's revelations contemplated the past and the future, he also focused on the present task of building Zion, both the "city of Zion" in Jackson County, Missouri, and the "stake of Zion" in Kirtland. In August 1831, Joseph had identified the spot on which the temple in Independence should be built, and a December 1832 revelation had instructed church members to build a "house of the Lord" in Kirtland. Joseph came to use the terms "house of the Lord" and "temple" interchangeably. He envisioned two temples, one in Missouri and one in Ohio.

By June 1833, Joseph had grown frustrated that construction of the Kirtland "house of the Lord"—on the property purchased from Peter French—had not yet begun. Church leaders met to discuss the dimensions of the planned temple. At the meeting, Joseph dictated a revelation that specified the building's shape and purpose. It would look much like a Protestant church from the outside, albeit enormous by rural Ohio standards. The inside would be more distinctive. Rather than a single large room with a balcony, Joseph and his associates designed two main floors, a "lower court" and an "upper court." There would be ample space for worship and large assemblies, but also rooms for the School of the Prophets and more intimate meetings. Hyrum Smith and other men broke ground on June 7, and the cornerstones were laid on July 23. By the fall, workers had finished the building's stone foundation.[16]

Joseph had even more grandiose aspirations for Independence. The city plat—a chart of lots—was for a one-mile square, divided into forty-nine blocks. Farms would surround the city on every side. Most of the blocks were subdivided into twenty half-acre lots for homes, while the three central blocks were for "public buildings," including twenty-four temples that would serve as "houses of worship [and] schools." Joseph envisioned that fifteen thousand to twenty thousand people would live in the city. The first one-mile square was just the start. When the Saints had laid it out and filled it up, they would "lay off another in the same way"—until Zion filled the entire world.[17]

By the summer of 1833, there were around twelve hundred church members in Jackson County, and more eastern Saints were making plans to move there. The Mormon influx alarmed other settlers. The Saints didn't intend to build churches here and there like the Baptists or Methodists. Instead, as one of Joseph's revelations had instructed, they intended to buy the "whole region of country." In July 1833, the church's *The Evening and the Morning Star,* which wasn't nearly as boring as Joseph complained, openly announced that the Saints would "take possession of this land." William Phelps, the paper's editor, cautioned that church members, unlike the ancient Israelites, would take possession through "regular purchases" rather than through the "shedding of blood," but that hardly put other settlers at ease. The Saints already comprised around a third of Jackson County's population, and their rapid growth was discouraging non-Mormons from coming.[18]

In 1832 and early 1833, a few anti-Mormon agitators threw bricks and stones through the windows of Mormon homes, and there were plenty of threats and abusive remarks. Then in mid-July 1833, anti-Mormons circulated a petition that demanded that the Saints leave. The petition bandied about a host of accusations. The Mormons were religious fanatics who spoke in tongues and pretended to have worked miracles. They were from the dregs of Ohio and New York, lazy and idle men and women.

The petition also introduced a new charge, that the Saints had been "tampering with our slaves" and were "inviting free Negroes and mulattoes from other states to become Mormons and remove and settle among us." The accusation stemmed from a piece that Phelps had published, in which he excerpted a Missouri statute that forbade any "free negro or mulatto" from entering or settling in the state. Phelps did so to warn church members against transgressing Missouri law. At the same time, though, he commented that the church itself had "no special rule . . . as to people of color." Elsewhere in the same issue of the paper, Phelps observed that "in connection with the wonderful events of this age, much is doing towards abolishing slavery, and colonizing the blacks, in Africa." Upon word that his remarks had offended Jackson County slaveholders, the editor quickly published a clarification, stating that the Mormons wouldn't admit any "free people of color" into the state or the church.[19]

Complaints about miracles and fear of slave revolts were smoke-screens for the primary concern. Other Missourians feared being over-run and overpowered. In Jacksonian America, majorities ruled, and they often tyrannized minorities. Once the Mormons gained a majority, they would fill Jackson County's offices. Other Missourians would be living under a Mormon sheriff and Mormon judges. The anti-Mormons argued that their only recourse was to expel the Saints before they achieved power. They expressed their intention to rid Jackson County of the Mormons "peaceably if we can, forcibly if we must." Several hundred Missourians signed the manifesto.[20]

On July 20, a large gathering of anti-Mormons met in Independence and drafted a set of resolutions. The demands included that no additional church members move into Jackson County and that those already present agree to leave within a reasonable time. The anti-Mormons also insisted that Phelps immediately cease publication of the *Star* and that the Saints close all of their shops and other businesses. They brought the ultimatum to Partridge, Gilbert, Phelps, and the other church leaders and demanded their assent. The Mormons asked for three months to respond, probably hoping to consult with Joseph. The mob gave them fifteen minutes to agree. They refused.[21]

The anti-Mormons concluded that force was necessary. A mob numbering in the hundreds razed the printing office. Phelps was partway through printing the *Book of Commandments* containing Joseph's revelations. The vigilantes scattered the pages onto the dirt street. Vienna Jacques, a well-to-do New Englander who had sold her property and moved to Missouri, scrambled to collect them. "Madam," a member of the mob told her, "this is only a prelude to what you have to suffer." The mob also tarred and feathered two Mormon men, including Bishop Partridge. Sidney Gilbert persuaded the anti-Mormons to spare his store by promising to have everything packed to go as quickly as possible.[22]

Three days later, on the same day that the Ohio Saints were laying the temple cornerstones in Kirtland, hundreds of vigilantes ran and rode into Independence, brandishing guns, clubs, and whips, some waving red flags, many terrifying the Saints with their yells. The attackers seized several Missouri church leaders. They threatened to whip them mercilessly, destroy more property, and have their slaves trample Mormon crops. Outnumbered and outgunned, church leaders agreed to leave the county. They would gather that year's harvest and be gone before spring.

The Saints hoped that state officials would make their departure unnecessary. The actions against the Mormons were popular among other
white Jackson County settlers, but many Missouri politicians and journalists
denounced the mob. The St. Louis *Missouri Republican* described the vigilantism as "wholly at war with the genius of our institutions and . . . subver-
sive of good order." Missouri governor Daniel Dunklin seemed to agree.
"Ours is a government of laws," he reassured church leaders. Dunklin urged
the Saints to take their complaints to justices of the peace, obtain warrants
for the arrest of anyone who had broken the law, and seek relief from the
courts. The governor added that if the courts failed the Mormons, he
would take the necessary steps to ensure the execution of state law.[23]

Vigilantism elsewhere in the United States should have made the
Saints skeptical that Dunklin would keep his word. Just a few weeks after
the destruction of the church's printing press and the tarring and feath-
ering of its bishop, a Protestant mob burned the Ursuline convent in
Boston. The chief perpetrators were either acquitted or pardoned. These
were not isolated examples. Courts also refused to convict vigilantes who
beat or destroyed the property of Irish immigrants, political opponents,
and African Americans. President Andrew Jackson condemned rioters
who burned abolitionist mail in Charleston, South Carolina. Like most
white Americans across the country, Jackson loathed abolitionists, but he
did not think that their offensiveness excused vigilantism. "This spirit of
mob-law is becoming too common and must be checked," Jackson maintained. As both Jackson and Dunklin understood, it was far easier to denounce mob violence than to check it.[24]

Missouri Mormon leaders had kept Joseph informed about the
mounting tension. He had counseled them to eschew violence. "Renounce war and proclaim peace," a revelation had commanded. The
Saints should fight their enemies only after repeated provocations. After
the mob attack, Oliver Cowdery rushed to Kirtland to obtain Joseph's
guidance. When he reached Kirtland, Cowdery found the prophet on the
porch, washing his face and hands. When Joseph learned what had transpired in Jackson County, his face was soon wet with tears.[25]

Kirtland leaders met that evening. Was it now time for war instead of
peace? Or should the Saints sell their lands and leave Zion? Cowdery
dashed off a letter to Missouri that allowed that the Saints might have to
sell some properties but should retain the temple lot. A week later, Joseph
had a different message. The Saints would not leave Jackson County. He
had received "the word of the Lord that you shall be delivered from your

danger and shall again flourish." They would establish another printing office in Missouri. They would keep Sidney Gilbert's store. Above all else, they would keep their land. "Let those who are bound to leave the land," Joseph counseled, "make a show as if to do until the Lord deliver." They should stall. They should stall because Joseph didn't know what to do. "We wait the command of God," Joseph concluded. "If he shall say go up to Zion and defend thy brethren by the sword, we fly." But not yet.[26]

The news of Missouri mobs heightened Joseph's fear that similar persecution could take place in Ohio. "We are no safer here in Kirtland than you are in Zion," he wrote. "The cloud is gathering around us with great fury." As had been the case with Ezra Booth and Symonds Ryder, a former church member fomented the fury. Doctor Philastus Hurlbut was a good-looking and fast-talking Methodist lay preacher who converted to Mormonism and was ordained an elder in March 1833. "Doctor" was his given name; he was not a physician. After his baptism, Hurlbut soon departed on a mission, preaching in western Pennsylvania.[27]

Hurlbut's mission didn't last long. The new elder liked women more than he liked his new church. In June 1833, a council in Kirtland excommunicated him in absentia for "unchristian conduct with the female sex." Hurlbut rushed to Kirtland, made a "liberal confession" of his errors, was restored, then was again "cut off" when more evidence emerged about his transgressions.[28]

Hurlbut next became the world's first professional anti-Mormon. He resumed preaching in western Pennsylvania and northeastern Ohio, now against the church that had just excommunicated him. He had heard rumors that the Book of Mormon resembled a story written by Solomon Spalding, an erstwhile Congregational minister and storekeeper who had died in 1816. After talking with Spalding's former neighbors in western Pennsylvania, Hurlbut was certain he was onto something that could bring down Joseph Smith for good. He wanted to travel east to interview Spalding's widow and other witnesses, but he needed money to do so. Grandison Newell, a wealthy resident of Mentor, Ohio, financed Hurlbut's investigation.

Matilda Spalding Davison gave Hurlbut what her late husband had titled "Manuscript Found." Unfortunately for Hurlbut, it was obviously not Joseph Smith's source for the Book of Mormon. The tale instead narrates the adventures of a group of Christian Romans who cross the Atlantic Ocean and encounter two Native peoples, one "barbarous" and one lighter-skinned and "civilized." Other than the rather common tropes of a hemispheric crossing and differently hued Indians, the manuscript did not bear any resemblance to the Book of Mormon.[29]

Hurlbut was undeterred. He collected statements from Spalding's brother and several others who remembered that Spalding had written another novel. This second manuscript, they were sure, was the source for the Book of Mormon, down to the names Lehi and Nephi. Hurlbut developed the idea that Sidney Rigdon had met Spalding, obtained the manuscript, and had helped Joseph Smith fashion it into the Book of Mormon. It made sense to Hurlbut that the more educated and accomplished Rigdon was the prime mover behind the "Gold Bible." Neither Hurlbut nor anyone else could locate Spalding's lost manuscript, however, and there is no evidence that Rigdon met Joseph Smith prior to the fall of 1830. Hurlbut arrived back in Kirtland in December 1833. He brought a sheaf of affidavits from Joseph Smith's former neighbors in and around Palmyra, New York. The statements described an ignorant, idle young man who deceived his neighbors with tales of buried treasure.[30]

Joseph was worried. "The people are running after him [Hurlbut]," the prophet informed the Missouri Saints, "and giving him money to break down Mormonism, which much endangers our lives." The March 1832 attack on Joseph and Sidney Rigdon had come on the heels of Ezra Booth's strident critiques. Joseph now expected fresh salvoes against him in area newspapers, and he feared for his physical safety.[31]

In mid-November, Joseph was awakened well before dawn by a knocking at the door. It wasn't the mob. "Come get up," a friendly man told him, "and see the signs in the heavens." Along with many other townspeople, Joseph walked outside and stared up at the night sky. "[I] beheld to my great joy," he wrote in his journal, "the stars fall from heaven yea they fell like hail stones." The meteors, an unusually intense occurrence of the annual Leonid shower, were so bright that they woke many Americans from their sleep. Joseph concluded from the display in the heavens that "the coming of Christ is close at hand." Ancient prophecies, and his own revelations, were being fulfilled.[32]

The Bible predicted great tumult prior to the return of Jesus Christ, and a few weeks later Joseph received word of further tribulations suffered by the Missouri Saints. Joseph's advice to stall and seek redress hadn't worked. Once it became apparent that the Missouri Saints did not intend to leave Jackson County, their opponents resumed their campaign of harassment and violence.[33]

The results were deadly and, for the Saints, disastrous. With the support or tacit sanction of Jackson County officials, the mobs tore down houses and whipped Mormon men. In some instances, church members fought back. On November 4, at a settlement above the Big Blue River in the far western part of the county, the mob tracked down and fired upon a group of thirty Mormons. The Saints shot back, killing two of their assailants. One church member was mortally wounded in the exchange. Other Mormon settlements were scenes of chaos and confusion. Families staggered through the prairie, mostly making their way north and crossing the Missouri River to Clay County. They slept in tents, shanties, or even on the cold late-fall ground. They suffered from exposure and malnourishment. Bishop Edward Partridge watched the meteor shower from his camp on the north side of the Missouri River opposite Independence. The thousands of shooting stars "stream[ing] down thick as rain" served as a reminder of God's power. Nothing else could return them to their homes.[34]

The need for Joseph's direction was now acute. How long would the Saints wait for Zion's liberation, its "redemption"? And by what means would God return them to their land? In a letter to the Missouri church leaders, Joseph confessed that he still did not have an answer to these questions. "The Lord will not show me," the prophet confided.[35] On one point, however, Joseph was firm. The Saints should not sell their Jackson County lands. God had punished the Saints because many of them had transgressed, but they would return to their properties.

A mid-December revelation likened Zion to a vineyard inadequately tended and guarded by its servants. They had allowed the enemy to ravage it. Now, however, the "Lord of the vineyard" had asked one of his servants—a subsequent revelation identified this figure as Joseph—to reclaim it. He was to gather "warriors ... young men and they that are of middle age." The specifics were not clear, but Joseph would recruit an army and march to Missouri. In the meantime, he counseled the Saints to buy up as much land in and around Jackson County as possible and to petition the governor and the president of the United States for redress.[36]

Before Joseph began gathering his soldiers, he initiated a legal war in Kirtland. Doctor P. Hurlbut had returned with his affidavits and the Spalding manuscript and presented them as evidence of Joseph's fraudulency. Hurlbut announced his intention to publish a book that would prove the Book of Mormon a "*fiction* and *imagination*." In a letter to their

counterparts in Missouri, Ohio church leaders asserted that Hurlbut
"also made many harsh threats ... that he would take the life of
Brother Joseph if he could not destroy Mormonism without." On December 21, 1833, Joseph filed a complaint with John C. Dowen, a justice
of the peace in Kirtland, alleging that Hurlbut had threatened to do him
harm.[37]

The legal action heightened the tension. "It is said that the inhabitants have threatened mobbing [the Mormons]," wrote B. F. Norris, a
non-Mormon resident of nearby Mentor. "They [the Mormons] are
arming themselves with instruments of war such as guns, swords, dirks,
spontoons." Men guarded Joseph and Emma's home at night. In the days
before Hurlbut's hearing, vigilantes fired a cannon somewhere in town in
an attempt at intimidation. "They say they are not going to be drove
away as they were at Missouri," Norris reported.[38]

Jackson County officials summarily dismissed Mormon complaints,
but Justice Dowen issued a warrant for Hurlbut's arrest. A constable
brought him to Painesville, ten miles northeast of Kirtland. William
Holbrook, another justice of the peace, heard the case in the town's
Methodist church. Joseph was among sixteen witnesses who testified. According to the later recollection of Hurlbut's attorney, the prophet stated
that when he had first attempted to retrieve the Book of Mormon plates,
the devil or an unseen power had knocked him backward. Justice Holbrook did not rule on the merits of the Book of Mormon, but he found
merit in Joseph's complaint. He ordered Hurlbut to post a bond and appear before a county court in April.[39]

As the trial got underway, Joseph gathered with Bishop Whitney,
Oliver Cowdery, Frederick Williams, and Heber C. Kimball, bowed
down, and pleaded with God that he would prevail "against that wicked
Hurlbut and that he be put to shame." Residents of Chardon, the county
seat, turned out to see the prophet and his antagonist. The courthouse
"was filled, almost to suffocation." Witnesses for the prosecution testified
that in the wake of his excommunication and disillusionment, Hurlbut
had threatened "revenge" against Joseph. In his own testimony, Joseph
told the court that he "became afraid of bodily injury from the defendant." The judge ordered Hurlbut to pay a $200 bond to keep the peace
and to pay more than $100 in court costs.[40]

Joseph and his friends were elated. "We are not in any fear that the
kingdom will be overthrown by him [Hurlbut]," wrote Oliver Cowdery.[41]

Hurlbut's days as a professional anti-Mormon were over. He sold the materials he had collected to the *Painesville Telegraph*'s Eber D. Howe.

Between Hurlbut's January 1834 hearing and the April trial, Joseph had begun making preparations for Zion's liberation. Parley Pratt and Lyman Wight had arrived with the news that the exiled Jackson County Saints had survived the early winter with their lives and faith intact. Pratt and Wight, however, informed the Kirtland leaders that the Missouri Saints, now sheltering in Clay County, had grown desperate to know when and how Zion would be "redeemed from our enemies." At a church council, Joseph stood up and announced that he would go to Missouri. Who would join him? Several dozen men volunteered. The council selected Joseph as the "Commander in Chief of the Armies of Israel." A revelation declared that Joseph would lead the Saints as "Moses led the children of Israel." The army needed to be bigger, however. Joseph and others fanned out across the Northeast in an attempt to raise men and money.[42]

While visiting church members in nearby Norton, Ohio, Joseph, Sidney Rigdon, Oliver Cowdery, and Zebedee Coltrin withdrew into the woods to pray. They asked God to give Joseph the "strength, and wisdom, and understanding" he would need to lead the Saints back onto their lands. Then the three men laid their hands on Joseph and prayed that he would "return again in peace and triumph" to Kirtland. Their prayers would be answered only in part.[43]

CHAPTER FOURTEEN

General Smith (1834)

W HAT HAPPENS WHEN A prophet gets it wrong? Or when his plans fail? Would Moses have kept his leadership intact had the Hebrews been turned back at the Red Sea?

History is full of failed prophets. The American Baptist minister William Miller predicted that Jesus Christ would return sometime between March 21, 1843, and March 21, 1844. Thousands of Americans awaited the Second Coming with rapt anticipation. When Jesus did not appear on schedule, the "Great Disappointment" led to some prophetic recalculation, the splintering of the movement, and the abrupt loss of Miller's influence.

Another early nineteenth-century figure more closely resembled Joseph Smith. Tenskwatawa, the Shawnee prophet and brother of Tecumseh, had a series of visions beginning around 1805 in which he discerned that his people and other Natives should reject European ways. In June 1806, he gained credibility when he predicted a looming darkness a few days before a solar eclipse. As the historian Adam Jortner explains, Tenskwatawa became "the man who made the sun go dark at midday." He taught that the "Master of Life" wanted Indians to gather together into a single nation. European Americans called it Prophetstown, a Native city in the Indiana Territory. Alarmed by its growth, in 1811 General William Henry Harrison led an expedition against the Indian "city-state." Tenskwatawa promised his people safety from American weapons, but they suffered heavy casualties in the Battle of Tippecanoe. Prophetstown was destroyed. Tenskwatawa's influence was eclipsed by the defeat.[1]

Joseph Smith had staked a great deal on his identification of Independence as the millennial New Jerusalem to which Jesus Christ would return. In response to Joseph's revelations, hundreds of church members had moved there. Now, Joseph had proclaimed that he would lead an army to redeem their stolen land.

It was by far the riskiest act of Joseph's prophetic career to date. The Mormon prophet was comfortable with long odds but, unlike William Miller, Joseph hedged his bets. Christ would come soon, but Joseph never set a date or a year. Zion would stand forever, if the Saints were faithful.

In early May 1834, Joseph presided at a conference in Kirtland that declared that henceforth, the church would be known as "The Church of the Latter Day Saints." The original name, "the Church of Christ," indicated the movement's universal aspirations but was too generic. The revised name pointed to continuity with Christ's ancient followers, and to the belief that church members lived in the "latter days" prior to their Savior's return.[2]

On May 5, Joseph and the "Camp of Israel"—later known as "Zion's Camp"—left Kirtland. The day before their departure, Joseph called together his recruits. "We were all sealed up to eternal life by Joseph," remembered Reuben McBride. If McBride and the other men remained righteous, their salvation was assured. They would "come forth in the day of the Lord Jesus." It wasn't exactly a holy war Joseph had in mind, but it was at least a holy march.[3]

"General Smith" and his camp intersected other recruits as they journeyed west, eventually becoming two hundred men strong. A dozen women and some children accompanied the camp. At its full strength, the camp had twenty wagons, each pulled by two or three horses.

Despite the rhetoric about "warriors," Joseph did not intend the Camp of Israel to retake Jackson County by force of arms. In February, Governor Dunklin had ordered state militia troops to protect church members if the latter returned to their Jackson County homes. He also promised protection during any trials stemming from the outrages of the past year. Joseph, therefore, only had to lead his men to Clay County, from which they would accompany the expelled Saints back to their properties.[4]

Meanwhile, Jackson County's rabble-rousers were ready. They knew that an armed company of Saints was coming. The church had published a broadside of Joseph's December 1833 revelation that talked of "warriors" redeeming Zion. Rumors of an approaching Mormon army spread like a prairie fire. Residents of Jackson County assembled in preparation for war. They burned dozens of Mormon houses.[5]

For Joseph and the other members of Zion's Camp, the next six weeks were a mixture of adventure and tension, camaraderie and contention. The journey was arduous. At the outset of the march, the ground froze at night. Then when it rained, bedding became waterlogged. At times their supplies of food ran low. Nor did they always have access to clean water. George A. Smith, the prophet's sixteen-year-old cousin, recalled that a few weeks into the trip they "were compelled to drink water from sloughs which were filled with living creatures." They clenched their teeth and strained out the "wrigglers."[6]

Joseph's endurance of these hardships endeared him to his men. Two weeks into the march, along a soggy portion of the National Road in eastern Indiana, Moses Martin "saw the prophet wade in the mud over the tops of his boot legs and help draw the wagons out." On his prior trips to Missouri, Joseph had sometimes traveled by stage while other men had walked. During the march, the prophet walked nearly the whole way, just like everyone else. He slept in the same tents and ate the same scanty food. It wasn't easy. His feet were sore and blistered, and he was bothered by what he described as "a little touch of my side complaint," probably lingering pain from the 1832 mob attack. Still, at age twenty-eight Joseph was in his physical prime, and he held up well to the trip's rigors.[7]

The army's cohesion did not hold up as well. One point of recurrent tension was a dog given to Joseph by a church member near the outset of the march. Joseph quickly became devoted to the dog, Major, who returned his affection by guarding the prophet a bit too zealously. Major also sometimes barked at night. Ten days into the march, just over the Ohio-Indiana border, Sylvester Smith—no relation to Joseph—snapped. He threatened to kill the dog. "General Smith," wrote Martin, "severely reproved him, showing him that he possessed the same scent and worse than the dog." The two Smiths both had hot tempers.[8]

Some distractions were more welcome. After the marchers crossed the Illinois River in early June, they encountered a series of large burial mounds. Archaeologists date the mounds to the Hopewellian exchange period, about two millennia ago. Like many other Europeans and white Americans, the Saints couldn't resist the chance to dig into Native graves. They excavated the top of a large mound and discovered the bones of a very large man, along with a stone arrowhead that they presumed had killed him. His thigh bones were enormous, even longer than Joseph's, and one of them was broken. Soon after the excavation, Joseph reported a vision in which the Lord had shown him that the remains were those of a "mighty prophet." Joseph later identified the man as Zelph, a warrior who had served under a prophet named Onandagus. (Neither figure is mentioned in the Book of Mormon.) According to the journal of marcher Wilford Woodruff, Joseph said that Zelph "was a white Lamanite." After he repented and turned to the Lord, God took away his dark skin. "The curse was taken from him or at least in part," Joseph explained. Joseph also asserted that the broken thigh bone had resulted from "a stone flung from a sling in battle" years before his death. Like Joseph, Zelph had walked with a bit of a limp and pain for the rest of his life.[9]

Near the mounds they found "altars" or "fortifications." Joseph wrote Emma that they were "wandering over the plains of the Nephites, recounting occasionally the history of the Book of Mormon." Joseph and his followers traversed a sacred landscape. The prairies and hills revealed clues of ancient civilizations. The skeleton and the arrowhead connected the marchers to warriors who had come before them. They were "modern Zelphs."[10]

The army ferried over the Mississippi River on June 5. While waiting his turn, Levi Hancock, a member of Sylvester Smith's company, whittled a fife from an elder tree. The company then proudly marched single file into camp as Hancock blew his shrill instrument. The noisy procession alarmed Joseph's dog, who made to attack the men. No harm was done, but Sylvester Smith again threatened to kill the dog. Major made matters worse by barking that night. In the morning, according to Brigham Young, there was "considerable complaint and murmuring concerning the dog." The prophet threatened to whip anyone who harmed Major. "If that dog bites me I will kill him," Sylvester Smith told Joseph. After the prophet repeated his threat, some wondered whether his "spirit" was appropriate. Joseph "then said that he had descended to that spirit in order to show the spirit which was among them," for their edification. It wasn't the best explanation, but eventually everyone simmered down.[11]

Joseph and the other officers had prepared for what might await them should they attempt to cross into Jackson County. They had a flag made by Levi Hancock. It was white and tipped with red. Hancock drew an eagle on one side and wrote the word "Peace" in big letters on the other. Attached to a staff, it became the Army of Israel's standard. When the men had the energy, they did a modest amount of military training. On one occasion, recorded Moses Martin, the leaders sounded an alarm at night to see "how quickly we could be formed in a line fit for action." Three minutes, it turned out. The men also staged a "sham fight which terminated in a large amount of sport." The closer they got to Jackson County, the more serious such matters became. On June 10, Joseph selected "twenty swordsmen for a life guard" and "twenty of the best riflemen for rangers." According to George A. Smith, Joseph himself carried a horse pistol from the War of 1812, a rifle, and a sword. If he had had a uniform, Joseph would have cut a decent military figure.[12]

As the camp approached western Missouri, Joseph dispatched Parley Pratt and Orson Hyde to consult with Governor Dunklin in Jefferson City. It remains unclear exactly what the governor conveyed to Joseph's messengers. Earlier in the month, Dunklin had written a political ally that "the Mormons have no right to march to Jackson county in arms." Private citizens could not "levy war," even in defense of their own rights. He probably told Pratt and Hyde as much. For months, Joseph had maintained hope that Dunklin would direct state forces to restore the Saints to their Jackson County lands. By this point, Joseph must have realized that despite his prior statements, Dunklin would not support them. Regardless, when the emissaries returned to the camp, its leaders held a council and decided to "go on armed and equipped." Bishop Partridge met the camp on June 15 and warned them that violence would ensue should they enter Jackson County.[13]

On June 17, after they ferried across Wakenda Creek in Carroll County, Missouri, Joseph ordered the camp to proceed and spend the night on a large prairie. It was beautiful country, with waist-high corn, and black raspberries ripe for picking. But Lyman Wight, Joseph's second in command, concluded that the camp would be less exposed to attack if they remained in the woods. After all, they were only two days from reaching Clay County. There was no doubt that members of the Jackson County mob were watching their movements. Wight, Sylvester Smith, and their men remained behind. When the companies reunited, Joseph was livid with the rebels. Joseph grabbed the camp's French horn and threw it. Sylvester Smith thought the prophet had aimed the horn at him. Not even the specter of mob violence could stop the marchers from fighting among themselves. Wight apologized and promised his future obedience.[14]

Missouri officials now attempted to mediate the dispute. Circuit court judge John F. Ryland invited the Clay County Mormon leaders and a committee from Jackson County to negotiations in Liberty, the Clay County seat. The committee proposed that one side buy out the other for an arbitrated price of twice the land's value, with payment due within thirty days. The anti-Mormons in Jackson County negotiated from a position of strength. They occupied the ground and they had burned most of the Saints' houses. They also knew that the Saints would be unable to raise the funds needed to buy out the county's non-Mormon settlers, who held title to the vast majority of Jackson County's land. The church representatives promised an answer within a week, after they consulted with Joseph. In the meantime, the anti-Mormons also made clear their willingness to fight. "The whole county is in an uproar," reported a correspondent in Lexington, thirty miles to the east. "Should they cross the river, there will be a battle, and probably much blood shed."[15]

Joseph and his army reached Clay County on June 19. The tension was as high as the corn, which now reached their shoulders. They made camp between the forks of the Fishing River near a Baptist meetinghouse. That night, according to camp member Charles Coulson Rich, there was "an alarm of an attack." In their later recollections, several of the Saints reported that there were hundreds of non-Mormon men on the banks of the Fishing River preparing to mob them. The attack never came. Instead, the camp experienced what Moses Martin termed "one of the most shockingest storms ever known." For six hours, "the whole canopy of the wide horizon was in one complete blaze." The thunder claps were deafening, and the rain came down in torrents. No mob would have dared to cross the swollen river. Some of the Saints took shelter from the stormy blast in the Baptist church. The next day, they found evidence of a tremendous hailstorm to the north. Half-pound hunks of ice had destroyed crops and other vegetation.[16]

On June 21, Judge Ryland, Clay County sheriff Cornelius Gilliam, and several other would-be peacemakers visited the camp, now four miles north of Fishing River at church member John Cooper's farm. Joseph spoke to them, professing that his people had no intention of provoking bloodshed. He and other church leaders then prepared a counteroffer for the Jackson County committee. If given a year to raise the funds, the church would buy out all residents who could not abide the presence of Mormons in the county.[17]

Joseph probably knew that the anti-Mormons would not accept his offer. The only real choice was whether his followers would fight the mobs. Besides Joseph's concern to avoid violence, success in a war was unlikely, particularly if the non-Mormon residents of surrounding counties joined the fight. Indeed, on June 23, a Lafayette County committee of more than one hundred residents declared that they were prepared to prevent "foreign Mormons" from invading Jackson County. Joseph and the other Saints realized that they lacked the power to achieve their objectives on their own, and no other power would come to their aid.[18]

Not even God. The day after the meeting with Ryland and Gilliam, Joseph dictated a revelation. In it, Jesus Christ maintained that Zion would be redeemed, but not yet. Why not? The answer was the same that Joseph's revelations had given for the Saints' expulsion from Jackson County: transgression. The Saints had brought misfortune upon themselves. Not enough men had volunteered to fight. The Saints hadn't given enough money. And those who had marched lacked unity. Therefore, the Lord declared, they would "wait for a little season for the redemption of Zion." Until that time, the Saints should purchase as much land in Jackson County and surrounding areas as possible, and the Army of Israel should grow until it had enough soldiers to overpower its enemies. The elders should return to Kirtland and receive "a great endowment" of spiritual power and blessing in the temple.[19]

Thus, even before the anti-Mormons had responded to his proposal, Joseph had abandoned the campaign. While many camp members were relieved at the prospect of returning to their families, others felt that the revelation betrayed the cause of Zion. George A. Smith, the prophet's cousin, recalled that "several of the brethren apostatized because they were not going to have the privilege of fighting." Their long journey had been for naught.[20]

The camp remained together for a few more days. Then, on June 25, people started getting sick. It was cholera. Over the next week, fifteen church members died. The dead included Jesse J. Smith, Joseph's cousin; Betsy Parrish, who had accompanied her husband Warren on the march; Sidney Gilbert, Bishop Newel K. Whitney's erstwhile partner and a key figure in the church's Missouri affairs; and Phebe Murdock, a daughter of John Murdock. Dozens of others became ill. Grief compounded the misery of failure.

As the cholera struck, the Camp of Israel began to disperse into companies. Its members started on their return journeys in early July. An Indiana newspaper observed later that month they looked "like the remnant of a scattered army ... quite a contrast to their outward bound appearance." Back in Ohio, the Saints were on tenterhooks waiting for news. In mid-July 1834, a newspaper near Kirtland reported that while leading his army in an attempted crossing of the Missouri, Joseph had been wounded in the leg, had had his leg amputated, and had died several days later. More accurate reports quickly dispelled the rumors. Joseph safely returned to Kirtland in early August, but it proved much harder to overcome the discontents created by the march's inglorious conclusion.[21]

"I was met in the face and eyes as soon as I had got home," Joseph lamented. "The cry was Tyrant! Pope! King! Usurper! Abuser of Men!"[22] Had the Camp of Israel succeeded, Joseph could have brushed aside the accusations as the idle talk of malcontents. But the camp's failure led to talk that Joseph was a false prophet.

Sylvester Smith had reached Kirtland several days earlier. He remained angry at the way that Joseph had rebuked and insulted him during the march. He also alleged that Joseph had filched money consecrated for the march. Sylvester Smith was one of the twelve members of the Kirtland High Council, a position of some authority that lent gravity to his charges. He did more than grouse to his friends in private. On Saturday, August 9, at some sort of public meeting, he accused Joseph "of prophesying lies in the name of the Lord."[23]

Joseph and his associates moved to quash the challenge. On August 11, they convened a council, held just west of the temple site in a newly built schoolhouse. Joseph spoke about the events of the past several months, explained the circumstances that had led him to chastise Sylvester Smith, and defended his financial stewardship. Sylvester Smith at first made a "partial confession," then reneged once he was no longer facing the prophet and his defenders.[24]

"I have not been able to regulate my mind," Joseph wrote in mid-August. Joseph had known failure before, from the loss of the Smith family farm to the unsuccessful treasure quest to the loss of the first Book of Mormon manuscript. In those instances, Joseph responded to setbacks by devoting himself to a new project, usually grander than the last. In this case, he wasn't ready to let go of Zion. Perhaps to allay criticism, he pinpointed a deadline for its liberation. September 11, 1836, "is the appointed time for the redemption of Zion," he declared. On the same date in 1831, a revelation had specified that God would maintain a "stronghold" in Kirtland for five years. If church members prepared appropriately, the Saints would return to Zion at the end of that five-year period. By looking to the future, Joseph created some breathing room. Without giving up on Zion, the church could move beyond the camp's failure and focus on the Kirtland Temple.[25]

Meanwhile, with Bishop Newel K. Whitney presiding, the Kirtland High Council assembled in late August to hear charges against Sylvester Smith. It took two days to hear a string of Camp of Israel participants testify about conflicts over camp food, the dog, and the French horn. According to Brigham Young, Joseph had upbraided Sylvester Smith when he had refused to share bread with Parley Pratt, who in consequence had no bread to eat one night. Young and others insisted that Sylvester Smith had deserved the sharp reproofs from Joseph. Whitney then rendered his decision. In order to remain a member of the church, Sylvester Smith had to acknowledge in print that he had "willfully and maliciously lied" in all of his accusations.[26]

Backed into a corner, Sylvester Smith signed his name to the council's decision. He prepared a statement for the *Latter Day Saints' Messenger and Advocate*, the church's new monthly newspaper, confessing that the "errors" of which he had accused Joseph "did not exist, and were never committed by him." He expressed deep contrition. "I have received testimony from the heavens," he concluded, "that the work of the Lord, brought forth by means of the book of Mormon, in our day, through the instrumentality of bro. JOSEPH SMITH Jr. is eternal truth." In late September, Sylvester Smith formally lost his place on the Kirtland High Council, but that body decided that he should retain his standing as a high priest. It was an ideal solution, keeping Sylvester Smith in the church but putting an end to his public criticism of the prophet.[27]

Most of the marchers, moreover, retained their faith in Joseph. In fact, many of Joseph's most loyal associates in the years ahead were among those who had walked with him to Missouri. Men like Brigham Young and Heber C. Kimball had spent far more time with Joseph in the span of a few weeks than they had since their conversions. As Young put it, the Camp of Israel "gave us an experience that Kirtland could not buy." These stalwart Saints did not follow Joseph because his leadership was perfect or because his choices and predictions always panned out.

They followed him because they believed that the Book of Mormon and Joseph's revelations pointed them to Christ's one true church. At times, Joseph was short-tempered, but he also was quick to forgive. Like them, he had left his family to help the Missouri Saints. He had waded into the mire right next to them and had endured the same storms. They would stick by him. They directed their anger not toward their prophet but against the enemies who had assaulted their brothers and sisters in Zion.

When the mobs had first driven the Saints from their Jackson County homes, church members expected or at least hoped that judges and Missouri politicians would help them secure justice. It proved impossible to pursue charges against their assaults in court, and Dunklin betrayed them with his equivocation and passivity. Church leaders had also appealed to President Andrew Jackson. Secretary of State Lewis Cass, however, rebuffed the request. "The president cannot call out a military force to aid in the execution of state laws," Cass insisted in early May, "until the proper requisition is made upon him by the constituted authorities."[28] The suffering of the Saints garnered sympathy in some quarters, but no one would help them. Even so, Joseph and his people weren't ready to give up on the country and its constitution. Their faith in the American republic was shaken, not shattered.

CHAPTER FIFTEEN

Blessings (1834–1835)

W HEN JOSEPH RETURNED TO Kirtland from Missouri in early August 1834, he found Emma, Julia, and young Joseph all healthy. The previous year, the family had moved to a property that lay just north of the temple site, the first time since Joseph and Emma had left Harmony that they had a house of their own. It was a short walk to Sidney Rigdon's home and Oliver Cowdery's printing office. Other church members built residences near the temple site over the next few years, and the Whitney stores and residence were a few hundred yards to the north. Joseph's parents lived on a farm owned by Frederick G. Williams across the river to the northeast. For the next two and a half years, Joseph was rarely far from Kirtland, his family, and his friends.

The intra-church hubbub surrounding Joseph's behavior on the march to Zion subsided, but external critics sharpened their attacks on the prophet. In November, Eber D. Howe's *Painesville Telegraph* announced the publication of his book, *Mormonism Unvailed*. Like Palmyra's Abner Cole, Howe was a religious skeptic with a deep disdain for what he perceived as irrationality and spiritual excess. And in this case, it was personal. Two of Howe's sisters and his wife belonged to the church that he skewered. In April 1834, Sophia Howe—one of what her husband called many "fanatical females"—had contributed $7.60 to the Camp of Israel. Eber Howe didn't want to inflame mobs, and his newspaper lamented that the Missouri "victims of delusion" had suffered violence and expulsion. Still, Howe aimed to land a decisive blow in print against Joseph Smith and his church.[1]

Mormonism Unvailed combined Ezra Booth's letters, a sampling of Joseph's revelations, Hurlbut's affidavits, and Howe's own commentary. Howe constructed an entertaining and biting narrative about the origins of the Book of Mormon. After years of vain searches for treasure with his divining rod and peep stone, "Jo Smith" had concocted the story of the plates and authored the Book of Mormon with the aid of Solomon Spalding's now-lost manuscript. If this "farrago of nonsense" only separated the gullible few from their senses and money, some combination of mockery and pity might have sufficed. But Howe insisted that Mormonism threatened all Americans. As their numbers grew, and as they recruited the Indians to their cause, the Mormons would seize power, first in Jackson County and Kirtland, then in the United States as a whole. Joseph would rule "by immediate revelations." Echoing what Sylvester Smith had alleged after his return from Missouri, Howe warned that "we shall then have Pope Joseph *the First*, and his hierarchy." Howe calculated that if the debacle of Jackson County and the "army of Zion" hadn't broken the faith of the fanatics in their prophet, nothing would, but he hoped his exposé would inoculate other Americans against the contagion.[2]

Howe's book didn't halt the growth of Joseph's church, but it left a lasting mark nevertheless. The assertion that the Book of Mormon rested upon a missing Spalding manuscript retained currency for decades and still plays a role in debates about the origins of the Book of Mormon.

Mormonism Unvailed reinforced the necessity for Joseph to get his own message into print. After the mob had scattered the unbound pages of the *Book of Commandments*—containing most of Joseph's revelations through 1831—onto the streets of Independence, Joseph and his associates made plans for a second attempt in Kirtland. It was urgent, Joseph and his associates explained, as "the church was evil spoken of in many places." The new volume, *Doctrine and Covenants*, appeared in the summer of 1835.[3]

The first portion of the volume consisted of seven "lectures as delivered before a theological class." An Elders School had met in Kirtland, a successor to the earlier School of the Prophets. Alongside Sidney Rigdon and Hyrum Smith, Joseph sometimes taught in these sessions, held in the schoolroom beneath the Kirtland printing office. Rigdon probably was the foremost author of the published lectures, which drew on the Bible and the Book of Mormon for doctrines about God, Jesus Christ, and the

Holy Spirit. At least in their structure, the lectures resembled the theological systems and creeds of other Christian churches. The "Lectures on Faith," as the series became known, were intended to refute representations of the church as "disbelieving the Bible ... [or] being an enemy to all good order." The second portion, the "covenants," referred to Joseph's revelations, about a hundred of which appeared in the volume.[4]

Just as Joseph's early revelations finally appeared in print, the pace with which he produced them slowed to a trickle. Joseph had dictated dozens of revelations in the early 1830s, sometimes bringing them forth day after day. On a number of occasions, Joseph dictated long, theologically rich messages that took his scribes many hours or even multiple days to write down. Going forward, there were only a handful of such texts. New directions and doctrines now emerged through church councils or simply through Joseph's discourses. Perhaps after the Jackson County debacle, he had lost a measure of revelatory confidence. Or perhaps Joseph felt changed circumstances required new methods. Regardless, the development points to a reason for Joseph's resilience and success. He wasn't a one-trick prophet. He set aside his seer stone. He dictated fewer revelations but improved his rhetoric. Joseph was a constant innovator.

In the fall and winter of 1834–1835, Joseph's innovations focused on building unity and harmony within the church and within his circle of family and friends. One way Joseph encouraged cohesion was through a proliferation of ecclesiastical quorums and positions, which he imbued with sacred purpose through rites of ordination. He also introduced new rituals of blessing that connected scores of men and women to the church, to each other, and to God.[5]

Shortly after Joseph had been ordained as "President of the High Priesthood" in early 1832, he had installed Sidney Rigdon and Jesse Gause as his counselors. After Gause's apostasy, Joseph chose Frederick G. Williams as a replacement. What about Oliver Cowdery? He had been Joseph's primary Book of Mormon scribe and was the church's "second elder" at the time of its 1830 establishment. Rigdon, however, had supplanted him as the prophet's scribe and the church's foremost preacher. This was partly because of Rigdon's talented preaching, but also due to Cowdery's jealousy and a scandal he had caused when he proposed marriage to a young woman and then jilted her. Cowdery felt the sting of other men surpassing him.[6]

Now Cowdery was back in the prophet's good graces for reasons that remain unclear. Perhaps the passage of time had dulled the scandal and the past tension between the two men. After the destruction of the church's Independence printing press, Joseph tasked Cowdery with acquiring a new one and overseeing its operations in Kirtland. Then, at a December 1834 meeting, Joseph made Cowdery an "Assistant President" alongside Rigdon and Williams.[7]

Cowdery's record of the occasion gives a sense of the dignity with which Joseph conducted ecclesiastical business. Joseph prayed to God, laid his hands on Cowdery, ordained him to his new position, and blessed him effusively. "Endow him with power from on high," Joseph asked God, "that he may write, preach, and proclaim the gospel. . . . Prolong his life to a good old age, and bring him in peace to his end, and to rejoice with thy saints." The prophet then blessed Rigdon and Williams in the same manner. Joseph added his father and his brother Hyrum to the church's expanding presidency as well.[8]

Joseph Smith Sr. was also ordained as the church's patriarch, having the authority to bestow fatherly blessings on church members.[9] The new office grew out of scriptural precedents and existing practices of blessing in the church. In the Book of Mormon, Lehi blesses his sons toward the end of his life, just as the biblical Jacob blesses his sons prior to his death. Prominent men in the church sometimes blessed their sons, and Joseph Jr. gave blessings to family and friends. Joseph Smith Sr.'s blessings, though, assumed a particular significance. The elder Smith blessed his progeny and other church members, especially those who lacked fathers among the Saints. The intention was to strengthen bonds within family and to bind others within a chain of priesthood and lineage that stretched back to the ancient Israelite patriarchs. A scribe preserved patriarchal blessings in a record book, and individuals kept copies of them.[10]

A few days after the ordinations, Joseph's parents, siblings, and their families came to his house for a "feast," evoking a biblical "feast of fat things." Rather than a celebration, it was a solemn assembly, meant to convey rich spiritual blessings to those present. In keeping with a sense of decorum and order, the members of the Smith family took their seats "according to age."[11]

Joseph Sr. then arose. "I am now old, and my head is white," he began. He looked back on a life full of hardship and "folly." Later in the evening, he expanded on his missteps. It hadn't just been bad luck.

Rather, the prophet's father had often been "out of the way, through wine." Others had scorned him. He didn't elaborate, but Doctor P. Hurlbut's affidavits provided plenty of evidence that neighbors in Palmyra and Manchester looked down on him for his economic failures and for his treasure-hunting activities. Finally, Joseph Sr. grew sorrowful. "I look round upon you before me," he lamented, "and I behold a lack: three seats are, as it were, empty." Two of his sons had died at birth or in infancy. And Alvin was taken in the "bloom of youth." Family ties on earth were fragile.[12]

From his oldest to his youngest, Joseph Sr. laid his hands on the heads of his children and their spouses. He declared that his progeny were the descendants of the biblical Jacob, of the house of Ephraim. When the patriarch came to Joseph Jr., his third-eldest living child, he noted that his prophet son had "suffered much" in his youth, that the "poverty and afflictions" of the family had grieved his soul. Yet he had responded to his father's shortcomings with "perfect love." Joseph Jr. was like Shem, the biblical son of Noah, who covered up his naked and drunk father instead of laughing at him. Joseph had made his flawed father a patriarch. It is easy to imagine the eyes of both men welling up with tears. Joseph Sr. echoed the Book of Mormon's identification of his namesake as "a choice seer." God would prosper Joseph Jr. just as he had his ancient progenitors. Through him the lame would walk, the deaf would hear, and the blind would regain their sight. Zion would be redeemed. Tens of thousands would embrace the true gospel through his ministry, and he would stand on the earth to see the Savior return. One day Joseph Jr. would rejoice with his many descendants and with all of the other Saints in the celestial kingdom.[13]

Emma was up next. She had endured a great deal since attaching herself to the Smith family. Wicked men had attacked her husband, and her own parents and siblings hadn't joined the church. Worst of all, she had endured the loss of four children. "Thou art not to be blamed," Joseph Sr. reassured his daughter-in-law. He also blessed her with great promises. Some of her family would be saved, she would bear more children, and she would live to see Jesus Christ.[14]

In the months and years that followed, other Saints sought out Joseph Sr. and received blessings at his hands. Many church members, like Emma, were spiritual "orphans." Their parents had died or had rejected the church. "Thou art blessed of the Lord," the patriarch told John Murdock, "and shall have a parental blessing." The priesthood would remain established in his posterity. "Thou mayest no longer be an orphan," he blessed Levi Jackman. No one who embraced the truth would lack for kinship and connection.[15]

Sometimes the patriarch veered in more somber directions. He told sixty-one-year-old Lovina Wilson that because she was already so "aged," she wouldn't remain alive until the Second Coming. Instead, she would "soon go down to the grave." The patriarch was a bit stumped by William Phelps, the rather freethinking newspaper editor. "Well the Lord has put it into my heart to say," he finally proceeded, "that you are a *strange man*." "That I know," Phelps replied. Joseph Sr. added that Phelps was a "speckled bird" and prone to arrogance. Nevertheless, he would be an instrument in the salvation of many and, unlike Lovina Wilson, he would live until he met his redeemer.[16]

As was true of Joseph Jr.'s prophecies of Zion's redemption, not all of Joseph Sr.'s promises were fulfilled. Missions sometimes failed, family members lost the faith, and, as it turned out, nobody lived until Christ's return. Church members treasured the blessings anyway. The words of the two Josephs, patriarch and prophet, provided comfort amid setbacks and hardships. Each Saint had a glorious lineage. A future in Christ's millennial reign. And a place within Christ's church, connected to friends and kin.

The season of ecclesiastical organization and blessings continued into the early months of 1835. On February 8, Joseph asked Brigham and Joseph Young to come to his house after a Sunday meeting. The Young brothers sang to Joseph, and "the Spirit of the Lord was poured out." Joseph explained that God had given him a vision that he should call a meeting of those men who had marched to Zion with him. The revelation Joseph had dictated at Fishing River the previous June had promised a "great endowment and blessing." The endowment of power waited on the Kirtland Temple's completion, but Joseph was ready to bestow the blessings.[17]

The camp veterans assembled a week later, joined by a large congregation. Joseph read the fifteenth chapter of the Gospel of John. "Greater love hath no man than this," Jesus told his disciples at his last meal with them, "that a man lay down his life for his friends." Joseph then spoke about the trials and sufferings on their journey to Zion. They had been willing to sacrifice their lives if necessary. Some had perished, but it hadn't been in vain. They had proven themselves. God now intended that they should be ordained to "go forth to prune the vineyard for the last time," to find those men and women who would embrace the truth prior to the Second Coming. He asked his former Zion's Camp marchers to stand to signal their agreement. They all rose.[18]

Then Joseph announced that Oliver Cowdery, David Whitmer, and Martin Harris—the three Book of Mormon witnesses—would select twelve men to be ordained as apostles. With only one exception (John F. Boynton), the men chosen were soldiers in the Army of Israel or already in Missouri at the time of the march. Joseph felt that these men had proven themselves. The ordination of twelve apostles, parallel to Christ's twelve disciples in the New Testament and Book of Mormon, fulfilled a long-standing promise in Joseph's revelations. Their mission, Joseph explained two weeks later, was to be "a travelling high council." They would preside over branches of the church outside Missouri and Kirtland. For the most part, though, they would be the church's premier evangelists. The witnesses, and possibly Joseph as well, laid their hands on the apostles and pronounced blessings. They would work miracles. They would be mighty witnesses across the earth and would live until the return of Christ.[19]

Dozens of other Camp of Israel veterans needed blessings. In the New Testament, Jesus had selected an additional seventy followers to travel in pairs from place to place, preaching and working miracles. Beginning on February 28, 1835, dozens of men, all of whom had marched with Joseph, were blessed and ordained as members of the "Seventy." Bestowing the blessings took two days. Again, many of the promises were outrageous. Almon Babbit learned that he would have "power over diseases and plagues." Sylvester Smith, reconciled with Joseph, would "preach to kings, and have power over great men." Not everyone who had marched received a blessing at this time, but in the coming months others would receive their "Zion Blessing" from Joseph, his father, or other high-ranking church leaders.[20]

Joseph still wasn't finished. Other men hadn't marched to Zion but had demonstrated their faithfulness by working on the House of the Lord. By this point, workers had completed the walls of the temple and would soon start on its roof. Church members had donated their labor and their wealth to bring about this progress. Another long series of blessings ensued, some men being ordained to various offices at the same time. A few men were ordained as missionaries "to the Lamanites," an indication that Joseph had not fully set aside his hope of evangelizing Natives.[21]

The blessings provided ballast for a church shaken by the loss of Jackson County. Both Christ's return and Zion's redemption had been delayed. Many of the more far-fetched predictions would not come to pass. At the same time, the Saints in Kirtland could see the House of the Lord rising before their eyes. They could envision the Twelve and the Seventy taking the Latter Day gospel to distant lands. Joseph and his followers would make good on these promises.

CHAPTER SIXTEEN

Abraham (1835)

I N EARLY SUMMER 1835, a merchant came to Kirtland hoping for a windfall. Irish-born Michael Chandler, who had immigrated to the United States in the late 1820s, transported unusual wares: four mummies, two papyrus scrolls, and some additional papyrus fragments. The artifacts came from tombs in the ancient city of Thebes, dug up between 1817 and 1822. At the time, French and British officials were accumulating Egyptian grave relics for sale to museums and private collectors. The mummies that Chandler eventually brought to Kirtland were disinterred by workers hired by Antonio Lebolo, an agent of Bernardino Drovetti, France's consul general in Egypt. After Lebolo's death, his heirs authorized the sale of a set of eleven mummies that had remained in his possession, and they were transported to New York City and then Philadelphia.[1]

European and American fascination with ancient Egypt had exploded after Napoleon's 1798 invasion of Egypt. In the European (and American), Christian imagination, Egypt represented beauty, wisdom, and mystery. Collectors such as Thomas Jefferson acquired Egyptian sculptures, settlers named towns for places such as Memphis and Alexandria, and obelisks became a popular choice for grave markers and monuments. And ordinary Americans turned out in droves to see mummies.[2]

After their initial display in Philadelphia, exhibitors carted the mummies and scrolls to cities such as Pittsburgh, Baltimore, and New Orleans. Thousands of people paid 25 cents each to look upon the "posthumous travelers." Along the way, most of the mummies were sold. The actor Junius Brutus Booth, the father of Abraham Lincoln's future assassin, bought two of them in Louisville.[3]

Chandler exhibited the last mummies in Cleveland. "To realize," observed one visitor, "that I was viewing one of my own species who had lived ... three or four thousand years ago, produced a sensation like that of associating with people of another world." Americans who gazed at the embalmed corpses often felt a connection with them. For some, it was a sacred, mystical encounter. "Curiosity immediately becomes excited," editorialized one of the city's newspapers, "and the visitor before he is aware of it, will become absorbed in meditation and awe."[4]

By this point, Chandler wanted to sell his remaining merchandise, so he rolled into Kirtland, set up his collection at a hotel, and told the locals that he had heard that Joseph Smith Jr. possessed "some kind of power or gifts by which he had previously translated similar characters." He also let it be known that if he couldn't find someone who could translate the papyri, he would take the scrolls to London.[5]

The mummies and especially the scrolls intersected with Joseph's long-standing passions. He loved graves and their relics, an interest that had persisted through treasure hunts, the Book of Mormon plates, and the excavation of Zelph. The prophet anticipated that the scrolls might reveal mysteries about biblical figures such as Abraham and Joseph, who according to the Old Testament both spent time in Egypt. Joseph's own texts pointed to this convergence of ancient Israelite and Egyptian cultures. The Book of Mormon begins by asserting that Lehi's record "consists of the learning of the Jews and the language of the Egyptians," and near the end Moroni identifies the characters with which he writes as "reformed Egyptian."

Joseph was still engaged in his quest to recover the "pure language" spoken by Adam. Like many of his contemporaries, Joseph speculated that Hebrew and Egyptian were closely related and contained at least echoes of that earliest human speech. In May 1835, William Phelps, who had just returned to Kirtland from Missouri, sent his wife "a specimen of some of the pure language," which added hieroglyphic characters to the words on the "sample" Joseph had produced several years earlier.[6] For Joseph and Phelps, ancient languages were far more than an academic concern. They represented esoteric secrets that could unlock spiritual knowledge and power.

When they learned of Chandler's arrival, Joseph and Oliver Cowdery visited him right away. The prophet interpreted a portion of the hieroglyphics for Chandler on the spot. Engaging in some flattery, Chandler signed a certificate pronouncing that Joseph's interpretation was in accord with the opinions of the "most learned." A decade earlier, the French Egyptologist Jean-François Champollion had used the Rosetta Stone discovered by Napoleon's troops to begin decoding ancient Egyptian hieroglyphics. That work remained inchoate and largely inaccessible to English-language readers. In other words, the "most learned" Americans could not have translated the writing, but Chandler didn't let anyone's ignorance interrupt his potential sale.[7]

The mummy merchant's asking price was a steep $2,400. Joseph didn't hesitate.

What exactly had Joseph bought? Oliver Cowdery described the scrolls as "beautifully written . . . with black, and a small part, red ink or paint." Most of the writing is in hieratic script, a cursive form of hieroglyphics, accompanied by illustrations. A Cleveland newspaper lamented that the contents of the papyri and the names of their authors "will *never* be unfolded." Joseph was more optimistic. Either during his initial inspection of the scrolls or soon afterward, he identified them as "the sacred record kept of Joseph in Pharaoh's court in Egypt and the teachings of Father Abraham." At least some of the time, Frederick Williams stored the mummies at his house, but the scrolls remained with the prophet.[8]

Ten years after her husband's death, Emma Smith sold the mummies and papyri. In a series of transactions, some of the materials went to the Chicago Museum and were incinerated in the great fire that destroyed much of the city in 1871. Other fragments ended up in New York City's Metropolitan Museum of Art and were acquired by the Church of Jesus Christ of Latter-day Saints in 1967.[9]

Scholars have identified the surviving fragments as mortuary texts, scrolls laid in the arms of the dead to help them achieve eternal well-being. Several of the pieces come from a Book of Breathing for a Theban priest named Hôr, who lived in the early second century B.C.E. The fragments contain incantations that would enable the deceased to secure resurrection and eternal life. For instance, one vignette shows the god Anubis bringing a man back to life. The text explains that "[Anubis] has writ[ten] for you a Breathing Document with his own fingers, so that [your *ba*-spirit] may breathe." Other fragments are pieces of a book for a woman referred to as Ta-Sherit-Min (the daughter of Min, god of fertility). The spells in this text would keep her safe from demonic enemies,

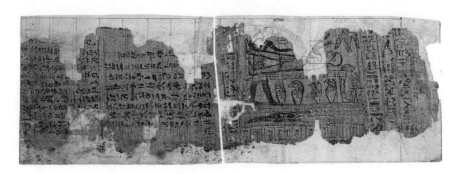

Fragment of Book of Breathing for Horos, ca. 200 B.C.E.
(© By Intellectual Reserve, Inc.)

permit her to move safely in the underworld, and allow her to consume food and drink rather than excrement and urine. While now-lost portions of the collection may have contained other texts, there is no reason to believe that they included anything about Abraham and Joseph.[10]

The prophet started working with the scrolls right away.[11] Joseph's foremost partner was Phelps, who was boarding with the Smiths that summer. Like Joseph, Phelps had a capacious and speculative mind, and he approached the Egyptian project with enthusiasm. Joseph's scribes copied characters and illustrations into notebooks, and the prophet identified their meaning. One snippet identified "Katumin, Princess, daughter of Onitas King of Egypt." In the 1840s, when Lucy Mack Smith showed the mummies to visitors, she told them that they were the remains of Onitas and his household, presumably including his daughter Katumin.[12]

Joseph began dictating what Phelps labeled "the book of Abraham written by his own hand upon papyrus and found in the catacombs of Egypt." It started with Abraham's desire to become "a high priest, holding the right belonging to the fathers, from the beginning of time," stretching back to Adam. Phelps copied characters from one of the papyri in a column to the left of the text. After a few sentences, though, Joseph stopped dictating his text.[13]

For the rest of July, Joseph, Phelps, and Cowdery "engaged in translating an alphabet to the Book of Abraham, and arranging a grammar of the Egyptian language as practiced by the ancients."[14] They pored over the hieroglyphs and pictures on the papyri and made copies of them. Next, they sketched out a possible alphabet and created a "Grammar and

Alphabet of the Egyptian Language." Most of the characters in the alphabet and grammar were taken from the papyri, but, perhaps because
portions of the scrolls were damaged, Joseph and his scribes also included other symbols. Some came from the pure language samples, others may have come from almanacs or may have been original creations.
The Egyptian project became a mishmash of language and ideas,
mapped onto characters from the papyri and interwoven with biblical
inspiration.[15]

For each character, Joseph sketched out five "degrees" of meaning, in
the process transforming glyphs into mini-narratives. He identified one
character as *Ah brah-aam*, which in the fifth and most complex degree
meant "a father of many nations, a prince of peace, one who keeps the
commandments of God, a patriarch, a rightful heir, a high priest." In
some instances, Joseph and his scribes took inspiration from the vignettes, including a striking image of a woman paddling a boat. They
transliterated a character underneath the vignette as *Iota toues Zip Zi.*
They then stipulated its first-degree meaning as "the land of Egypt first
seen under water" and sketched a fifth-degree story: "The land of Egypt
which was first discovered by a woman while under water, and afterwards
settled by her sons she being a daughter of Ham." She had brought "the
record of the fathers [i.e., Noah and his ancestors]" and the "art of em-
balming" with her to Egypt. Joseph identified another character as representing Queen "Kah tou mun" or Katumin, one of the four mummies he
had purchased. She was descended from this daughter of Ham.[16]

This burst of lexicographical activity paused around the end of July.
"Nothing has been doing in translation of the Egyptian record for a long
time," a frustrated Phelps wrote in mid-September, "and probably will
not for some time to come." Joseph, however, resumed the Egyptian
project at the beginning of October. "The system of astronomy was unfolded," Cowdery noted. Joseph, Cowdery, and Phelps identified characters from the papyri as representing stars and planets, but also notions of
time, power, and the divine government of the universe. Joseph sketched
out a cosmos that consisted of "fifteen moving planets" and "fifteen fixed
stars." Another character represented an individual "with delegated and
redeeming power, second in authority," meaning Jesus Christ. There
were also "millions of planets," multiple systems, revolving around God,
the source of all light. Joseph added that one of those fixed stars, named
Kolob, "signifies the first creation nearer to the celestial, or the residence
of the Lord." A day on Kolob was like a thousand years on earth.[17]

Why the focus on astronomy in a narrative written by Abraham? The "Grammar" explained that "the most aged of all the fathers" had sought this knowledge "by means of the Urim and Thummim," objects placed in the breastplate of the high priest of ancient Israel and used for divination. The upshot was that Abraham had obtained this "system of astronomy" from God and had brought it to Egypt. The idea was not original to Joseph Smith. The first-century Jewish historian Josephus maintained that Abraham had brought the sciences of mathematics and astronomy to the Egyptians, who in turn passed them along to the Greeks. The writings of Josephus were popular in the early American republic.[18]

Some of Joseph's ideas—"fixed stars," innumerable worlds, and the motion of systems around an ultimate center—resemble the thoughts of contemporary thinkers, including the Scottish philosopher Thomas Dick. As several scholars have pointed out, Dick's works were discussed widely in American newspapers and excerpted in the church's own *Messenger and Advocate*. But the prophet was not simply aping Dick or any other author. Instead, he was drawing on commonplace if controversial notions of his time: an enormous and expanding universe, inhabitable planets, solar systems rotating around the throne of God. Poets, philosophers, and theologians articulated and debated these concepts, which challenged traditional Christian understandings of the cosmos. Joseph grabbed hold of ideas that caught his attention and developed them, degree by degree.[19]

Joseph likewise envisioned an ever-expanding church ordered around a fixed center. Over the previous year, he had created a host of new offices and filled them with men he regarded as trustworthy. Joseph now found how hard it was to maintain unity and harmony.

In late September, the twelve apostles returned to Kirtland. Several disputes had developed during their mission. According to one report, they had neglected to solicit funds needed for the temple's completion, a key part of their assignment. Joseph alleged that the apostles had made themselves "an independent counsel subject to no authority of the church—a kind of outlaws." The prophet also reprimanded two members of the new quorum, Orson Hyde and William McLellin, for having criticized Sidney Rigdon's leadership of a Kirtland school at which male church members learned grammar, penmanship, and mathematics.[20]

The Twelve met with Joseph the day they returned from the east. Hyde and McLellin apologized for insulting Rigdon, but the apostles convinced Joseph that they otherwise had fulfilled their mission faithfully and were not acting independently of his authority. The prophet pronounced that "all things were settled satisfactorily." The next week, the apostles came to Joseph's house, where he showed them the "ancient [Egyptian] records." Joseph then attended one of their meetings. He instructed the Twelve that it was "the will of God" that they take their families to Missouri in the spring. In the meantime, they should attend "the School of the Prophets" and prepare themselves for their "endowment with power" in the temple. The apostles voiced their agreement.[21]

Joseph's associates usually assented to his counsel when they were face-to-face with him. After all, when their prophet told them that his counsel was "God's will," what could they say? If they objected to his instructions, they would be rejecting his prophetic leadership. In this case, however, the apostles remained sore that Joseph had questioned their behavior. Moreover, there were also some discontents within the quorum. Joseph had insisted that his younger brother William be ordained as one of the Twelve, over the objections of Oliver Cowdery and David Whitmer. The nepotistic selection wasn't Joseph's most inspired choice. His younger brother had an "inflammatory disposition," as Joseph put it.[22]

The Smith brothers came together in early October when their father became severely ill. As commanded by his own revelations, the prophet brought Joseph Sr. "mild herbs," and he returned each of the next several days. The efforts seemed to no avail, as the patriarch was "failing very fast." On Sunday, instead of preaching, Joseph Jr. spent the morning in "secret prayer." By himself, communing with the Lord, he received an answer: "Thy father shall live." Joseph was at his father's side the rest of the day. That evening, David Whitmer came to the home. He and Joseph prayed together and laid their hands on the old man. "Our aged father arose and dressed himself, shouted and praised the Lord," Joseph Jr. reported. He called William Smith to the room so that they could join together in songs of praise.[23]

A breach emerged between Joseph and William, however, during a late October meeting of the Kirtland High Council. William Smith had accused David Elliott of whipping and beating his fifteen-year-old daughter, Lucena. It was a grim case. Lucena Elliott had gone to a neighbor's house, showed the bodily marks of her whipping, and spoke of hanging herself "to get rid of her trouble and affliction." Apparently, she had contemplated suicide for several years.

Joseph testified in the case. David Elliott had marched with him to Missouri in the spring of 1834, and Joseph had recently visited the Elliott home in Chagrin. The prophet averred that "the girl was in the fault, and that the neighbors were trying to create a difficulty." The high council gave a mixed judgment that while the charge against Elliott had some merit, it had not been "fully sustained." The council added that had Elliott trained his daughter properly, he shouldn't have had to beat her at the age of fifteen.[24]

That should have ended the matter, but William Smith refused to accept the rather unsatisfying judgment. He sharpened his accusation, now alleging that Mary Elliott, Lucena's mother, had not only abused her but also had beaten "the rest of her children." Joseph was called back to the high council and asked to preside. When Lucy Mack Smith gave testimony against Mary Elliott, he objected. As far as the prophet was concerned, the case had already been settled.[25]

William Smith was livid. First, Joseph had testified in support of individuals William had accused of abuse. Now, his elder brother had interrupted their mother, in the process "invalidating or doubting" her testimony. Joseph never took kindly to challenges to his authority. He told William that he was "out of place" and should sit down. A fraternal standoff ensued. William said he wouldn't sit down unless Joseph "knocked him down." Joseph began to stomp off, but Joseph Sr. convinced him to stay and told both of his sons to simmer down. Business resumed. David and Mary Elliott both made confessions, acknowledging their guilt and demonstrating contrition. The council forgave them.[26]

William and Joseph were not ready to forgive each other. The brothers attempted to talk through their differences two days later. Joseph proposed that each give his side of the story, confess any faults, and then allow Warren Parrish and their brother Hyrum to "decide the matter." William had seen this gambit before. At the very least, Parrish—hired two days earlier as Joseph's scribe—would support his boss and prophet. William complained that Joseph was "always determined to carry [his] points whether right or wrong and therefore he would not stand an equal chance." Finally, each brother spoke, but when Hyrum began to weigh in, William grew angry. He declared that he wanted nothing more to do with the church, stormed off, sent his preaching license to Joseph, and began telling everyone who would listen about his mistreatment.[27]

The breach was painful and awkward. The Kirtland High Council had chastised David Elliott for his failure to maintain a peaceful household.

How did it look to have the prophet's own brother criticizing him in the streets? How could Joseph foretell the restoration of Zion when unity proved so elusive within the church and within his own family?

While the dispute with his brother persisted, Joseph made a renewed attempt to restore harmony with the Twelve. He leaned on the full weight of his prophetic mantle, dictating a revelation in which the Lord pronounced them "under condemnation" for their lack of humility and a failure to divide resources equally among themselves. In the revelation, Jesus Christ singled out several of the Twelve—Orson Hyde, William McLellin, and David Patten—as particular offenders but noted that all of the apostles needed to "repent speedily." The revelation also predicted that William Smith would return and become a "polished shaft" in the Lord's "quiver," but warned that if he failed to repent he would be "brought low." He would lose his position.[28]

The revelation did not set things in order. William remained estranged from his brother, and others among the Twelve were uneasy. Indeed, Joseph seemed dissatisfied with nearly everyone that fall. The prophet announced that the Lord had condemned William Phelps and John Whitmer for unspecified "iniquities." Joseph also corrected Sidney Rigdon after Rigdon rebuked John Smith, the prophet's uncle. Even Emma Smith received some withering criticism when she left a Sunday meeting before the Lord's Supper. She "manifested contrition by weeping." It seemed to many in and around Kirtland that they could do no right in the prophet's eyes.[29]

Why was Joseph so critical and combative? He could be hot tempered, as illustrated by his clashes with Sylvester Smith during the march to Missouri. Such outbursts were usually episodic and interspersed with his more typical sociability. Throughout the fall of 1835, however, Joseph's mood remained sour. Was he frustrated with the Egyptian project? Perhaps, but Joseph had worked on his Bible revision in a similar start-and-stop fashion. What seems most likely is that Joseph's rupture with William affected him to the point of disrupting his other relationships. Regardless of the source of Joseph's disquiet, everyone around him looked forward to its passing.

Joseph spent an evening with nine of the Twelve at their request in mid-November. He insisted that despite any errors, he was doing his best to lead the church and to uphold its members. Joseph urged them to look ahead. He instructed the apostles in the necessity of "the washing of feet," a ritual practiced at the outset of the 1833 School of the Prophets but that Joseph now understood as preparatory to the coming "solemn assembly" in the temple. Joseph encouraged the apostles that great blessings were in store for them should they remain faithful. "All who are prepared and are sufficiently pure to abide the presence of the Savior," Joseph promised, "will see him in the solemn assembly." If the apostles humbled themselves, if they repented, if they washed each other's feet, if they kept themselves spiritually clean, they would see the Lord. The blessings the prophet described, coupled with his tacit admission of his own shortcomings, helped the apostles look past Joseph's stretches of truculence.[30]

As of mid-November 1835, Joseph and his scribes had produced a large volume of material derived from their encounter with the Egyptian papyri. Notebooks were filled with characters, transliterations, and degrees of definitions. But to this point, Joseph had only dictated a few paragraphs of the Book of Abraham. Then, over the course of a week, Joseph unveiled a story.

The characters, definitions, and ideas became a narrative woven into the fabric of the King James Bible. In this case, Joseph sandwiched a story between the eleventh and twelfth chapters of Genesis, just before Abraham—then Abram—leaves Chaldea. In Joseph's text, Abraham is distraught over his father's abandonment of the true priesthood. (The biblical Book of Joshua states that Abraham's father "served other gods.") His kin are under the sway of a "priest of Pharaoh" who has sacrificed three virgin daughters for their refusal to worship idols. Abraham is the intended next victim. He cries out to the Lord, who appears to him in a vision, sets him free, and smites the wicked priests. The Lord instructs Abraham to leave Chaldea and the idolaters, including his kin, who live there.[31]

The Book of Abraham then digresses into an origin story for Egypt, using the death of the priest of Pharaoh as a segue. The reader learns that Egypt was "discovered by a woman" at a time when the land was under water after the flood. She is a daughter of Ham and thus a granddaughter of Noah. Here Joseph's scribes placed the character from underneath the vignette of the paddling woman (*Iota toues Zip Zi*). Her son, named Pharaoh, establishes "the first government of Egypt." The genealogy is a critical point, as the text explains that Pharaoh is of a "lineage by which he could not have the right of Priesthood." The line of Ham is cursed.

In the Book of Genesis, Ham's mistreatment of Noah, his father, leads to a curse of servitude on his son Canaan and Canaan's posterity. (Although the passage specifies that it is Canaan's offspring who bear the curse, it became known as the Curse of Ham.) Genesis does not connect the curse with dark skin, nor does it place the descendants of Canaan in Africa. Nevertheless, Jews, Christians, and Muslims came to identify the Canaanites with dark-skinned African peoples brought to the Mediterranean world as slaves. Similarly, many Christians presumed that the mark God placed upon Cain as punishment for having murdered his brother Abel was dark skin. The belief that Black Africans were the cursed descendants of Cain and Canaan was ubiquitous.[32]

Joseph had incorporated these ideas into his revisions to and expansions of Genesis. He had specified that the "seed of Cain were black," and he also had added the detail that a "veil of darkness shall cover" Canaan. Now, in the Book of Abraham, Joseph connected the twin Cain and Canaan curses. The woman who discovers Egypt comes from the "loins of Ham," and the text suggests that she is a descendant of Cain through her mother.[33]

These were not arcane points in the antebellum United States, and Joseph drew links between the Book of Genesis and American slavery. In the spring of 1836, Joseph cited the curse of Canaan as a justification for his opposition to abolition. "The curse is not yet taken off the sons of Canaan," the prophet asserted. Joseph's immediate successor, Brigham Young, excluded Black men from the priesthood and Black church members from participation in certain sacred rituals. Joseph himself did not reach that conclusion despite the Book of Abraham's discussion of a cursed lineage. The prophet did not object to the 1836 ordination of Elijah Able, an African American convert who later became a Seventy and served a mission to Canada. For Joseph, race and slavery were episodic rather than central concerns, and his views on these subjects were unsettled.[34]

For a week, Joseph dictated the Book of Abraham, and his assistants transcribed characters alongside his narrative. Then the prophet came down with a severe cold. Joseph expected to resume his translation in a few days, but he didn't. The Egyptian project stalled yet again.

After spending a small fortune on the mummies and papyri, and after announcing that he had discovered the writings of Abraham and the biblical Joseph, the prophet had produced what amounted to only about ten manuscript pages. Back in 1828 and 1829, Joseph had dictated scores and then hundreds of pages of the Book of Mormon in a few months. Now he translated in fits and starts, and he made no immediate plans to publish the results. He returned to the Book of Abraham again a few years later, but he never fashioned a grand narrative. Indeed, Joseph never came close to matching his early literary output. He had a story in mind and some new ideas about God and the cosmos, but he brought forth very little text. The Mormon prophet remained an author whose first novel proved a niche hit but who could never finish the second book.

Did Joseph believe that he possessed scrolls written by Abraham and Joseph? Or did he simply make up a fanciful story? Scholars cannot access the Book of Mormon plates, but some of the Egyptian materials have been preserved. While they confirm that Joseph was wrong about the contents of the scrolls, his Egyptian project wasn't a straightforward act of deception. The labor of creating notebooks, alphabets, and the *Grammar* points to a serious, if misguided, effort. Joseph could have dictated a text in a much less arduous fashion, as he did with the Book of Mormon. This time around he wanted to demonstrate his bona fides as a translator, and he continued to tell people that he could interpret the hieroglyphics.

One reason for Joseph's detour from the Book of Abraham was his budding fascination with another ancient language, Hebrew. As was not the case with Egyptian, there were people who could help Joseph learn to read Hebrew. In early November 1835 Joseph traveled to Willoughby, Ohio, to hear a lecture by Dr. Daniel Peixotto, a Jewish physician. Oliver Cowdery then went to New York City and acquired a Hebrew Bible, lexicon, and grammar.[35]

Joseph began with the Hebrew alphabet. He loved it. Joseph still had the thirst for learning and self-improvement evidenced by the earlier creation of the School of the Prophets. Over the coming weeks, he often spent whole days either studying by himself at home or gathering with a few friends to work together. The prophet anticipated that learning the biblical language would help him decipher the papyri and that both Hebrew and Egyptian might take him closer to the language of God.

Joseph turned thirty years old in December 1835. The prophet spent his birthday studying Greek—another occasional interest—and showing the Egyptian papyri to visitors. A tall, muscular man, he was less scrawny than he had been at the time of the church's founding. He remained youthful in appearance, retaining a full head of light-brown hair. Although Joseph was a bit lame because of his boyhood infection and the 1832 mob attack, he hadn't lost his vigor. He still loved to wrestle, and he still usually won.

On Christmas Eve 1835, a church member named Jonathan Crosby arrived in Kirtland. Like the large majority of converts, Crosby had joined the church without having met its prophet and president. He reached Kirtland after dark, stopping at John Johnson's tavern and inn. Getting directions from Johnson, he went to Joseph's house and knocked. Joseph answered the door himself, invited Crosby inside, and questioned him about his background and conversion. Several other men were present, including Hyrum Smith and Martin Harris. Emma served cider and then supper.

"I thought he was a queer man for [a] prophet of God," Crosby later wrote. He had imagined the translator of the Book of Mormon and president of the church to be more austere, not so convivial. Joseph invited Crosby to stay the night and through breakfast. The prophet showed his guest "the records of the mummies" and told him that as they were written in the language of the Book of Mormon, he could read them. Joseph's hospitality and charm put newcomers at ease. "I could not help liking him," Crosby explained.[36]

Joseph had not invited William Smith to share in his Christmas feast and festivities. The breakdown in fraternal relations had worsened in mid-December. Joseph attended a meeting of a debating society at William's house, speaking in the affirmative on the question of whether it was "necessary for God to reveal himself to man to render them happy." A few days later, Joseph returned for the conclusion of the debate. As a boy, Joseph had participated in a Palmyra debating club, but he had misgivings about the society in Kirtland. He felt that it encouraged contention and sophistry. When those present began to discuss whether they should continue the society, William grew upset. It was his house, and if he wanted to continue having debates in it, no one should interfere. Joseph interfered and told William that he "was as ugly as the devil."[37]

The brothers' father tried to calm them down, but it was too late. Joseph snapped that he had helped finish the house and had supported William's family. He had a right to a say. William started toward Joseph, who took off his coat, ready to fight. This time, Joseph lost. His weak side gave way. Other men present had to rescue him. Joseph limped home, unable to sit down or stand up without assistance.[38]

Meanwhile, Joseph attempted to resolve the now months-long discontents of Orson Hyde. The apostle was upset with both of the feuding Smith brothers. Hyde was among the apostles who had criticized Sidney

Rigdon's school leadership the previous summer, and he had objected to Joseph's recent revelation condemning the Twelve. Now he was complaining that a church store—run by the temple building committee—was extending credit to William Smith while refusing it to him. "If one has his support from the 'public crib,' " Hyde maintained, "let them all have it." Shouldn't the Twelve be treated equally? Why was the prophet favoring his brother among the apostles? Hyde petulantly informed Joseph that he wouldn't study Hebrew in such circumstances.[39]

Hyde expressed the above in a letter that he handed to Joseph the day before the prophet's fight with William. Joseph, whose feelings were "lacerated" by the accusations, "lost" Hyde's letter. Now, as Joseph convalesced, the apostle turned up with another copy and read it aloud. The aching prophet gritted his teeth, conceded that the committee hadn't treated Hyde fairly, and patched things up.[40]

Joseph's parents came by that evening. They were "sorely afflicted" over the fraternal rift. It seems that they placed the bulk of the blame on William, with whom they had been living. They accepted Joseph's invitation to move into his household. Even so, Joseph Sr. and Lucy Mack Smith wanted their children to be at peace with each other. Joseph Jr. wasn't giving any ground. He insisted that he "had acted in righteousness in all things." The next day, Hyrum appeared with a conciliatory letter from William, who apologized and offered to abandon his office as an apostle. Joseph didn't let his brother off easily. He wrote William a long response in which he detailed their recent conflict and defended himself. "It seems to me," Joseph wrote, "that you still retain an idea, that I have given you reasons to be angry or disaffected with me." He kept William dangling instead of accepting his apology.[41]

Joseph began 1836 filled with despair. He was still estranged from William, and that was only one of many instances of disunity. There were conflicts within the Smith family, divisions among the Twelve, bickering among other church members. The House of the Lord was almost finished. Workers had been plastering the interior, and it would soon be ready for the "endowment of power" Joseph had said the elders needed before the redemption of Zion. Satan was doing his utmost to stoke conflicts that would "prevent the Saints from being endowed," he reflected. As Joseph looked ahead, he prayed that God would "burst" Satan's cloud and usher in heaven's blessings.[42]

CHAPTER SEVENTEEN

Jubilee and Pentecost (1836)

JOSEPH'S NEW YEAR'S PRAYERS were answered. Within the span of a fortnight, the animosities of the past several months were put to rest.

Later in the day on January 1, 1836, William Smith came to see his brother. Joseph, William, their brother Hyrum, their uncle John, Joseph Sr., and Martin Harris withdrew into a room to settle the fraternal conflict. Joseph Sr. began by expressing that the rift had deeply wounded him. Chastened, the two brothers found their hearts softened. William went first, confessing that he had abused his brother and asking Joseph's forgiveness. The prophet reciprocated. The pair then covenanted to be reconciled and to "build each other up." They would stop paying heed to gossip and stop finding fault with each other.

Emma and Lucy Mack Smith joined the men, and the brothers repeated their covenants. Tears flowed from everybody's eyes. Joseph's scribe referred to the occasion as a "jubilee," a biblical reference to a year of forgiveness and freedom. The next day, the Kirtland High Council heard William's confession and restored his standing in the church.[1]

A few days after his reconciliation with William, Joseph assembled several dozen church members in the nearly finished temple to organize the Hebrew school. Joseph had been dabbling with the language for weeks, but he and others were eager for the arrival of an instructor. In fact, in the absence of a teacher, even Hebrew became a point of contention. The day after the school's organization, Joseph and Orson Pratt, a member of the Twelve, got into a spat about Hebrew pronunciation. Fortunately, William McLellin soon returned with news that he had hired Joshua Seixas, a member of a prominent New York City Jewish family who had been teaching at a nearby college.[2]

In mid-January, the Twelve asked to meet with Joseph and his counselors Frederick Williams and Sidney Rigdon. The apostles came with bruised feelings and a long list of complaints, some old and some new. Thomas Marsh, president of the Twelve by seniority of age, laid it all out. From the previous summer, they remained upset that Joseph had suspected and punished them on the basis of uncorroborated allegations. The Twelve also wondered about their place in the ecclesiastical pecking order. At a recent council meeting, Joseph had asked the church's various councils and quorums to give their assent to a set of regulations for the temple. Joseph called on the apostles after the high councils of Kirtland and Zion, respectively. The Twelve felt slighted and disrespected. Why didn't Joseph trust them and honor their position?

Joseph maintained the spirit of reconciliation with which he had begun the year. Although he made it clear that the apostles were not without blame, he allowed that he had sometimes "spoken too harsh from the impulse of the moment" and had "wounded" their feelings. He provided an explanation for the order of business at the recent meeting and affirmed that their authority was next to the church's presidency and thus above the Kirtland and Zion High Councils. Rigdon and Williams also made apologies, and everyone present entered into a covenant to uphold each other and to give no credence to unproven allegations in the future. The men took each other by the hand and pronounced blessings on each other.[3]

The meeting with the Twelve was a breakthrough. Joseph was now ready to prepare for the temple's dedication and the solemn assembly that would take place within it. Joseph envisioned the latter as a grander reprise of the covenants and rituals of purification he had introduced in conjunction with the 1833 School of the Prophets. The church's elders would receive an "endowment of power" at the assembly. The phrase alluded to the instructions of Jesus that, following his death and resurrection, his apostles should wait in Jerusalem until they were "endued with power from on high." This promised endowment came at Pentecost, when the fire of the Holy Spirit descended on the apostles, enabled those present to hear them in their own languages, and led to the mass conversion of thousands. Joseph's Bible-literate followers would have anticipated an outpouring of spiritual power.[4]

As he looked forward to the solemn assembly, Joseph introduced rituals of washing, blessing, and anointing designed to prepare church leaders for their endowment. The evening after his reconciliation with the Twelve, Joseph invited to his home Oliver Cowdery and John Corrill, who had overseen the last phases of the temple's construction. Joseph and his two guests undressed and "wash[ed] each other's bodies" with "pure water." Then they "bathed" each other "with whiskey, perfumed with cinnamon." Martin Harris joined them, and they scrubbed and perfumed him as well.[5]

Such intimate, physical ritual washing was distinctive on the landscape of American Christianity. Indeed, any sort of bathing was an unusual experience for most rural Americans in the 1830s. There were some proponents of bathing, however. Reformers from John Wesley to Sylvester Graham urged washing or bathing in cold water as a way to cure all sorts of physical and spiritual ills. Some physicians, moreover, specifically recommended whiskey baths as a means to restore health. In keeping with such advice, Joseph's "Word of Wisdom" had recommended "strong drinks . . . for the washing of your bodies."[6]

Popular fads may have provided some impetus for the ceremonial washing, but Joseph and his associates took inspiration from ancient practices. The first washings took place on a Saturday night. According to Cowdery, the purpose of the ritual was to make themselves "clean before the Lord for the Sabbath." The outward washing reflected an inward purity achieved through the confession of sin and a covenant "to be faithful to God." Cowdery noted that the priests of ancient Israel "used to wash always before ministering before the Lord" in the temple. Similarly, Latter-day Saints should cleanse themselves through confession and ritual washing.[7]

A large congregation gathered at the schoolhouse the next morning. Joseph began the meeting by "organiz[ing] the several quorums present": the presidency, the Twelve, the Seventy, then the high councils of Kirtland and Zion. The deliberate procedure reminded the Saints of the importance of a properly ordered church. The Twelve, no doubt, were gratified to be recognized after the presidency.[8]

Then the members of the presidency—Joseph, Sidney Rigdon, and Frederick Williams—confessed their sins. Other church leaders did so as well. Many in the congregation, overcome with emotion, sobbed and wept. "I cried as little children cry in earnest," wrote William Phelps. Repentance gave way to rejoicing. "There was speaking and singing in tongues, and prophesying, as on the day of Pentecost," Phelps continued.[9]

A few days later, on January 21, Joseph gathered with the presidency and the church's two bishops—Edward Partridge and Newel K. Whitney —in the schoolroom on the temple's upper floor. In addition to washing and perfuming, church leaders needed to be anointed with oil, as Moses had anointed Aaron and his sons. Joseph Sr., the church's patriarch, took a seat, and the others formed a circle around him. Joseph Jr. took a vial of oil, and the other men raised their right hands in the air and blessed it. As they laid their hands on the patriarch, Joseph anointed his father's head with the consecrated oil and blessed him. Then, in order of their age, Joseph Sr. anointed the members of the church presidency. When he came to his son, the patriarch poured oil on Joseph Jr.'s head and "sealed upon [him] the blessings, of Moses, to lead Israel in the latter days."[10]

After the anointings, "the heavens were opened." Joseph described a series of visions. He saw "the celestial kingdom of God" with its streets of gold. Within this heaven were Adam, Abraham, and the archangel Michael. His parents were also there, as was his brother Alvin, who had died before the restoration of Christ's true church and had not been baptized into it. How had Alvin attained celestial glory? Joseph and his family had worried about Alvin's eternal fate, as did many families whose loved ones died either prior to April 1830 or without having joined the church. The Lord answered that all those who died without "a knowledge of this gospel, who would have received it," would have a place within the celestial kingdom. The visions rolled on. Joseph saw the Twelve enduring hardships, working miracles, preaching the gospel, and eventually residing in the celestial kingdom. He also saw Zion's redemption.[11]

The Kirtland and Missouri High Councils now joined Joseph in the schoolroom. As the men blessed one another and sang hymns and shouted hosanna, many of the men also had visions. Some saw Jesus Christ. Angels appeared to others. Finally, well after midnight, Joseph dismissed the meeting with a blessing as the men lifted up their hands toward heaven. Joseph and the others were too overcome by what had transpired to concentrate on Hebrew in the morning.[12]

Language learning continued to suffer as Joseph presided over the anointing of other groups of men over the next several days. After the last such gathering, Joseph returned from the temple late at night with a deep sense of satisfaction and comfort. The conflicts and turmoil of the fall had dissolved into harmony and spiritual euphoria. Joseph's brother William had shared in the anointing, blessing, and visions. Sylvester Smith,

once a sharp critic of the prophet, was now working as his scribe. The
Twelve were content and faithful. Joseph's penchant for the creation of
quorums and councils caused confusion and jealousy, but it also meant
that scores of men had received an anointing and a blessing. What Joseph
wanted was for every man to have a place and to know his place.

Joseph lay in his bed but couldn't sleep. "My soul cried hosanna to
God and the Lamb through the silent watches of the night," he shared.
"And while my eyes were closed in sleep, the visions of the Lord were
sweet unto me and his glory was round about me." It was a foretaste of
Zion.[13]

These were satisfying weeks for Joseph in other ways as well. Each
morning save Sunday he attended the school of Joshua Seixas. There
were many Hebrew enthusiasts in Kirtland, or at least many eager to
share in one of the prophet's pursuits. A nearby newspaper reported that
"some of the men in the middle age peruse their Hebrew till 12 o'clock
at night, and attend nothing else." The dozens of students soon made
enough progress to begin translating biblical sentences. "My soul de-
lights in reading the word of the Lord in the original," Joseph recorded.[14]

In mid-February, Joseph Coe, who had borrowed money to help Joseph purchase the Egyptian papyri and mummies, asked the prophet if
he could exhibit the artifacts at John Johnson's inn. The prophet agreed,
cautioning Coe to handle the manuscripts delicately. For the time being,
Joseph's focus had switched from the revelatory translation of Egyptian
characters to the scholarly translation of Hebrew. He was so avid that he
reviewed his lessons on Sundays and obtained additional instruction
from Seixas whenever possible.[15]

On at least one occasion, Joseph prayed that even as Seixas taught
them Hebrew, they might "become his teachers in the things of salvation" so that he might believe the Book of Mormon and be baptized. Although Seixas had quietly embraced some form of Christianity in the
early 1830s, there is no evidence that he considered a conversion to
Mormonism. As Seixas's seven-week term drew to a close in early March,
Joseph urged his instructor to remain in Kirtland for another session of
the school. Seixas tarried until the end of March, when upon his departure from Kirtland he provided Joseph with a certificate praising his
translation skills and stating that he was becoming "proficient in Hebrew." Joseph no doubt beamed when he looked at the attestation.[16]

Joseph's most tangible accomplishment since the publication of the Book of Mormon was the completion of the House of the Lord, the Kirtland Temple. It had taken a massive investment of money and labor to build what Joseph and his associates had sketched out three years earlier. The total cost is unknown, but it was probably at least $40,000.[17] For scant wages, men had hauled rock, raised and painted walls, and built pews and pulpits. Women had given their labor to make veils that could be hung to divide larger spaces into smaller compartments. The temple testified to the industry and dedication of the Latter-day Saints.

On top of a modest bluff, the House of the Lord loomed large over the scattered buildings in its vicinity and was visible from a great distance. "I cannot begin to describe the beauty of this fine building," Roger Orton wrote to his father. The temple's exterior was striking. A multicolored bell tower stood above an earth-red shingled roof reaching a height of 115 feet. The exterior walls, made of roughly hewn stone, were painted light blue, and the massive double doors were green.[18]

The building's three-story interior was even more distinctive. On each of the two main levels, four tiers of pulpits and seats faced the congregation at each end of the building. The pulpits on the left were marked with initials for various groups within the church's Melchizedek priesthood, including the First Presidency, the members of which occupied the highest tier. The pulpits and seats at the other end were for leaders of the "lesser [Aaronic] priesthood," including the church's bishops. The architecture represented Joseph's vision of ecclesiastical order and hierarchy. Everyone had a place.[19]

On March 27, 1836, a massive crowd gathered early in the morning for the temple's dedication. Joseph, Sidney Rigdon, and Oliver Cowdery entered at eight o'clock, and a thousand Saints soon filled the building to capacity. Hundreds were turned away disappointed. The presidency and other leaders took their seats in the tiered pulpits and seats. Joseph gave his father the place of highest honor, in the center of the west end's top tier.

Sidney Rigdon, who presided over the morning services, preached for two and a half hours, focusing on Jesus's words: "The foxes have holes, and the birds of the air have nests; but the Son of man hath not where to lay his head." Despite all of their toils and privations, despite the predictions of scoffers that they would never raise the walls that now surrounded them, they had persevered. Rigdon drew a stark contrast between other churches and Christ's true church. Yes, there were other magnificent structures, but "not one except this, on the face of the whole

Kirtland Temple pulpits, west end, 1934. (Photograph by Carl F. Waite; courtesy of
Library of Congress)

earth, that was built by divine revelation." Now Christ had his house, a
house built according to Joseph's revelations and through the labor and
donations of the hundreds of Saints sitting in the pews.[20]

When Rigdon finished his sermon, he asked the church presidency,
then other leaders, and finally the entire congregation to stand and acknowledge Joseph as "a Prophet and Seer." Everyone rose.[21]

After a brief intermission, during which nursing mothers left to breastfeed their infants, the choir—positioned in the four corners of the room—led the congregation in singing a hymn written by William Phelps. "The earth was once a garden place / with all her glories common," it began, "And men did live a holy race / And worship Jesus face to face / In Adam-ondi-Ahman." The name drew on Joseph's sample of "pure language"; it referred to the place where Adam had blessed his posterity at the end of his life. The hymn continued by evoking the blessings, fame, and peace of Enoch's Zion and urged the Saints to anticipate their "Savior's second comin'," when they would enjoy "a holy home / Like Adam-ondi-Ahman." The dedication of the House of the Lord made this future glory seem close at hand.[22]

Then it was Joseph's turn to preside. He asked the congregation to rise and acknowledge his fellow presidents as "Prophets and Seers," then to acknowledge the other layers of ecclesiastical authority. There was no dissent. This was the unanimity Joseph craved, the harmony lacking the previous fall, the unity he had restored through the confessions and forgiveness earlier that year. Everyone had his place.[23]

Joseph then offered a long prayer that he and his associates had composed the day before. He beseeched God for the redemption of Zion and for the success of the preaching missions that would follow the sacred assembly. "Let the anointing of thy ministers," Joseph prayed, "be sealed upon them with power from on high: let it be fulfilled upon them as upon those on the day of Pentecost." He asked for an outpouring of tongues and that God's glory would fill the house like a rushing wind.[24]

The choir sang another of Phelps's hymns as the meeting reached its climax. "The Spirit of God like a fire is burning," it began. "The latter day glory begins to come forth / The visions and blessings of old are returning / The angels are coming to visit the earth." As the elders distributed the bread and wine, Joseph testified that Phelps's words were true. Angels had visited him, leading to the Book of Mormon and the restoration of priesthood. Frederick Williams, a member of the church's presidency, stood up and said that he had seen an angel that very morning, sitting between him and Joseph Sr. while Rigdon had prayed.[25]

The congregation moved toward the conclusion of the meeting with three loud shouts of "Hosanna! Hosanna! Hosanna to God and the Lamb, Amen, Amen and Amen!" The apostles Brigham Young and David Patten stood up and each "sang a song of Zion in tongues," then spoke in tongues. Finally, eight hours after they had first entered the building, Joseph gave a blessing and dismissed the meeting.[26]

Joseph asked the elders in the congregation to return to the House of the Lord after several hours. When the men reassembled, Joseph reminded them that they were latter-day links in a chain of priesthood authority that stretched back to the early Christian apostles and to Solomon's Temple. They had been washed and anointed like ancient Israelite priests. Soon they would wash each other's feet like Jesus's disciples. Accordingly, they would receive the same blessings as their predecessors. Their neighbors might scoff at their claims to speak in tongues and heal the lame, but God had not changed, and neither had the order of the Lord's House. There was another outpouring of spiritual power that night, replete with visions and prophesying. It was a "a continuation of our Pentecost," Stephen Post recorded.[27]

The dedication of the House of the Lord was preparatory to the solemn assembly planned for several days later. On Monday, Joseph rested. "Nothing worthy of note transpired," his scribe recorded. On Tuesday, the prophet attended Joshua Seixas's school for the last time, then met with four close associates in the temple. When they "sought for a revelation" about the timing of Zion's long-delayed redemption, "the voice of the Spirit" instructed them to gather additional church leaders, fast together, and remain in the temple all night. Joseph and around fourteen church leaders met that afternoon in what he described as "the most holy place in the Lord's house," probably by the west pulpits, closed off from the rest of the meeting space by a veil.[28]

Joseph and the other men washed their faces, hands, and feet. Then they washed each other's feet, with Sidney Rigdon beginning by washing Joseph's. Around dusk, they celebrated the sacrament of the Lord's Supper, but as a "feast," with generous amounts of bread and wine. "We prophesied and spoke in tongues and shouted hosannas," wrote Bishop Edward Partridge. The meeting continued until daybreak on Wednesday, March 30.[29]

After a short rest, Joseph and his tired but exhilarated associates went back to the temple for the long-awaited solemn assembly. In front of more than three hundred elders, Joseph stood in the pulpit and reflected on their many trials and afflictions in the six years since the church's founding. "This is a year of Jubilee to us and a time of rejoicing," he announced. They would have bread and wine "sufficient to make [their] hearts glad," he added.[30]

Tubs were filled with water, and towels were laid out. The members of the church's presidency began by washing the feet of the Twelve, and by noon all of the men had participated in the ritual. For hours on end, men prophesied, spoke and sang in tongues, and shouted hosanna. Church members blessed each other and called down "cursings upon the enemies of Christ who inhabit Jackson County." There was another feast of bread and wine after sunset. Then Joseph told the elders that they were ready. He had given them all of the instruction and preparation they needed. They would go out, build up the Kingdom of God, and redeem Zion. Joseph called on them to enter into a covenant "that if any more of our brethren are slain or driven from their lands in Missouri by the mob that we will give ourselves no rest until we are avenged of our enemies." The men "sealed" the covenant "unanimously by a hosanna and amen." A weary Joseph retired for the night as the spiritual outpouring continued until it was nearly dawn. According to Joseph, "The Savior made his appearance to some," and others saw angels. "It was a Pentecost and endowment indeed," the prophet concluded.[31]

The following Sunday, Joseph and Oliver Cowdery lingered in the temple after the afternoon service. The veils were lowered, leaving them secluded in the pulpit at the west end of the building. When they looked up after a time of silent prayer, "the veil was taken from their minds and the eyes of their understandings were opened." The two men then experienced a series of visions together. They saw Jesus Christ standing atop the pulpit in front of them. His hair was white; his eyes were like flames. As Joseph wrote of his youthful vision of Jesus Christ, his face shone "above the brightness of the sun." The Savior told the two men that they should rejoice because they had built a house acceptable to him. He would continue to appear to his people in the temple.

Joseph and Oliver then saw Moses, Elias, and Elijah. The latter figure announced that his appearance fulfilled Malachi's prophecy that he (Elijah) "should be sent before the great and dreadful day of the Lord come, to turn the hearts of the fathers to the children, and the children to the fathers." The "day of the Lord" referred to the judgments on the world that would accompany Christ's Second Coming. "Therefore," Elijah told Joseph and Oliver, "the keys of this dispensation are committed into your hands." For years, Joseph's revelations had emphasized that he and his associates held the "keys" of priesthood authority, given to preside over Christ's church, to receive revelations, to baptize, and to commune with Jesus Christ and God the Father.[32]

By the time of the joint visions, Joseph and his associates had signed hundreds of preaching licenses for the church's elders, who soon left Kirtland on their missions. After the fits and starts of the Bible revision and the Egyptian project, after the loss of Zion and the Army of Israel's failure to reclaim it, Joseph had now enjoyed a clear triumph. He had presided over an outpouring of spiritual gifts in a magnificent temple. No wonder he proclaimed it a "year of Jubilee."

It had been a decade since Joseph had traveled to the Susquehanna River Valley to work for Josiah Stowell as a treasure hunter. It had been six years since the first members of the Church of Christ had accepted him as their seer, translator, and prophet. The roughly fifteen hundred Saints living in and around Kirtland and the dedication of the House of the Lord were tangible signs of the church's growth, as well as indications of Joseph's talents. Joseph used ritual—blessings, feasts, washing, anointing—to bind these people together, bind them to him, and bind them to God.[33]

CHAPTER EIGHTEEN

Follies (1836–1837)

THE GROWTH OF KIRTLAND and the temple's dedication earned the Mormon prophet some grudging respect from other residents of northeastern Ohio. Caleb Peck, who lived in nearby Chardon, remembered Joseph as industrious, temperate, and "usually in an excellent humor." He observed that countless individuals had benefited from Joseph's generosity and hospitality. Peck added that Joseph was "a very fine looking man viewing him with a full face—but not as good looking from a profile view," perhaps because of his Roman nose.[1]

Joseph's successes came at a steep price. A decade earlier, the Smith family hadn't been able to obtain the credit they had needed to retain their farm. Now banks and individuals gladly loaned money to Joseph. John Corrill, who oversaw the completion of the Kirtland Temple's interior, estimated that church leaders were around $13,000 or $14,000 in debt at the time of the building's completion. There were also other debts as well as plans to purchase additional land in both Kirtland and Missouri. Joseph was comfortable taking on significant financial risk.[2]

In partnership with Sidney Rigdon and Oliver Cowdery, Joseph also borrowed money for a merchandizing operation. The idea came naturally to him. His parents had run such businesses in Vermont and Palmyra. Joseph and his partners obtained goods on credit from merchants in Buffalo and New York City. "He was close in money matters," recalled Caleb Peck, "could drive a sharp bargain—always having the advantage on his side." The Saints, however, had too little money for sharp bargains, so Joseph extended credit and charity to those without the means to pay. "Money was scarce," recalled then church member Oliver Olney. "Almost to a man, they wanted to borrow." Many of them borrowed from Joseph. He anticipated that Kirtland's growth and prosperity would enable him to meet his obligations, but as the debts piled up, so did the financial pressure.[3]

The prophet took a different sort of risk shortly after the temple's dedication. This step imperiled the familial and ecclesiastical bonds he had worked so hard to cultivate. Sometime in the late spring and early summer of 1836, Joseph had an intimate relationship with a servant girl named Fanny Alger. She was more than ten years younger than him, born in New York but raised mostly in northeastern Ohio, where her parents were baptized into the Church of Christ. Benjamin F. Johnson, who became acquainted with her after he moved to Kirtland in 1833, remembered her as a "very nice and comely" girl.[4]

Fanny worked for the Smith family, though in what precise capacity remains unclear. Emma's need for assistance became more acute after the June 1836 birth of Frederick (named after Frederick G. Williams, Joseph's counselor). Joseph Smith III was now three years old, and Julia Murdock Smith turned five that spring. Fanny may have helped Emma with the many tasks inherent in childrearing and housekeeping. It is also possible that she may have worked as a dairy maid on Hyrum Smith's farm.[5]

Most information about the relationship between Joseph and Fanny comes from later comments by individuals who wanted to either sully or defend the prophet's posthumous reputation. Still, enough evidence exists to reconstruct the basic contours of the episode.

The relationship was intimate. Emma Smith confided in apostle William McLellin that she "looked through a crack [in a barn] and saw the transaction!!" When he shared this report, McLellin had been excommunicated from the church for several decades. He considered Joseph Smith a fallen prophet. But Benjamin Johnson, faithful to the prophet and the church, also recalled that Joseph and Fanny "were *spied upon* and found together."[6]

Oliver Cowdery gained at least some knowledge of what had taken place. "The storm became so furious," narrated Ann Eliza Young, "that Joseph was obliged to send, at midnight, for Oliver Cowdery . . . to come and endeavor to settle matters between [him and Emma]." Emma settled those matters by demanding that Fanny Alger leave her household.

Whether or not Young's thirdhand report is true, there is other evidence that Cowdery was upset with Joseph's behavior. He later referred to a "nasty, filthy affair" between Joseph and Fanny.[7]

In the early 1840s, Joseph was sealed in marriage to more than thirty women. Some church members believed that Fanny Alger was a first step or false start in Joseph's practice of polygamy. Mosiah Hancock, son of Levi Hancock, was born in 1834. He had no firsthand knowledge about Joseph's relationship with Fanny Alger. However, according to an account he wrote based on information from his father, he maintained that it was a marriage that began with a quid pro quo. As of early 1833, the then unmarried Levi Hancock wanted to marry Clarissa Reed, another servant in the Smith household. He sought Joseph's permission. "I want to make a bargain with you," Joseph offered. "If you will get Fanny Alger for me for a wife you may have Clarissa Reed." In other words, Joseph would forego a potential plural marriage to Reed if Levi Hancock would help him secure Fanny as a wife. "I love Fanny," Joseph added. Levi Hancock was the brother of Fanny Alger's mother, so he was an ideal intermediary. He presented the idea to Fanny's parents, who told him he could ask his niece himself. He did, and she agreed. Levi Hancock performed the ceremony, repeating the words as Joseph dictated them to him.

It is an intriguing story, but not true. Hancock added that Clarissa Reed expected to become one of Joseph's wives because she and Emma Smith "were on the best of terms." It seems highly unlikely that Clarissa Reed would have been aware of this possibility in early 1833. Joseph had no plural wives at the time, and Emma certainly wouldn't have wanted her husband to marry a servant girl regardless of how well she got along with her. Moreover, Hancock's story of a marital bargain only makes sense if a marriage to Fanny Alger occurred about the same time that Levi Hancock married Clarissa Reed, and their wedding took place in March 1833. Had Joseph married Fanny Alger and maintained a relationship with her, he could not have kept it secret from Emma for several years.[8]

Other church members, however, also believed that the relationship between Joseph and Fanny was a marriage. "Fanny Alger's mother says Fanny was sealed to Joseph by Oliver Cowdery," stated Eliza Jane Webb, Ann Eliza Young's mother. Eliza R. Snow, who herself was later sealed in marriage to the prophet, lived with the Smiths that summer. Snow considered Fanny Alger Joseph Smith's first plural wife.[9] Still, there is reason to be cautious with these recollections. Given Oliver Cowdery's description of the scandal as a "nasty, filthy affair," he certainly hadn't sealed Joseph and Fanny in marriage. Perhaps Joseph had explained the relationship to Fanny as in some way sanctioned by God. "I do not know that the 'sealing' commenced in Kirtland," wrote Eliza Jane Webb, "but I am perfectly satisfied that something similar commenced." She gave as her source of information "what Fanny Alger told me."[10]

Emma immediately put an end to what she simply understood as her husband's unfaithfulness. "Emma Smith turned Fanny out of her house because of Joseph's intimacy with her," recalled Eliza Jane Webb. Fanny stayed for a few weeks at the Kirtland home of Webb and her husband.[11]

Joseph, meanwhile, left Kirtland in haste. On July 25, 1836, he traveled east in the company of Oliver Cowdery, Sidney Rigdon, and Hyrum Smith. Before Joseph departed, he asked Levi Hancock for a favor. Hancock had marched with the Army of Israel and was ordained as a Seventy. Joseph trusted him. "I saw Joseph Smith," Hancock recalled. "He told me to take Fanny Alger and go." Joseph wanted her out of the way. The prophet's own trip lasted seven weeks, plenty of time for Hancock to arrange Fanny Alger's transport to the west, and perhaps enough time for Emma's anger to subside.[12]

The Alger family stopped in Indiana for the winter, where Fanny married Solomon Custer, a nineteen-year-old man who was not a member of the church. Fanny's parents continued to Missouri and eventually to Utah. She kept quiet about her relationship with the Mormon prophet. Fanny drifted away from the church, but her parents and at least one of her siblings remained faithful Latter-day Saints.

Emma forgave Joseph rather quickly. It is likely, therefore, that Joseph described his actions as a momentary lapse or misunderstanding rather than a marriage, as the latter would have produced a more serious rupture with Emma. Whispers about the Alger affair grew over the next two years, however, and other church members who knew or learned about the episode were less forgiving.

Joseph made his departure on the same day that he received a troubling letter from Missouri. Since the expulsion of the Mormons from Jackson County, church members had taken refuge in Clay County, north of the Missouri River. Residents of Clay County initially had welcomed or at least accepted the Saints as refugees, but as their numbers grew, and as they purchased land, non-Mormon settlers became antagonistic. In an attempt to defuse tensions, Missouri church leaders laid plans to purchase lands beyond Clay County to the northeast.[13]

Before the Saints could leave on their own terms, mobs forced them out. On June 28, two vigilantes whipped a Mormon man almost to the point of death. After the attack, a committee of Clay County men—some of them sympathetic to the Saints—sought to maintain the peace. The proposed solution was straightforward. The mobs would cease their attacks if the Saints left. It was the only way to avoid a "civil war." The committee would allow the Mormons to gather that year's crops, and large landowners could stay until they could get a fair price for their property. There was no time for the Missouri Saints to consult with Joseph. In his absence, William W. Phelps, Bishop Edward Partridge, and the other Missouri leaders agreed. They sent a letter to Joseph to keep him abreast of developments.[14]

It was less than two months before the September 11, 1836, deadline Joseph had set for Zion's redemption. At the solemn assembly in the temple, Joseph had vowed that if more church members were driven from their lands, the Saints would not rest until they were "avenged." However, when word of the Clay County capitulation reached Kirtland, there was no angry or anguished council meeting, no talk of raising an army. Instead, Joseph and the other members of the church's presidency dashed off a letter to the Clay County committee. Joseph expressed a desire for peace above justice. He also sent a short letter to Missouri church leaders that affirmed their decision. Joseph then departed Kirtland that same evening. In his rush to escape the fallout from his relationship with Fanny Alger, Joseph did not take the time to provide the beleaguered Missouri Saints with more detailed guidance.[15]

Joseph's party went by boat to Rochester and then continued east via the Erie Canal. Oliver Cowdery observed that many of the towns that had sprung up along the canal had now withered away. They next traveled by rail—a first for Joseph—from Schenectady to Albany, then on a steamer down the Hudson River. They saw another reminder of the ephemeral nature of human achievement once they reached New York City. A fire the previous December had engulfed more than a dozen city blocks. The conflagration had reduced the Merchants' Exchange Building to a "heap." Grand new buildings were under construction, and the streets were crowded with stagecoaches.[16]

The travelers next proceeded to Salem. As a boy, Joseph had accompanied his uncle to the coastal city as he recovered from the leg infection that had nearly killed him. This time around the prophet was hoping for financial recuperation. A church member named Jonathan Burgess had given Joseph a tip that "a large amount of money had been secreted in the cellar of a certain house in Salem, which had belonged to a widow." No one else knew that the money was there, so if Joseph and the others could purchase, rent, or otherwise gain access to the house, they could solve their money troubles in short order. It was a new treasure quest.[17]

Nathaniel Hawthorne—who lived not far from where Joseph stayed in Salem—published a short story about a maniacal search for a "hoard of precious metals" in a decaying family home. In the end, the protagonist rips apart his house and discovers a chest, only to find that it contains worthless colonial-era provincial notes. The tale resonated because many Americans yearned to find hidden Spanish treasures and riches, to "heap up gold by the bushel and the cartload, instead of scraping it together, coin by coin." Joseph, likewise, after years of cobbling together contributions from church members, hoped to find a cache of gold or silver that would pay off the church's debts in one fell swoop and leave enough to purchase new properties in Missouri.[18]

Alas, Joseph's 1836 treasure quest was no more successful than his earlier ventures. When the prophet and his companions reached Salem, Burgess met them, but he was no longer able to identify the house with certainty. The day after their arrival, Joseph dictated a revelation. Despite their "follies," the Lord was "not displeased" that they had made the journey and promised that he had "much treasure in this city" for them. "Concern not yourselves about your debts," the revelation continued, "for I will give you power to pay them." Joseph and the others stayed in Salem for a few weeks. They toured the East Indian Marine Society museum and went to see "witch hill," where victims of the 1692 witchcraft trials had been hanged. They also visited the remains of the Catholic convent that a mob had burned down three years earlier. In the latter case, all but one of the mobbers escaped conviction, and the order received no compensation for its loss. The parallels to the Mormon experience of persecution in Jackson could not have escaped Joseph and his companions.[19]

It was hard to set aside the thought of hidden riches, however. By mid-August, Joseph had become hopeful. "We have found the house since Brother Burgess left us," he wrote Emma, "but the house is occupied and it will require much care and patience to rent or buy it." Either their patience was quickly exhausted, or they rented the house but found no treasure in the cellar. By the end of August, the travelers left New England, no richer than when they had come.[20]

"Believe me that I am your sincere friend and husband," Joseph entreated Emma from Salem. It reads like a plea for forgiveness. If so, Emma was mollified. It would be years before she and Joseph faced renewed strain in their marriage.[21]

Joseph apparently took the words of the Lord to heart. The prophet gave every appearance of being completely unconcerned about debt. He and associates made several significant land purchases in September and October 1836, and they also bought nearly $2,000 worth of goods on credit for their merchandizing operation. In most instances, other men also signed their names to the deeds or promissory notes, but creditors would look to Joseph to settle the debts.[22]

Mormon Kirtland was rich in land and labor, but most church members had little cash. It was an endemic problem in Jacksonian America. Specie was scarce. Paper money was plentiful, but unregulated. Individuals wrote promissory notes, businesses printed banknotes, chartered and unchartered banks circulated their own notes, and counterfeiters put fake notes into circulation. It all hinged on confidence. As long as people believed that they could exchange their banknotes for specie, the notes promoted commerce. But if there was reason to doubt a bank's ability to stand behind its paper, their value plummeted.[23]

Questions of confidence became more acute in the wake of Andrew Jackson's successful war against the Bank of the United States. The institution had served as a check against financial recklessness by demanding payment in specie on notes from state-chartered banks. Banks that lacked sufficient reserves of hard money collapsed, but this weeding-out process enhanced confidence in the remaining banks and their paper. Notes of the Bank of the United States circulated at par across the country, giving the United States the beginnings of a national currency.

President Jackson, however, saw the bank as a "Monster," a rival center of power whose directors could destroy state banks as they saw fit. In 1832, four years before the national bank's charter would expire, Nicholas Biddle, the bank's director, persuaded Congress to renew it. Biddle hoped that Jackson would acquiesce in order to avoid controversy during an election year. A defiant Old Hickory told Martin Van Buren, his running mate in that year's presidential campaign, that "the bank is trying ... to kill me, *but I will kill it.*" Jackson killed the bank with a veto of the renewal bill. The president then transferred federal specie deposits to the state banks. Finally, in one of his last significant actions as president, Jackson in July 1836 issued what became known as his Specie Circular, which required payment for federal land purchases in gold or silver. The mandate forced individuals to redeem banknotes, which drained bank reserves.[24]

Kirtland's residents relied heavily on the Bank of Geauga in nearby Painesville. The bank's directors included Grandison Newell, who had financed Doctor Hurlbut's campaign against Joseph. Given this situation, Joseph decided that Kirtland needed its own bank and currency for the sake of its prosperity. The prophet and his companions had discussed the idea during their recent stay in New York City, and they now decided to move ahead. They named their bank the Kirtland Safety Society.

Starting a bank required printing plates, paper, investors, and a high tolerance for risk. The prophet had the latter in spades and got to work on the rest. In October, Joseph sent Oliver Cowdery and Hyrum Smith to New York City, where they purchased a safe and ordered plates. Meanwhile, dozens of church members began investing in the enterprise by subscribing for shares worth $50 each, purchasing them for a small fraction of their face value. Joseph bought three thousand shares—worth a stated value of $150,000—with an initial payment of $1,342.69. Altogether, more than a hundred investors made payments on their stock purchases. Some of the payments were made in specie, but many were in the notes of other banks, and it remains unclear how much silver and gold the bank had on hand when it commenced operations. At an early November meeting, the society's stockholders appointed Sidney Rigdon the bank's president and Joseph its cashier.[25]

Joseph and his associates hoped to obtain a charter for their bank from the Ohio state legislature. Apostle Orson Hyde went to Columbus, where hard-money Democrats received the charter proposal coolly. The Kirtland bank's leaders responded with creative determination. Cowdery brought the firm's printing plates to Kirtland by the end of December, and bank officers began printing notes in denominations from $1 to $100. In what was probably an attempt to circumvent an 1816 state law against unchartered banks, church leaders renamed their institution the Kirtland Safety Society Anti-Banking Company. They clumsily altered some of the notes by stamping "ANTI" and "ING CO." in small print around the word "BANK." The society's officers soon abandoned the practice and reverted to the prior name, further evidence of the amateurish character of the whole endeavor.

Kirtland Safety Society $1 bill. (© By Intellectual Reserve, Inc.)

Safety Society leaders used a tiny stamp to indicate that theirs
was an "ANTI-BANK-ING CO[mpany]." (© By Intellectual Reserve, Inc.)

The bank lacked the state's sanction, but Joseph revealed that it had
God's blessing. On January 6, 1837, the prophet told the men present in
the Deposit Office—built the previous fall to conduct the bank's business
and store its materials—that he had received the "word of the Lord upon
the subject of the Kirtland Safety Society." It was more than the still
small voice of the Spirit. Alone by himself, Joseph had heard "an audible
voice." Joseph kept the contents of the message to himself, but he reassured his followers that "all would be well" if they heeded the Lord's
commandments.[26]

For a few weeks, everything did go well. Bank directors made short-
term loans that put $10,000 worth of notes into circulation. The in-
creased money supply gave Kirtland's economy a jolt. Willard Richards
informed his sister that new homes were "going up almost every day"
and that craftsmen could "command any price." The price of land rose

accordingly. Some "who were not worth a dollar one year ago are now worth their thousands and tens of thousands," Richards added. Many well-connected church members borrowed from the bank and purchased land in and around Kirtland.[27]

Non-Mormons took note. In mid-January, the nearby *Cleveland Daily Gazette* complained about "an emission of bills from the society of Mormons . . . showered upon us." The paper asserted that the bank was unstable, deceptive, and illegal. Unstable because the Safety Society might lack the specie—or other assets—necessary to redeem its notes upon demand. "They seem to rest upon a spiritual basis," the paper opined. Deceptive because of the insertion of "ANTI" on the notes, which unsuspecting individuals might overlook. And illegal, the paper alleged, because the society and its notes violated Ohio law. There was the 1816 law, which threatened individuals who operated an unchartered bank with a $1,000 fine. Moreover, an 1824 state law declared that the notes of unchartered banks were "void" and accordingly worthless.[28]

The society soon came under pressure. The Bank of Geauga, which had extended a $3,000 loan to the Safety Society's directors, refused to accept Kirtland notes, which made it difficult for the Mormon money to gain acceptance in the region. Even worse, Grandison Newell orchestrated a run on the bank by buying up the Mormon notes and taking them to Kirtland for redemption. By the end of the month, the Safety Society temporarily suspended specie payments. Those who held the bank's notes became nervous.[29]

Joseph tried to stave off the bank's failure. He sent apostle Orson Hyde back to Columbus in a more serious attempt to obtain a charter. Hyde managed to secure a vote in the state senate, but it failed. At the same time, Joseph traveled around Lake Erie to the west and acquired a controlling interest in the Bank of Monroe. Through the purchase the Kirtland bank could become a branch of the latter institution, chartered by the State of Michigan. The problem with the strategy was that the Bank of Monroe was itself on the verge of collapse. The merger of two shaky banks strengthened neither. The Bank of Monroe was forced to suspend specie payments in March.[30]

It was a terrible time to try to save a bank. The nation's banking system was already under duress from Andrew Jackson's specie circular and from a decision by the Bank of England to restrict credit to American banks and merchants. Scores of banks across the country failed in what became known as the Panic of 1837. The Kirtland Safety Society was already faltering before the panic, but the national financial meltdown made its demise a near certainty.[31]

In early April 1837, Joseph presided over a reprise of the solemn assembly at the Kirtland Temple, replete with speaking in tongues, visions, and prophesying. At the assembly, Joseph addressed the banking crisis. The debts of the church's leaders caused embarrassment, he acknowledged. Yet he was unbowed. They had begun poor, were often afflicted, and nevertheless they had sacrificed to preach the gospel and "build a house for the Lord." If the Saints brought their money to Kirtland, the church's debts could be settled and the town would flourish. Joseph shared that he had received a vision of Kirtland's future. Commerce by steamboat and railroad would turn Kirtland into a rich metropolis. The Saints would build houses of worship and "beautiful streets." The rulers of the earth would come to look on the city's glory.[32]

Joseph's florid vision of Kirtland's future did not instill present confidence. Rigdon soon noted that "many of the Church had refused Kirtland currency." In other words, even the Saints would not accept Kirtland Safety Society notes any longer.[33]

On April 13, Wilford Woodruff and Phebe Carter were married in Joseph's home. The couple had expected the prophet to solemnize their marriage, but Joseph was on the lam. Grandison Newell had sworn a complaint before a Painesville justice of the peace that Joseph had threatened to kill him. (A court eventually acquitted the prophet of the charge.) Newell's complaint stirred up local opposition to Joseph, who left his home in order to evade both arrest and mobs. "His life was so beset and sought for by wicked and ungodly men," explained Woodruff.[34]

Joseph traveled east to Palmyra, New York, where he stayed with Martin Harris. The prophet intended to be gone for just a few days, but Hyrum sent word that it remained unsafe in Kirtland. In her husband's absence, Emma struggled to run a household in circumstances that were straitened by the banking crisis and Joseph's debts. Although she called her family "small," there were twenty individuals living in her home by that June, including their three children, Joseph's parents, boarders, visitors, and help. When Emma told Julia and Joseph III that their father would remain away longer than he had planned, she "could hardly pacify" them.[35]

Joseph's creditors were even harder to pacify. "It is impossible for me to do anything," Emma wrote her husband, "as long as everybody has so much better right to all that is called yours than I have." Creditors pursued "every particle" of property that they could "lay their hands on."[36]

Longtime supporters abandoned Joseph as the crisis worsened. John Johnson, who in the early 1830s had invited the prophet to live in his Hiram, Ohio, home, gave up on the Safety Society and Joseph Smith at the same time. He went to the bank and redeemed his shares for every penny of the $600 he had invested. John Johnson, Elsa Johnson, and several others in their family withdrew from the church. As individuals who held the Kirtland notes sought to rid themselves of them, their value plummeted. By late May, they circulated at half their face value. Later in the summer, they were nearly worthless. The Kirtland land bubble also popped. Property prices, already rising with the influx of immigrants, had soared because of the infusion of bank notes earlier in the year. Individuals now divested themselves of properties, which they held in their own names but which had been part of the church's strategy for the development of Kirtland. John Johnson transferred or sold a large number of properties to his own family members and to others who had become critical of Joseph, eliminating a significant financial backstop for the church.[37]

Joseph took steps to stabilize his personal finances. He had recently sold three properties to apostle Parley Pratt for the sky-high price of $2,000, with a down payment of $75. Pratt estimated that Joseph had paid less than $100 when he had acquired the properties. Shortly after Joseph returned to Kirtland in mid-May, he turned over Pratt's debt to the Safety Society, either for cash or as part of another transaction. Sidney Rigdon, as an officer of the bank, then demanded payment from Pratt. Caught in what he described as a "snare," Pratt offered Rigdon the three properties as a way to settle the debt. Rigdon refused to show any mercy and demanded Pratt's house as payment. Pratt couldn't gain an audience with Joseph, so he aired his discontent in a blistering letter. He blamed Joseph and Rigdon for "leading this people astray" through "false prophesying and preaching." Joseph had made a "sacred promise" that Pratt "would not be injured" through the land transaction, and the apostle now faced ruin.[38]

Joseph's role in the rise and fall of the Kirtland Safety Society was not the only cause of ecclesiastical dissent. Warren Parrish, formerly Joseph's scribe, had learned about Joseph's intimacy with Fanny Alger. Oliver Cowdery, who had not made peace with the prophet's behavior, might have been Parrish's informant. Regardless, Parrish told others what he had heard. The twin scandals—one financial, one sexual—posed the most severe threat to Joseph's authority since the organization of the church. By late May 1837, there was a cadre of disaffected high-ranking church members, including Parley and Orson Pratt, their fellow apostle Lyman Johnson, President Frederick G. Williams, Book of Mormon witness David Whitmer, and Warren Parrish.

Parrish denounced Joseph's behavior in a Sunday meeting, and Lyman Johnson and Orson Pratt sent a message to Bishop Newel K. Whitney accusing Joseph of "lying, and misrepresentation—also for extortion—and for speaking disrespectfully against his brethren behind their backs." Joseph's supporters brought charges of their own against several of the dissenters. The Kirtland High Council met in the House of the Lord to discuss the latter charges. Joseph did not attend, a sign he did not want a direct confrontation with his opponents. The members of the council discussed the procedure for trying the charges, then "dispersed in confusion." The previous year, in the months leading up to the temple's dedication, Joseph repeatedly had taught church members to respect the careful organization of the church's quorums and councils. Now, order gave way to ecclesiastical chaos.[39]

Joseph tried to put the banking disaster behind him. On June 8, he, Emma, and his parents transferred all of their Safety Society shares to Oliver Granger and Jared Carter, church members faithful to him who applied the stock toward Joseph's outstanding debts. Dozens of other individuals withdrew their shares over the next two weeks. Joseph and Sidney Rigdon resigned as officers of the bank, leaving it to the direction of Warren Parrish and other antagonists. Later in the summer, Joseph publicly condemned the "speculators, renegades, and gamblers" who operated the bank. Kirtland money now circulated for pennies on the dollar.[40]

That month Joseph contracted a severe illness. At one point, Rigdon confided that "he should not wonder naturally speaking if he [Joseph] did not live until night." Joseph told a visitor that when he became too weak to pray, Satan "strove with all his power to get his spirit," to end his life. During those moments, a "good spirit" protected him, and he asked Emma and friends to pray on his behalf. In the midst of his illness, Joseph also found spiritual consolation. He "was blessed at times with such glorious visions as made him quite forget that his body was afflicted." Loyal Saints gathered in the House of the Lord, where they fasted and prayed for him all night long. Jared Carter had a vision of "a grave open to receive him (Joseph Smith) but saw the earth fall in of its own accord with no person in [it]." It was a hopeful omen.[41]

During Joseph's illness, his opponents became more public in their criticism. At a Sunday morning meeting in the temple, Parley Pratt proclaimed that "nearly all the church had departed from God and that Brother J[oseph] S[mith] had committed great sins." A disgusted Sidney Rigdon hastened to dismiss the congregation. The afternoon meeting also became contentious. According to Mary Fielding, who married Hyrum Smith that December, for the first time since the Saints had completed the House of the Lord, Sunday passed without a celebration of the Lord's Supper.[42]

When the meeting broke up, Fielding walked home past Joseph's house, "not knowing whether he live[d] still." Within a few days, however, the prophet was up and about, and he soon reconciled with Parley Pratt. Joseph remained formidable. When he met his critics face–to-face, he could often persuade or cajole them into contrition, and through his preaching, Joseph could remind them of why they had accepted him as God's prophet in the first place. On the other hand, Joseph left Kirtland several times that summer and fall and, with each trip, disorder within the church grew.

As the financial panic swept the country, Joseph's creditors demanded payment as they tried to meet their own obligations, and local non-Mormon antagonists happily used his indebtedness to harass him. On July 27, as Joseph and Sidney Rigdon traveled through Painesville on their way to visit branches of the church in Canada, they were detained repeatedly by the sheriff, Abel Kimball, for a failure to pay debts. In each instance, Joseph either paid the debt or posted bail to pledge his later appearance in court. Frustrated, Joseph finally decided to retreat to Kirtland. As he did, Kimball leapt into Joseph's carriage, seized the reins, and served him yet another writ. Joseph gave the sheriff his watch and started for home. The next day, Joseph and his associates bypassed Painesville as they set off again for Canada, traveling thirty miles east to catch a steamboat at Ashtabula.[43]

Conflict between the prophet's detractors and defenders intensified during Joseph's trip. At another Sunday meeting in the temple, Joseph Smith Sr. criticized Warren Parrish in relation to the Safety Society. Parrish charged at the church's patriarch. Joseph Sr. called on Oliver Cowdery, who was a justice of the peace, to detain Parrish. Cowdery sat like a statue. Before Parrish could pull Joseph Sr. out of the pulpit, William Smith grabbed Parrish and began carrying him toward the door. Dissident apostle John Boynton drew a sword and threatened to "run him [William Smith] through" if he took another step. According to Eliza Snow's later recollection, other men drew pistols and bowie knives. A melee ensued, while some church members "tried to escape from the confusion by jumping out of the windows." Everything was falling apart.[44]

Meanwhile, Joseph attempted to evade his non-Mormon enemies during his return to Kirtland. When his party docked at Ashtabula, he and Sidney Rigdon disguised themselves and headed for home in the carriage of church member Sampson Avard. Someone had spotted them, however, and four miles short of Kirtland they were arrested and brought back to Painesville, where "a gang of mobbers were thirsting for their blood." Joseph and Sidney feared a reprise of the attack five years earlier that had nearly killed them. Fortunately, Kimball detained his prisoners at a tavern owned by a Painesville Saint, Horace Kingsbury, whose housekeeper let them out the kitchen door.[45]

Joseph and Sidney fled into the woods, their enemies pursuing them with torches. They took refuge in a swamp and lay down next to an old log. Joseph told his exhausted friend to try to breathe more quietly if he wanted to avoid recapture. Their pursuers didn't find them, and the two men climbed fences, stumbled through bushes, and walked through cornfields until they found the road to Kirtland, which they reached shortly before dawn.

It was Sunday. Joseph went to the House of the Lord and "spoke in a very powerful manner," related Mary Fielding. "The Saints felt the blessing and left the house rejoicing abundantly returning their blessing upon him." Just as he had preached the morning after he had been tarred and feathered in 1832, so Joseph now stood tall again in the face of persecution.[46]

Joseph also stood up to his internal critics. That summer, while on a visit to Kirtland from Missouri, the apostles Thomas Marsh and David Patten heard talk that Joseph had committed adultery. Patten discussed the matter with Warren Parrish and Oliver Cowdery. Parrish told him Joseph was guilty. Cowdery's response was coy. He "cocked up his eye very knowingly," hesitated to answer, but "conveyed the idea that it was true." Patten marched off to confront the prophet. "David insulted Joseph," Brigham Young recalled. "Joseph slapped him in the face and kicked him out of the yard." With his words as well as his fists, Joseph convinced the two apostles of his innocence. The prophet also learned from David Patten that Cowdery had offered less than a full-throated defense of his conduct. Cowdery was "in transgression," Joseph wrote the Saints in Missouri.[47]

The prophet mended fences with several of the dissenters, but by September Joseph recognized that his position in Kirtland was becoming untenable. His extensive debts made it possible for his enemies—or even indifferent creditors—to assail him with lawsuits. His property was at risk, and his efforts to evade arrest by extended absences from Kirtland hampered his ability to conduct church business.

Given these challenges, it was natural for Joseph's thoughts to return to Missouri. In December 1836, the Missouri legislature had created Caldwell County in an attempt to sequester the Saints from their non-Mormon antagonists. Even before the legislative act, the church's Missouri leaders had purchased Caldwell County land near Shoal Creek, which became the town of Far West. By July 1837, there were a hundred buildings in Far West, and fifteen hundred Missouri Saints assembled to break ground for a temple. That September Joseph decided that it was time for him to visit.[48]

En route to Far West, Joseph stopped in Dublin, Indiana, where Fanny Alger Custer lived with her husband. There is no record of whether she attended any of the three meetings Joseph and his companions held in Dublin, but the prophet's thoughts must have turned to her during his stay.[49]

The prophet reached Far West in early November. The new settlement pleased Joseph, who concluded that it would provide "sufficient room" for ongoing Mormon migration. The prophet attended a conference, held in part to resolve ongoing concerns about the loyalty of certain leaders. As Joseph had done on several occasions in Ohio and Missouri, he asked church members whether they affirmed their leaders, who were introduced in sequence. The process had become an ecclesiastical ritual within the church, one that customarily produced few surprises.

There was drama on this occasion. When the prophet nominated Frederick G. Williams as one of his counselors, several men objected. Joseph and Emma had named their second living son after Williams, but the Safety Society had driven a wedge between the two men. According to Lucy Mack Smith, Joseph suspected Warren Parrish—and perhaps Williams himself—of having stolen bank deposits. Joseph had demanded that Williams, in his capacity as a justice of the peace, issue a search warrant in an attempt to find the deposits. Joseph then threatened to drop Williams from the church presidency when he refused the demand. Jo-

seph and Williams had patched things up by the end of the summer, but
a letter that Williams sent to Missouri church leaders reopened the conflict. The conference voted against Williams, who was replaced by
Hyrum Smith. There were also objections raised against David Whitmer
and John Whitmer as members of the church's Missouri presidency,
though they retained their positions for the time being.[50]

Joseph didn't even nominate Oliver Cowdery as one of his counselors. It was a pointed omission. The two men, however, engaged in a
heartfelt conversation in which they agreed to "drop every past thing."
They would not talk about Fanny Alger any longer. Cowdery stayed in
Missouri when Joseph returned to Ohio.[51]

Joseph was back in Kirtland by December 10. His legal and financial
standing had grown more precarious in his absence. Joseph and Sidney
Rigdon had been tried in absentia by a Geauga County court, charged
with violating Ohio's 1816 law against unchartered banking. The defendants' attorney argued that an 1824 statute had suspended the earlier
statute, but the judge in the case instructed the jury that the 1816 law remained "in force." Accordingly, the jury convicted the two men and fined
them $1,000 each. The statute specified that the proceeds be divided be-
tween the state and the individual who brought the complaint. In this
case, Grandison Newell had orchestrated the suit, so he stood to benefit
from the conviction. Newell pursued legal actions to collect the debt
and, if necessary, have Joseph's property seized to pay it.[52]

Dissent within the church had reached new heights while Joseph was
in Missouri. Prominent among the dissenters were Martin Harris and
Warren Parrish, along with apostles Luke Johnson and John Boynton.
"They hold meetings every week," wrote Vilate Kimball. "The tenor of
their worship is to expose the iniquities of this church." She added that
Sylvester Smith, Joseph's antagonist during the 1834 Zion's Camp
march, "denies the existence of a God." Grandison Newell attended the
dissenters' meetings and plotted strategy against Joseph and those faithful to him. According to Thomas Marsh's account, the dissenters
"claimed themselves to be the old standard [and] called themselves the
Church of Christ." They saw Joseph as either a fallen prophet or "a liar
from the beginning" whom God had nevertheless used to bring forth the
Book of Mormon and the earlier revelations.[53]

The source of the estrangement between Joseph and Oliver
Cowdery was widely known by this point. Joseph felt the need to defend

himself against suggestions of sexual immorality. At a tumultuous meeting in the temple, Joseph asserted that Cowdery had confessed to making a false accusation of adultery against him.[54] The prophet's supporters also tried to impose ecclesiastical discipline against the Kirtland dissenters. In what John Smith, Joseph's uncle, referred to as a "mighty pruning," the Kirtland High Council in late December excommunicated nearly thirty individuals, including Martin Harris.[55]

Joseph couldn't cut off his creditors and legal opponents, and they moved to ruin him. The judgments in the illegal banking case and other lawsuits empowered sheriffs and constables to seize property to satisfy fines and debts. In early January, Abel Kimball, Joseph's least favorite sheriff, announced a fire sale: the church's printing press and type; a collection of furniture; and copies of the Book of Mormon, the Doctrine and Covenants, and hymnals. The sheriff also seized and sold Joseph's Egyptian materials. "Mummies sold," reported Hepzibah Richards, "records missing." As it turned out, church members helped Joseph regain possession of the papyri and mummies. Joseph and his associates also had transferred and mortgaged the Kirtland Temple and its land, respectively. The prophet could preserve little else, however. "They were stripped of everything," Vilate Kimball wrote, "even to food and raiment." Soon the constable would come for Joseph's land and house.[56]

Joseph's final Kirtland revelation told the prophet to take his family to the west as soon as possible. "Get out of this place," the Lord put it bluntly, "or there shall be no safety for you."[57] Joseph understood that he would be risking his life if he stayed in Kirtland. He fled on horseback that same evening, traveling overnight and reaching the town of Norton, Ohio, by morning. Emma—early in the second trimester of another pregnancy—and their three children soon joined him, and they and the Rigdons began the journey west. Joseph would never return to Kirtland.

In the wake of Joseph's flight, Kirtland was a shambles of chaos and violence. Sheriff Kimball sold the printing office. An actual fire soon followed the fire sale. Residents awoke in the middle of the next night to find the printing office ablaze. The press and the office's other contents had just been auctioned. "In one hour it was consumed with all its contents," reported Hepzibah Richards. "The temple and other buildings badly scorched." It was arson. Several men sympathetic to Joseph were arrested, but Justice of the Peace Warren Cowdery (Oliver Cowdery's brother) dismissed the charge. Meanwhile, the "old standard" Church of Christ secured the keys to the House of the Lord and planned to hold Sunday meetings there. "They will have it, if it is by the shedding of blood," Richards explained.[58]

It was an inglorious end to Joseph's seven years in northeastern Ohio. The Latter-day Saint community in and around Kirtland had grown and thrived under Joseph's leadership. With the optimistic but not unreasonable expectation that rising property values would enable him to sell parcels and settle debts, Joseph had borrowed money to purchase land and build the temple. He had chosen to "go ahead" to get ahead, very much in keeping with the spirit of Jacksonian America. Several of Joseph's choices—his relationship with Fanny Alger, the establishment of the bank, his absences from Kirtland in the midst of crisis—shook the foundations of what he had built. Now he had been forced to "get out." Unfortunately for Joseph, he also had many antagonists in Missouri.

CHAPTER NINETEEN

East of Eden (1838)

I N MID-MARCH 1838, two months after fleeing Kirtland, Joseph, Emma, and their children arrived in Far West. A delegation of Missouri Mormon leaders had met the prophet and his family eight miles from their destination and escorted them to what Joseph dubbed "little Zion."[1]

Joseph drafted what he termed a "motto" for the church, a document akin to a brief manifesto. In it, Joseph called for "peace and good order" along with "wholesome laws and virtue." There was no necessary conflict between his church and American ideals, the prophet insisted. Joseph praised the U.S. Constitution, and he honored the blood that had purchased their liberty in the American Revolution. Joseph sought "aristarchy," meaning "government by excellent men." He wanted to dispel the disunity and disputatiousness that threatened the church. "Woe to tyrants, mobs, aristocracy, anarchy, and Toryism," he warned, "and all those who invent or seek out unrighteous and vexatious lawsuits." The motto signaled the desire of Joseph and other Saints for a fresh start in Missouri.[2]

It would not be easy. Fallout from the twin Kirtland scandals— Fanny Alger and the bank—followed Joseph west. As the Saints migrated to Missouri, moreover, anti-Mormons in the western part of the state grew determined to drive them out. Joseph worked quickly to establish the peace and order he craved and that the church would need as it attempted to withstand its enemies.

Joseph and Oliver Cowdery had agreed to "drop every past thing" during the prophet's November 1837 visit to Far West. But Joseph hadn't done so. Instead, he had stated publicly in Kirtland that Cowdery had confessed to having made a false accusation of adultery against him.

Cowdery's brothers Warren and Lyman informed him about Joseph's assertion. Oliver Cowdery was incensed and demanded that Joseph "correct" himself. "Until which you and myself are two," Cowdery added. In a letter to his brothers, he described what he had told Joseph. "I did not fail to affirm that what I had said was strictly true," Cowdery declared. "A dirty, nasty, filthy affair of his and Fanny Alger's was talked over . . . as I supposed was admitted by himself." Cowdery had been uneasy since he had learned about the prophet's intimacy with Fanny Alger. Now he felt the prophet had insulted his character. Cowdery expressed solidarity with the "good cause" led by Warren Parrish in Kirtland.[3]

Joseph had no intention of correcting himself. He anticipated further trouble with Cowdery, and the prophet also suspected the disloyalty of the church's Missouri presidency: John Whitmer, David Whitmer, and William Phelps. Objections to Phelps and the Whitmer brothers had been raised at the November 1837 conference. Joseph by letter asked apostle Thomas Marsh to lay the groundwork for action against the four men. In January, the Missouri High Council accused them of selling their Jackson County land and of ignoring the Word of Wisdom by drinking tea and coffee. Joseph's revelations had forbidden the land sales, but the men "declared they would not be controlled by any ecclesiastical power or revelation whatever in their temporal concerns." The council deposed the Missouri presidency, and Thomas Marsh and his fellow apostle David Patten took over as acting presidents, joined by Brigham Young a few months later. In early March, a church council presided over by Marsh and Patten excommunicated Phelps and John Whitmer.[4]

Cowdery's church trial, before the Missouri High Council and its bishopric, took place in mid-April. Bishop Edward Partridge sent Cowdery a list of nine charges. They included "falsely insinuating that [Joseph Smith] was guilty of adultery." The prophet testified at the trial and "gave a history respecting the girl business," though the clerk discreetly omitted the details from the minutes. Cowdery did not attend his trial. In a letter he stated his intention to withdraw from the church.[5]

Oliver Cowdery had been one of Joseph Smith's most significant partners for over a decade. He was Joseph's principal Book of Mormon scribe, had helped Joseph organize the Church of Christ, and

had written many of Joseph's early revelations. At the trial, Joseph referred to Cowdery as his "bosom friend," someone he had "entrusted . . .
with many things." That relationship had been episodically fraught.
Cowdery didn't always like playing second fiddle to Joseph. Still,
Cowdery was close enough to Joseph to work with him on the Egyptian
project, and it was Cowdery who, alongside Joseph, had seen Jesus and
Elijah behind the veil in the Kirtland Temple.[6]

Bishop Partridge and his assistants, along with the high council, declared that Cowdery was no longer a member of the church. David
Whitmer and the apostles Lyman Johnson and William McLellin soon
joined the growing ranks of the excommunicated. Book of Mormon
scribes, men who had sworn that they had seen the golden plates, early
financial supporters, bosom friends. They had rejected Joseph's leadership. The previous summer and fall, the prophet had sought long, heartfelt audiences to settle his differences with these men. He now wanted
them out of the way.

In late April 1838, Joseph dictated a revelation in which the Lord clarified that the church should be called "the Church of Jesus Christ of Latter Day Saints." The revelation also commanded the Saints to begin
preparatory work on a new "House of the Lord," at the spot selected by
Phelps and John Whitmer. The Saints should break ground on July 4.
Since the expulsion from Jackson County, Joseph had not instructed the
Missouri Saints to build a temple or even publish a newspaper. Far West
was different. It was a new place of gathering. The prophet threw himself
into the task of building up Mormon settlements in the region. Joseph's
tried-and-true strategy featured land purchases, ecclesiastical organization, merchandizing operations, a printing press, and a temple.[7]

Joseph left Far West in mid-May to inspect potential settlements in
newly created Daviess County, about thirty miles to the north. As when
Joseph and the Saints had discovered the bones of "Zelph" on their 1834
march to Missouri, the prophet had his mind on the land's sacred past.
He named one spot Tower Hill because of what he understood as "the
remains of an old Nephitish altar and tower." Lyman Wight, a church
member, had recently made his home there. The prophet identified another parcel of land that sloped down to the banks of the Grand River as
Adam-ondi-Ahman. Several years earlier Joseph had described Adam-
ondi-Ahman as a valley in which Adam had blessed his posterity shortly
before his death. Now Joseph added that it was where Adam, as the "An-

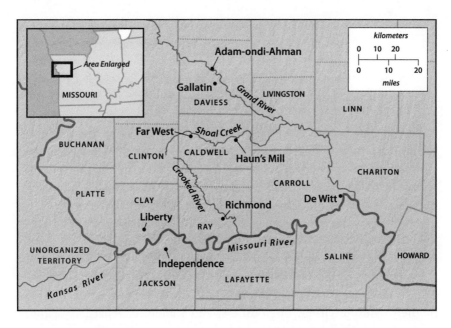

Joseph Smith's activities in Missouri. (Map by John Hamer)

cient of Days" referenced in the Book of Daniel, one day would "come to visit his people." If Adam and Eve had come to Adam-ondi-Ahman after their expulsion from Eden, it followed that the garden would have been nearby. Joseph was soon teaching that the Garden of Eden had been in Jackson County. Regardless, the land near the river was fertile. Within weeks, church members began settling Adam-ondi-Ahman, which they often shortened to Diahman.[8]

Joseph hurried back to Far West. On June 2, Emma gave birth to Alexander Hale Smith, the couple's third living son. The months of her pregnancy had been tumultuous and arduous. With insufficient preparation, Emma and her family had journeyed a thousand miles in the dead of winter. After they reached Far West, the prophet and his family took shelter with George W. Harris, then relocated to a house that Samuel Musick had operated as a tavern, and finally—when Alexander was three weeks old—moved to a home that Joseph bought from George Hinkle.

At the end of June, Joseph presided over the organization of Diahman as a "stake of Zion," with its own presidency, council, and bishop. He also authorized the purchase of land in the town of De Witt, about fifty miles to the southeast in Carroll County. It was risky to establish Mormon settlements outside of Caldwell County. The Saints had never formally agreed to confine themselves to a single county, but non-Mormons, state legislators, and church representatives understood the tacit arrangement. Joseph, by contrast, envisioned Far West as a hub for stakes of Zion in other counties.[9]

As Joseph and his associates established new settlements for Mormons coming to Missouri, they took steps to get unwanted persons to clear out. Oliver Cowdery and the other recent excommunicates were still in Far West. Joseph feared a reprise of Kirtland, where dissidents and apostates had used alternative church meetings and lawsuits to undermine his authority.

A group of church members loyal to the First Presidency plotted to drive out the dissenters. Among the ringleaders of the group was Sampson Avard, a physician and erstwhile Campbellite preacher. With the obvious sanction of the First Presidency, Avard's group in mid-June drafted a letter to Cowdery, Phelps, Johnson, and the Whitmers, accusing them of theft, counterfeiting, litigiousness, and slander. "Depart, or a more fatal calamity shall befall you," the letter bluntly warned. It gave the excommunicants precisely seventy-two hours to leave. "We will put you from the county of Caldwell," the letter concluded. "So help us God." Eighty-three men signed the warning, including Hyrum Smith.[10]

Sidney Rigdon delivered the same message before a Far West congregation on June 17. "If the salt have lost his savor," he read from the Gospel of Matthew, "it is thenceforth good for nothing, but to be cast out, and to be trodden under foot." Rigdon didn't name names in what became known as his "salt sermon," but everyone knew who and what he meant. Rigdon threatened "to erect a gallows on the square of Far West and hang them up as they did the gamblers at Vicksburg [in 1835]." In that instance, the leading citizens of Vicksburg had warned the city's gamblers to leave town within twenty-four hours. Five who lingered were hanged. Joseph stood up after Rigdon's sermon, cautioned that he didn't "want the brethren to act unlawfully," but suggested—contrary to the New Testament—that Judas "was hung by Peter." Joseph supported the pressure brought to bear against his former friends.[11]

The threats worked. "These men took warning," Joseph's scribe wrote, "and soon they were seen bounding over the prairie like the scapegoat to carry off their own sins." With the exception of Phelps, who attempted to reconcile with church leaders, the dissenters took refuge with apostle-turned-apostate William McLellin in Clay County.[12]

Those who had circulated the letter now organized themselves into a militia. They called themselves the Society of the Daughter of Zion, the Brother of Gideon, and the Big Fan, but became more commonly known as the Danites. Joseph came up with the name, alluding to a passage in the Book of Judges about a group of warriors from the tribe of Dan. The warriors confiscate idols from the home of Micah, then proceed to conquer a town. The biblical reference was a bit obtuse, but the idea was that the Danites would be stalwart warriors like their ancient namesakes.[13]

The Saints had already organized a Caldwell County regiment of the state militia. The Danites operated as an extralegal group. According to John Corrill, members "entered into solemn covenants, before God, and bound themselves under oath to keep the secrets of the society." Danite officers included Carter and Avard, and also George W. Robinson, who was Joseph's scribe. "We have a company of Danites in these times," wrote Robinson, "to put to rights physically that which is not right, and to cleanse the church of very great evils." The Danites vowed that no one in Caldwell County would be permitted to speak against the church's presidency. "All tattling, lying, and backbiting must be put down," Corrill later explained, "and he that would not submit willingly should be forced to it, or leave the county."[14]

Going forward, maintaining a militia—whether chartered or extralegal—was an additional prong in Joseph's strategy for building up Mormon gathering places. The expulsions from Jackson County and Clay County illustrated the need for the Saints to protect themselves against the threat of mobs. Joseph also wanted to intimidate critics within the church. Historians have argued at length about how much Joseph knew about certain Danite actions. In some cases, evidence is sparse. In broad strokes, though, the prophet understood the group as a new way to protect himself and the church.

During the July 4 festivities in Far West, at which the church dedicated the four cornerstones of the planned temple, both county and Danite officers received recognition, and members of both companies marched. Sidney Rigdon delivered an even saltier speech at this occasion. After paeans to the founders of the American republic, and calls for the religious liberty of all Americans to be respected, Rigdon recounted the many persecutions the Saints had suffered in the eight years since the church's founding. Church leaders knew that what had happened in Jackson County and Clay County could occur in Daviess, Carroll, or even Caldwell County. Rigdon announced to any would-be persecutors that "from this hour, we will bear it no more, our rights shall no more be trampled on with impunity." The Saints would never leave their homes again. "That mob that comes on us to disturb us," Rigdon threatened, "it shall be between us and them a war of extermination." It was a Mormon declaration of independence from mob rule.[15]

Joseph heartily approved of Rigdon's fiery talk. According to Ebenezer Robinson, who worked as a church clerk and editor, the prophet followed "with the shout of Hosanna, Hosanna, Hosanna." He encouraged church members to purchase a pamphlet of the address.[16]

For the July 4 celebration, church members had chopped down the largest tree they could find and erected it as a liberty pole. The Stars and Stripes fluttered in the wind as thousands of Saints listened to Rigdon denounce mobs. Several days later, the liberty pole was shattered by a lightning bolt during a thunderstorm. It seemed an ominous sign.[17]

Over the summer, scores of Mormon emigrants from Kirtland and elsewhere arrived in Missouri. One company of Canadian Saints reached Diahman in late July, and apostles Orson Hyde and Heber Kimball returned from England with news that they had baptized more than a thousand people. Many English converts began making plans to emigrate. By the fall, there were by rough estimates between eight and ten thousand church members in western Missouri.[18]

Joseph spent much of July in Diahman, where he organized a branch of the Danites. William Swartzell, who was initiated into the group, recorded a description of the proceedings in his diary, a portion of which he published after he left the church. About fifty new recruits came to the meeting, held in a grove near Lyman Wight's house. Wight presided. He was a "rough looking man [who] had his sleeves rolled up and [went] about bare headed." On this occasion, he wielded a cowhide strap with a pound of lead at the end. Wight recommended the weapon to all Danites. Joseph preached, providing instruction on what it meant for a church member to be *"a man of God, and a son of Thunder."* Then Wight asked each recruit to swear an oath that he would never betray the secrets of the organization at pain of death. Swartzell and the other new Danites also learned a sign—a clap of the right hand to the right thigh, then raised to the right temple—that they could use to signal distress to each other.[19]

The wave of Mormon emigrants coincided with Missouri's election season. The new arrivals weren't eligible to vote, but church members who had been in the state for at least a year were. There were few non-Mormon settlers in Caldwell County, so Mormon control of the county's politics was relatively uncontroversial. In other places, and in statewide politics, the increasing number of Saints stoked tension, in part because they were expected to vote as a bloc.

As early as May, Missouri politicians began paying calls on Mormon leaders. A few days after a Whig candidate for Congress visited and spoke in Far West, Sidney Rigdon bluntly reminded the Saints that "the politics of this Church (with but few exceptions only) are that of Democracy [the Democratic Party]." In Joseph's presence, Rigdon added that "all of the first presidency" agreed. The church's forthright proclamation of its political stance did not stop other Whig candidates from attempting to secure a Mormon endorsement. Church members comprised around one-third of Daviess County's eligible voters, meaning that they likely held the balance of power. According to Rigdon, "all the candidates" in Daviess County made "proposals" to Lyman Wight, believing that he could deliver Mormon votes. Among them was William Peniston, another Whig candidate for the House. Wight flatly turned him down because Peniston had supported earlier efforts to expel the Saints from the county.[20]

Men went to polling places across the state on August 6. Joseph was in Far West, where voting proceeded calmly. The next morning, however, the prophet received word that two or three church members had been killed in Gallatin, the Daviess County seat. The attackers had not allowed the Mormons to retrieve their fallen brethren, whose corpses remained on the ground. Joseph joined a company of men who rushed to Diahman. At its head were the Danite officers Elias Higbee, Sampson Avard, and George Robinson. When they reached Lyman Wight's house, they gained a more accurate sense of what had transpired. In Gallatin, Peniston had climbed atop a barrel and denounced the Mormons, jawing that they had no "more right to vote than the n[——]s." Fighting words led to a fight. A drunk anti-Mormon struck one of the Saints. Church member John Lowe Butler recalled the covenants he had made the previous summer, which he thought obliged him to defend his fellow Danites. Butler grabbed a stick and commenced striking the anti-Mormons. "They fell as dead men," he recounted. No one died, but there were cracked skulls and other serious injuries on both sides. Even with some of the Saints unable to vote, Peniston lost his bid for a seat in Congress.[21]

What had taken place at Gallatin was not all that unusual by the standards of Jacksonian-era elections. Drunkenness, profane insults, and fisticuffs were common at or near polling places, and other religious divisions fueled political violence. Catholics and Protestants brawled on election days in cities like Philadelphia and New York, for instance. Democrats and Whigs on the frontier routinely tried to stop their opponents from voting. The difference in western Missouri was that the anti-Mormons knew that they might be able to expel their political opponents.

On the morning of August 8, well-armed Mormon representatives went to the house of Adam Black, a Daviess County justice of the peace who lived near Diahman. There were rumors that Black was supporting the organization of a mob that would attack and drive out the Diahman Saints. The Mormons who went to Black's house asked him to sign a statement promising that he would enforce the law. Black refused. He told them he was already bound by the law and his oath to do them justice.

Black's answer didn't satisfy the Mormon men. After a long and heated argument, they began leaving. Black warned them not to spread lies about him. "You mob, you black son of a bitch," a Mormon man responded, "shut your head, or I'll cut it off." Black ordered the men to get off his land.[22]

They did, but Joseph and a larger group of at least one hundred Mormons soon returned. Black asked Joseph to come inside and discuss matters with him directly. Joseph later stated that while he found Black "hostile in his feelings" toward the Saints, the ensuing conversation was cordial, with the exception of some "highly insulting language" employed by Mary Black, the judge's wife. In the end, Black refused to put his name to the document that the Saints had drafted, but he wrote his own statement, signed it, and gave it to Joseph. The next day, several sympathetic non-Mormon Daviess County figures came to Lyman Wight's house and entered into a "covenant of peace." Joseph returned to Far West thinking that he had defused the threat.[23]

It is difficult to understand why Joseph and other church leaders thought a statement signed by Black under such circumstances would be of any value. It wasn't. Black promptly signed an affidavit in which he alleged that "one hundred armed men called Mormons" had surrounded his house. It was the Mormons who had formed a mob, he asserted. Black explained that he had subscribed to the previous declaration only in order to avoid "instant death." He called on the Daviess County militia and the militia of adjoining counties to disperse the Mormon mob and to "maintain the supremacy of the law." William Peniston, defeated at the polls, swore an affidavit alleging that the Mormons had threatened to kill him as well. Circuit court judge Austin King issued a warrant for the arrest of Joseph and Lyman Wight. Both refused to accompany a sheriff who came to take them into custody. The prophet insisted on being tried in Caldwell County as he didn't think he could get a fair hearing in Daviess County. A legal standoff ensued.[24]

Joseph and the Saints found themselves in a familiar dilemma. When church members prepared to defend themselves, or when they responded to provocations, their opponents used it as evidence of a growing Mormon threat. Anti-Mormon vigilantes now gathered in Daviess County to harass the Saints, and citizens in Daviess, Carroll, and other counties formed committees demanding that church members abandon their settlements. These dynamics had played out in Jackson County and then again in Clay County, ending with the Saints' expulsion both times. Joseph understood that if the Saints fought back, opposition to them would increase. On the other hand, if they eschewed violence, there was no guarantee that forbearance would bring peace.

"This looks a little too much like mobocracy," wrote George W. Robinson, Joseph's scribe and a Danite officer. "It foretells some evil intentions, the whole upper Missouri is all in an uproar and confusion." Concerned about the potential for violence in several counties, and also in response to reports of "Indian disturbances," Governor Lilburn Boggs ordered several militia officers to raise nearly three thousand "mounted men armed" to quell any unrest.[25]

On September 4, Major General David Atchison, head of the state militia's third division, came to Far West. Atchison brought with him Alexander Doniphan, an officer under his command. Atchison and Doniphan shared a law office in Liberty, and church leaders were already acquainted with both men. The pair had worked to shepherd the bill creating Caldwell County through the state legislature, and Doniphan had represented the Saints during their expulsion from Jackson County. Church leaders now retained the two lawyers to assist them in the present crisis. Atchison promised to "do all in his power to disperse the mob." He started by brokering a legal compromise. Joseph and Lyman Wight would attend a hearing before Austin King in Daviess County, but just over the Caldwell County line. Even so, the Saints were nervous. Church leaders placed "an army of men" on the Caldwell side of the line.[26]

The hearing was anticlimactic. Judge King held that there was sufficient evidence that the two men had threatened Adam Black and ordered them to post bond that they would appear before a Daviess County circuit court in early November.

The legal process did not defuse the tension between the Saints and their neighbors. On September 9, a Caldwell County militia company intercepted a shipment of Jäger rifles intended for the Daviess County mob. Captain William Allred impounded the arms and ammunition and apprehended the three men who were transporting them. Around the same time, anti-Mormons seized two church members in Daviess County, and officials there complained that other Mormon men involved in the Adam Black incident were resisting arrest. Doniphan and his troops persuaded both the Saints at Diahman and their opponents to stand down.[27]

Meanwhile, there was violence between the Saints and anti-Mormons in Carroll County. Back in June, Joseph had ordered John Murdock—the biological father of the prophet's adopted daughter, Julia—to purchase half of the township of De Witt, and Mormon immigrants continued to settle there throughout the summer and early fall. Beginning in early July, anti-Mormon citizens held a series of meetings in Carrollton, the county seat. They issued demands that the Mormons leave. When General Doniphan dispersed the mob in Daviess County, many of its members went straight to Carroll County and joined anti-Mormon forces gathering a few miles outside of De Witt. On September 22, Mormon settlers at De Witt signed a letter to Governor Boggs. They stated that the mob, now upwards of one hundred armed men, had given them until October 1 to leave the county and "if not gone by that time, to exterminate them, without regard to age or sex, and destroy their chattels, by throwing them in the river." The Saints begged Boggs to put down the mob. The governor, commander in chief of the state militia, sent no response.[28]

There were skirmishes after the deadline passed. "The mob," wrote John Murdock, "continued to harass us day and night by shooting at our people in the woods, in cornfields, in town, and into our camps." The Saints fired back. They also pleaded with state militia officers to restore peace. General Atchison dispatched a brigade commanded by Major General Hiram Parks to De Witt. A committee from Howard County sought to broker peace. Its members secured an offer from non-Mormon leaders in Carroll County. If the Saints would vacate the county, they would receive 10 percent above fair value for their property. Church leaders refused.[29]

On October 6, Joseph and General Parks both arrived at what threatened to become a field of battle. Along with the prophet came sev-

Lilburn W. Boggs, ca. 1830s. (Courtesy of State Historical
Society of Missouri)

eral dozen reinforcements from Far West and Diahman. They were
ready to fight. Parks's militia troops, by contrast, were not, or at least not
to protect the Mormons. Parks found that the bulk of his men favored
the mob. "I can do nothing but negotiate between the parties," Parks lamented to Atchison.[30]

Militia officers and church leaders appealed to Governor Boggs. "If
one of the [non-Mormon] citizens of Carroll should be killed," another
state militia general informed the governor, "before five days I believe
there will be from four to five thousand volunteers in the field against
the Mormons, and nothing but their blood will satisfy them." According
to an incredulous St. Louis newspaper report, Boggs "could see no cause
to interpose, thus leaving the parties to fight it out!" A messenger dispatched to the governor confirmed that Boggs would not act.[31]

No journal entries, letters, or other sources reveal Joseph's thoughts
during the standoff. Joseph had vowed that the Saints would not suffer
another expulsion from their homes. He had seconded Sidney Rigdon's

vow to wage a war of extermination against any mob that molested them. He had supported a crackdown on internal dissent and had presided over the formation of a semi-secret militia force. He had sought assistance from state officials. Now there were only two options: retreat from De Witt or fight a war against impossible odds. Church leaders in Missouri had made similarly tough choices in Joseph's absence earlier in the decade. This time, the prophet was in the field, and it was his choice.

Joseph chose to abandon De Witt and agreed to the previously offered terms. On October 11, several hundred Mormon settlers began a multiday, seventy-mile trek to Far West. The Saints never received compensation for their property.[32]

The retreat emboldened the Saints' enemies, many of whom now went to Daviess County. If the Mormons would abandon De Witt, why should anyone expect them to fight to defend Diahman, or even Far West? For the Saints, however, there was a difference. As church member Albert P. Rockwood noted, "De Witt was not an appointed stake of Zion." Adam-ondi-Ahman was, and Joseph had imbued it with sacred, biblical significance. It could not be so readily discarded.[33]

Joseph gave every indication that his people would fight for Diahman. On Sunday, October 14, he preached a war sermon, taking as his text the words of Jesus from the Gospel of John: "Greater love hath no man than this, that a man lay down his life for his friends." Joseph told the congregation of his "determination to put down the mob or die in the attempt." According to church member Warren Foote, Joseph warned that "those who would not turn out to help to suppress the mob should have their property taken to support those who would." At sermon's end, Joseph ordered those who were willing to fight to assemble the next day.[34]

On Monday morning hundreds of men greeted the prophet. He reminded them that the Saints had beseeched Governor Boggs, county officials, and militia officers for help, all to no avail. "All are mob," Joseph declared. "The governor is mob, the militia is mob, and the whole state is mob." It was time for church members to take matters into their own hands. "We have yielded to the mob in De Witt," Joseph explained, "but I am determined that we will not give another foot." The prophet had concluded that persecution was worse than fighting. He and several hundred Mormon men marched to Diahman to take the fight to their enemies.[35]

On October 18, David Patten, Lyman Wight, and Seymour Brunson led raids on the Daviess County communities of Gallatin, Millport, and Grindstone Fork. As non-Mormons fled before them, the Latter-day Saint vigilantes pillaged stores and burned homes and other buildings. A Mormon mob even captured a cannon that their opponents had buried near Gallatin. The Saints brought it and other plunder, including some cattle from Grindstone Fork, back to Diahman. Most non-Mormons fled the county, but some fought back and burned outlying Latter-day Saint homes. In the end, though, it was a rout. "We have driven most of the enemy out of the county," John Smith noted in his diary. Judge Austin King seconded this assessment in a letter to Governor Boggs. "At this time there is not a citizen in Daviess except Mormons," he wrote. What was Joseph's role in the vigilante operations? According to the later testimony of Latter-day Saint militia officer George Hinkle, "Neither of the Mr. Smiths [Joseph or Hyrum] seem to have [had] any command as officers in the field, but seemed to give general directions."[36]

When he returned to Far West, Joseph learned that apostles Thomas Marsh and Orson Hyde had abandoned the church. Marsh in particular had been a stalwart support of Joseph, but recent events had changed his mind. The apostate apostles went to Richmond, in Ray County, where Marsh signed an affidavit that detailed and decried the recent raids on non-Mormon settlements. He also asserted that there was a "company of . . . true Mormons, called the Danites, who have taken an oath to support the heads of the Church in all things." Some of Marsh's charges reflected either the wild talk of church leaders at the time or his own hyperbole. Marsh alleged that church leaders had appointed a "destruction company" prepared to raze the towns of Liberty and Richmond. He went so far as to suggest that Joseph's overarching plan was "to take the state . . . the U.S., and ultimately the whole world." Joseph would become an American Mohammad and "make it one gore of blood from the Rocky Mountains to the Atlantic Ocean." Missourians had two choices: "Jo Smith or the sword." They could permit Joseph to expand his prophetic kingdom in their midst or they could fight him in battle.[37]

One escalation led to another. Fearing additional attacks, non-Mormons in the areas surrounding Caldwell County stepped up their surveillance and harassment. Samuel Bogart, a Methodist minister and captain in the Ray County militia, obtained permission to "range" the county line and prevent a Mormon "invasion." Bogart ranged very aggressively. His men harassed church members who lived in the southernmost part of Caldwell County, destroyed property, and seized three Latter-day Saint men as captives. At least one of the Mormon prisoners belonged to a "spy company" that had patrolled into Ray County.[38]

News of the captives reached Far West on the evening of October 24. Around midnight, church leaders resolved to attack Bogart's company and free their brethren. Apostle David Patten—known as "Captain Fearnaught" —commanded a company of roughly sixty men who rode south from Far West and crossed the county line. At daybreak, they found their enemies, who were well positioned near the banks of Crooked River. Shots rang out, and Patten realized that his exposed men would prevail only if they charged forward. The strategy worked, but at a great cost. As Bogart and his men retreated, however, they inflicted heavy casualties on their attackers. One Mormon died in the battle, as did one non-Mormon. Two of the Mormon prisoners had managed to flee when firing commenced. The other captive was wounded by gunfire, as were eight other Saints, including Patten.[39]

Joseph and several other church leaders met Patten six miles south of a settlement at Log Creek. The prophet laid his hands on Patten and prayed for healing. With the wounded men, they continued on to another church member's home, where Patten's wife joined the group. "Ann, don't weep," the apostle told her. "I have kept the faith and my work is done." Patten then succumbed to his injuries, as did one of the other wounded men.[40]

The news grew even grimmer. A church member named Jacob Hawn owned a mill on the banks of Shoal Creek in eastern Caldwell County. About fifty Latter-day Saints lived in the immediate vicinity, and the settlement became known as Hawn's Mill. Good relations with nearby non-Mormons turned sour after the outbreaks of violence in other parts of western Missouri. Bolstered by refugees from Daviess County, mobs in southwestern Livingston County (to the east of Caldwell County) rode into the settlement and confiscated weapons. Meanwhile, some Mormon families on their way to Far West stopped and took shelter at Hawn's Mill, whose population swelled in late October.[41]

On October 30, two or three hundred vigilantes, led by erstwhile Livingston County militia officer Thomas Jennings, gathered themselves into three companies and rode for Hawn's Mill. The Saints there recently had engaged in negotiations with their non-Mormon counterparts, so they weren't expecting an attack. Women and children fled into the woods, in some cases narrowly escaping gunfire. One woman, Mary

Stedwell, was shot in the hand when she raised her arms to surrender. Nearly three dozen men and boys took shelter in the blacksmith shop.

It was an indefensible position. The Mormon men were badly outnumbered, and their enemies could shoot bullets through the shop's windows and the cracks between its log walls. A number of men fled. Some made it, while others were shot down. Sixty-two-year-old Thomas McBride was wounded during his escape attempt, then captured by the vigilantes. A man from Daviess County shot McBride in the chest after he surrendered and then used a corn cutter to mutilate his dying body. When the mob finally breached the shop, they stripped wounded men of their clothing and left them to die.[42]

The vigilantes also discovered several boys cowering inside. Nine-year-old Charles Merrick ran outside, and the mob shot him. Merrick died a month later. Sardius Smith (no relation to Joseph), ten years of age, didn't try to flee. Instead, he begged for his life. The mob had already killed his father and wounded a brother. One of the raiders pointed his gun at the lad, fired, and blew off a portion of his head. Some of his fellow vigilantes objected. "Damn the difference!" another responded. "Nits make lice!" Some white Americans had used the same phrase to justify the execution of Native children.[43]

A macabre and doleful evening ensued after the vigilantes left. Seventeen Saints were dead. "It was sunset," wrote Amanda Smith. "The dogs were filled with rage howling over their dead masters; the cattle caught the scent of innocent blood and bellowed." Once they felt it safe to emerge from hiding, women tended to the wounded and wondered what to do with the corpses. It would take a long time to bury the dead, and the assailants might return. The survivors filled a nearby well with the bodies of their loved ones. Amanda Smith and one of her other sons placed Sardius Smith's bloodied and mutilated corpse in the well and then covered it with dirt and straw.[44]

Meanwhile, the Saints in Far West stared down their own annihilation. Governor Boggs responded to reports of outrages in Daviess County by concluding that the Mormons "had made war upon the people of this state." He ordered Major General John B. Clark and several other state militia commanders to raise volunteers, rendezvous, and await further instructions. "The Mormons must be treated as enemies," Boggs declared, "and must be exterminated or driven from the State." Boggs's directive had not reached the perpetrators of the Hawn's Mill Massacre prior to their decision to attack the settlement, but men in many western Missouri counties now joined militia units and prepared for war.[45]

Militia generals Atchison, Lucas, and Doniphan marched their men to Far West. Even after Mormon reinforcements from Diahman rushed south, there were only a few hundred Saints under arms to oppose thousands of militia troops. As his troops neared Far West, Atchison received word that Boggs had appointed General Clark as the overall commander of the militia operation. The governor likely made the decision because he doubted that Atchison would take a firm anti-Mormon stance. Atchison retired from the field, believing that he had been in effect dismissed, while Lucas decided to take charge until Clark arrived. Lucas was from Jackson County and had played a role in the negotiations that led to the expulsion of the Saints in 1833. Regardless of who commanded them, there was a thin line between a Missouri militia company and a mob. If Lucas attacked Far West, there would be a bloodbath.[46]

Joseph again had to choose whether his people would fight or back down. By this point, the prophet probably knew that capitulation would mean the complete abandonment of Mormon Missouri. He at first expressed resolve. Joseph assembled the Mormon militia on Far West's public square. If the mob came, he vowed, "we will play hell with their apple carts." They were outnumbered, but angels would fight alongside them. The Saints spent the night erecting breastworks around the city.[47]

The next day, October 31, Joseph's resolve melted. He sent a delegation to "beg like a dog for peace." According to John Corrill, the prophet's calculus was simple. He didn't want his people slaughtered. Colonel George W. Hinkle, commander of the Caldwell County militia, led the Mormon delegation. Hinkle was accompanied by Corrill and Reed Peck, and William W. Phelps and Arthur Morrison later joined the negotiation. The men held military or civic offices in Caldwell County, but they also had objected to elements of Joseph's recent leadership, including the Daviess County raids and the Danite society.

General Lucas showed the Mormon representatives Boggs's "extermination order." Then Lucas dictated harsh terms. Joseph and several other top church leaders had to give themselves up to be tried and punished. The rest of the Mormons would surrender, give up their arms, and prepare to leave Missouri. Hinkle asked to have the night to respond. Lucas agreed, but with a caveat. The Saints could consider the terms overnight only if Joseph, Sidney Rigdon, Lyman Wight, Parley P. Pratt, and George Robinson delivered themselves "as hostages." If the Saints rejected the terms the next morning, Lucas promised to return the hostages prior to an attack.[48]

As Hinkle brought copies of Boggs's order and Lucas's terms back to Far West, Lucas told his troops to get ready. If the Mormon leaders did not turn themselves in, they would attack before sunset. Joseph made that contingency unnecessary. He and the other "hostages" presented themselves. The next day, Hinkle accepted Lucas's terms, and the Saints surrendered their arms.

Joseph subsequently alleged that Hinkle was a "traitor" and had "decoyed us unawares." The prophet had expected a conference with Lucas, not his arrest. Hinkle, Reed Peck, and John Corrill, by contrast, all insisted that Joseph understood the situation and voluntarily made himself Lucas's prisoner. "Smith himself was the first man that agreed to the proposals," Corrill wrote. Hinkle stated that, the morning after his arrest, Joseph himself sent word instructing the Saints at Far West to surrender. Diahman and other communities soon followed suit.[49]

Regardless, Joseph didn't expect the treatment he and his fellow prisoners received. The prophet asked Lucas for permission to spend a final night with his family. The general refused. Joseph and the others were marched to Lucas's camp, serenaded by the "hideous yells" of their enemies. They spent the night lying on the ground during a dismal rain. The next day, after the Saints surrendered, Lucas marched his prisoners—who now also included Hyrum Smith and Amasa Lyman—back to Far West.[50]

That night Lucas organized a court-martial, at which the seven prisoners were tried in absentia and sentenced to be shot. The trial was a sham, because Joseph and several of the other prisoners held no military office. Lucas intended to have the condemned prisoners brought into Far West's public square early the next morning and executed. Doniphan told Lucas his proceedings were illegal, not to mention extremely brazen, prior to General Clark's arrival. He also visited the prisoners. "By God you have been sentenced to be shot this morning," Hyrum Smith recalled Doniphan's words, "but I will be damned if I will have any of the honor of it or any of the disgrace." Then he marched his men out of Far West. Doniphan's protest halted the planned executions. Looking to save face and avoid punishment, Lucas later denied that he had tried the prisoners by a court-martial, let alone intended to execute them.[51]

It was a reprieve, not a release. Lucas allowed each of the men to collect a few belongings from their homes. Emma was relieved to see Joseph alive but was not allowed a private moment with her husband.

One of the militia troops thrust Joseph III away from his father. "God damn you," he shouted at the boy. "You get away you little rascal or I will run you through." Lucas had decided to send the prisoners to his headquarters in Independence. He had them bundled into a wagon with the covers tied down. Lucy Mack Smith rushed to the scene in an attempt to bid her sons farewell. The soldiers wouldn't allow her to see them, but Joseph and Hyrum reached their hands out for her to hold. A cry was raised, and horses pulled the wagon away. The prophet finally was going back to Zion, but not as its redeemer.[52]

CHAPTER TWENTY

Hell Surrounded with
Demons (1839)

As JOSEPH AND THE other prisoners were transported to Independence, Mormon settlements became scenes of chaos and violence. Militiamen-turned-vigilantes plundered homes, shot animals, and harassed and assaulted now-defenseless men. William Carey, a recent emigrant from Ohio, had his skull split open when a soldier landed "a full blow with the breech of his gun upon his head." Hannah Johnston, raped by a soldier after the surrender at Far West, delivered a baby girl the following summer. Both she and the child died soon after the birth.[1]

"What outrages may be committed by the mob I know not," Joseph wrote Emma, "but expect there will be but little or no restraint." The prediction was correct. Whether or not he had duped the prophet into surrendering, George Hinkle took advantage of Joseph's arrest for his personal gain. Joseph had purchased a house from Hinkle the previous spring. According to Emma Smith, Hinkle now entered the home and "used coercive measures to drive" her and her family from the premises. He then stole clothing, furniture, and a horse. Former apostle William McLellin also picked over the prophet's property, taking everything from buttons to Hebrew books. Joseph agonized over his inability to protect his family.[2]

In contrast to those he had left behind, Joseph was treated well once he left Far West. In the custody of Brigadier General Moses Wilson, the prisoners reached Independence on November 4, 1838. "We have been protected by the Jackson County boys," he wrote Emma, "in the most genteel manner." Despite a heavy rain, hundreds turned out to see the captured prophet. General Wilson permitted the prisoners to secure lodging at an inn and stroll about without a guard. They walked to the temple lot just west of Independence, the spot Joseph had identified by revelation back in 1831. William Collins, a non-Mormon resident of Independence, accompanied them, saying he "presumed the place did not look as it would had [they] been permitted to have remained in this country." General Wilson invited the prisoners to dinner the next evening, and he promised that if they remained in Independence for an extended period of time, they would be allowed to send for their families.[3]

The genteel treatment soon ended. General Clark sent orders taking custody of the prisoners and ordering their transport to Richmond in Ray County. They reached Richmond on November 9. General Clark had arrived earlier in the day. He ordered Joseph and the other six men placed in an old log house under close watch. There would be no more comfortable beds, let alone walks about town or fine dinners.

The next morning, General Clark appeared before Joseph and his companions. He tersely informed them that they would be charged with treason, murder, and other crimes. Clark then had the seven prisoners chained together by their legs. "We are bound together in chains as well as the cords of everlasting love," Joseph wrote Emma. Like Samuel Lucas, Clark wanted to try the prisoners, especially Joseph, by a military tribunal, but both his superiors and Missouri state officials advised against the idea. Instead, Judge Austin King convened a court of inquiry. King's task was to determine whether there was probable cause that the accused had committed the crimes in question. If so, they would be bound over to stand trial.[4]

Back in early September, King had presided over the hearing at which Joseph answered charges that he had threatened Adam Black. At the time, Judge King exhibited no particular animus against Joseph or his church. "Until lately I thought the Mormons were disposed to act on the defensive," he explained to Governor Boggs in late October. The offensive in Daviess County and the Battle of Crooked River changed his mind. "They are the aggressors," he asserted. "They intend to take the law into their hands." Now Joseph's liberty rested in King's hands.[5]

Clark arrested dozens of additional Mormon men in early November, and King called a parade of witnesses to provide evidence. Many were former members of the church: John Whitmer, the Book of Mormon witness excommunicated the previous spring; William W. Phelps, who had worked with Joseph on the Egyptian papyri; George M. Hinkle, who had commanded the Caldwell County militia until the surrender of Far West; and Sampson Avard, the Danite general.[6]

Avard, who had stood with Joseph and watched the erection of bulwarks around Far West, testified that Joseph had been the "prime mover and organizer" of a secret society bent not only on the expulsion of dissenting church members, but on the very destruction of the United States. Joseph had instructed his underlings to pillage non-Mormon homes and stores in Daviess County, and he had presided over the dispersal of the resulting booty. Avard produced a copy of the Danite constitution, and also the threatening letter to the dissenters that Sidney Rigdon had written back in June.[7]

Joseph denounced the hearing as a "mock examination."[8] There were dozens of defendants, and it wasn't clear at the outset which church members were charged with which crimes. The defendants weren't present for at least most of the testimony against them. Their lawyers apparently did not have the opportunity to cross-examine all of the state's witnesses, and they had difficulty bringing their own witnesses to Richmond.

At the inquiry's conclusion, Judge King ruled that there was sufficient reason to believe that Joseph, Hyrum, Lyman Wight, Sidney Rigdon, Alexander McRae, and Caleb Baldwin had committed treason. Defendants awaiting trial on charges of treason could not post bail, so King remanded them to the Clay County jail in Liberty. King also concluded that five other church members, including apostle Parley Pratt, should stand trial on charges of murder connected to the Battle of Crooked River. They stayed in the Ray County jail in Richmond. The judge ruled that twenty-four other defendants should face trial on charges such as arson and burglary, though he granted them bail. King dismissed charges against nearly thirty other men.

Joseph and his five co-defendants were placed in a wagon and transported to Liberty, which they reached on December 1. They traveled under the guard of Captain Samuel Bogart, whose troops had been scattered in the Crooked River battle and who considered the Saints "the most odious set of fanatics that ever disgraced God almighty." When the prisoners reached their destination, they walked down a flight of stairs and through a pair of "screeching iron doors." The jail was a forbidding structure, with four-foot walls constructed of limestone, loose rock, and oak. Joseph wrote a hasty note to Emma, reassuring her that they were "all in good spirits." Captain Bogart delivered the message.[9]

Joseph described Liberty Jail as a "hell surrounded with demons." The jailer and other guards occupied the upper floor, where the prisoners sometimes spent their days. A trapdoor led to the "dungeon," where they slept. Two tiny windows provided the only glimmers of natural light. Townspeople banged on the doors and mocked them through the windows. If the prisoners kept warm with a fire, they choked on the smoke that filled the room. They rested on filthy and decaying straw mattresses. They were given scraps of bread and meat, placed in a basket in which chickens had roosted. The guards told them that the meat was human flesh, which they called "Mormon beef." The prisoners drank the dregs of coffee and tea and suspected that the guards had mixed poison into the drinks. "It vomited us almost to death," Hyrum recounted. The days stretched into weeks. The hunger, cold, and abuse weakened their bodies and sapped their will.[10]

The prisoners weren't alone in their suffering. After Joseph's capitulation, the Daviess County Saints had relocated to Caldwell County, where most church members spent a bleak winter. Many families had abandoned their harvests and now went hungry. Refugees crowded into homes and cabins; others slept in tents, wagon boxes, and makeshift huts. Lucy Mack Smith recalled that the land in front of her house was "covered with beds laying in the open sun where men, women, and children were compelled to sleep in all weather." Vigilantes ranged the area and harassed those Saints who attempted to retrieve crops and other belongings from their properties.[11]

In the midst of these trials, the church faced a leadership vacuum. Joseph and his counselors in the church's First Presidency—Sidney Rigdon and Hyrum Smith—were in jail. A majority of the Quorum of the Twelve Apostles were excommunicated, disaffected, or dead. Bishop Edward Partridge for years had managed many of the church's property and business transactions in Missouri. Now, like many other Saints, he felt compelled to place his family's needs above church affairs.

Some church members wrestled with ongoing questions about Joseph's leadership. The year 1838 had begun with the collapse of Mormon Kirtland. It ended with the worst disaster in the church's short history. There had been violence during the expulsion of the Mormons in Jackson County, but nothing on this scale. The Saints blamed their enemies, but especially after the defection of high-ranking and long-trusted

Liberty Jail, ca. 1878. (Courtesy of Church History Library)

church leaders, many church members wondered whether Joseph had led them astray. At a mid-December church meeting in Far West men stood up to declare that Joseph was "not a fallen prophet." Some endorsements were less than ringing. Simeon Carter, a member of the Missouri High Council, "thought perhaps Joseph had not acted in all things according to the best wisdom yet how far he had been unwise he could not say." It is telling that those present felt the discussion was necessary.[12]

In January 1839, Joseph informed Brigham Young and his fellow apostle Heber C. Kimball that "the management of the affairs of the church devolves on you that is the Twelve." For the moment, there was no grand plan for the future. "The gathering of necessity [is] stopped," Joseph conceded. He instructed Young and Kimball to ordain replacements for those apostles who had fallen away or died. Given Thomas Marsh's defection, Joseph told them that the oldest of the original apostles should now preside over the quorum. That guidance elevated Young, who was thirteen days older than Kimball.[13]

Young and Kimball quickly took charge. They organized a removal committee to oversee the church's exodus from Missouri, and hundreds of Saints covenanted to "never desert the poor . . . till they shall be out of the reach of the exterminating order."[14] Church leaders sold land for a fraction of its value, including properties in Jackson County. Although the agreements reached with militia generals permitted the Saints to remain until the spring, most chose to leave in the dead of winter because of the scarcity of food and fuel and because of ongoing harassment by mobs. Beginning in January, families headed east toward the Illinois border, usually traveling in small groups.

It was a Mormon trail of tears, and a trail of frostbite and blood as well. The Saints slept on the prairie in tents made from blankets, which provided little shelter from the elements. Church leaders later stated that "women and children marked their footsteps on the frozen ground with blood," as ice lacerated bare or poorly protected feet. A thousand church members were underway in February, including Emma and the children, followed by Joseph Sr. and Lucy Mack Smith. It took most families around two weeks to reach the banks of the Mississippi River. After crossing by ice or by ferry, they found refuge in and around Quincy, Illinois. Joseph Smith III remembered walking across the frozen river. He and his sister Julia held their mother's dress on either side, while Emma carried Frederick and Alexander in her arms.[15]

Joseph and his five fellow prisoners chafed at their continued separation from their families and fellow Saints, not to mention the prospect of execution should a court convict them of treason. In late January, the prisoners sent a habeas corpus petition to the Clay County court, asking Judge Joel Turnham to rule on the legality of their incarceration. At the hearing's conclusion, Turnham granted bail to Sidney Rigdon, who hadn't been in Daviess County during the Mormon offensive, but he sent the others back to jail. Warned that the mob would kill him upon his release, Rigdon endured another ten days in jail, then slipped away at night with the sheriff's assistance.[16]

The prisoners now tried extralegal means to gain their freedom. On February 7, while receiving several visitors and their supper in the jail's upper room, they made a break for it. Hyrum Smith grabbed Samuel Tillery, the deputy jailer, shoved him aside, and he and the others made to burst through the doors. Tillery shouted at the guards to shoot the prisoners if they tried to run, which induced them to stop.[17]

Foiled once, they tried a second time the next month. Friends passed augers and an iron bar through the windows, and they started boring through the walls of their dungeon. It was risky. According to Hyrum, the guards included "a few religious bigots ... willing to shoot us." By

March 4 they were ready to breach the jail's outer stone wall. "We expect to make our escape without fail," Lyman Wight wrote in his diary. The plan miscarried when a friend on the outside developed loose lips. Incensed townspeople volunteered to guard the jail "till it was mended," and the prisoners were now watched "day and night." Still, they didn't fully give up on the plan. On March 17, the jailer discovered an auger handle during an inspection of the dungeon. The jailer left, returned with twenty-five men, had them search the room thoroughly, and threatened to put Joseph and the others "in chains." The guards became less accommodating when visitors came to the jail.[18]

While awaiting his legal fate, Joseph wrote and dictated letters. He hadn't seen Emma since January and urged her to send news of his children. "Tell me all you can and even if Old Major is alive yet," Joseph pleaded, referring to his beloved dog. As for his own welfare, he confided to Emma that he was worn down. "My nerve trembles from long confinement," Joseph excused his handwriting, even worse than usual. He could barely hold the pen.[19]

In long letters that Joseph dictated to the church as a whole, though, he was both reflective and resolute. He had questions for God. "O God, where art thou?" How long would God permit the Saints to "suffer these wrongs and unlawful oppressions" before his heart softened? He explained that letters from Emma, Don Carlos Smith (Joseph's brother), and Bishop Partridge had refreshed his spirit. Through them, God answered his pleas. "My son," he heard. "Peace be unto your soul. Thine adversity and thy afflictions shall be but a small moment." Yes, he and his fellow prisoners had suffered, and the other Missouri Saints had endured bitter persecutions. But their persecutors wouldn't succeed. "Hell may pour forth its rage like the burning lava," he vowed, "and yet shall Mormonism stand . . . God is the author of it." God's truth would prevail over thick walls, iron doors, and demonic guards.[20]

Joseph denounced mobs, Governor Boggs, the Missouri legislature, and even his own attorneys, but he reaffirmed his faith in the United States and its constitution. "It is a heavenly banner," Joseph wrote, "to all those who are privileged with the sweets of liberty." Again and again, Missourians had deprived the Saints of their liberty, but Joseph expected his people to find fair treatment from other Americans.[21]

In early April 1839, Joseph and his fellow prisoners were transported to Gallatin in Daviess County, where a grand jury would choose whether to indict them on charges of treason, riot, and other crimes. "This night," he wrote Emma on the eve of their departure, "is the last night we shall try our weary joints and bones on our dirty straw couches in these walls."[22] Two days later, they arrived in Gallatin, where six months previously Mormon troops under the command of Lyman Wight—one of the defendants—had ransacked stores and burned the courthouse. The prisoners stayed at a home a mile outside of town, which doubled as the courtroom during the day.

Irregularities abounded at the hearing. The presiding judge, Thomas Burch, had been the prosecuting attorney at the November 1838 preliminary hearing. Even more shockingly, several members of the impaneled grand jury had participated in the Hawn's Mill Massacre. Other jurors guarded the prisoners at night, and the defendants' lawyers slept in the same room as well. It was cramped, but the prisoners didn't mind. "Slept last night in a bed for the first time for five months," Hyrum noted.[23]

Joseph was the star of the show. Peter Burnett, one of the defense attorneys and later California's first elected governor, recalled that despite the prophet's stature, Joseph's "appearance was not prepossessing." Moreover, his "limited" education was readily apparent, and he was "awkward but vehement" in conversation. Even so, Burnett noted, "he was much more than an ordinary man," in part because he deemed himself "born to command," displayed a keen "native intellect," and was intensely sociable. Townspeople, curious to have their former antagonist among them, came and chatted with the defendants all day and late into the night. Soon the guards let Joseph outside to talk with the crowds who pressed for a word with him.[24]

Joseph's physical strength was intact. The guards heard that their most famous prisoner was a "skillful wrestler." They dared the prophet to accept a challenge from the best man in the county. Joseph demurred with the excuse that wrestling might not be appropriate for either a prisoner or a minister. The guards talked him into it with the promise that they wouldn't make it an occasion for gambling. But any illicit bets on the prophet paid off, as Joseph threw his opponent with ease.[25]

The criminal charges were harder to shake, and the atmosphere in the makeshift courtroom became tense when defense witnesses implicated some of those present in the murders at Hawn's Mill. How could they get a fair hearing before men who had shown such little regard for Mormon lives the previous fall? The outcome was never in doubt, though. The jury indicted the defendants on charges of treason, rioting, and arson. Judge Burch denied bail, but he granted a change of venue to Boone County because of his prior role as a prosecutor in the case.

The judge dispatched the five prisoners to Columbia (in Boone County) in the care of only five guards. They spent the first night in a Diahman cabin that Lyman Wight had built and that William Bowman, one of the guards, had appropriated after the Saints' expulsion. By now, Joseph and the others knew that despite their indictment on capital charges, they would soon be free. Judge Burch had told the guards to let the prisoners make their escape. While some citizens in western Missouri still wanted revenge against Mormon leaders, others—including Governor Boggs and Judge King—were satisfied with the fact that nearly all church members had left the state.[26]

The night of April 16, Sheriff William Morgan told the prisoners it was time. Joseph bribed the guards with a promissory note for $150 in exchange for two horses. The prisoners also bought their captors a jug of whiskey. "I shall take a good drink of grog and go to bed," Morgan told them, and the other guards did the same. Joseph, his brother, and the three others took their freedom.[27]

The escapees now shared in the suffering of the thousands of others who had made the exodus. With only two horses among five men, they had to walk most of the hundred miles to the Mississippi River. "I jumped into the mud," Joseph recalled several years later. "When I got to water . . . my boots [were] full of blood."[28] Eschewing well-traveled roads in order to avoid detection, they hurried on all the next day and late into the night.

On April 22, a "pale and haggard" man stepped ashore the banks of the Mississippi in Quincy. Dimick Huntington, sent by Emma to learn if there was any news from the west, scrutinized the newcomer's appearance. He was unshaven and wore "an old pair of boots full of holes," torn pants, a blue cloak with an upturned collar, and a wide-brimmed black hat with its rim "soaped down." When he got close to Huntington, the man raised his head. "My God is it you, Brother Joseph?" Huntington exclaimed. Joseph told him to hush. He wasn't sure whether he was out of legal danger. Joseph asked Huntington to take him to his family. When he reached Emma's temporary residence four miles outside of the city, she spotted him immediately and "met him halfway to the gate." Joseph embraced his wife and four children.[29]

It was just over a year since Joseph had arrived in Far West after his flight from Ohio. He and his fellow Saints had endured persecution in

New York, Ohio, and across western Missouri. County after Missouri county had expelled his people and threatened them with extermination. Anti-Mormon violence had cost several dozen men, women, and children their lives, and the loss of property imposed a staggering financial burden on the church and its members. Joseph's legal fees from the last half year alone amounted to around $50,000.[30]

Joseph would never forget the haunting scenes of Liberty Jail. At the same time, his suffering confirmed his sense of prophetic calling. Jesus had warned his disciples that they would endure persecution and be thrown into prison, and Paul and other early Christians had been put in chains. The Mormon prophet also compared himself to "Joseph of Egypt," who while in jail did not know whether his family still lived.[31]

Joseph emerged from prison unbowed, ready to throw his opponents the way he had thrown the best wrestler in Daviess County. Instead of abandoning the principle of gathering, he would build a bigger city. Scarred by the defeats in Kirtland and Missouri, he sought the power to protect himself and his church from future mobs.

Keys (1839–1840)

ENERAL JOHN B. CLARK advised church members after the surrender at Far West to "scatter abroad." They should not organize themselves "with bishops, presidents, etc. lest [they] excite the jealousies of the people." Out of necessity, the Saints had dispersed during the exodus, and Joseph had put the brakes on gathering to the west. These were only temporary concessions. Through Joseph's revelations, Jesus Christ had commanded the Saints to build Zion in preparation for his return. They would listen to Christ rather than Clark. By the time Joseph and his fellow prisoners made their escape, they had a new plan in place, one that the Mormon pursued with his customarily kinetic energy.[1]

The previous fall, a group of Saints fleeing Far West had veered to the north, crossed the Des Moines River, and ended up in the southeastern corner of the Iowa Territory near the town of Montrose. Several of their number, including Israel Barlow, learned that a land speculator and occasional physician named Isaac Galland held extensive claims in the area, known as the Half-Breed Tract (a parcel of land once set aside for Sac and Fox individuals of mixed descent). Galland had a roguish past. He divorced his first two wives and married a third before the second divorce was finalized. After some preliminary discussions with Barlow, Galland offered the church twenty thousand acres for $2 per acre, paid over twenty years without interest. Galland was also prepared to sell parcels of land across the river in Commerce, Illinois.[2]

Joseph was kept abreast of these developments while in Liberty Jail and urged church leaders in Quincy to make the deal. They hadn't done so by the time Joseph reached Quincy, so the prophet took matters into his own hands. Just a few days after his reunion with Emma and his children, Joseph headed north, met with Galland, and purchased several tracts of land, the start of a wave of acquisitions over the coming weeks and months.

By May 3, 1839, Joseph was back in Quincy. Wilford Woodruff, who that day saw Joseph for the first time in two years, reported that Emma Smith was "truly happy." So was Joseph. Woodruff found him "frank, open, and familiar as usual." Joseph presided over a general conference of the church, held at a Presbyterian camp-meeting ground two miles north of town. It was the first time in half a year that Joseph had addressed a large congregation. Only with difficulty could he overcome his emotions. The moment filled him with "peculiar feelings" and gratitude.[3]

The Saints at the conference rejoiced at the reunions they experienced in Quincy, and church leaders made plans to move north to Commerce and Montrose. But it was impossible to move ahead without looking back. The Saints planned to gather affidavits documenting their persecutions and to petition Congress and President Van Buren for redress. Andrew Jackson had ignored their plea for help in 1834. But this time was different, or should have been different. Their losses were on a grander scale. Thousands of Saints had been forced to abandon their property or sell at cut-rate prices. Newspapers across the country published articles about the slaughter at Hawn's Mill. Most other Americans sympathized with, or at least pitied, the Mormons. The conference resolved to send Rigdon to Washington as the church's delegate.[4]

Joseph left Quincy on May 9 with Emma and his children on the fifty-mile trip to Commerce. The family's goods included the Egyptian mummies and papyri, which somehow had survived the flight from Kirtland and the expulsion from Missouri.[5]

It was yet another new beginning. The prophet and his family moved into a "small log house" in Commerce that was part of the recent land purchases. Their new home was situated on a bend of the Mississippi River, a peninsula that consisted of marshy, shrubby flatland backed by seventy-foot bluffs to the east. The area had once been known as Quashquema, after a Sauk leader. As its Native inhabitants moved west of the Mississippi, the U.S. government appropriated the land for veterans of the War of 1812. Speculators bought out the ex-soldiers. The arrival of the Saints meant that those investments finally paid off. Mormon refugees quickly turned what had been a small village into a bustling town. Other church members purchased farms in outlying areas of Hancock County or across the river in Iowa.[6]

The Saints continued to acquire property over the course of the summer. In early July, Joseph crossed the river to examine a large parcel of land in the Half-Breed Tract that the church had recently purchased from Isaac Galland. Joseph also waded into the Mississippi to baptize Galland. In the end, however, Galland was more interested in profits than prophets. He also had a clear-eyed sense of what might unfold as the Saints built a new place of gathering. "[They] will probably continue to buy out the settlers," Galland wrote an acquaintance a few weeks after his baptism, "until they again acquire a sufficient quantity of '*honey comb*' to induce the surrounding thieves to rob them again." He predicted that the Saints would then "no doubt have to renounce their religion; or submit to a repetition of similar acts of violence, and outrage." The Mormons, after all, attracted hostility wherever they settled in large numbers.[7]

For now, any renewed hostility was in the future. The Saints streamed into the region. Most families initially slept in wagons or in tents, many in the yard out in front of Joseph and Emma's new house. Although circumstances remained rough, it was a big improvement from the past winter, and there was time to build homes that summer and fall.

As the Saints established new communities in Illinois and Iowa, Joseph prepared the Quorum of the Twelve Apostles for a long-planned mission to Europe. He presided over a late-June council that restored a contrite Orson Hyde—who had abandoned the church the previous fall—to his place among the Twelve. Then Joseph spent several days providing the apostles with theological instruction. He revealed what he called "keys to the kingdom of God," teachings that, if understood, unlocked spiritual power and authority. For instance, Joseph told the apostles how to distinguish between angels and devils. They should offer to shake hands. An angel, he told them, "is a Saint with his resurrected body," whereas Satan might appear in the guise of a man but lacked a physical body. "By observing this key," Joseph explained, "we may detect Satan." The advice pointed to the fact that the Saints lived in a world in which angels and Satan were very real to them. It also reflected Joseph's belief that angels and humans—and perhaps God and Jesus Christ—were the same sort of being, albeit at different stages of progression.[8]

Isaac Galland, ca. 1850. (Courtesy of Church History Library)

Mobs had stolen the Saints' property and treated them like vermin, but Joseph described an alternate, loftier reality. Church members were not "damned Mormons," as the Missourians had called them. Instead, the Saints had Israelite blood in their veins. Joseph meant it literally. When the Holy Ghost came upon a "Gentile" (a non-Jew) at his baptism into the church, the effect was "to purge out the old blood and make him actually of the seed of Abram." This spiritual blood transfusion often produced side effects, which explained why some church members experienced ecstasy and physical manifestations.[9]

Joseph promised the apostles even greater things should they remain faithful. They had received the "first comforter," the Holy Ghost. If they humbled themselves, their "calling and election" would be "made sure." They would receive a second "comforter," Jesus Christ himself. They would be blessed in the ways that Moses, Isaiah, and Paul were blessed. The Savior would teach them "face to face," reveal the Father to them, and show them "visions of the heavens." The spirit of revelation would come upon them like "pure intelligence."[10]

Joseph unlocked these and other mysteries because he "held the keys" of priesthood authority. Priesthood, he instructed, was a chain that extended back to Adam, who had received the "First Presidency" and the "keys" from God. There had been others, such as Noah, Moses, and then Jesus's disciples Peter, James, and John. Only one man or group of men held this authority at any given time. As Joseph explained in a history he worked on about this time, the latter three had then ordained Joseph and Oliver Cowdery to the Melchizedek priesthood in 1829. Now Joseph, his counselors in the First Presidency, and the apostles held the keys.

In the near future, Joseph taught, Adam would hold a council with his posterity and deliver up the "keys of the universe" to Jesus Christ. "Those men to whom these keys have been given will have to be there," Joseph explained. They and the most ancient earthly prophets were all connected, and they needed each other. "We cannot be made perfect without them," Joseph insisted, "nor they without us." The prophet, his counselors, and the apostles would return to Adam-ondi-Ahman and reign as priests and kings over a millennial earth.[11]

Promises of their millennial reign did not prevent the apostles from worrying about their precarious present. Who would provide for their families while they were abroad? What if the apostles were attacked or imprisoned during their mission? Joseph and his fellow counselors in the presidency—Hyrum Smith and Sidney Rigdon—laid their hands on the men and their wives and "sealed" blessings upon them. Joseph warned them not to betray the church despite any hardships, even to the point of death. But he also had words of comfort. "If we were faithful," Wilford Woodruff recorded, "we had the promise of again returning to the bosom of our families." They would stand firm against persecution, win "many souls as seals of [their] ministry," and find their families safe upon their homecoming. Joseph anticipated that European converts would flock to the church's American places of gathering.[12]

As the summer temperatures peaked, the Saints learned why other Americans had avoided the swampy flats in Commerce and across the river. The marshy areas bred mosquitoes that carried malaria. Countless church members fell sick.

Joseph and Emma tended the hundreds of Saints who had pitched their wagons and tents on their property. They welcomed as many as they could into their home. Every day, Joseph visited the sick, laid his hands on them in prayer, anointed them with oil, and brewed tea for them. "The prophet was our only doctor," recounted Oliver Huntington, whose mother died that July. "In fact, he was doctor to all the brethren." Zina Huntington, Oliver's sister, remembers Joseph bringing "warm drink" into their tent as succor.[13]

Joseph himself succumbed to the disease for a spell, but by July 22, he had recovered enough to visit the sick in Montrose. "Joseph went through the midst of them," recorded Wilford Woodruff, "taking them by the hand and in a loud voice commanding them in the name of Jesus Christ to arise from their beds and be made whole." Many did just that, and the newly healthy "followed Joseph from house to house." The prophet's ministrations sustained the Saints, but the sickly season persisted into the fall. A number of children died, and parents watched others linger at the precipice of death. Many of the apostles were ill or weak when they left on their missions in September and October.[14]

The fact that parts of Commerce were "a *deathly sickly* hole," as Joseph put it, did not dent the prophet's enthusiasm. He oversaw additional land purchases in the summer and the early fall, and church leaders submitted a plat for newly surveyed portions of the area. At a church conference in early October, Joseph stated that it was "made known to him that it [Commerce] shall be sanctified and be a place of gathering." The conference declared that Commerce was a stake of Zion. The Saints could drain the swamps and remove the scourge of malaria. Church members could purchase lots and build homes. The Saints gave their new place of gathering a new name, Nauvoo, which Joseph explained was a Hebrew word meaning "a beautiful situation, or place, carrying with it, also, the idea of *rest*." The river and the bluffs were indeed beautiful, but rest would prove elusive.[15]

In late October 1839, Joseph and Elias Higbee joined Sidney Rigdon on his journey to the nation's capital. Joseph's parting with Emma and the children was fraught. Three-year-old Frederick was sick with a fever. "I shall be filled with a constant anxiety about you and the children until I hear from you," Joseph wrote from Springfield. He knew that Emma would bear a heavy burden in his absence but explained that his "sense of humanity" compelled him to undertake the sacrifice. "Shall I see so many perish and not seek redress?" he asked.[16]

Emma's burden was indeed heavy. Frederick recovered quickly, but Joseph III became feverish and "bled at the nose until he was very weak." Emma also ran an informal infirmary for other church members. The

Joseph Smith in Iowa and Illinois. (Map by John Hamer)

day of Joseph's departure, Orson Hyde and his wife and daughter—all sick—moved into the home, as did James Mulholland, Joseph's scribe, who died several days later.[17]

Sidney Rigdon was suffering from malaria when he and Joseph left Nauvoo. By the time they reached Columbus, Ohio, it was clear that Rigdon was not fit to keep going, so he remained behind, and Joseph continued on in the company of Elias Higbee.[18]

The pair arrived in Washington on November 28. More than forty thousand people resided in the nation's capital, which Charles Dickens derided as the "headquarters of tobacco-tinctured saliva" during a visit to the city a little more than a year later. Unlike on his earlier trip to New York City, Joseph did not take the time to describe his surroundings or the social conditions of Washington. He was focused on his political mission.[19]

The prophet established good relations with the Illinois congressional delegation. Senator Richard Young loaned Joseph $500 to finance his party's stay in Washington. Illinois representative John Reynolds took Joseph and Higbee to the President's House (later known as the White House), where they obtained a meeting with Martin Van Buren. Other than humble roots—Van Buren was the son of an innkeeper—the president and the prophet had little in common. A local newspaper described Joseph as "a tall, muscular man . . . a plain yeoman," who made up for his limited education and poor diction with sincerity and firmness. Van Buren was more than twenty years Joseph's senior, more than half a foot shorter, rotund, and far more calculating and expedient. The "Little Magician," as he was known, did not hesitate to put party before principle.[20]

The Saints hoped that Van Buren would mention the persecution of their people in his annual message to Congress, thereby helping their petition find favor in the House and Senate. When brought into the president's parlor, Joseph handed Van Buren letters of introduction from Illinois politicians. Van Buren glanced at one and frowned. "What can I do?" he sighed. "I can do nothing for you. If I do anything, I shall come in contact with the whole State of Missouri." Joseph pressed the president to consider what his people had suffered. Had Joseph been shrewder, he might have pledged the Mormon vote in an attempt to win Van Buren's support. The president extended his sympathy but would not support their cause. His annual message, published later that month, was silent on the subject.[21]

The church delegation and their political allies continued to work on their memorial to Congress. They assembled scores of affidavits documenting the suffering of church members in Missouri. Joseph preached in Washington, then spent several weekends with a fledgling branch of the church in Philadelphia. While there, he visited a phrenologist, Alfred Woodward, who used a "reading" of the prophet's skull to postulate aspects of his personality. Joseph scored highest for "individuality," or his powers of observation, and lowest for "order" and "alimentiveness," or appetite for food. (Joseph wasn't a glutton, but he enjoyed his meals.) The prophet had his head examined on two other occasions. Despite the pretensions of phrenologists, most Americans regarded such readings as good fun, somewhat akin to consulting almanacs or other forms of astrology. The fact that Joseph's several phrenological readings differed wildly in their conclusions made the prophet skeptical of their usefulness.[22]

Joseph was back in the nation's capital at the end of January 1840. Matthew L. Davis, a journalist who attended a Latter-day Saint meeting in Washington, described the prophet to his wife as "what you ladies would call a very good looking man." Joseph, aware that a notorious reputation preceded him, did his best to cut a respectable figure. He dressed unostentatiously, and he spoke plainly and with evident sincerity. Joseph also did his best to appeal to the Protestant sensibilities of his audiences. "We teach nothing but what the Bible teaches," he insisted, adding that "all who would follow the precepts of the Bible, whether Mormon or not, would assuredly be saved." At the same time, Joseph gently introduced some distinctive principles, for instance, that God and human spirits were both eternal. Davis informed his wife that he had no opinion on "matters of *faith*," but Joseph persuaded him that the Mormons deserved sympathy and a measure of respect.[23]

The church's memorial was now ready. It patiently documented the manifold persecutions the Saints had endured in Missouri, from their arrival in Jackson County to their expulsion the previous winter. The memorial crescendoed with the macabre details of the massacre at Hawn's Mill, when the mob had shot ten-year-old Sardius Smith in the head and had hewed an elderly man to pieces "with an old scythe." The Saints claimed to have lost $2 million worth of property, all because of a "difference in religious sentiment." Where else could they turn for redress? The governor of Missouri had ordered their expulsion or extermination. They could not return to Missouri to sue in its courts. "For ourselves," the petitioners concluded, "we see no redress, unless it be awarded by the Congress of the United States."[24]

Richard Young introduced the memorial in the Senate. Lewis Linn of Missouri promptly objected, stating that the Senate lacked jurisdiction over the affairs of a "sovereign state." When Senator Young suggested that the hundreds of affidavits amounted to a "hard case" against the actions of certain Missourians, Linn countered that "the Mormons were the aggressors, and brought upon themselves the punishment." Kentucky's Henry Clay, twice defeated as a presidential nominee and the chamber's most prominent Whig, advised his colleagues to settle the question of congressional jurisdiction in the matter. The Senate accordingly referred the memorial to its Committee on the Judiciary.[25]

Joseph did not wait for the senators to reach a final judgment on the matter. "My heart is entwined around you and those little ones," he had written Emma from Philadelphia.[26] He left for home in mid-February. Elias Higbee remained in Washington.

The prophet reached a Nauvoo that had changed for the better in his absence. Newspapers that spring reported that the Saints had built around three hundred homes. "Our church here is prospering," Joseph wrote. "There is now every prospect of our having a good society, a peaceable habitation and a desirable residence here."[27] The malaria outbreak of the previous summer and fall had abated, at least for the time being.

One reason for Joseph's sunny outlook was his optimism that the church's petition would succeed in Washington. "The affair now before Congress was the only thing that ought to interest the Saints at present," he told a council of church leaders. Joseph sent instructions to Higbee not to accept anything short of the requested $2 million as compensation for their Missouri losses. Joseph had come away convinced that most members of the Senate favored their memorial. With Henry Clay and "other influential men" as "warm advocates," how could they fail?[28]

They failed because they actually did not have very many advocates, and major figures like Clay considered it a minor matter. Only three of the five members of the Senate Committee on the Judiciary bothered to attend the hearing on the church's memorial. Those senators heard testimony from Higbee, and Missouri politicians and a St. Louis newspaper editor spoke against the Mormons. The church's claims might have received more attention had Joseph remained in Washington and spoken before the committee himself. After several days of testimony, reported Higbee, the committee concluded that "redress can only be had in Missouri, [in its] courts and legislature." The national government claimed no jurisdiction over Missouri's treatment of its citizens.[29]

A church conference denounced the committee's report as "unconstitutional" and "a great insult," especially in its expectation that the Saints should depend on the "magnanimity of the state of Missouri for redress." Joseph was stung by the rebuff of President Van Buren, whom he derided as a "fop or a fool." Back in Nauvoo, Joseph mocked Van Buren's girth. The prophet joked that the president "would continue to grow fat, and swell and, before the next election, burst!" Joseph intended to puncture Van Buren's chances in Illinois. He told a congregation that "he did not

wish to have any political influence," but he let it be known that in November's presidential election he would be voting for William Henry
Harrison.[30]

Joseph could not ignore politics, as the persecution of the Saints demanded a political solution. And why wouldn't the Saints support Van
Buren's opponent, when the president had dismissed their plea for help?
But Joseph couldn't throw his weight behind one candidate or party
without risking the other side's ire. The Saints, upon their arrival in Illinois, enjoyed sympathy from both Whigs and Democrats. Joseph would
have needed considerable tact and skill to maintain bipartisan support.
Tact, however, was not one of the Mormon prophet's talents.

Saviors on Mount Zion (1840)

By the summer of 1840, several thousand church members had gathered on the Illinois and Iowa sides of the Mississippi River. New arrivals bought land from church leaders on credit, and the makeshift settlements of the previous year grew into a fledgling city. "The brethren begin to roll in like clouds," Joseph commented. He rhapsodized about Nauvoo's future, prophesying that it would become "the greatest city in the world." He vowed to build a temple as glorious as Solomon's, and he promised that the task "shall impoverish no one but enrich thousands." The Saints would hear the clinging of coins in their pockets, and they would gain access to spiritual power in the Lord's House.[1]

Church members needed Joseph's optimism to tide them through their travails. Despite the rapid growth, present circumstances in Nauvoo remained challenging for the Saints. "Goods are so dear here," wrote Vilate Kimball to her husband in England. "It costs almost a fortune to clothe a family comfortable." In addition to poverty, there was sickness and death. Malaria returned with the summer, and although the epidemic did not match the previous season's severity, dozens of Saints died.[2]

The prophet's own family experienced both growth and hardship. In June, Emma gave birth to another son, whom she and Joseph named Don Carlos, after one of Joseph's brothers. There were now four boys in the family, along with the couple's adopted daughter, Julia. "They are as

David H. Smith, *Bend in the River,* ca. 1868. (Photograph by
Lachlan Mackay; courtesy of Community of Christ Archives)

smart children as can be found anywhere, and perhaps a little smarter,"
Emma bragged to David Hale, her brother.[3]

The children and a larger household—there were usually relatives
and boarders as well—made for a great deal of work, so Emma and
Joseph secured help. In May 1840, Bishop Edward Partridge, weakened
by the Missouri persecutions and Nauvoo fevers, died at the age of forty-
six. Two of his daughters, nineteen-year-old Eliza and sixteen-year-old
Emily, eased the financial burden on their widowed mother by joining
the prophet's household. "Joseph and Emma offered us a home in their
family," Emily later recalled. "They treated us with great kindness."
Emily Partridge looked after little Don Carlos. Sadly, the baby only lived
a little more than a year.[4]

Joseph also wanted more help. He faced the twin burdens of making
payments on the debts he had assumed and of meeting the insatiable

demands of newcomers for land and assistance. Joseph asked other church leaders for a break from the press of business so that he could "devote himself exclusively to those things which relate to the spiritualities of the church." He wanted to get back to the "Egyptian records" and even return to the translation of the Bible that had occupied him in the early 1830s. Other church leaders in Nauvoo were sympathetic to Joseph's request, of course, but they regarded the prophet as indispensable when it came to real estate. After all, Joseph was "responsible for the payment of the city," debts that exceeded $150,000. Still, they appointed a clerk to oversee land sales and promised to provide for the "wants" of Joseph and his counselors in the First Presidency.[5]

Joseph made good on his desire to focus on "spiritualities." In sermons over the course of the summer, the prophet introduced what Phebe Woodruff—wife of apostle Wilford Woodruff—called "strange things" and "strong meat." Joseph suggested that the ten "lost" tribes of Israel had been removed from the earth, along with a large chunk of the planet. At the time of Christ's Second Coming, they and the planetary fragment would return and the earth would be "reeling to and fro like a drunken man." It was Joseph's twist on the many theories Jews and Christians had advanced about the lost tribes and the apocalypse.[6]

The prophet surprised the Saints with other literal but idiosyncratic readings of the Bible. In his first letter to the Corinthians, Paul comments that he "die[s] daily." Surely Paul didn't mean that he experienced physical death on a daily basis. Perhaps he referred to acts of self-abnegation or his willingness to risk his life for the gospel's sake. In the same passage, Paul refers to having "fought with beasts at Ephesus." Some ancient and modern commentators took the second verse to mean that Paul had contended against actual animals, perhaps in the arena. Others believed that the "beasts" were Paul's human opponents, or perhaps demons. Joseph put the two verses together and hypothesized that "the beasts that he fought with at Ephesus often killed him and he came to life again." Phebe Woodruff's two-year-old daughter Sarah Emma was among the Saints who died in the summer of 1840. Stirred by Joseph's explication of scripture, she wondered, "Why may not our little Sarah be raised to life again?"[7]

Death was capricious. It snatched away not only vulnerable infants but men and women in their prime, such as Bishop Partridge. Another loss in the summer of 1840 was that of Seymour Brunson, a War of 1812 veteran who had served missions, survived battles and hardships in Missouri, and held a place on the Nauvoo High Council. In July 1840, he caught cold after getting up in the night to drive some stray cattle off of his property. A few weeks later he was dead.[8]

Joseph was at Brunson's deathbed. The dying man urged the prophet "not to hold him any longer" because he had experienced a vision of David Patten, the apostle killed in the Battle of Crooked River. "He wants me," Brunson told Joseph, "and the Lord wants me, and I want to go." Shortly before Brunson expired, he told Joseph that the "room [was] full of angels . . . come to waft my spirit home." He bid his family and friends farewell and "fell asleep in Jesus."[9]

Thousands of Saints attended Brunson's funeral, forming a mile-long procession to his grave. Joseph preached on the resurrection. "A more solemn sight I never witnessed, and yet the day was joyful because of the light and glory which Joseph set forth," Vilate Kimball observed. It was joyful also because the Saints felt assured of the dead man's salvation. He had "always been a lively stone in the building of God," the church's *Times and Seasons* noted, and Brunson had died full of faith.[10]

In the funeral crowd Joseph noticed Jane Neyman, whose grown son recently had died outside of the church. Were there any glad tidings for her? Yes, the prophet proclaimed. Joseph pointed to the biblical text he had chosen for the occasion: "Else what shall they do which are baptized for the dead," the apostle Paul asked the early church in Corinth, "if the dead rise not at all? Why are they then baptized for the dead?" The passage had perplexed Christians down through the centuries. For the Mormon prophet, it answered a vexing theological question.[11]

Most American Protestants understood baptism as a sign of an individual's conversion or inclusion within the church. It was important, but not strictly necessary for salvation. For Joseph, by contrast, baptism was essential, and not just any baptism. Individuals needed to be baptized by those who held priesthood authority in Christ's one true restored church. God would welcome infants and children who died before the age of eight into the celestial kingdom, but men, women, and older children who died unbaptized would fall short of the fullness of eternal glory. Joseph insisted that he had the Bible on his side. "Except a man be born of water and of the Spirit, he cannot enter into the kingdom of God," Jesus had taught. No baptism, no remission of sins, no salvation.

It was a deeply personal question for the Smith family. Joseph gradually had backed away from the horrible possibility that Alvin, who had died in 1823, was in hell. After his Kirtland Temple vision of Alvin in the celestial kingdom, Joseph proclaimed that those who died "without a knowledge of this gospel, who would have received it . . . shall be heirs of the celestial kingdom of God." Joseph suggested that those who died without the chance to be baptized "must have it hereafter." But how could the dead be baptized?[12]

A suggestion came through word of a curious vision experienced by a woman on the other side of the Atlantic Ocean. Brigham Young included the details in a letter that reached Nauvoo about six weeks before Seymour Brunson's death. Ann Booth, a Methodist convert to the church in Manchester, was "carried away in a vision to the place of departed spirits." She saw David Patten holding a key and unlocking the door to the topmost of twelve prisons. When Patten went inside, he was greeted by none other than John Wesley, the founder of Methodism. Patten preached the necessity of baptism for the remission of sins. A river of clear water appeared, and Patten baptized Wesley and ordained him into the priesthood. Then Wesley baptized the other prisoners, who included many of Ann Booth's loved ones, who had all "lived and died Methodist." She foresaw a heavenly reunion with her family. Booth's vision of posthumous spirit baptism induced Joseph to contemplate a way that living Saints could bring about the salvation of their deceased loved ones. Joseph's solution was that church members could be baptized on their behalf.[13]

Meanwhile, Joseph Smith Sr.'s life on earth drew to a close. He was near death by the time of Seymour Brunson's funeral, then lingered for another month. In mid-September, he suffered "an eruption of a blood vessel" and vomited a considerable amount of blood. Joseph Jr. and Hyrum rushed to their parents' house. The brothers laid their hands on their father and prayed for him, but they knew it was the end.[14]

Joseph Jr. returned to his father's bedside the next day. They talked about baptism for the dead, and Joseph Sr. asked his prophet son to be "baptized for Alvin immediately." He summoned the rest of his children and blessed them as the biblical Jacob had blessed his sons. A few minutes before his death, Joseph Sr. stated that his senses grew unusually keen. Lucy Mack Smith recorded his final words: "I see Alvin." His father's death shook the prophet deeply. The elder Smith had been infirm for several years, but Joseph Jr. blamed his final illness on "ruthless mobs" whose persecutions had weakened the old man.[15]

By the time of the church's October 1840 conference, Joseph was ready to instruct the Saints about baptism for the dead. Ann Booth's vision had become well known within the church. Joseph told the congregation that he didn't "wholly [discard] Sister Booth's vision," but he disagreed with some of its particulars. "John Wesley can receive this work, but how can his spirit be baptized in water?" Joseph asked. Spirits couldn't be baptized, Joseph taught, but they could deputize living Saints to undergo the rite. As soon as church members were baptized on their behalf, spirits would be "released from prison." Their family would "claim them in the resurrection and bring them into the celestial kingdom." Church members could be baptized for their deceased parents, grandparents, siblings, uncles and aunts, and children, bringing about the eternal reunions of families in heaven. As Joseph put it with a biblical phrase, they could become "saviors on mount Zion" for their loved ones.[16]

The Saints quickly embraced the new teaching. Even as the October conference continued, the waters of the Mississippi were "continually troubled," Vilate Kimball reported, with baptisms. The elders stood in the river, and Latter-day Saint men and women waded in to save their loved ones. "They are going forward in multitudes," Phebe Woodruff wrote. Some were being baptized for more than a dozen individuals in a single day. Woodruff had planned to wait until her husband returned from England to be baptized for her mother, but she grew impatient. "The last time Joseph spoke about the subject," she wrote, "he advised everyone to be up and . . . liberate their friends from bondage as quick as possible." There was a lull over the cold winter months, but large numbers of baptisms resumed the next spring.[17]

Members of the Smith family participated in the rite. Emma Smith was baptized for her father and a deceased sister. Lucy Mack Smith did the same work for her parents and one of her sisters. Hyrum, rather than Joseph, was baptized for Alvin Smith; it is possible that Joseph officiated at this proxy baptism.[18]

Some church members disregarded Joseph's caution that the Saints should be baptized only for their close relatives, not "for acquaintances." Three individuals, including Don Carlos Smith, the prophet's brother, were baptized for George Washington, and a woman was baptized for Martha Washington. The Saints supported William Henry Harrison in this world and the next. More than two-thirds of Hancock County voters cast ballots for Harrison over Martin Van Buren in the 1840 presidential election. Then, after the newly inaugurated Harrison died, Ebenezer Robinson was baptized for him.[19]

Other Christians, whether Protestant or Catholic, understood baptism as a once-in-a-lifetime ritual, and a ritual that one underwent for one's own sake. For the Saints, baptism was an ordinance that one could and should do repeatedly for several different reasons. Excommunicated Saints, or those who had drifted away from the church and wanted to return, were brought back into the fold through rebaptism. Joseph began encouraging all church members to embrace rebaptism as an act of repentance and commitment. At the conclusion of the church's semi-annual conference in April 1841, the Saints walked to the banks of the river. Joseph and Sidney Rigdon waded into the waters of the Mississippi and baptized each other. Joseph then explained that "the door was open for the Saints to do as they had done, namely, repent and do their first works." Hundreds of church members followed their example. Joseph also taught that the Saints could enter the baptismal waters in order to be healed of sickness and infirmity. For their sins, for their bodies, for their dead, the Saints should immerse themselves again and again.[20]

Joseph knew that most Americans couldn't fathom his church's growth. "Why is it this babbler gains so many followers and retains them?" the prophet once asked. Joseph's answer was simple. People followed him because he "possess[ed] the principle of love." But it was also because Joseph offered them compelling solutions to their deepest needs. Most Americans did not accept those solutions. "Surely the Gentiles will mock," Vilate Kimball predicted when she wrote her husband about baptism for the dead. She was right. Newspaper editors and other critics loved the idea that the Mormons were frolicking in the Mississippi in order to save George Washington for eternity. It was easy to ridicule religious innovation, but many Americans agonized about loved ones who had died bereft of the faith that Protestant Christians insisted was necessary for their salvation. Joseph's doctrines and rituals went to the heart of these theological anxieties. It is no wonder that thousands of men and women were willing to move across the country and to sacrifice so much for the church and for its prophet.[21]

One baptism had a profound influence on the remainder of Joseph's life. In the summer of 1840, Joseph received a series of letters from John C. Bennett, a militia officer who also held a ceremonial title as quartermaster general of Illinois. Thirty-six years of age, with salt-and-pepper hair atop his short, thin frame (Joseph called him a "little man"), Bennett was a consummate huckster. An erstwhile Methodist preacher, he peddled diplomas, sold medicinal tonics, and later became a semi-successful breeder of chickens. Above all else, Bennett was a self-promoter, and he

John C. Bennett, ca. 1842. (Courtesy of Church History Library)

presented himself to Joseph as a political ally and strategist. With Joseph's encouragement Bennett moved to Nauvoo and was baptized.[22]

Joseph had a penchant for latching onto new arrivals who seemed in a position to advance his church's cause. In this case, he was desperate for the political wonders that Bennett promised to work. The Saints had failed to win redress for their past losses, and Joseph and the others who had fled their Missouri captors feared extradition and a return to prison. Bennett offered to write legislation that would incorporate the city of Nauvoo and provide its residents with a safe haven from future persecution. Bennett's rapid rise in Joseph's esteem was evident at the October 1840 conference, at which he spoke several times. Bennett discussed the outlines of a proposed city charter, and he urged the Saints to vote for those politicians who had "held out the hand of friendship" during their afflictions. The conference appointed him the church's delegate to the legislature in Springfield.[23]

Bennett delivered. The Illinois legislature, the governor, and the state supreme court all assented to the proposed act. "Each party," recounted Thomas Ford, an Illinois judge and consummate political insider, "was afraid to object to them for fear of losing the Mormon vote, and each believed that it had secured their favor." Stephen Douglas, a prominent young Democrat and the Illinois secretary of state, helped move the act through the Illinois House of Representatives. Abraham Lincoln, an up-and-coming Whig, congratulated Bennett after the charter's passage.[24]

The legislation chartered the city of Nauvoo and granted its residents a panoply of powers and protections. If officers of the law from other jurisdictions came to arrest one of its residents, Nauvoo's city council could issue a writ of habeas corpus, freeing a defendant until a Nauvoo court ruled on an arrest's legality. The act also created the Nauvoo Legion, a contingent of the state militia at the disposal of the mayor. The individual provisions reflected precedents from other Illinois city charters. Collectively, though, they were unusual in their scope. Although the legislation made no mention of the church or of religion in any way, it provided a legal framework whereby church leaders could control Nauvoo's governments and courts and deploy their own militia to defend the city's residents and their property. The Saints had fashioned their own city-state on the Mississippi.[25]

Bennett returned to Nauvoo in triumph. In February, Nauvoo's citizens elected him the city's first mayor, and he also received the rank of major general in the Nauvoo Legion.

The legion's officers chose Joseph as the militia's lieutenant general. The prophet's rank was a matter of considerable hubris. The only other American who had held the rank was George Washington, following his appointment as commander in chief of the U.S. Army in 1798. The Saints' military appointments received little scrutiny. Governor Thomas Carlin signed Joseph's commission.[26]

Two years earlier, Joseph had spent the winter in Liberty Jail after the loss of the church's Missouri settlements. Now the prophet had rekindled his vision of gathering the Saints into a great city in the last days before the return of Christ. Already one company of English converts had arrived in the fall. He looked upon the city rising on the banks and the bluffs by the Mississippi and saw an expansive future. Mormon men had started quarrying stone for the temple, which church leaders planned to erect on the city's high ground. Nauvoo would have a university, also chartered in the recently passed legislation. There also would be a hotel or inn—the Nauvoo House—in which Joseph and his family would live and to which they would welcome visitors to the city.

Joseph's message was simple. "Let the Saints come here," he proclaimed as the word of the Lord. "There is no other way for the Saints to be saved in these last days," Joseph added. Thousands of church members in the United States and Europe answered his call.[27]

Sealings (1841–1842)

B APTISM FOR THE DEAD solved long-standing Christian anxieties. Another innovation, however, created a cascade of problems for the prophet. It was very "strong meat," and Joseph shared it only with his most trustworthy friends.

In the fall of 1840 Joseph went across the river to the home of Joseph Bates Noble in Montrose. Noble had marched to Missouri with the prophet and had remained loyal through the tribulations of Kirtland and Far West. Joseph Smith had a deep connection with the family of Noble's wife, Mary. Her father, Alva Beman, was the "great rodsman" among the budding seer's treasure-hunting associates in the mid- to late 1820s. The Bemans joined the church and were baptized in Kirtland. Alva Beman died in 1837; his widow, Sarah, died in August 1840.[1]

Louisa Beman, Mary Noble's younger sister, was present when the prophet visited. Mary Noble apparently was not. The prophet shared that he had received a revelation on "the principle of celestial marriage or 'a plurality of wives,' " and that an "angel of the Lord had commanded him . . . to move forward." Louisa Beman was the one with whom Joseph intended to move forward.[2]

The prophet didn't share his new doctrine with Sidney Rigdon, his longtime counselor in the church's First Presidency. Still not fully recovered from the illness that had interrupted his trip to the nation's capital, Rigdon was thinking about moving his family to the east, away from Nauvoo's swampy climate. Joseph also did not confide in William Law, a well-to-do newcomer who ascended to the church's First Presidency after Hyrum Smith became church patriarch. Nor did he tell Hyrum. And Joseph certainly did not broach the subject with Emma.

Joseph didn't speak publicly about his marriages, nor did he keep records in a private journal. A number of his wives attested to the "sealings" in later years, and some provided intimate details. Other women remained circumspect. Any historian writing about Joseph's polygamy has to admit a significant degree of uncertainty, about everything from the number and timing of the marriages to the nature of these relationships. It is not easy to sift through the gossip, obfuscation, and defamation. What follows in this and subsequent chapters is based on the best available documentation, but given the nature of the sources, it is an incomplete and imperfect reconstruction. During Joseph's lifetime, only he knew the full story, and he took great pains to obscure it.

Before he discussed the doctrine with Joseph Bates Noble and his family, Joseph Smith had thought about polygamy, at least on and off, for more than a decade. When he dictated the Book of Mormon, the text prohibited polygamy, with one loophole. Men could take additional wives if God commanded them to do so in order to "raise up seed," to cause his people to reproduce more quickly. Joseph may have thought more about the possibility of multiple wives during or after his relationship with Fanny Alger in Kirtland. By 1835, moreover, he was teaching that Latter-day Saint marriages could persist "forever" instead of only "till death."[3] Proxy baptism underscored the potential eternity of family bonds. Polygamy enabled Joseph, and eventually other men, to expand those families and thus broaden those eternal bonds.

What about sex? Polygamy was hardly the simplest way for an American man to arrange intercourse with other women. At the same time, the accusations of adultery in the wake of his dalliance with Fanny Alger had sown doubts about Joseph's leadership. Plural marriage provided a biblical and theological framework in which sexual relationships with other women were righteous.

There was an even more obvious reason why Joseph contemplated polygamy. He read the Bible. When Joseph dictated a revelation on the subject, it began by referencing that he had asked God why Abraham, Isaac, Jacob, Moses, David, and Solomon had been "justified . . . [in] having many wives and concubines." Joseph modeled his life after theirs. Like Moses, he delivered the words of God to the people and served as their political and military leader. Like Solomon, he built temples. If these ancient prophets and patriarchs had more than one wife, why shouldn't the prophets and patriarchs of the latter days?

The next spring, on April 5, 1841, Joseph Bates Noble took his sister-in-law across the river. In the creeping darkness of an early Nauvoo evening, the two Josephs and Louisa Beman stood underneath an elm tree. Louisa disguised herself as a man with a coat and hat. Noble quietly repeated the words Joseph told him to use. "It was done in a whisper," Noble recalled. It wasn't a marriage akin to others the church had performed in recent years. Instead, Noble explained, it was "the first sealing ceremony in this dispensation." By the authority of the priesthood, Louisa Beman would be Joseph Smith's wife for eternity.[4]

And not just for the afterlife. In a court deposition five decades later, Joseph Bates Noble testified that the prophet consummated his first plural marriage. "I saw him in bed with her," he stated bluntly. Noble left the pair in his just-built Nauvoo home.[5]

When the prophet discussed polygamy with Joseph Bates Noble, he made it clear that polygamy was a privilege and a commandment for other righteous men. According to one report, Noble had set his heart on a woman he wished to add to his family. He "pressed [Joseph] to seal the contract but he never could get opportunity." Another opportunity arose, however. Two years to the day that Noble had sealed the prophet to Louisa Beman, a church member named Sarah Alley became Noble's plural wife.[6]

Joseph had few documented interactions with Louisa Beman after the night of their sealing. The prophet provided her with some sort of financial support, and he rebaptized her, one of his other plural wives, and Sarah Alley on the same day in May 1843. Shortly after Joseph's death, Beman became the polygamous wife of Brigham Young, with whom she had five children, all of whom died in infancy. The first pair of twins were named Joseph and Hyrum. In 1850, she died of breast cancer in Salt Lake City.[7]

On April 6, 1841, the morning after the first sealing, Joseph oversaw a grand celebration of the church's eleventh anniversary. The Nauvoo Legion assembled, along with two volunteer militia companies from Iowa. Joseph arrived in "full military costume," accompanied by four aides-de-camp and twelve guards, themselves "in splendid uniforms." Church editor Robert Thompson commented that the officers' dress "would have become a Bonaparte or a Washington." The militia greeted Joseph with salutes, the sounding of trumpets, and the firing of cannons. A delegation of Mormon women gifted him a "beautiful silk national flag," and Joseph reviewed the 650 troops.[8]

One of Joseph's recent revelations had identified Nauvoo as "a cornerstone of Zion." The same text instructed the Saints to build a temple, which would contain a font for baptisms for the dead and provide space for solemn assemblies and other rituals. Church leaders had selected a temple ground, on the bluffs about a mile east of the peninsula at the river's edge.[9]

Joseph asked Latter-day Saint men to consecrate a tenth of their days to temple labor, and by the anniversary they had dug a foundation and built walls to a height of five feet. After reviewing the Nauvoo Legion, Joseph led its members to the temple ground, which they enclosed in a hollow square. Nearly ten thousand people watched Joseph preside over the laying of the temple's cornerstones.

Thomas Sharp, non-Mormon editor of a Whig paper in nearby Warsaw (soon to be renamed the *Warsaw Signal*), attended the April 6 dedication and praised the "respectable appearance" of the Nauvoo Legion. Stephen Douglas, now a member of the Illinois Supreme Court, visited Nauvoo in early May, along with Cyrus Walker, an influential lawyer and Whig. They addressed a Sunday congregation and gave every indication that they welcomed Nauvoo's growth and would protect its people's liberties. Joseph wrote a letter for the church's *Times and Seasons* periodical in which he noted that Douglas and Walker, as "champions of the two great parties" in Illinois, laid aside strife and extended "courtesy, respect, and friendship" to the Saints.[10]

Nauvoo's era of good feelings proved fleeting. Thomas Sharp recognized that as the Mormon population increased, church members would dominate Hancock County's politics. The 1840 vote for William Henry Harrison aside, Mormon leaders typically supported Democratic candidates. Sharp expressed his displeasure when a church member ran against two non-Mormons in a bid for county school commissioner. He also objected when Stephen Douglas appointed John C. Bennett, recently elevated to the church's First Presidency, to a minor political office. The editor maintained that the Mormons deserved religious liberty but complained that the prophet exercised "inordinate power."[11]

Joseph fired off a pugnacious letter to Sharp, asking to discontinue his subscription to a paper he regarded as "that filthy sheet, that tissue of lies, that sink of iniquity." Sharp obliged Joseph's request to publish his cancellation notice but noted that he still owed $3. "Come, Josey," the editor jabbed, "fork over, and for mercy's sake don't get a revelation that it is not to be paid." The prophet settled the debt.[12]

Neither man settled the quarrel, however. Sharp's newfound antagonism toward Joseph was good business and good politics. The Whig editor warned that a Mormon majority in Hancock County threatened the republican liberties of other citizens. The Saints would vote as a bloc as their prophet dictated, making Joseph the county's power broker. "If it comes to this," he asked, "that Joe Smith is to control the majority of votes in our county, are we not in effect, the subjects of a despot?—might we not as well be serfs to the autocrat of Russia?" Sharp also pointed to the Nauvoo Legion. Why did a church need an army? Sharp portrayed Joseph as pope and potentate, a dangerous union of church and state. For their part, church publishers heaped insults upon "Thom-ass Sharp," mocking his "far-famed" nose and referring to him as a "Fat Turkey" and the "Devil" incarnate.[13]

Given what had transpired in Missouri, Joseph might have opted to lie a bit low in the church's new home. He instead paraded at the head of hundreds of militia troops and basked in the support of politicians. The prophet emphasized that all people irrespective of creed were welcome in Nauvoo and the church's other settlements, but the fact that both he and associates such as John C. Bennett held civil, military, and political offices provided fodder for Sharp's complaints.

Meanwhile, old enemies tried to settle old scores. In early June 1841, Joseph was arrested as he was returning from a trip to Quincy, where he had met with Governor Carlin. Just a few hours after the prophet left Carlin's home, the governor had received a request from Missouri asking for his assistance in extraditing Joseph to face the charges—including treason—that he had fled two years earlier.

Missouri officials initially hadn't pursued legal efforts to retrieve Joseph and his fellow prisoners. Indeed, they gave Joseph every opportunity to escape once it was clear that the Mormons were leaving the state. But Missouri governor Lilburn Boggs changed his mind after church leaders persuaded Carlin to extradite a group of Missouri vigilantes who had abducted four Mormons in Illinois. When Carlin made that request, Boggs in return demanded Joseph and the other Mormon fugitives from Missouri justice. Carlin made only a half-hearted effort to uphold his end of the bargain. He sent a sheriff with a warrant to Nauvoo, but Joseph was away at the time. Thomas Reynolds, Boggs's successor as governor of Missouri, had renewed the legal effort, and everyone knew where Joseph was. Carlin sent a posse to arrest the prophet.[14]

The lawmen caught up with Joseph at a hotel in Bear Creek and brought him back to Quincy. At this point, the Missourians' plans unraveled. Joseph obtained a writ of habeas corpus from a county judge, meaning that a court would rule on the legality of his arrest. And who would issue that judgment? None other than Stephen Douglas himself, who came to Quincy on the evening of Joseph's arrest and arranged to hear the case two days later in Monmouth, fifty miles northeast of Nauvoo.

The atmosphere in the courtroom was tense. Some of the lawyers who argued for Joseph's extradition did their best to "inflame the passions of the people against the defendant and his religion," but Joseph had assembled a crack legal team of his own, including prominent Whig lawyers Orville H. Browning and Cyrus Walker. In court, Browning cited Boggs's extermination order and the cruelties the Saints had suffered during their exodus. "Shall this unfortunate man, whom their fury has seen proper to select for sacrifice, be driven into such a savage band?" Browning asked. Douglas did not rule on the merits of whether Missouri had the right to extradite Joseph and try him on charges of treason. He instead invalidated Joseph's arrest on a technicality. When the sheriff in the fall of 1840 had returned the warrant to Governor Carlin, it had become void.[15]

Joseph was free, but the resolution implied that Missouri could obtain his extradition with a valid warrant. Indeed, even before Douglas's ruling, Carlin had signed a new warrant for the arrest of Joseph and several of his co-defendants. The governor asked a sheriff to apprehend the accused, but because they were elsewhere, nothing came of it. Joseph's political friends shielded him for the time being. Already, though, there were familiar, troubling signs: anti-Mormon conventions in Warsaw and Carthage. "Persecution is kindling up again against the Saints," Don Carlos Smith, the prophet's brother, wrote that summer.[16]

Shortly before Independence Day 1841, the apostles began returning home from what had been a wildly successful mission across the Atlantic. Thousands of English men and women had been baptized in just the prior year. Joseph perceived several of the apostles—Brigham Young, Heber Kimball, John Taylor, Wilford Woodruff, Willard Richards, George A. Smith—as among his most loyal supporters. Joseph now took them further into his confidence. According to George A. Smith, his cousin "astonished" him by revealing the "doctrine of patriarchal marriage" upon their return to Nauvoo. To a man, the apostles recalled their shock and initial horror. Brigham Young commented that it was the "first time in my life that I had desired the grave." He and the other apostles worried about what polygamy would mean for their own families and for the church. "When it was revealed to us," John Taylor reminisced, "it looked like the last end of Mormonism. For a man to ask another woman to marry him required more self-confidence than we had." Joseph helped them find the confidence. All of these men eventually became prolific polygamists.[17]

The prophet set the example. He married two sisters in the closing months of 1841. Zina and Presendia were the daughters of William and Zina Huntington. The Huntingtons had been strict, Sabbath-keeping Presbyterians in upstate New York, but they became disaffected because of a gulf they perceived between their church and biblical Christianity. They read the Book of Mormon and, in 1835, were baptized. Zina met Joseph when her parents moved to Kirtland. She recalled the prophet's "light auburn hair [and] blue eyes" and that when he talked to the Saints "with the spirit of revelation or inspiration ... his countenance would look clear and bright." Both Zina and Presendia were full of faith. They saw angels, spoke and sang in tongues, and rejoiced in a church that had restored the spiritual gifts described in the Bible.[18]

The Huntington sisters were also full of friendship toward their church's prophet. Presendia visited Joseph twice during his months in Liberty Jail, though the jailer denied her entry in the second instance. "My heart rejoiced at the friendship you manifested," Joseph wrote her. Zina lived for a short while in the Smith home after the death of her mother in the summer of 1839.[19]

Unlike Louisa Beman, Joseph's second and third plural wives were already married to other men. In early 1841, Zina had accepted a marriage proposal from Henry Jacobs, an upright young man who had been ordained a Seventy. Jacobs was a partner in a coffin-making business with one of Zina's brothers (a smart move, given the malaria), and he was a talented violinist. Nauvoo mayor John C. Bennett married the couple in March 1841. They moved into a very modest log house, with a dirt floor and a dry-goods box for their table. Although Zina later described an unhappy marriage, Henry looked back on sweet spiritual communion. "We could say our prayers together and speak together in tongues and bless each other in the name of the Lord," he recalled.[20]

Zina Huntington, who later became the plural wife of
Brigham Young, with their daughter, Zina Presendia Young,
ca. 1856. (Courtesy of Church History Library)

The fact that Zina had a second suitor complicated matters between
the couple. Either before or after Zina's marriage to Henry Jacobs, Joseph proposed that she become his plural wife. The prophet didn't approach her directly but instead used her brother Dimick as his
intermediary. "Tell Zina," the prophet instructed, "I put it off and put it
off till an angel with a drawn sword stood by me and told me if I did not
establish that principle upon the earth, I would lose my position and my

life." According to her reminiscence, Zina needed little convincing. God had prepared her to accept the teaching. "I had dreams that I could not account for," she related. "When Joseph Smith revealed this order, I knew what it meant." In late October 1841, when she was more than six months pregnant, Dimick sealed his sister in marriage to Joseph. Zina soon gave birth to a son, Zebulon William Jacobs. DNA analysis has confirmed that Zebulon was Henry's son, not Joseph's.[21]

Zina's older sister, Presendia, had powerful spiritual experiences at Protestant revivals, both as a girl and again shortly after her 1827 marriage to Norman Buell. Then, after Zina brought them a Book of Mormon in 1835, Presendia and Norman were baptized. Before and after their conversion, the couple suffered loss and heartache. Between 1833 and 1838, four of their five children died, most soon after birth. Norman also lost his faith in the church, becoming disaffected during the war and persecutions in Missouri. After their exodus from the state, the couple lived in Lima, Illinois, twenty miles south of Nauvoo. Some of Presendia's friends and relatives urged her to separate from her husband because of his apostasy. She didn't leave Norman Buell but, like Zina, Presendia accepted Joseph's proposal. Dimick Huntington sealed a second sister to the prophet.[22]

Joseph was just getting started. In January 1842, Brigham Young sealed Joseph to his widowed sister-in-law, Agnes Coolbrith Smith. Don Carlos Smith, the prophet's younger brother, had died the previous summer. Several scholars have described Joseph's sealing to Agnes as a "Levirate marriage," following the biblical commandment that when a woman's husband died without having borne him a son, "her husband's brother shall go in unto her, and take her to him to wife." The idea was that the brother would produce a son and heir. In this case, Joseph did not beget a son (or daughter) with Agnes, which indicates that if the marriage was consummated, sexual intercourse was infrequent. Joseph married Agnes not to provide her with a son, but rather to provide for her eternal glory.[23]

Joseph and his scribe Willard Richards dined at Agnes Smith's home eleven days after the sealing. Richards noted in his journal that a "Sister Harris" was present. Lucinda Pendleton Harris probably became Joseph's wife about this time. Back in 1826, her first husband, William Morgan, was killed after making plans to publish an exposé of Masonic rites and practices. Four years later, Lucinda married George Harris and moved from western New York to Indiana. After another four years, she and her second husband were baptized by Orson Pratt. They moved to Far West and met Joseph when the prophet and his family stayed in their home after Joseph and Emma's flight from Kirtland. Small world, indeed. In Nauvoo, the Harrises lived "just across the street" from the Smiths. A visitor to the city described Lucinda as short of stature, "with light hair and very bright blue eyes, and a pleasant countenance." Lucinda's sealing to Joseph did not alienate George Harris from the church. After the prophet's death, he stood in the Nauvoo Temple as a ceremony confirmed his wife's eternal sealing to Joseph.[24]

On February 8, 1842, Joseph was sealed to twenty-three-year-old Sylvia Lyon (née Sessions).[25] Several years earlier, Joseph had officiated when Sylvia had married Windsor Lyon in Far West. By the time Sylvia became Joseph's plural wife, she and Windsor had two children. One month after Sylvia's sealing to Joseph, she was present when her own mother was sealed to the prophet.[26] Like Sylvia, Patty Sessions was already married to a church member in good standing.

Mary Rollins Lightner was sealed to Joseph in late February. She was pregnant, carrying her third child by Adam Lightner, who was friendly toward the church but not a member. A niece of Sidney Gilbert, Mary had been baptized at the age of twelve in Ohio, then moved with her family to Jackson County. In Missouri, she experienced the ecstasy of speaking in tongues and the horror of persecution and expulsion.[27]

When Joseph introduced the subject of plural marriage to Mary Lightner, he told her that God had first instructed him to marry her back in 1834. Joseph added that more recently an angel had appeared to him three times and told him to "obey that principle or he would slay" him. The third time, the angel stood with a "drawn sword" before him. Joseph emphasized to Mary that he had no choice. He also revealed that despite her marriage to Adam Lightner, she always had been meant for him. "I was created for him before the foundation of the earth was laid," she recalled. Finally, Joseph encouraged her that their marriage would ensure her salvation. "I know that I shall be saved in the Kingdom of God," the prophet stated. "All that he [God] gives me I shall take with me for I have that authority and that power." Mary must have felt intense pressure. Joseph was her prophet. His life was at stake, and so was her eternal glory.

Mary Lightner nevertheless remained skeptical about the prophet's proposal. Joseph assured her that God would provide her with a witness to the truth of what he had taught. She prayed about the matter and discussed it with Brigham Young. Then one night, she saw a "personage" standing in front of her bed. The figure was white, bright, and beautiful. "Those eyes piercing me through, and through," she wrote, "I could not endure it." She hid under the covers, but she understood the vision as spiritual confirmation of Joseph's teaching. Mary continued to live with Adam Lightner. They moved to a small community about fifteen miles from Nauvoo.[28]

By the middle of 1842, the prophet had around a dozen plural wives.[29] At the time of their sealings to Joseph Smith, the women ranged in age from seventeen to fifty-three. The majority of women were already married at the time of the sealings, but others were widowed or previously single. The diversity of cases makes generalization challenging. One of the few constants in the sealings is that, as had been the case with Louisa Beman and the Huntington sisters, Joseph knew these women well, or at least knew and trusted members of their families. Joseph approached those he thought would accept the doctrine. Most of them did, though it sometimes took considerable persuasion and pressure. A significant number of women and their families were willing to do something that they at first considered repugnant because they believed so strongly in Joseph as God's prophet.

In all known instances, already married women continued to live with their first husbands during Joseph's lifetime. At some point, these men learned of their wives' sealings to Joseph, if not from their wives or from the prophet himself then through rumor. Nevertheless, most first husbands remained on good terms with Joseph. That amicability suggests that Joseph or their wives told the men that the sealings would not affect their marriages. Joseph presumably underscored the eternal benefits for the families of his plural wives, including for those first husbands who belonged to the church.

What was the nature of these plural marriages on earth? There is strong evidence that Joseph consummated many of the sealings to unmarried women, though the fact that none of those women had children by Joseph suggests that the sexual encounters were limited. Did Joseph have sex with already married women? In an interview many decades later, Zina Huntington affirmed that she had become Joseph's wife "for eternity," but she gave terse and contradictory answers when pressed about whether she was also Joseph's wife "for time." Most nineteenth-century individuals—monogamous or polygamous—did not divulge such intimate matters. It is possible that Joseph had sex with some or even all of the already married wives, but it is also possible that the sealings were ceremonial, only for eternity and not for earth.[30]

Joseph told women that he had no choice but to take plural wives, but why so many? And what was the rush? Other than Solomon, the biblical patriarchs were more limited in their marrying than Joseph. Some of the prophet's followers later connected the size of a man's family to the extent of his celestial glory, and it seems likely that Joseph thought along such lines. If Joseph "lusted for kin," as his biographer Richard Bushman asserted, he also thirsted for eternal glory and power. It is the simplest explanation for the proliferation of marriages, one that fits within the reality that in many instances, there was little relationship— sexual or otherwise—after the sealings.[31]

Joseph's marriages also fit into a pattern of growing recklessness, present as well in his finances and political strategy. Joseph was imprudent. It would have been wise to cultivate good relationships with both political parties in Illinois or at least to have formed enduring ties with one. Instead, Joseph blatantly traded Mormon votes for political promises, in the end antagonizing both sides. It would have been wise to eschew a heavy debt burden after the collapse of Mormon Kirtland, but Joseph quickly put himself in a similar bind in Nauvoo. And even if convinced of the righteousness or theological necessity of plural marriage, it would have been wise to move slowly.

Joseph's polygamy was a principle without a plan other than its rapid expansion. Once he embraced plural marriage, he pursued it with audacity and incaution. Joseph, it turned out, enjoyed living dangerously. Clandestine sealings and meetings were exhilarating. He knew how risky these actions were and swore his wives and confidants to secrecy. "The very walls had ears," Zina explained. "We spoke of it only in whispers." With an expanding circle of women and families, however, other eyes and ears saw the trysts and heard the whispers.[32]

CHAPTER TWENTY-FOUR

Upper Rooms (1842)

I N EARLY 1842, JOSEPH stood behind the counter of his newly completed red-brick store, on the banks of the Mississippi River and just
down the street from the Smith family's Nauvoo residence. The
store opened for business on January 5. Joseph greeted a throng of
customers who were eager to purchase their sugar, coffee, and tea from
the prophet, and who often persuaded him to gift them necessities because of their poverty. As in Kirtland, Joseph's store did not become profitable, but the building became the hub of church and political activity.
Joseph established an office on its second floor, which also contained a
larger room used as a meeting space. Joseph rarely oversaw the store's
commerce, but he was present upstairs most days. It was here that Joseph
steered Nauvoo's government, married some of his plural wives, and introduced sacred rituals.

It was also where Joseph returned to a project he had set aside. For
years he had spoken about his desire to get back to his translation of the
Egyptian materials, and he continued to show the mummies and papyri
to visitors. Now, he finally prepared for publication what he had dictated
back in 1835. "The Lord is blessing Joseph," apostle Wilford Woodruff
wrote in his diary that February, "with power to reveal the mysteries of
the kingdom of God, to translate through the Urim and Thummim ancient records and hieroglyphics as old as Abraham or Adam."[1]

The fruits of Joseph's labor appeared in several spring 1842 editions
of the church's *Times and Seasons*. The first installment featured a facsim-

Sutcliffe Maudsley, *Portrait of Lucy Mack Smith*, ca. 1842.
Gouache on paper. She sits under a framed vignette from the
Book of Abraham papyri, and she is holding a Book of Mormon.
(Courtesy of Church History Museum)

ile of one of the vignettes in the papyri along with Joseph's annotations.
The original Egyptian vignette still exists. Egyptologists interpret it as
the god Anubis reanimating a corpse. According to Joseph's interpretive
notes, by contrast, the pictures depict Abraham in Chaldea, bound on an

TIMES AND SEASONS.

"Truth will prevail."

Vol. III. No. 9.]   CITY OF NAUVOO, ILL. MARCH, 1, 1842.   [Whole No. 45.

A FAC-SIMILE FROM THE BOOK OF ABRAHAM.
NO. 1.

EXPLANATION OF THE ABOVE CUT.

Fig. 1,—The Angel of the Lord.

2. Abraham, fastened upon an Altar.

3. The Idolatrous Priest of Elkenah attempting to offer up Abraham as a sacrifice.

4. The Altar for sacrifice, by the Idolatrous Priests, standing before the Gods of Elkenah, Libnah, Mahmachrah, Korash, and Pharaoh.

5. The Idolatrous God of Elkenah.

6. The   "   " " Libnah.

7. The   "   " " Mahmachrah.

8. The   "   " " Korash.

9. The   "   " " Pharaoh.

10. Abraham in Egypt.

11. Designed to represent the pillars of Heaven, as understood by the Egyptians.

12. Raukeeyang, signifying expanse, or the firmament, over our heads; but in this case, in relation to this subject, the Egyptians meant it to signify Shamau, to be high, or the heavens: answering to the Hebrew word, Shaumahyeem.

Facsimile published with Joseph Smith's translation of the Book of Abraham.
(© By Intellectual Reserve, Inc.)

altar while an "idolatrous priest" prepares to sacrifice him. Following the vignette was the opening text of the Book of Abraham, identified as "the writings of Abraham, while he was in Egypt . . . written by his own hand." God rescues Abraham from the priest, reveals to him knowledge of priesthood and astronomy, and sends him away from the idolatrous Chaldeans to the land of Canaan.[2]

As the first pages rolled off the press, Joseph started on the next section of text. He resumed where he had left off in 1835, with Abraham and Sarah journeying to Egypt because of a famine in Canaan. Before their departure, Abraham receives instruction through the Urim and Thummim. He sees great stars, including one named Kolob, nearest to the throne of God. The Lord teaches Abraham that just as one star was always greater than another, so also "if there be two spirits . . . one shall be more intelligent than the other." All spirits were eternal, without beginning or end, but they attained different degrees of intelligence, glory, and power.

How did these eternal intelligences come to be on the earth? The Lord shows Abraham "the intelligences that were organized before the world was." It is a vision of spirits in their premortal existence. The Lord selects as his "rulers" a number of noble and righteous souls, including Abraham. This group of spirits also includes "one that was like unto God," Jesus Christ. "We will go down," Jesus declares, "for there is space there, and we will take of these materials, and we will make an Earth whereon these may dwell." God asks whom he should send to carry out this plan. "Here I am, send me," responds Jesus. Another spirit also volunteers. God chooses the first, leaving the second—Satan—full of wrath. In this premortal realm of human existence, righteous spirits align themselves with Jesus Christ, while others side with Satan.

God moves ahead with the plan. "Let us go down," he says. The Book of Abraham next recapitulates the story of creation from the first two chapters of Genesis, but with a significant grammatical correction. "They went down at the beginning," he dictated, "and they organized and formed (that is, the Gods) the heavens and the earth." Creation was not the work of one God. It was the work of many gods. The change resulted from Joseph's study of Hebrew. The Hebrew word rendered as "God" in Genesis 1 is *Elohim*. Joseph had learned from Joshua Seixas that the word's ending typically signified a plural noun. "The word *Elohim* ought to be the plural all the way through," Joseph later commented. The gods created light, land, living creatures, and—finally—men and women in their image.[3]

Another annotated Egyptian vignette accompanied the second *Times and Seasons* installment of the Book of Abraham. The original was from a hypocephalus, a circular papyrus placed under a deceased person's head. It depicts an array of Egyptian deities, worshipped by the creatures who appear before them.[4] Joseph, by contrast, understood multiple images as representing God sitting upon his throne, revealing "the grand key words of the Holy Priesthood" to figures such as Adam, Noah, and Abraham. What Joseph had in mind were words such as *Ahman*, which the prophet had revealed as the name of God in the original, pure language. Knowing and speaking that name enabled humans to access divine power and unlock the heavens.[5]

Joseph left some pictures and Egyptian writing untranslated. He stated that one part of the vignette "contains writing that cannot be revealed unto the world; but is to be had in the Holy Temple of God." Joseph always promised his followers that there was more revelation to come. They could take their place alongside the biblical prophets and receive the same grand key words. Like their priesthood predecessors, they were God's chosen rulers.[6]

Joseph had reflected on these ideas at a late-January gathering in his home. God the Father, Joseph began, "was once the same" as those who came after him. He had "redeemed a world [and] became the eternal God of that world." Then Jesus Christ followed in his father's footsteps and "redeemed this earth." He had become his Father's equal. One god had begotten another. This cycle of creation, redemption, and exaltation was a model for human existence. "All the Saints," Joseph promised, would in their turn receive a similar "celestial glory." Alluding to the New Testament, they would become "gods many and lords many." Men could become gods. Degree by degree, men could obtain that which would bring about their celestial glory and power.[7]

Joseph plumbed ancient texts, the ideas of church associates like Parley Pratt and William Phelps, and the culture that surrounded him. One of these sources of inspiration was Freemasonry. When Joseph dictated the Book of Mormon, Freemasonry was mired in the scandal caused by the murder of William Morgan, the first husband of Joseph's plural wife Lucinda Pendleton. By the early 1840s, anti-Masonry had faded as a political movement and social force. Lodges began to recover their respectability and regrow their memberships. John C. Bennett was a Mason, as were Stephen Douglas and many state politicians and aspiring officeholders.

Joseph, meanwhile, had developed an appreciation for Freemasonry's emphasis on secrecy. In Missouri, he had supported the Danites, a society of loyalists who swore oaths to defend the church and its prophet against vigilantes and dissenters. Joseph felt an even keener need for secrecy and loyalty as plural marriage expanded in Nauvoo. "I can keep a secret till doomsday," the prophet declared, but he knew that not everyone was so circumspect.[8]

Despite the anti-Masonic flavor of Joseph's early texts, he became attracted to the motifs and themes of Masonic ritual. In order to achieve the rank of Master Mason, a blindfolded candidate assumes the role of Hiram Abiff, understood as the architect of Solomon's Temple, and reprises his "death, burial, and resurrection." In the rite, the candidate—as Abiff—is murdered for refusing to reveal the secret "Master's word." The master of the lodge, playing the role of King Solomon, raises the candidate and whispers in his ear a "substitute for the Master's word." Along the way, initiates act out the consequences they will suffer if they, unlike Abiff, betray Masonic secrets. They will have their throats slit and their abdomens disemboweled. However, should they remain true, they can anticipate a glorious eternity. According to William Morgan's 1826 exposé, Master Masons looked forward to the time that Jesus Christ would return to the earth. Those men "found worthy, by his pass-word . . . [would] enter into the celestial Lodge above, where the Supreme Architect of the Universe presides." Here is a source for Joseph's promise that the Saints would receive the "grand key words" in the temple.[9]

The Mormon prophet loved Freemasonry's theater and pageantry, its aprons, scepters, and swords. The rites contained handgrips and passwords and secret names. In the higher degrees of Royal Arch Masonry, candidates recover the secret sacred name of God, a quest that resonated with Joseph's own interest in the name of God in the pure original language of heaven. Like Solomon and Hiram Abiff, Joseph was building a temple in which men and women would prepare themselves to come into the presence of God.

In mid-March 1842, Abraham Jonas, the Grand Master of Masonic Grand Lodge of Illinois, came to Nauvoo and oversaw the formal establishment of a lodge. On March 15, with three thousand onlookers thronging the route, the members of the Nauvoo Lodge paraded from Joseph's red-brick store to a grove near the temple, where Jonas delivered an address on the subject of "ancient York Masonry." That evening, members withdrew to the "lodge room" in Joseph's store. Joseph and

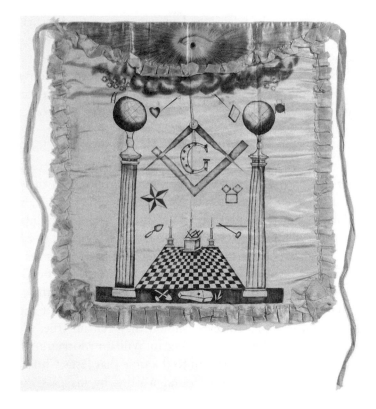

Joseph Smith's Masonic apron. (Photograph by Val Brinkerhoff;
courtesy of Community of Christ Archives)

Sidney Rigdon were initiated as "Apprentice Masons." The next day, they were raised to the "degree" of "Fellow Craft Mason" and then elevated to the "sublime degree" of "Master Mason." It was unusual for new initiates to advance so quickly. In the coming weeks, scores of men joined the Nauvoo Lodge, making it by far the largest in Illinois. The rapidity of the initiations underscored the prophet's newfound enthusiasm for Masonry.[10]

On February 6, Emma delivered a stillborn son, the fifth child she and Joseph had lost. Joseph was sealed in marriage to Sylvia Lyon two days later, but he also was attentive to his first wife's health and grief. The prophet approached Anna and William McIntire, parents of three-month-old twin girls. He asked Anna if "she would let him have one of them." Joseph and Emma thought that if she nursed the girl, it would fa-

Joseph Smith's red-brick store, ca. 1886. (Courtesy of Church
History Library)

cilitate her recovery from the pregnancy. McIntire reluctantly agreed
upon Joseph's promise to return the infant each night. "After [Emma] became better in health," another of McIntire's daughters recalled, "he did
not take our baby anymore." Emma endured another sorrow, however. In
late February or early March, she learned of the death of her mother,
Elizabeth Hale, whom she had not seen since she and her husband left
Harmony in 1830.[11]

On March 17, 1842, the day after Joseph and Sidney Rigdon became
Master Masons, Emma and around twenty other women gathered in the
same upper rooms of the prophet's store. They came to organize a chari-
table society for female Saints. Joseph along with apostles John Taylor
and Willard Richards presided over the first, organizational meeting of
the group.

Several Nauvoo women had proposed a "Sewing Society" to provide
clothing and other necessities for men working on the temple. Eliza R.
Snow, talented with both the needle and the pen, drafted a constitution,
which Sarah Kimball submitted to Joseph. It was good, the prophet
told them, but he could give them "something better," something involving more than charity. "I have desired to organize the sisters in the
order of the priesthood," he stated. "I now have the key [authority and

knowledge] by which I could do it." The society would instruct Nauvoo's women in the principles of Masonry and prepare them to participate in priesthood rites. At a meeting later that month, Joseph told the women that he would "make of this society a kingdom of priests" as in the days of Enoch.[12]

The pattern of the priesthood, Joseph explained, meant that the women should establish a presidency. The women unanimously selected Emma Smith, which Joseph explained fulfilled his 1830 revelation that she would be an "Elect Lady" who would "expound the scriptures." Apostle John Taylor laid his hands on her head and blessed her, "that she might be a mother in Israel and look to the wants of the needy." It was the most visible position of leadership Emma ever occupied within the church.[13]

The next order of business was the society's name. Sarah Cleveland and Ann Whitney, chosen as Emma's counselors, proposed the Nauvoo Female Relief Society, but apostle John Taylor, supported by Joseph, preferred "Benevolent" to "Relief." Just as communities in recent years had formed lyceums and debating societies, so too there were women's benevolent societies across the country. Emma stepped in and asserted herself. Nauvoo's women intended something more "extraordinary" than other institutions. Her argument prevailed. The society's members unanimously agreed to call their organization the Female Relief Society of Nauvoo. Scores of women joined, making the Relief Society a female counterpart to the Nauvoo Lodge, although for the time being without the ritual and pageantry.[14]

The Relief Society had another purpose as well. Its members, Joseph explained at their first meeting, were tasked with "correcting the morals and strengthening the virtues of the female community." This was a delicate matter. "Deal with them," Joseph taught, "and keep all your doings within your own bosoms." If members of the society conducted themselves improperly, their transgressions should be handled, but with discretion.[15]

Joseph soon revealed why he was so concerned about secrecy. At the society's next meeting, he asked Emma to read a complaint he had submitted, which accused a young woman named Clarissa Marvel of making "scandalous falsehoods on [his] character." Little is known about Marvel, a young woman apparently working by herself in Nauvoo. The minutes of the meeting do not elaborate on the nature of her alleged "falsehoods," but it is easy enough to read between the lines. Marvel either lived or had lived with Agnes Smith. She had witnessed something she considered inappropriate in Joseph's visits to his brother's widow.[16]

It was an awkward meeting. Agnes Smith and several of Joseph's other plural wives were in the room, as was Emma, who was not privy to her husband's secret marriages. Also present was Lucy Mack Smith, who heard an implicit allegation that her son had engaged in improper behavior with her widowed daughter-in-law. Joseph was nearby in his office and could listen to everything. Agnes Smith stammered that she had not seen anything "amiss" in Marvel's character. The society selected two women to discuss matters with the young woman in private. "We must avoid the appearance of evil," stressed Ann Whitney.[17]

Joseph opened the next meeting of the Relief Society by complimenting the women's "zeal," but he observed that "sometimes their zeal was not according to knowledge." Yes, they should "purge out iniquity," but they should proceed with extreme caution.[18]

The women then received a report that Clarissa Marvel "appeared like an innocent girl." Who, then, was the source of the derogatory gossip? Apparently two other women—Laura Jones and Hannah Burgess—had spread the rumors. Ann Whitney appointed two more women to demand the appearance of Jones and Burgess at the society's next meeting. Elizabeth Durfee, one of the two appointees, objected. She did not want the assignment, perhaps because she herself had or soon would become one of Joseph's wives. Emma told Durfee to serve unless she could find a more capable substitute.[19]

Emma Smith then read a letter from her husband in which Joseph cautioned the society that men were trying to "debauch" Latter-day Saint women by claiming that he and other church leaders sanctioned sex outside of the confines of marriage. They should not believe such lies, he warned. Joseph, curiously, left open the possibility that he might teach them things "contrary to the old established morals and virtues and scriptural laws." If so, they would learn it from his own "mouth, by actual revelation and commandment." Joseph suggested that his instructions would test whether the society's members were "sufficiently skilled in Masonry as to keep a secret." He wanted to know whether he could trust the women.[20]

The chatter was already spreading throughout Nauvoo, however. At the church's semi-annual conference in early April, Hyrum Smith—in the dark about the polygamous sealings—denounced a rumor that he and members of the Twelve had shut a young woman "in a room for several days, and that they had endeavored to induce her to believe in [a man] having two wives." The woman in question was Martha Brotherton, a seventeen-year-old recent arrival from England. The apostles hadn't locked her in a room for three days, but Young, who had befriended her while on his mission, had asked her to become his first plural wife. Joseph had counseled Brotherton to accept his teachings on marriage and to accept Young as her husband. The horrified Brotherton and her parents soon left Nauvoo.[21]

Joseph now publicly delivered the same warning he had given privately to the Relief Society. In a Sunday sermon, he "pronounced a curse upon all adulterers and fornicators and unvirtuous persons and those who had made use of his name to carry on their iniquitous designs." He added that he would cleanse the church of all immorality.[22]

At a mid-April Relief Society meeting, Sarah Cleveland—sealed to Joseph sometime that spring—announced that Clarissa Marvel had signed a certificate stating that she had never "heard anything improper or unvirtuous in the conduct or conversation of either President [Joseph] Smith or Mrs. Agnes Smith." The young woman had placed "her mark," an X in lieu of a signature, on the document. Cleveland warned the society's members that God would judge them if they spoke evil of Joseph or Emma.[23]

What was Emma's role throughout the investigations? What, if anything, did she know about her husband's polygamy? Was she eager to undertake a Relief Society campaign against iniquity in order to safeguard her husband's reputation—and her own—or did she suspect his infidelity and want to get to the bottom of things? Unlike Joseph, Emma seemed more interested in uncovering immorality than in maintaining secrecy. She surely had heard whispers about her husband's alleged marriages or affairs. Given Joseph's Kirtland relationship with Fanny Alger, Emma might have worried about his fidelity, but she did not countenance gossip that Joseph had married other women. Such behavior remained unfathomable.

The uproar did not deter Joseph from pursuing additional plural marriages. On April 9, 1842, the prophet asked Marinda Hyde to arrange a discreet meeting with Nancy Rigdon, Sidney Rigdon's nineteen-year-old daughter. Hyde was the wife of apostle Orson Hyde, who was in the midst of an arduous three-year mission to Europe and Jerusalem. (Circumstances became so trying that Hyde, suffering from hunger on a longer-than-expected trip at sea, was forced to eat snails along the shores of the eastern Mediterranean.) The previous December, Joseph had dictated a revelation in which God urged Marinda Hyde to "hearken to the counsel of my servant in all things whatsoever he shall teach her." According to Marinda Hyde's later statement, Joseph had already taught her the principle of plural marriage. She accepted it. The timing of Marinda's sealing to Joseph is uncertain, but it took place either before mid-April 1842, while her husband was still on his mission to Jerusalem, or the following spring. Either way, she became a "polygamy confidante," and Joseph used her as an intermediary for an especially risky proposal—risky because Joseph had not introduced Sidney Rigdon to the principle of plural marriage.[24]

Marinda Hyde escorted Nancy Rigdon to the *Times and Seasons* printing office, which doubled as a residence for Hyde and her two young daughters. Joseph was waiting. When the prophet proposed marriage, a shocked Nancy rejected him. Joseph would have anticipated a need for persuasion. In this case, he sent Nancy a letter. "That which is *wrong* under one circumstance," he explained, "may be, and often is, *right* under another." Solomon, he continued, had asked God for wisdom, but then received "every desire of his heart," including, Joseph implied, hundreds of wives and concubines. Joseph added that obedience to God's commandments would bring joy, peace, and happiness, blessings that, if rejected, God would bestow on others. Nancy remained unconvinced.[25]

The Nauvoo Lodge and the Relief Society were both mass social organizations. Three hundred men joined the lodge in its first several months. Five hundred female Saints were members of the Relief Society. Both organizations were designed to prepare church members for rituals that would grant them spiritual power and blessings. In a May 1, 1842, sermon, Joseph explained that he would reveal "certain signs and words" to the elders upon the temple's completion.

A select number of elders did not have to wait that long. On May 4, again in the upper floor of his red-brick store, Joseph met with nine associates, including Hyrum Smith, Newel K. Whitney, and apostles Brigham Young, Heber C. Kimball, and Willard Richards, all of whom were Masons. Joseph wanted to prepare church members en masse for the temple, but he also wanted a smaller group of men that he could trust.[26]

Historians usually refer to these events as the introduction of what became known as the Nauvoo "endowment," though the term may not have been used at first. Joseph's scribes did not write down the contents of what Richards termed "instructions concerning the priesthood."[27] According to

Brigham Young's recollection, he and the other initiates were taken into a side room or office, "where we were washed and anointed and had our garments placed upon us." Joseph gave each man a "new name," and he taught them "key words" that included "signs, tokens, and penalties." Then they proceeded into the large upper room, which had been divided into several compartments with curtains. As they progressed through these spaces, Joseph provided them with further instruction. Richards explained that the purpose was to "secure the fullness of [their] blessings" so that they would be able to "come up and abide in the presence of Eloheim [God] in the eternal worlds." They would repeat the signs, tokens, and key words in order to pass by angelic sentries into God's celestial presence.[28]

Joseph's "instructions concerning the priesthood" bore a palpable resemblance to the Masonic rites in which the prophet had participated earlier in the year. Freemasonry was the inspiration for the key words, oaths, and penalties, including gestures symbolizing the macabre punishment individuals would suffer should they reveal the ritual's content. The robes, caps, and aprons also represent Masonic influence.

The initiates understood this connection. "There is a similarity of priesthood in Masonry," Heber Kimball informed Parley Pratt that summer. Joseph taught that "Masonry was taken from priesthood but has become degenerated, but many things are perfect." Willard Richards later observed that "in this council was instituted the ancient order of things for the first time in these last days." Joseph had restored Masonic rites to their original divine pattern, much in the way that his translations had restored the missing and corrupted portions of the Bible.[29]

In keeping with that idea of restoration, the rite bore the marks of the prophet's longer-term interests. Well before his intensive engagement with Masonry, Joseph had spoken of handshakes as a means to distinguish angels (who according to Joseph had bodies) from Satanic spirits (who did not). Since the early 1830s, moreover, Joseph had evidenced a fascination with lost names and words as conduits for spiritual power. The story of Hiram Abiff and Solomon's Temple resonated with the prophet, but as Joseph continued to develop the Nauvoo endowment, he took inspiration from the Genesis stories of creation, the Garden of Eden, and Adam's transgression.

The May 1842 initiations created another inner circle bound by ritual oaths and secrecy, a circle that mostly overlapped with those men Joseph had taken into his confidence about polygamy. At the same time, Joseph intended the "ancient order" for many more Saints, and not just

Sutcliffe Maudsley, *Joseph Smith in Nauvoo Legion Uniform*, ca. 1842.
Gouache on paper. (Courtesy of Church History Museum)

for men. Joseph had told the women of the Relief Society that "the keys of the kingdom are about to be given to them . . . as well as to the elders."[30] The washings and anointings of the Kirtland endowment had been for the men only, but Joseph planned to expand the Nauvoo rite in ways that incorporated women.

There was one final similarity with Masonry. In the lodges of Freemasonry, men advanced through a series of degrees before achieving the rank of Master Mason. Even then, though, there were always possibilities for further advancement, whether through the degrees of Royal Arch Masonry or in a whole panoply of auxiliary degrees. Likewise, in the months and years ahead, Joseph introduced additional priesthood instruction, rites, and degrees. Joseph's enthusiasm for ritual was never sated.

Nauvoo was outwardly peaceful and booming. "Emigration is like bees, swarming by flowers from all parts," Wilford Woodruff reported to his fellow apostle Parley Pratt. There were approximately four thousand Saints in Nauvoo itself and probably several thousand more in the surrounding area. Large crowds thronged the church's Sunday meetings. Baptisms for the dead moved into the basement of the temple. They took place in a font modeled after the "molten sea" standing "upon twelve oxen" in Solomon's Temple.[31]

On May 7, 1842, Joseph presided over a general parade of the Nauvoo Legion's two thousand troops. Visitors for the occasion included Stephen Douglas; William Wilson, chief justice of the Illinois Supreme Court; and several other prominent politicians. At midday, a steamboat delivered around forty Saints, emigrants from England. In the afternoon, Joseph hosted a dinner for the legion's staff, including Major General John C. Bennett, and their wives. He then delivered a speech to the reassembled troops. At the conclusion, Joseph and Emma enjoyed a ride around the temple grounds. Joseph basked in the order, unity, and power projected by the legion's parade and the visible concord between Mormon Nauvoo and state leaders.[32]

"Why stand in the way?" Joseph asked the members of the Relief Society that spring. God had chosen him to lead the church. He was "continually rising" despite "everything bearing him down." Joseph expressed confidence that he could overcome all opponents and challenges, be they financial, political, legal, or spiritual. "After all," the prophet observed, "[I] always come out right at the end." That confidence was soon put to a severe test.[33]

CHAPTER TWENTY-FIVE

World on Fire (1842)

O N APRIL 29, 1842, Willard Richards wrote that Joseph had learned about a "conspiracy against the peace of his household." At the center of the trouble stood John C. Bennett, who was both engaging in sexual misconduct and threatening to expose Joseph's polygamy.[1]

Bennett was mayor of Nauvoo, major general in the Nauvoo Legion, grand secretary of the Nauvoo Masonic Lodge, and an assistant in the church's First Presidency. Careful observers of Joseph's activities, however, would have noticed that Bennett was not in Joseph's innermost circle. Especially after the Twelve returned from their mission to England, Joseph spent countless evenings with them, not with Bennett.

It is unclear how much Bennett knew about Joseph's plural marriages. When Joseph was sealed to Louisa Beman, Bennett was still living with the prophet and could identity Joseph Bates Noble as the man who had performed the sealing. However, while Bennett later claimed to have been present for some of Joseph's proposals and liaisons, it does not seem that the mayor was a polygamy insider.[2]

Even so, Bennett was aware of the many rumors, and he used them to facilitate his own sexual pursuits. William Law, another member of the First Presidency who later broke with Joseph, deemed Bennett a "thorough scoundrel." According to several reports, Bennett seduced women by telling them that Joseph sanctioned extramarital sex and had engaged in such behavior. Bennett's immorality was about the only thing on which everyone in Nauvoo would agree.[3]

In early May, Abraham Jonas—Illinois's leading Freemason—sent a letter to Nauvoo informing its leaders that Bennett was a man of poor character who had been expelled from a lodge in Ohio. Bennett denied the charges "in toto," but Mormon hierarchs had heard enough to investigate and sideline him. Bennett's leadership in the Nauvoo Lodge was over. Church officers drafted a notice announcing that they were "withdraw[ing] the hand of fellowship from Gen. John C. Bennett." They held off publishing the notice, however, in the hope that Bennett would confess and make amends. Joseph wanted to punish Bennett for his transgressions without precipitating a public scandal. The prophet understood that Bennett could cause trouble.[4]

It was becoming harder and harder for Joseph to tamp down polygamy rumors. Sidney Rigdon had learned about the prophet's overture to his daughter. Also, Nancy Rigdon had shown Joseph's letter to Francis Higbee, who had been courting her. Higbee then put the story "in circulation." On May 12, Joseph dictated a letter to Sidney Rigdon "concerning certain difficulties or surmises." The next evening the two men had a heartfelt conversation, but Rigdon remained uneasy.[5]

While Joseph sought to squelch polygamy rumors and address John C. Bennett's transgressions, he got wind of a brazen crime in Missouri. On May 6, an assailant had fired a pistol through a window of the Independence residence of Lilburn Boggs. The former governor, who had ordered the Mormons to leave his state or face extermination, was reading a newspaper after dinner. His son heard the crack of the gun, rushed into the room, and found blood gushing from his father's head and neck. Two balls had penetrated Boggs's skull, and one lodged in his neck. Physicians and family members did not expect him to survive the attack.[6]

Word that Boggs had died soon reached Nauvoo. Church leaders announced what they regarded as good news during a Sunday meeting. Apostle Wilford Woodruff noted that "the vengeance of God has overtaken him at last and he has met his just deserts." In his journal, Woodruff drew an arrow lodged in Boggs's head.[7]

An investigation into the shooting yielded a suspect, a silversmith named Tompkins, but he was cleared. Newspapers spread rumors that Joseph had ordered Boggs's assassination. The Burlington, Iowa, *Hawkeye and Patriot* published an anonymous letter stating that a "suspicious stranger seen lurking around for several days before the murder . . . is supposed to be a *Mormon.*" Other papers reported that Joseph had prophesied that Boggs would suffer a violent death. "I should not entertain a doubt that it was done by some of Joe's minions at his instigation," the postmaster in Montrose informed Missouri's governor, Thomas Reynolds.[8]

Joseph wasted no remorse on Boggs, but he denied any role in the former governor's death. "My hands are clean and my heart pure," he maintained. William Smith, the prophet's brother, speculated in the church-owned *Wasp* that Boggs had been shot "by one of his own negroes."[9]

It turned out that Boggs hadn't been exterminated after all. He recovered. He blamed Joseph Smith for his brush with death. And he wanted justice.

The extent of Joseph's legal danger rested on the willingness of Illinois's governor to cooperate with Missouri officials in any extradition attempt. Under the terms of the state constitution, Thomas Carlin, the incumbent, couldn't seek a second consecutive term. In August, voters would elect his successor, who would take office in December. Joseph endorsed the Democratic nominee, Adam Snyder, whom the prophet praised because of his prior support for the Nauvoo Charter. The endorsement antagonized the Whig candidate, former governor Joseph Duncan, who made opposition to the Mormons and their charters the centerpiece of his bid.[10]

Snyder's May 14, 1842, death upended the campaign. Thomas Ford, a member of the state supreme court, replaced him as the Democratic nominee. Ford expressed wariness about both the Nauvoo Charter and anti-Mormon demagoguery. Joseph now stated that he would "not cooperate or vote with either the Whig or Democratic parties."[11] It was uncertain whether Illinois's next governor would be an ally or an antagonist of the Saints.

Nauvoo's internal politics were in flux as well. John C. Bennett resigned as the city's mayor on May 17. Joseph, who had been serving as vice mayor, became acting mayor. The city council met two days later to ratify Joseph's ascension to the office.

As the council conducted the election, Joseph quickly scribbled down a revelation and "threw it across the room to Hiram Kimball," a city alderman and prosperous merchant. Kimball was not a member of the church but had joined the city's Masonic lodge. Kimball's wife, Sarah

Kimball, was one of the founders of the Relief Society. "Verily thus saith the Lord," read Joseph's revelation, "Hiram Kimball has been insinuating evil and forming evil opinions against you." If Kimball persisted in his gossip and scheming, the revelation warned, he would be cursed.[12]

What sort of evil opinions? No contemporary sources elaborate, but Hiram Kimball likely was talking about Joseph's polygamy. The merchant had the inside scoop because Joseph had proposed marriage to his wife. Like Nancy Rigdon, Sarah Kimball had turned him down. "I asked him to teach it to someone else," she recalled. The prophet tossed the revelation to Hiram Kimball in an attempt to forestall opposition to his election as mayor and discourage talk about the failed proposal.[13]

The council voted eighteen to one in Joseph's favor. Hiram Kimball presumably was the lone dissenting vote, though he and the prophet quickly reconciled. He was baptized into the church the next summer, and he and his wife remained faithful Latter-day Saints until their deaths. Neither Kimball ever married plurally.[14]

After the vote, the city council adopted a resolution thanking Bennett for what he had done for Nauvoo. Joseph also put some pointed questions to his predecessor. Did Bennett know anything against him? Joseph asked. Bennett denied having stated that Joseph had "given [him] authority to hold illicit intercourse with women." He insisted that he had "no difficulty with the heads of the church" and hoped that he would be restored to his "former standing." Joseph pressed. Did Bennett know anything against his character? The ex-mayor maintained that Joseph was an honorable man. The prophet wanted to have these affirmations of his character on the record.[15]

Shortly after the city council concluded its business, the Relief Society held its weekly meeting. Emma Smith told the women that it was "an evil day." They had not been sufficiently diligent in their mandate to uncover and root out iniquity. "The time had been," she continued, "when charity had covered a multitude of sins—but now it is necessary that sin should be exposed." Emma didn't mince words. She noted that "some in authority" had behaved immorally and had claimed her husband's sanction for their behavior. The president of the Relief Society demanded action.[16]

Other church leaders agreed, at least when it came to the sins of certain individuals. The Nauvoo Stake High Council, which handled local ecclesiastical discipline, met several times over the following week. At a decided risk to their own reputations, multiple women testified that

Chauncey Higbee, brother of Francis Higbee and Bennett's aide-de-camp, had seduced them. Catherine Warren provided shocking testimony. She stated that she had slept with Higbee, Bennett, and other men, including William Smith. Warren also alleged that Bennett had promised to "attend to it" with medicine should she become pregnant. The council excommunicated Chauncey Higbee. It did not pursue charges against the prophet's brother, whom another witness also implicated. The leaders of the high council probably had received word that they should keep their investigations within certain bounds.[17]

Joseph still hoped to keep the scandal out of the public gaze. On May 26, the day after Warren's testimony, Bennett made a confession to the Masonic lodge "concerning females in Nauvoo." Joseph pleaded with the men to forgive Bennett. They did so and agreed to keep matters confidential.[18]

That afternoon, Joseph and Emma attended another meeting of the Relief Society. A remarkable scene unfolded before a room so crowded that many could not get inside. Joseph explained to the women that because of their "refined feelings and sensitiveness," they were prone to be overly zealous and rigid when it came to matters of morality. He had worked hard to bring iniquity to light. Now they needed to forgive those who repented and sought restoration. Excessive zeal was dangerous. "A little tale will set the world on fire," he warned. They should not make public the transgressions of church members. Nor should they proceed recklessly in their crusade for moral reformation, "lest in exposing these heinous sins, we draw the indignation of a gentile world upon us." In other words, they might have to allow some sins to go undetected or unpunished in order to protect the church.[19]

Emma stood up when her husband had finished speaking. She agreed that the women should set aside "idle talk" and gossip. Still, she insisted that "sin must not be covered." Moreover, anyone who refused to expose men and women who had committed "heinous sins" themselves became offenders. Whereas Joseph's primary concern was to protect himself and the church from scandal, Emma was bent on rooting out sexual immorality and getting to the truth. Joseph still had not told her about his plural marriages. Perhaps Emma hoped that rigorous investigations would clear her husband's name or, if the rumors proved true, bring him to repentance. Joseph let Emma have the last word.[20]

It is hard to gauge Joseph's mood during these weeks. The prophet worried that Boggs's shooting would place him in legal jeopardy, and there had been no shortage of tumult in Nauvoo because of scandal and rumor. At the same time, the establishment of the Masonic lodge and the Relief Society were signal accomplishments, as was the ritual that became known as the endowment. "Brother Joseph feels as well as I ever see him," apostle Heber C. Kimball commented in mid-June. "One reason is he has got a small company, that he feels safe in their hands." Joseph expected trouble from Bennett and Boggs but possessed the self-confidence that he could overcome all enemies.[21]

On June 18, Joseph called a special church meeting. Thousands of men and women gathered near the temple and heard the prophet detail John C. Bennett's "iniquity, wickedness, and corruption." It is unclear what precipitated the final break. Joseph probably suspected that Bennett planned to collaborate with the church's enemies in Illinois and Missouri and wanted to get ahead of his antagonist. Bennett soon left Nauvoo, in keeping with his long history of skipping town in the wake of his frauds and scandals.[22]

Joseph's next step was to publish a host of charges against Bennett in the church's Nauvoo newspaper. The prophet outlined a long history of adultery and slander, and he included evidence in the form of letters dating back to the spring of 1841. (Thoughtful readers might have wondered why Joseph had continued to elevate a man with demonstrably poor character.) Church leaders also included Bennett's mid-May testimony that Joseph had not sanctioned "illicit intercourse with women." Joseph warned the Saints that Bennett would malign the church and attempt to destroy it.[23]

Bennett got right to it. He wrote letters, which Springfield's *Sangamo Journal* published in support of Joseph Duncan's anti-Mormon gubernatorial campaign. Bennett's charges were a blend of fact, fancy, and hyperbole. "Holy Joe" threatened to unleash his band of Danites to murder Bennett and other opponents. The prophet was a swindler trying to hoodwink creditors and gullible church members. And then there was polygamy, a sordid tale of alleged marriages, botched proposals, and rank adultery. The prophet's "clandestine wives"—single and married—surpassed King Solomon's accumulation of women. Holy Joe had made Nauvoo a prophetic pottage of corruption and sex.[24]

The former mayor had spread his allegations in Nauvoo before his departure. Bennett had obtained Joseph's letter to Nancy Rigdon and may have spoken with her family about the matter. Joseph visited the

Rigdons on June 28. Both Bennett and Willard Richards wrote second-hand accounts of the meeting. According to Bennett, the prophet at first tried to "deny the attempted seduction." Nancy Rigdon then "told him he was a cursed liar." Richards, by contrast, reported that "Elder Rigdon's family ... were confounded and put to silence by the truth from President Joseph." Sidney Rigdon did not fully accept Joseph's explanation, however. He sent Joseph a note in which he asked for the prophet's company on a ride out onto the "prairie," the land to Nauvoo's east. Rigdon assured Joseph of his friendship and hoped that they could "settle forever all difficulties." It seems that Joseph ignored the request. He suspected that Rigdon and his family had aligned themselves with Bennett.[25]

Bennett also asserted that while apostle Orson Pratt was away from Nauvoo on his mission to England, Joseph had paid a series of visits to his wife, Sarah. Joseph repeatedly had pressured her to become one of his plural wives. Sarah Pratt repeatedly had turned him down. Then, on a final visit, Joseph had forcibly kissed her. Sarah Pratt supported at least the substance of Bennett's allegations, which made it harder for Joseph to parry the charge. Instead, Joseph publicly countered that Sarah Pratt had engaged in an illicit relationship with Bennett. The prophet didn't mince words. The *Sangamo Journal* reported that in a July 14 speech, Joseph declared that Sarah Pratt "had been a w[hore] from her mother's breast."[26]

As far as Orson Pratt was concerned, the allegations of John C. Bennett and Joseph Smith were equally dreadful. "I am a ruined man!" Pratt wrote. Either the man he regarded as a prophet had proposed a polygamous marriage to his wife, or his wife had slept with Bennett. "My sorrows are greater than I can bear!" he concluded. "Where I am henceforth it matters not." It was a suicide note. On the morning of July 15, Pratt was missing, and his letter was found along a road in Nauvoo.[27]

Joseph sprang into action. He organized the men of the city to search for Pratt, "lest he should have laid violent hands on himself." He also called a meeting at the grove, where he denounced Bennett, "especially with regard to Sister Pratt." That night searchers found Orson Pratt sitting on a log fifteen miles south of Nauvoo.[28] The apostle returned to the city but remained deeply troubled. "His feelings are so wrought up," Brigham Young informed Parley Pratt, Orson's brother, "that he did not know whether his wife is wrong, or whether Joseph's testimony and others' are wrong ... he is all but crazy about matters." Like Sidney Rigdon, Orson Pratt was anguished and confused but uncertain whether he wanted to break with the man he had accepted as God's prophet.[29]

The turmoil surrounding John C. Bennett did not deter Joseph from pursuing additional plural wives. On June 29, 1842, the day after Joseph met with the Rigdons, Brigham Young sealed Eliza R. Snow to the prophet. Snow, secretary of the Relief Society, lived with Sarah Cleveland, another of Joseph's many wives, who stood as a witness to the sealing.[30]

Snow wrote a terse and cryptic entry in her journal: "This is a day of much interest to my feelings." She was single at the time of the sealing, unlike many of the women Joseph had married over the past year. At the age of thirty-eight, she probably expected to remain so. But as she later explained, even before anyone broached the idea to her, she had received an "intimation" that God would restore the practice of plural marriage. Snow had boarded with the prophet's family in Kirtland and had taught his "family school." She recalled his "kindness," "expansive mind," and humility in private devotions.[31]

The next month Joseph was sealed to Sarah Ann Whitney, the seventeen-year-old daughter of Newel and Elizabeth Ann Whitney. The Whitneys had been among Joseph's most steadfast followers since the day they had welcomed him into their Kirtland home. Newel was one of the men washed, anointed, and sealed by Joseph in May 1842, and Ann Whitney was one of Emma's counselors in the Relief Society presidency. Joseph confided the principle of plural marriage to Newel, who talked about the matter with Ann. Newel and Ann were visionaries who had had many powerful spiritual experiences over the past dozen years, and they asked God to give them "some special manifestation concerning this new and strange doctrine." God granted their request. "A halo of light encircled us," Ann Whitney later wrote.[32]

The vision did more than convince them about the correctness of the new doctrine. It persuaded them to give their daughter to Joseph. The prophet dictated a revelation to Newel Whitney for the occasion. It is the first contemporaneous record that presents Joseph's theology of marriage in detail. In the revelation, the Lord promised that the entire Whitney family—"both old and young"—would be "crowned ... with honor and immortality and eternal life." How could they be sure? The promise rested on "the lineage of ... priesthood" that stretched back to Melchizedek and other ancient patriarchs. The sealing bound together two families and their lineages, ensuring their connection and exaltation for eternity.

The revelation provided the words for the sealing, which Newel Whitney performed. Joseph and Sarah Ann promised to be each other's companions forever. They vowed to preserve themselves "for each other and from all others," with one rather large caveat: "reserving only those rights which have been given to my servant Joseph by revelation and commandment and by legal authority in times past." In other words, Sarah Ann promised to not have sex with any other men, and Joseph promised not to have sex with women who were not sealed to him in marriage or, in Emma's case, civilly married to him. With those vows made, Sarah became Joseph's wife, with "all the rights . . . that belong to that condition," including sexual intimacy. Sarah Ann and her parents undoubtedly wondered and worried about how the sealing would affect her life.[33]

Joseph also encouraged men he had introduced to the principle of plural marriage to move ahead. Apostle Brigham Young quickly recovered from Martha Brotherton's stinging rejection. On June 14, Joseph sealed Young to Lucy Ann Decker in the first well-documented instance of another Latter-day Saint man entering polygamy. Like many of the prophet's plural wives, Decker was already married to another man.[34]

The rifts with Sidney Rigdon and Orson Pratt were troubling to Joseph, but he probably believed that he could patch things up with both men over time. Another of Bennett's accusations posed a more existential threat. Nauvoo's ex-mayor alleged that after foretelling Lilburn Boggs's death, the prophet had sent his friend Orrin Porter Rockwell to Independence to fulfill his words. Bennett urged Illinois governor Thomas Carlin to issue a writ for Joseph's arrest and extradition, offering—for rhetorical effect—to serve the writ himself. "I regard him as a foul and polluted murderer," Bennett declared, and when he left Illinois, he took that message with him to St. Louis. Days after Bennett's accusations appeared in Missouri newspapers, Boggs swore affidavits that Rockwell was his shooter and that he possessed evidence that Joseph Smith "was accessory before the fact."[35]

Was there any truth to the allegations? Porter Rockwell was in Independence at the time of the attempted murder. He had taken his wife to be with her parents there during the late stages of a pregnancy, and he had returned to Nauvoo shortly after the shooting. Rockwell thus had motive and opportunity, and he surely had the means as well. It does not seem, however, that any witnesses connected Rockwell to the crime. Nor was there evidence—besides Bennett's accusation—that Joseph Smith had dispatched Rockwell to do the deed.

Boggs's affidavit was enough for Thomas Reynolds, the victim's successor as Missouri's governor. Reynolds requested that his Illinois counterpart, Thomas Carlin, issue writs for the arrest of Porter Rockwell and Joseph Smith so that they could be dealt with according to Missouri law.[36]

The prophet was worried, and for good reason. Joseph still feared that a mob would kill him if he was brought to Missouri. Moreover, he had heard rumors that Governor Carlin felt that he deserved to be "shot." When Joseph wrote Carlin to denounce Bennett's perfidy and seek reassurances, Carlin coolly responded that he had heard that Joseph had prophesied "that Boggs should die a violent death and that I should die in a ditch." While the governor maintained that he would try to suppress any mobs, he advised Joseph that he and his followers should be more careful with their words.[37]

Church leaders lobbied Carlin to shield Joseph from arrest. At a large meeting in Nauvoo, Wilson Law, a member of the city council and brigadier general in the Nauvoo Legion, presented a resolution declaring that Joseph was a "virtuous, peaceable, and patriotic man," the opposite of the moral monster that John C. Bennett described. The resolution passed overwhelmingly, but several men voted in the negative, including Orson Pratt. The prophet put Pratt on the spot, asking if he had any direct knowledge of the alleged misbehavior. "Personally, toward the female sex, I have not," he conceded. Pratt's dissent marred the occasion, but eight hundred men signed a petition asking Governor Carlin to defend their "peaceable rights." A thousand members of the Relief Society signed a second petition lauding Joseph's "virtue, philanthropy, and benevolence" and asking that Carlin protect him from injury.[38]

Emma Smith and Eliza Snow, now married to the same man, joined a delegation to Quincy. Wilson Law presented the petitions to Carlin, who, according to Snow, assured them of his protection and fidelity to the law.[39]

On August 1, shortly after the delegation returned to Nauvoo, Illinois voters went to the polls at the end of a heated gubernatorial campaign. Throughout the summer, Whig newspapers accused the Democrats of having made a "corrupt bargain" with "Joe Smith." Joseph made his feelings about the Whig candidate plain when he named a recently acquired horse "Joe Duncan." Shortly before the election, the Nauvoo *Wasp* published what amounted to an endorsement of Thomas Ford, the Democratic candidate. It turned out that Ford did not especially need Joe Smith to beat Joe Duncan. He won the election handily.[40]

Governor Carlin, however, remained in office until Ford's December inauguration. The day after the election, Carlin signed a warrant for Joseph's arrest. He sent the Adams County deputy sheriff, Thomas King, and two other officers to bring the prophet and Rockwell into custody. On August 8, the posse arrested the two men in Nauvoo.

Church leaders had prepared for this eventuality. The Nauvoo Charter authorized the city's municipal court to grant writs of habeas corpus in cases pertaining to city statutes. However, that authority would not free individuals from arrests on alleged violations of state or federal law. Stephen Douglas had invalidated the last warrant for Joseph's arrest and extradition, but Joseph and his friends did not want to count on non-Mormon judges this time around. Accordingly, the city council had passed a law that "no citizen of this city shall be taken out of the city by any writs, without the privilege of investigation before the municipal court, and the benefit of a writ of habeas corpus." In other words, the municipal court could thwart an extradition attempt.[41]

On the day of the arrests, the council met again and passed a bill that went further. Even if the "writ or process" used to arrest a Nauvoo resident was valid, the municipal court should "fully hear the merits of the case" before delivering up that individual to another jurisdiction. For instance, the ordinance mandated the discharge of a prisoner arrested for reasons of "religious or other persecution." The summer 1842 city ordinances turned the Nauvoo Charter's habeas corpus provision into a much broader tool of legal protection. It was a risky stratagem, however, one that hinged on the willingness of state courts to uphold the city's statutes and on the goodwill of politicians to leave the charter intact.[42]

The strategy proved expedient in the short term. Joseph petitioned Nauvoo's municipal court for a writ of habeas corpus, as did Rockwell. The justices agreed and immediately ordered the arresting officers to bring the prisoner before their court. Sheriff King was not sure what to do, so he left the pair in the custody of the city marshal and went to consult Governor Carlin. By the time King returned, Joseph and Rockwell were nowhere to be found.[43]

CHAPTER TWENTY-SIX

David (1842–1843)

ETERMINED TO KEEP HIMSELF free from his Missouri enemies, Joseph had slipped away before the posse could arrest him again. The prophet spent most of the next three months in hiding, governing the church in absentia and meeting clandestinely with family and friends.

Joseph first went to his uncle John Smith across the river in the Mormon settlement of Zarahemla, Iowa. A few days later, he arranged to meet Emma and a group of trusted allies after dark on one of the islands near the Iowa bank of the Mississippi. It was a "sacred night," when bonds were strengthened against the backdrop of oppression. "They were my friends," he reflected. "I now meet them in adversity, and they are still my warmer friends."[1] The reunion was brief, however, because of rumors that the governor of Iowa—like his Illinois counterpart—had issued a warrant for Joseph's arrest. His friends escorted him to the farm of Edward Sayers, a few miles upriver. Everyone took great care to avoid detection, as Sheriff King and another officer lingered in Nauvoo.

The prophet received encouragement from a steady stream of visitors, including "undaunted, firm and unwavering, unchangeable, affectionate Emma," a tireless comfort and advocate during these weeks. She traveled to Joseph's hideouts, and she directed letters to his legal counsel and political antagonists alike. All the while, she managed her large household, including their four children. When Joseph contemplated moving far away from Nauvoo, to the "Pine Country" of the Wisconsin

Territory, he assured Emma that he would go only if she joined him. Joseph instead took advice from Major General Wilson Law of the Nauvoo Legion and relocated within the city limits. On the night of August 17, Emma accompanied her husband to the house of Carlos Granger.[2]

Joseph referred to Emma as the "wife of my youth," alluding to a biblical proverb, but he also sought the company of a much more youthful wife. On August 18, he wrote Newel K. Whitney, Elizabeth Ann Whitney, and their daughter Sarah Ann and asked them to visit him. Newel Whitney should go ahead of the others and knock at a window on the southeast corner of Carlos Granger's house.

The prophet stressed the need for secrecy, but not because of the sheriff. "Find out when Emma comes," he told his friends. "Then you cannot be safe, but when she is not here, there is the most perfect safety." He advised the Whitneys to "burn this letter as soon as you read it." They ignored him on that point.

The fact that Joseph addressed this letter to three Whitneys complicates its meaning. "My feelings are so strong for you since what has passed lately between us," he wrote. He "could not live long" in this "dreary" and "lonesome" state. He desired "succor." It is unclear whether the words were meant for all three of the Whitneys, or for Sarah in particular. Nor does any evidence reveal what sort of succor Joseph envisioned. At the very least, though, Joseph sensed Emma would be suspicious if she learned that Sarah Ann Whitney had visited the safe house, even in the company of her parents.

Joseph's stated reason for the invitation was that he wanted to "get the fullness of my blessings sealed upon our heads." No sources indicate whether the Whitneys visited Joseph on the night of the invitation, but the prophet soon made good on the promised blessings. Newel and Ann had given their daughter in marriage to him, and they were blessed—presumably by Joseph himself—with a promise that they, along with all of their "house," would have a "part in the first resurrection together." The Whitneys then were baptized for the remission of their sins, confirmed, and then blessed again. "I was blessed above others," Newel wrote, "with long life, the keys of the priesthood, [and] a double portion of the spirit." Joseph bestowed rich spiritual rewards for their fidelity and friendship.[3]

On August 19, with Sheriff King having left Nauvoo, Joseph risked a return home. Amid rumors that another sheriff was in town incognito, Joseph proceeded with caution, confining himself to his house and the upper floor of his store. Joseph had eluded his captors for the time being, but he knew they would return, and he was prepared for a protracted legal struggle.[4]

Joseph needed to do more than evade arrest and extradition. John C. Bennett's salacious salvoes threatened to sunder Joseph's relationships with key associates and sully the church's national reputation. The prophet mounted a vigorous counterattack. He directed scores of men to disperse across the country to preach and publish against Bennett. Joseph wanted to bring Orson Pratt and Sidney Rigdon back into the fold, but if he could not, the prophet and his allies would discredit them as well.

Several of Pratt's fellow apostles spent days urging him to repent of his public opposition to Joseph. When he refused to do so, he was removed from the Quorum of the Twelve Apostles and "cut off" from the church. The next day, though, Smith's clerk, William Clayton, noted that "Orson Pratt has also signified his intention of coming out in defense of the truth"—in other words, in defense of Joseph and the church. Pratt's intentions were unclear, and he did not join the ranks of elders who were leaving Nauvoo to counter Bennett's charges. When Joseph risked appearing at a public meeting a week later, he tore into Pratt. "Orson Pratt has attempted to destroy himself," the prophet mocked the wayward apostle's near suicide, "caused all the city almost to go in search of him." Joseph denounced Pratt as a would-be Judas prepared to betray him to his enemies on the basis of his wife's gossip. A "serious and dejected" Pratt sat behind the prophet at the meeting.[5]

Things soon got worse for Pratt. At the end of the month, church leaders published a collection of affidavits refuting Bennett's allegations. They included several statements about Sarah Pratt, including a Nauvoo woman's assertion that she had seen Bennett "taking his hands out of her bosom" and "lying down over her." Jacob B. Backenstos, sheriff of Hancock County, and friendly to Joseph but not a member of the church, testified that Bennett had told him that Sarah Pratt "made a first rate go." One can only imagine the Pratts' embarrassment and horror at seeing such lurid accusations in print. It was cruel of Joseph and other church leaders to publish them.[6]

Orson Pratt's faith was so strong that it survived these assaults. "We intend to make NAUVOO OUR RESIDENCE," he proclaimed in print a few weeks later, "AND MORMONISM OUR MOTTO." He remained in Nauvoo, and he and Sarah remained together.[7]

Unlike Orson Pratt, Sidney Rigdon had more or less kept his discontents private. George W. Robinson, Rigdon's son-in-law and Joseph's former clerk, collaborated with Bennett and publicly broke from the church. Over the summer, Bennett repeatedly wrote about Joseph's proposal to Nancy Rigdon. Nevertheless, Sidney Rigdon tried to put the scandal to rest in mid-August. Before a Sunday meeting in Nauvoo, he shared that one of his other daughters, Eliza, had nearly died during a recent illness. Upon her recovery she had urged her father to remain "faithful in the cause" and warned that if Nancy "denied the faith . . . she would be damned." Sidney Rigdon denied reports that he had called Joseph a "fallen prophet."[8]

The matter didn't rest there, however. A few days after Rigdon's conciliatory address, Bennett published the purported "love letter" from "holy Joe" to Nancy Rigdon, in which Joseph explained that *whatever God requires is right*, NO MATTER WHAT IT IS."[9] Sidney Rigdon wrote a mealy-mouthed response. He observed that the letter wasn't in Joseph's handwriting and that publishing it was ungallant.[10]

Joseph noticed that Rigdon's statement wasn't exactly a rejection of the letter's authenticity. "As to all that Orson Pratt, Sidney Rigdon, or George W. Robinson can do to prevent me," he proclaimed, "I can kick them off my heels." Joseph kicked hard. Church leaders published an affidavit besmirching Nancy Rigdon's character. Nauvoo resident Stephen Markham claimed to have seen Nancy Rigdon and Bennett in a compromising position and asserted that they "were guilty of unlawful and illicit intercourse." Markham's affidavit appeared in a church broadside directly above Sidney Rigdon's statement.[11]

Sidney Rigdon did not ignore the attack on his daughter's honor. The *Sangamo Journal*, the outlet for Bennett's letters, published Rigdon's affidavit that "Markham is not to be believed" and had made a false statement under oath.[12]

Joseph kept Rigdon in his sights that fall. Rigdon was Nauvoo's postmaster, an office that Robinson previously had filled. Joseph accused them both of corruption, theft, and meddling, and he alleged that Rigdon permitted Bennett to purloin letters. Emma upbraided Rigdon and forbade him to allow anyone to take or open her husband's mail without express authorization. Rigdon explained that individuals from the church's printing office sometimes had collected mail for the prophet, but he defended his integrity. He wasn't letting Joseph's enemies read his mail. Unconvinced, in November Joseph organized a petition that requested the U.S. postmaster general to remove Rigdon from his office. The petition recommended Joseph as Rigdon's replacement. In all likelihood, Joseph wanted the position not for its salary but because postmasters could send and receive mail free of charge, and because it would have helped Joseph safeguard his communications and keep tabs on his opponents. The postmaster general ignored the petition.[13]

Meanwhile, Bennett published *The History of the Saints*, in which he expanded his exposé of Joseph's polygamy, ritual innovation, and financial misdeeds. Bennett landed some blows, such as when he alleged that Joseph had deeded properties to family members in order to shield them from his creditors. The accusation helped scuttle an application for bankruptcy that Joseph had filed the previous spring. In the end, though, Bennett was a critic without credibility. It was easy for church leaders to expose him as an adulterer, womanizer, and fraud, because he was all of those things. Rigdon and Pratt would have been more dangerous and credible antagonists, which made Joseph's vendettas against them risky.[14]

Within the church, Joseph's position was still strong. Outside of Rigdon and Pratt, other top leaders remained resolute, as did Emma Smith. While no sources document their private discussion of the subject during these months, she clearly believed her husband when he denied Bennett's allegations of polygamy. "I do not [do] the wrongs that I am charg'd with doing," Joseph told the Relief Society after his mid-August return to Nauvoo. Emma invited Eliza Snow to live in her house, unaware that Snow had been sealed to Joseph six weeks before.[15]

Joseph's most immediate danger remained arrest and extradition to Missouri. On September 3, as Joseph, Emma, and their children were eating their noontime dinner, three officers, including Adams County constable James Pitman, barged into the Smith residence. While another church member engaged them in conversation, Joseph slipped out the back door, walked through a small plot of corn, and hid himself in Newel K. Whitney's living quarters in the prophet's red-brick store. It was a narrow escape. Joseph soon moved to a less conspicuous location, and he put out a false notice that he had left the city. Joseph was in and out of Nauvoo for the next several months. The sheriffs and constables never found him.[16]

Church leaders worked with lawyers and state politicians to devise a solution to Joseph's legal jeopardy. Shortly after the August 1 election, Wilson Law had advised Joseph to remain in hiding "till the next governor takes the *chair*," hoping that despite his criticisms of the charter, Thomas Ford would end Thomas Carlin's cooperation with Missouri authorities. In the meantime, a Mormon delegation traveled to Springfield and met with Justin Butterfield, U.S. district attorney for Illinois. Butterfield had opposed Joseph's application for bankruptcy, but he bore the prophet no animus. In October 1842 Butterfield wrote Sidney Rigdon that Carlin should not have granted Missouri's request for extradition. Even if Joseph had instructed Porter Rockwell to shoot Lilburn Boggs, the prophet had not committed a crime in Missouri, nor had he fled from its jurisdiction. Illinois should not deliver him up.[17]

Ford at first disappointed the Saints when he took office in December. In his inaugural address, he termed the powers granted by the Nauvoo Charter "objectionable" and called for its amendment.[18] Still, knowing that Ford was their best hope, Butterfield accompanied several Mormon leaders to a meeting with the new governor. Ford agreed that Carlin's writ was illegal but hesitated to revoke it or otherwise interfere with an act of his predecessor. After consulting with the members of the Illinois Supreme Court, Ford encouraged Joseph to submit to arrest and then come to Springfield for judicial relief. Joseph took the advice.

Despite trepidation about leaving the protection of Nauvoo's courts, Joseph relished the trip after five months of off-and-on hiding. At private residences and in taverns, Joseph discoursed on everything from medicine to the millennium to American slavery. Joseph told one dinner party that he could never vote for a slaveholder and another that he would confine Black Americans "by strict laws to their own species [and] put them on a national equalization." The Mormon prophet regaled audiences with stories about the persecutions he had endured and overcome from New York to Missouri. Joseph loved being at the center of these evenings of conversation and mirth.[19]

The prophet's reception from Springfield's political elite was friendly. Governor Ford remarked to Joseph that he had heard that the Mormons were "different from other people, having horns or something of the kind." To his surprise, they "look[ed] like other people." Ford added that Joseph was "a very good looking man." The prophet cut a gentlemanly appearance, carrying a walking stick with a handle of "whale ivory" and a "sperm-whale tooth body." State politicians showed him and the other Mormons every courtesy. Samuel Hackleton, speaker of the Illinois House of Representatives, dropped by to inform church leaders that they could use the state capitol for their Sunday services. After a

Benjamin West, *Sketch of Joseph Smith*, 1843. (Courtesy of Abraham
Lincoln Presidential Library and Museum, Springfield, Illinois)

preliminary court appearance on Monday, January 2, 1843, Joseph dined
opposite Nathaniel Pope, the judge who would decide his legal fate.[20]

Justin Butterfield, Joseph's attorney, had filed a petition for a writ of
habeas corpus in the U.S. Circuit Court for the District of Illinois.
Among the visitors to the courtroom were a number of ladies, including
the recently married Mary Todd Lincoln. Despite the public interest, the
hearing's outcome was a foregone conclusion. The prosecution made a
lackluster effort, and Joseph's attorneys easily proved that he had been in
Illinois at the time of the assassination attempt on Boggs and thus was
not a fugitive. To deliver up a man who had not left the state contravened
the basic principles of American liberty, and to send him to Missouri
would be akin to sending him to the gallows. Judge Pope agreed. He set
Joseph free.[21]

The prophet had a final interview with Thomas Ford before he left
Springfield. The governor warned the prophet to "refrain from all electioneering." Joseph answered that he had always done so. He asserted

that the Mormons voted with unanimity not because of his direction, but because persecution forced them to oppose their enemies at the ballot box. That wasn't strictly true, but in any event, Ford was right to urge political discretion. The friendly reception in Springfield belied what had become bipartisan opposition to the Nauvoo Charter and its allegedly excessive prerogatives.[22]

Joseph and his companions enjoyed a triumphant homeward journey. Wilson Law and Eliza R. Snow composed "jubilee songs" to mark the occasion. The Saints celebrated not just Joseph's liberation, but the fact that their legal safeguards and political connections had worked. "The justice done a righteous cause," wrote Snow, "By those who stand in power / Does honor to our country's laws in this degenerate hour." The legal and political victory provided the Saints with assurance that the powers and principalities of Illinois were not like those of Missouri.[23]

A week later, Joseph and Emma presided over a large dinner party, which also marked their sixteenth wedding anniversary. The prophet read a letter that John C. Bennett had addressed to Orson Pratt and Sidney Rigdon. Bennett boasted that he was going to facilitate the prophet's arrest on the "old score from Missouri," the 1838 charges of treason, murder, and other crimes. Bennett no longer seemed an acute threat, however, and some of the fractures from the previous summer were healing.[24]

The fact that Orson Pratt showed Bennett's letter to Joseph was a sign of renewed loyalty, and the prophet now effected a full reconciliation. He gathered the Twelve and suggested that Pratt's expulsion from their ranks was invalid because too few of them had been present when the action was taken. Brigham Young observed that "all he had against Orson was when he came home [from his mission], he loved his wife better than David." It was an allusion to the close friendship between the biblical David and Jonathan. Young meant that Pratt had sided with his wife against the Lord's anointed. It was easy for the other apostles to sympathize with Pratt. Regardless of the particulars of this case, Joseph's sealings to already married women were unsettling. Even Joseph's most loyal followers worried about the possibility that Joseph would take their wives. Young once had a dream of seeing his first, civilly married wife, Mary Ann Angell, ride away with Joseph in a carriage.[25]

Joseph was ready to forgive Orson, but he was still tetchy about Sarah Pratt. "She lied about me," he insisted. "I never made the offer which she said I did." Joseph advised Orson to divorce Sarah "and raise a new family," but he promised not to "throw it in [his] teeth" if he stayed with Sarah. The restored apostle disregarded the prophet's advice, though Orson Pratt's subsequent embrace of polygamy produced discord in the couple's marriage.[26]

Orson and Sarah Pratt came to the banks of the Mississippi just before sunset. Some of those present had to "break the ice" on the river. The prophet and the Pratts waded into the frigid water, and Joseph baptized them for the remission of their sins.[27]

Joseph's vindication in court freed him to resume all aspects of his leadership. He was determined to see the Nauvoo Temple and Nauvoo House completed. There was the constant press of debts and land sales. And there was the matter of marriage. Now that he was safely back in Nauvoo, Joseph intended to resume the sealings that he had paused since the previous summer. As the number of sealings increased, so too would the difficulty of keeping polygamy secret from Emma.

Deep Water (1843)

JOSEPH WAS CHURCH PRESIDENT, mayor, and the Nauvoo Legion's lieu-tenant general. He frequently attended meetings of the Nauvoo Lodge and participated in the deliberations of the Nauvoo High Council. Nauvoo grew to rival Chicago as the biggest city in Illinois, and Joseph and his scribes oversaw an enormous number of property transactions. The press of business was constant and financial pressure remained acute. Joseph frequently borrowed money from church members in order to satisfy his many creditors. At the same time, he often gave city lots to newcomers and loaned money to Saints in need.

Joseph didn't only juggle a multiplicity of public responsibilities. The prophet's private life also was increasingly complex. There was the veneer of monogamy with Emma. And then there were the approximately fifteen other women who had become his plural wives over the previous two years. The sealings paused during his months of hiding out, but he now pursued additional marriages with renewed intensity. The result was unprecedented tumult in his domestic affairs.

As had been the case for several years, it would have been wise for Joseph to have proceeded with greater prudence. Caution was not his way, however. "Deep water is what I am wont to swim in," Joseph explained. Joseph acknowledged that he often plunged right into dangerous currents. "Excitement has almost become the essence of my life," he commented. "When that dies away I feel almost lost." Joseph rarely let the excitement die. Thus far, Joseph had confounded his enemies, but the paths he chose—and his own recklessness—would lead him and his church into peril again and again.[1]

The polygamous sealings did more than complicate Joseph's own life. They also created dilemmas for the women who married him and the families that he initiated into the practice.

Flora Woodworth was sixteen years of age at the time of her March 1843 sealing to Joseph. She was the daughter of Lucien Woodworth, the architect and foreman of the Nauvoo House project. Known as the "pagan prophet" (apparently because he had not yet been baptized into the church), Lucien became close friends with Joseph. The prophet, meanwhile, became smitten by the raven-haired Flora. He gave her a gold watch and took her on carriage rides. Joseph even deeded her a Nauvoo lot. Other plural wives received some of these favors, but Flora garnered an outsized share of the prophet's attention.[2]

Flora, however, also attracted other suitors, who did not know that she was unavailable as a prospective wife. One admirer was Orange Wight, the nineteen-year-old son of apostle Lyman Wight, and Flora did not discourage his attentions. One day, as they were walking near Joseph's house, the prophet drove up in his carriage and invited them to ride with him. After going to the temple and several other places, Joseph directed the carriage to the Woodworth home. Flora's mother, Phebe Woodworth, took Wight into a room and told him that Flora was Joseph's plural wife. Wight's courtship of Flora came to an abrupt end.[3]

Sarah Ann Whitney, sealed to the prophet in July 1842 at the age of seventeen, was a similarly tricky case. She had, like Flora Woodworth, reached an age at which young men would view her as a prospective wife. Because she was supposed to keep her marriage to Joseph secret, there was no easy way for her to rebuff suitors.

In March 1843, Joseph made a clandestine visit to the Whitney home. In the company of William Clayton, his scribe, the prophet left Nauvoo on March 21 for a visit to Shokokon, a town twenty-five miles up the Mississippi. Joseph had recently purchased some land there. The prophet and his scribe parted company near their destination, and Joseph snuck back into Nauvoo on March 23. That day, he wrote—in his own hand, a rarity—Sarah Whitney a blessing in which he reminded her that "if she remain[ed] in the everlasting covenant to the end," she would "come forth in the first resurrection . . . as also all her father's house." The conditional promise suggests that Sarah was struggling to accept her lot as one of Joseph's plural wives. She wanted more than an assurance of eternal glory. She needed clarity about her earthly circumstances.[4]

Joseph, however, had devised a creative solution, which he introduced during his secret visit to the Whitneys. The idea hinged on the cooperation of Joseph C. Kingsbury, Sarah's uncle by marriage. In the fall of 1842, Kingsbury's wife, Caroline (Newel K. Whitney's sister), had died during childbirth. The child had also perished. Kingsbury was crushed by their deaths. "I had lost some part of myself," he wrote. Joseph now comforted Kingsbury with an unusual offer. If Kingsbury would enter into a "pretended marriage" with Sarah, Joseph would seal him to Caroline for eternity. "No one [would] have power to take her from me," Kingsbury wrote. The still-grieving widower accepted Joseph's offer. The prophet laid his hands on Kingsbury's head and blessed him in the presence of Sarah Ann and her parents. He and Caroline would "be crowned and enthroned to dwell together in a celestial glory in the presence of God." Joseph also assured Kingsbury that they would be with their two deceased children. After bestowing the blessings on Sarah Ann Whitney and Joseph Kingsbury, the prophet headed back to Shokokon and returned to Nauvoo in William Clayton's company the next day.[5]

In April, Joseph officiated at Sarah Ann's sham civil marriage to Kingsbury, who moved into the Whitney home. No one would suspect that "Mrs. Kingsbury" was also "Mrs. Smith."[6]

Meanwhile, Eliza Snow left the Smith household in February 1843. Reminiscences attribute her departure to Emma's discovery that Snow had betrayed her through some sort of illicit relationship with Joseph. Emma pushed or pulled a pregnant Snow down the stairs, causing her to miscarry. In another version, Emma beat Snow with a broomstick. These later stories are not based on contemporary evidence. The obvious reason for Snow's departure is the fact that Lucy Mack Smith moved into the family home at that time. Snow left to make space for the prophet's mother. In mid-March Joseph and Emma together attended the last day of a school that Snow had taught that winter. Mormonism's first couple also went riding together on several occasions. It seems that Emma still trusted that she was Joseph's only wife.[7]

The prophet showed no apparent strain from navigating the secrecy and difficulties inherent in his many marriages. Indeed, he even played ball games in the streets of Nauvoo as winter turned into spring. Joseph, at the age of thirty-seven, retained his strength and vigor. When he took a mid-March trip to nearby Ramus, Joseph threw a man his clerk described as the town's "most expert wrestler." Joseph also liked competing at pulling sticks, a contest in which two men sat on the ground with their legs extended and soles pressed together. The opponents each held the end of a stick and tried to pull each other off the ground. Joseph prevailed with just one hand against Ramus's strongest man.[8]

Troubling news from Missouri dented Joseph's mood. In mid-March the prophet learned that Porter Rockwell, whom former governor Lilburn Boggs had accused of attempted murder, had been arrested during an unwise visit to St. Louis. Joseph also heard rumors—inaccurate, it turned out—that John C. Bennett's efforts had produced a fresh indictment against Joseph and other church leaders.

Joseph did his best to feign nonchalance. A few days after word of Rockwell's arrest, Joseph stretched himself out on his writing table, resting the back of his head on some law books. "I acknowledge myself a very great lawyer," Joseph jested. "I am going to study law and this is the way I study." The prophet fell asleep and began snoring.[9]

He was more worried than he let on. In the midst of discussions about Rockwell, Joseph related that he had dreamed of swimming in a clear river above a school of enormous fish. "I was astonished and felt afraid they might drown me," he shared. While Joseph prophesied that Rockwell "will get away from the Missourians," he did not want to leave it to chance. He corresponded with several attorneys and arranged Rockwell's defense. The potential of renewed extradition attempts weighed on Joseph's mind.[10]

The prophet remained convinced that Sidney Rigdon, his counselor in the First Presidency, was conspiring with Bennett. Joseph wrote Rigdon a blistering letter in late March. "You are in the exercise of a traitorous spirit against our lives and interest by combining with our enemies and the murderous Missourians," Joseph alleged. He stated that he would publish a notice that he was withdrawing fellowship from Rigdon and that he intended to raise the matter at the church's upcoming semiannual conference. Rigdon strenuously denied that he ever had countenanced Bennett's campaign.[11]

On the thirteenth anniversary of the church's April 6, 1830, founding, church members assembled on the "platform" of the under-construction temple. Walls of varying heights surrounded attendees. Once Joseph arrived, he made the first order of business a "trial" of the First Presidency. The Saints unanimously sustained Joseph as their president.

Then it was Rigdon's turn. After reminding the Saints that his health had precluded his attendance at recent church conferences, Rigdon stated that he had always regarded Bennett with suspicion. Dimick Huntington informed the congregation that Rigdon once had complimented Bennett as a "gentleman." Huntington's testimony was less than damning, and conference attendees voted almost unanimously that Rigdon should retain his standing. Still, the rift between Joseph and his counselor persisted. The two men did not trust each other, but as long as Rigdon professed his loyalty and friendship, Joseph did not feel that he could cast him off.[12]

The prophet took other men into his confidence, among them William Clayton, a talented writer and violinist. Clayton and his wife, Ruth, were recent emigrants from Lancashire, England. In February 1843, Ruth bore the couple's fourth child.

Soon after Clayton started working in Joseph's office as his scribe, his new boss sent Brigham Young to give him "some instructions on the priesthood," now a euphemism for polygamy. Unlike men like Young and Willard Richards, Clayton didn't need much convincing. Also unlike the apostles, who made only scattered and cryptic entries about polygamy in their private journals, Clayton recorded abundant detail as Joseph pursued additional wives and as those pursuits strained his other relationships. "During the last year of his [Joseph's] life," Clayton later recalled, "we were scarcely ever together, alone, but he was talking on the subject."[13]

Clayton told Brigham Young about a woman, Sarah Crooks, whom he had met prior to his emigration. They had become friends during his missionary work in Manchester, and Clayton confessed to his diary that he struggled with "impure affections" for her. Joseph soon took his scribe for a walk, told him it "was lawful . . . to send for Sarah," and even offered to foot the bill.[14]

Clayton did not wait for Crooks's arrival to marry plurally. He turned his attention to Margaret Moon, his wife Ruth's younger sister. Margaret, along with her mother, already lived in the Clayton household. She was engaged to marry another man, Aaron Farr, then away from Nauvoo on a mission. The obstacle proved surmountable. Clayton conversed with Margaret "on the priesthood." The overture prompted a visit from three of Aaron Farr's siblings, undoubtedly surprised and displeased at this turn of events. Undeterred, Clayton soon reported back to Joseph that Margaret "will submit to counsel with all her heart." Joseph

William Clayton, ca. 1855. (Courtesy of Church History Library)

then sealed Margaret to Clayton. Unlike Joseph, Clayton did not keep his plural marriage a secret from his first wife. In fact, on at least some occasions, he shared a bed with both sisters.[15]

The prophet's scribe soon had an opportunity to return the favor. Seventeen-year-old Lucy Walker had moved into the Smith household shortly after her mother's death. Her father had left Nauvoo on a mission to a warmer climate that might aid his health. Lucy helped care for Joseph and Emma's children. One day Joseph took Lucy aside and told her that God had commanded him to marry her. Sensing resistance, he asked Lucy whether she believed him to be "a prophet of God." When she answered in the affirmative, Joseph explained to her that "the principle of plural or celestial marriage . . . would prove an everlasting benefit to [her] father's house." Lucy was so stunned that she had little to say in response. Joseph told her to pray about it. She did, but instead of receiving the divine witness that he promised, she was in agony, wishing that she could join her mother in the grave.[16]

Joseph did not give up. He delivered an ultimatum to Lucy. She had one more day to submit to God's command. "If you reject this message," Joseph declared, "the gate will be closed forever against you." Lucy forbade Joseph from speaking to her on the subject again. He confidently told her that God would reveal the truth to her. After a sleepless night, she felt her soul fill with calm, peace, and happiness. Joseph was thrilled when Lucy shared the news of her acceptance with him. "He led me to a chair," Lucy recounted, "placed his hands upon my head, and blessed me with every blessing my heart could possibly desire." Joseph's pressure prompted a spiritual experience that convinced her to do something she at first had found repugnant.[17]

On the morning of May 1, 1843, William Clayton sealed Lucy Walker to Joseph at the Smith residence. Emma was away. Accompanied by Lorin Walker, Lucy's older brother, Emma had traveled to St. Louis to purchase items for the guest quarters of a new residence then under construction for the Smith family. "She [Emma] did not know anything about it at all," Lucy stated. The prophet's wife arrived home the next afternoon, not long after Joseph had enjoyed a ride with Flora Woodworth.[18]

Joseph briefly engaged a new translation project in the spring of 1843. A group of men in Kinderhook, Illinois, dug up a burial mound and reported that they had found six bell-shaped brass plates amid human bones. The plates, one of the men reported, "were completely covered with hieroglyphics that none as yet have been able to read." Many decades later, William Fugate admitted that he and a partner had etched the characters into the plates with acid and then staged the discovery of the plates as an elaborate joke at the expense of some local Mormons. Word of the alleged discovery quickly spread. Only seventy miles to the north was the nation's most famous—or notorious—translator of ancient plates. By the end of April, someone had brought the plates to Nauvoo.[19]

Joseph fell for the crude forgery. As with the Book of Mormon translation and the papyri, he saw Egyptian characters that shed light on ancient stories. Using the Egyptian grammar and alphabet he and his assistants had produced in the mid-1830s, the prophet got to work. By May 1, according to William Clayton, Joseph had "translated a portion." He asserted that the person buried in the mound "was a descendant of

One of the Kinderhook plates. (Courtesy of Chicago History
Museum, ICHi-074350)

Ham through the loins of Pharaoh king of Egypt." The plates contained
the story of his life. Apostle Parley Pratt reported that the man was one
of the Jaredites, a people whose history the Book of Mormon narrates.[20]

The plates, and Joseph's reaction to them, caused a stir in Nauvoo.
William Clayton and Brigham Young traced one of the plates and its
characters in their journals. Non-Mormons visited Joseph to see them as
well. "He compared them in my presence with his Egyptian alphabet,"
reported one man, "and they are evidently the same characters." The
prophet was confident he could "decipher them." Church editors printed
facsimiles of the plates and promised to publish the translation when Joseph finished it.[21]

Joseph had never stuck with any translation project other than the
Book of Mormon for very long. He didn't stick with this one either, and
didn't explain why. Perhaps he intended to return to the Kinderhook
plates, or perhaps he simply lost interest in them or suspected their inau-
thenticity. Building projects, Sunday sermons, land sales, and sealings left
little time for ancient texts.

Marriage assumed an increasingly central place not just in Joseph's activity, but also in his theology. That spring Joseph returned to one of his favorite biblical passages, in which the author of II Peter exhorts followers
of Jesus Christ to make their "calling and election sure." Back in the
summer of 1839, while Mormon refugees gathered in Commerce and
Montrose, Joseph taught that those Saints who remained humble and
faithful would have "calling and election . . . made sure" and would be
visited by Jesus Christ. They would be blessed with visions and revelations.
    Joseph now clarified that assurance of a place in God's kingdom re-
quired "a more sure word of prophecy," a word that men and women
"were sealed in the heavens." For many Protestants, a perennial question
was whether individuals could be certain of their salvation. That wasn't
Joseph's concern. For him, the key question wasn't an individual's salvation but rather the extent of his glory. "Knowledge is power," Joseph
taught, "and the man who has the most knowledge has the greatest
power." A decade earlier, Joseph had introduced the idea of three kingdoms of eternal glory, with the highest being the celestial. Now, he
added that "in the celestial glory there was three heavens or degrees."
What precisely did someone need to do in order to attain that highest
degree of celestial glory?[22]
    Joseph answered this question during a mid-May 1843 visit to the
home of Benjamin and Melissa Johnson in Macedonia, Illinois. The
prophet was connected to the Johnsons through friendship and marriage.
Two of Benjamin Johnson's sisters, Delcena Johnson Sherman and
Almera Johnson, were among his plural wives. Benjamin Johnson later
stated that during his visit to their home, Joseph "occupied the same
room and bed with my sister [Almera]." Johnson added that Joseph had
shared the same bed with another of his plural wives the previous
month.[23]
    The Johnsons, therefore, or at least Benjamin, were already polyg-
amy insiders. Joseph, however, took the occasion of his visit to explain

the connection between marriage and human exaltation. The prophet turned to William Clayton, who had accompanied the prophet on the visit. Joseph put his hand on his scribe's knee and explained that Clayton's eternal glory—his calling and election—was sure because he had "taken the step which is necessary for that purpose." He had "married for eternity." Such couples, Joseph continued, "will continue to increase and have children in the celestial glory." Individuals should always increase in progeny, glory, and power, and being sealed for eternity was the only way for a couple to have the fullest measure. "In order to obtain the highest [celestial glory]," Joseph insisted, "a man must enter into this order of the priesthood and if he don't he can't obtain it." It isn't clear from Clayton's notes of the conversation whether "this order of the priesthood" meant polygamy, but the Johnsons accepted its righteousness. Later that year, the prophet sealed Melissa Johnson to her husband.[24]

Joseph expressed "partiality" to a third Johnson sister, fifteen-year-old Esther. Benjamin told him that the family intended Esther to marry Melissa Johnson's brother, David LeBaron. Not easily deterred, Joseph talked with Esther. Both she and the family seemed bent on her prospective marriage to LeBaron, so the prophet "reluctantly" dropped the matter.[25]

In the spring of 1843 Joseph finally broached the subject of plural marriage with Emma. Continuing to deceive her was both undesirable and impractical. Rumors about Joseph's polygamy or affairs were rampant. Julia Murdock, Joseph and Emma's adopted daughter, later recalled that many in Nauvoo believed—incorrectly—that Joseph Smith was her father and that her mother "was some unfortunate girl that was betrayed by him." Emma surely heard the whispers as well, but she had chosen not to confront her husband. Perhaps she didn't want to know the truth.[26]

There is no record of how Joseph introduced the doctrine to Emma. Presumably he shared the same principles that he taught Benjamin and Melissa Johnson. He would have stressed the eternal connections and blessings that individuals and their families would receive. Joseph may not have told her that the marriages would involve sex, and he did not tell Emma about his prior sealings.

Emma tentatively accepted some version of Joseph's principle. She requested the prerogative of choosing her husband's plural wives, and she selected four young women who already were living in the household, women she knew and liked: Emily and Eliza Partridge, and Sarah and Maria Lawrence. Joseph had been appointed the Lawrence sisters' legal guardian after their father's death. These four young women already seemed part of the family.

In fact, unbeknownst to Emma, the Partridge sisters already had been sealed to her husband earlier that spring. Emily had come to suspect that Joseph wanted to make her one of his plural wives, but she had rebuffed his attempts to speak with her about the matter. Emily then agonized about the proposal that she had scuttled. "While I was struggling in deep water these few months," she later wrote, "I received a testimony of a truth of the words that Joseph would have said to me." If Joseph tried to raise the subject again, she was prepared to accept him.[27]

As Joseph did on several other occasions, he used a plural wife as an intermediary for the proposal. In early March 1843, Elizabeth Durfee went to Emily, told her that Joseph wanted her for a wife, and asked her to meet him at Heber C. Kimball's in the evening.[28]

Emily agreed. When she reached the Kimball house, neither Heber nor Vilate Kimball were there, only two of their children. Then Joseph and Heber arrived. Heber Kimball asked his children to leave because there was going to be a church council at the house that evening. For the sake of pretense in front of the children, he told Emily that she should return another time when Vilate was at home. Emily said goodbye. She felt spooked by the circumstances and, in her later words, "dreaded the interview." Before she reached the Smith residence, she heard Heber Kimball calling her softly, "Emily, Emily." She kept going for a while, but eventually he nearly overtook her. He brought her back to Joseph.[29]

The prophet told her "that the Lord had commanded him to enter into plural marriage, and had given [her] to him." She assented. Without delay, Heber Kimball sealed her to Joseph for time and eternity. "A strange way of getting married, wasn't it?" she later wrote.[30]

Sex followed sealing. In courtroom testimony many decades later, Emily affirmed that she and Joseph had intercourse but that the prophet did not spend the night with her. Presumably, they returned separately to the Smith residence. The next week Heber Kimball sealed Joseph to Emily's older sister, Eliza.[31]

Emma's selection of Emily and Eliza Partridge two months later thus necessitated some additional deception. "We were married in her presence again," recounted Emily, "because we thought proper to say nothing about the former marriage." Emma was present as a witness at the repeat sealings. According to Emily's later testimony, Emma took her (Emily's) hand and placed it on Joseph's, a symbol of her consent to their

Emily Dow Partridge, who later became the plural wife of
Brigham Young, with Emily Augusta Young and Edward Young,
ca. 1851. (Courtesy of Church History Library)

union. Although Eliza never discussed her marriages in as much detail as
her sister, there would have been a repeat of her sealing as well.[32]

Emma did not consent to what transpired after the sealings. Emily
Partridge spent that night with Joseph. Emma was alone in her room,
alone with the knowledge that her husband was sleeping with a nineteen-year-old woman who lived in her home and cared for her children.
"After the next day you might say that she [Emma] was bitter," Emily recalled. Emma forbade Joseph from spending any more nights with Emily
or with any other plural wives.[33]

Joseph also had kept his older brother Hyrum in the dark about his
plural marriages. Hyrum was appalled by the rumors and preached
against polygamy at a Sunday meeting while the prophet was out of
town. He took as his text a Book of Mormon passage, in which the Lord

proclaims that "there shall not any man among you have save it be one wife." Hyrum was not open to any departure from what he considered a "perpetual principle." He observed that he had heard talk about the biblical David and Solomon having many wives, but he insisted that such things were an offense against God.[34]

Alongside Emma, the church patriarch was one of a small number of people with sufficient credibility and clout to damage Joseph's authority. Indeed, Joseph was worried about precisely that eventuality. On May 23, William Clayton referenced "a plot that is being laid to entrap the brethren of the secret priesthood by brother H[yrum Smith] and others." Clayton probably meant that Hyrum intended to discover and expose the truth about Nauvoo polygamy.[35]

Hyrum confronted Brigham Young. "I am convinced something [has] not been told me," Hyrum complained to the president of the Quorum of the Twelve. Young agreed to tell him if he swore an oath to "never say another word against Joseph and his doing and his doctrine." Hyrum assented. Young then told him "the whole story," or at least that Joseph had a "good many wives" sealed to him. Hyrum wept and then went to his brother. They would go forward together. Despite Hyrum's moral and scriptural objections, the logic of celestial polygamy had obvious appeal for him. His first wife, Jerusha Barden, had died in 1837. Later that same year, he had remarried, to Mary Fielding. With whom would he spend eternity? Could both wives be his eternal companions?[36]

Joseph soon rewarded his followers who had accepted the principle. On May 26, the prophet met in the upper room of his store with eight of the men—including Hyrum—who had received the endowment one year earlier. The men repeated what Brigham Young termed "the first ordinances of the endowment." Joseph wanted the men to advance in their knowledge and power, however, so he gave them additional "instruction on the priesthood, the new and everlasting covenant." There is no record of the substance, but it was likely similar in content to what he had taught Benjamin and Melissa Johnson ten days earlier. If men wanted to progress in knowledge and power for eternity, they needed to be sealed in the new and everlasting covenant of marriage. That covenant included the acceptance and practice of polygamy.[37]

The group assembled again two days later. This time Emma joined them. By this point, nearly two dozen other women had been sealed to Joseph, and several of the other men present also had plural wives. Emma, by contrast, had been only civilly married to her husband.

According to Joseph's teaching, they would "cease to increase when they die, i.e., they will not have any children in the resurrection." Emma and Joseph now were sealed to each other for eternity. Other sealings followed the next day, as Joseph's most trusted associates brought their wives.

Robert Thompson, Mercy Thompson's husband, had died several years earlier. Could she be assured of an eternity with him? The prophet proposed a solution that built on the logic behind Joseph Kingsbury's blessing. Hyrum Smith could stand proxy as Joseph sealed Mercy to Robert Thompson for eternity. "Such a wedding I am quite sure [was] never witnessed before in this generation," recalled Mercy Fielding Thompson. Either as part of the same sealing or later in the summer, Joseph sealed Mercy to Hyrum "for time." She became his plural wife on earth. Similarly, Mary Fielding Smith (Mercy's sister) stood as proxy for Jerusha Barden, Hyrum Smith's first wife, ensuring that Jerusha and Hyrum would be eternal companions. Joseph also sealed Mary to Hyrum for time and eternity. It was a complex ritual solution to thorny questions that emerged through widowhood and remarriage.[38]

For Joseph, the sealings were a potential breakthrough. For two years, he had done his best to keep polygamy a secret from Emma and Hyrum. Now he had introduced plural marriage to two of the most significant figures in his life. They had both accepted it, but with one key difference. Hyrum discarded his prior opposition and fully embraced polygamy. He married at least one additional plural wife before the end of the year. Emma, by contrast, conceded the principle but resisted its practice.[39]

Joseph was full of swagger. The Sunday before his sealing to Emma, he preached in the under-construction Nauvoo Temple. Joseph had to press his way through the crowd to reach the stand. "If they did not keep clear," he joked, "[I] might sometime run up and down and hit some of them." Joseph knew he did not fit the country's image of a proper, sober religious leader. "Many think a prophet must be a great deal better than any body else," he commented, but he was after spiritual power rather than propriety. He could love a man "who swears a stream as long as my arm" if he cared for the poor. Joseph knew that he had his faults. "I don't want you to think I am very righteous," he instructed the Saints, "for I am not very righteous." He compared himself to a "rough stone rolling downhill." Perhaps he knew that he might hurt those with whom he collided, but that didn't stop Joseph from picking up speed.[40]

CHAPTER TWENTY-EIGHT

Anointed (1843)

"YOU HAVE A RIGHT to get all [the wives] you can," Joseph counseled William Clayton.[1] Joseph practiced what he preached. He continued to expand his family—without Emma's blessing. Emma regretted her initial acceptance of plural marriage and locked horns with Joseph again and again on the subject. Nothing that Joseph tried persuaded Emma that his marriages with other women were righteous, and her fierce opposition forced him to make some difficult concessions.

Joseph faced other conflicts that proved even harder to defuse. His enemies in Missouri demonstrated a remarkable tenacity, and Joseph was making new enemies in western Illinois. In particular, the prophet's political maneuvers in the run-up to the 1843 election inflamed anti-Mormon opposition in and around Hancock County. Whereas Emma had an enduring capacity to forgive Joseph, the church's political opponents were uninterested in reconciliation. As political and legal pressure mounted, Joseph responded by using Nauvoo's laws and courts to shield himself and his fellow Saints. The more he used these powers, the more he enraged his enemies, and the more determined they became to defeat him by any means necessary.

In the spring of 1843, apostle Heber C. Kimball broached the subject of plural marriage to his daughter, fourteen-year-old Helen Mar Kimball. After an initial discussion, he "introduced" Sarah Ann Whitney, Helen's good friend, as Joseph's wife. He then informed Helen of his plans for her. "Having a great desire to be connected with the prophet," Helen wrote, "he offered me to him." Heber's offer was a cruelty to her mother, Vilate, who had already endured the sacrifice and indignity of accepting her husband's first plural marriage. Heber Kimball gave his daughter a day to think about it, and the next morning Joseph came to teach Helen himself. "If you will take this step," he promised her, "it will ensure your eternal salvation and exaltation and that of your father's household and all of your kindred." Out of obedience to her father, for the sake of her family, Helen assented.[2]

Heber Kimball laid his hands on Helen's head and blessed her. William Clayton, Joseph's scribe and polygamy confidant, recorded Heber's words. "Thou shalt be blessed with immortal glory and enthroned with glory in the presence of the Lord," he promised her. On earth, and beyond the grave, she would have a "companion" who was "a man of God." He would provide her with "numerous" posterity, and her family would increase forever. Helen Mar Kimball became Joseph Smith's youngest plural wife.[3]

Did the marriage include sex? There is no way to know. Helen never divulged such intimate and personal information. In contrast to certain other plural wives, such as Flora Woodworth, Joseph does not appear to have paid much attention to Helen after the sealing. Given the mentions of "posterity" and "increase" in Heber's blessing, however, sex would have become an expected component of the marriage at some point.[4]

Around six weeks after the sealing, after he had left on a mission, Heber Kimball sent Helen a letter in which he encouraged her to keep the vows and covenants she had made and to "not make a breach." He knew that the path he had chosen for Helen would be difficult. Whether or not the marriage was consummated, the sealing reshaped Helen's life more than she expected. Her "youthful friends gr[e]w shy and cold," and she endured "poisonous darts from sland'rous tongues." Prior to the sealing, Helen had attended dances and relished opportunities to spend time with friends and prospective romantic interests. "No girl loved dancing better than I did," she later wrote. Now she was a "fetter'd bird with wild and longing heart." Joseph forbade her to attend dances at his residence to protect her from the attentions of other men.[5]

Joseph married all sorts of women, and the precise motivations of the parties involved varied from case to case. In this instance, Joseph married Helen because his friend and apostle Heber Kimball asked him to do so.

The marital variety continued in the late spring and summer of 1843: Elvira Holmes, at whose civil marriage Joseph had officiated; Rhoda Richards, the spinster sister of Willard Richards, and Joseph's oldest plural wife; Olive Frost, a single woman around twenty-seven years of age; and Nancy Winchester, only a dozen days older than Helen Mar Kimball.

As Joseph continued to accumulate wives, most of whom were unknown to Emma, his relationship with her remained brittle. As Emma's knowledge of Joseph's polygamy increased, she realized that many of her female friends and associates had known about or had even facilitated these marriages. It was humiliating. She couldn't trust anyone.

Joseph likewise did not trust Emma, fearing that she would attempt to get revenge. In late May, he asked William Clayton whether his scribe had "used any familiarity with Emma." Clayton denied the accusation, but Joseph soon warned Clayton that Emma "wanted to lay a snare," that she would use Clayton to get even with Joseph. "She thought that if he [Joseph] would indulge himself she would too," Clayton explained. There is no evidence that Emma ever pursued an extramarital relationship, but Joseph was concerned about her intentions.[6]

In mid-June 1843, Joseph and Emma traveled to Palestine Grove, 150 miles northeast of Nauvoo in Lee County, Illinois. A number of Emma's siblings and other relatives had settled in the region, so the journey reunited Emma with family members she had not seen for many years. One day after Joseph and Emma reached the home of her sister, Elizabeth Hale Wasson, they were surprised when William Clayton and Stephen Markham rode up to the house.

The two men brought troubling news. A Daviess County grand jury had indicted Joseph on charges of treason stemming from the 1838 Mormon War in Missouri. Governor Thomas Reynolds once again had asked his Illinois counterpart, Thomas Ford, to issue a writ for Joseph's arrest. Ford complied, but he did Joseph a favor by sending word to Nauvoo one day before he signed the writ. Meanwhile, two lawmen—Joseph J. Reynolds of Jackson County, Missouri, and Harmon T. Wilson of Hancock County, Illinois—learned where the prophet had gone and headed to Lee County to apprehend him.[7]

Reynolds and Wilson stopped at nearby Dixon and told its residents that they were "Mormon elders" who "wanted to see brother Joseph." After they gleaned where he was staying, they reached the Wasson home while the family was eating dinner. Overhearing their intention to search the house, Joseph slipped out the back door, planning to run to the barn. Wilson stopped him in his tracks. "They collared him," wrote Clayton, "and presenting cocked pistols to his breast threatened to shoot him dead if he made the least resistance." Before they forced him into a wagon, Joseph told Markham to go to Dixon, find a judge, and get a writ of habeas corpus.[8]

Joseph's captors brought him to a room at the Dixon Hotel. They intended to transport him to Missouri as soon as horses could be readied. An attorney located by Markham came to the hotel, but Reynolds shut the door in his face. "God damn you, I will shoot you," he yelled at Joseph. The prophet ripped open his shirt and repeatedly told him to "shoot away." A crowd had gathered at the hotel. Local Freemasons—non-Mormons—told the sheriff they would not let him "take Joseph away without a fair trial." Indeed, the attempted extradition more closely resembled a kidnapping than a legal procedure. Reynolds and Wilson backed down.[9]

Joseph had matched his enemies' bluster, and now he outfoxed them. Not only did Joseph's attorneys obtain a writ of habeas corpus from a local judge, they also brought multiple charges of their own against Reynolds and Wilson, including illegal detention as well as assault and battery. The Lee County sheriff took Reynolds and Wilson into his custody, though the two men obtained their own writs of habeas corpus. Soon both Joseph and his captors were on their way to Quincy, where they expected their respective writs to be heard by circuit court judge Richard Young.

The hijinks continued after Joseph, Reynolds, Wilson, and their lawyers left Dixon. No one intended to go to Quincy. One informant suggested that Reynolds and Wilson aimed to take Joseph on a steamboat that could spirit him downriver, from which they and collaborators could get him onto Missouri soil. Joseph, wise to their intentions, insisted on traveling overland. Along the way, several dozen members of the Nauvoo Legion joined the group as an escort. Reynolds and Wilson were powerless to prevent the party's divergence from the road to Quincy. Everyone now headed toward Nauvoo.[10]

On June 30, as Joseph approached the city, he saw the legion's band, with Emma and his brother Hyrum on horseback behind them, and an immense number of carriages and bystanders. Joseph embraced the moment. He left his buggy and mounted Old Charley, his beloved horse. Emma and Hyrum came up and took Joseph by the hand, and all three wept tears of joy. As Joseph proceeded into the city, the band played, men fired guns and cannons, and throngs of Saints lined the streets. When Joseph reached his house, his children flung their arms around him. "Pa, the Missourians won't take you away again will they?" exclaimed seven-year-old Frederick. Joseph then embarrassed Reynolds and Wilson by inviting them to dinner and seating them at the head of his table.[11]

Joseph's lawyers asked the Nauvoo Municipal Court to grant their client yet another writ of habeas corpus, as the writ Joseph had obtained in Lee County directed him to seek relief from a state court. The original Nauvoo Charter had empowered the city court to grant such writs only in cases arising under their own ordinances, not in cases pertaining to state law, but the city council had expanded the court's habeas corpus authority. The court granted the writ and planned to examine the validity of Joseph's arrest the next day.

The authority of Nauvoo's municipal court to issue a writ of habeas corpus was a quasi-religious principle to Joseph. The prophet knew that many Illinois politicians wanted to curb Nauvoo's power. "The legislature shall never take away our rights," he vowed. "I'll spill my heart's blood first." Otherwise, Joseph feared, his Missouri enemies would spill it.[12]

While huddling with his lawyers later that night, Joseph became even more forceful. "Governor Ford," he prophesied, "by granting the writ against me has damned himself politically and his carcass will stink on the face of the earth [and be] food for the carrion crow and turkey buzzard." Among Joseph's lawyers was Cyrus Walker, a Whig candidate for a seat in the House of Representatives. The Whigs had become vocal opponents of the Nauvoo Charter, but Walker was friendly toward the Saints and Joseph had decided to support his candidacy. "Cyrus Walker I have converted to the truth of habeas corpus," the prophet announced.[13]

The following day, Nauvoo's municipal court ruled that the warrant for Joseph's arrest was invalid and that the charge of treason was absurd in light of the fact that state authorities had permitted mobs to drive the Saints from their homes. Joseph was again at liberty. Reynolds and Wilson asked Governor Ford to issue another writ for Joseph's arrest and to ensure his appearance before a state court. Ford declined. Joseph had won this battle of wits and writs.

Emma and Joseph's joyful reunion masked their intense private conflict over polygamy. On July 12, Joseph and Hyrum discussed the dilemma in an upstairs office of the prophet's red-brick store. According to William Clayton, who was present, Hyrum encouraged Joseph to dictate his "revelation on celestial marriage." Joseph had been teaching his related doctrines of eternal marriage and plural marriage for several years, but he had never produced a revelation on the subject. Joseph mentioned, however, that he knew the revelation "perfectly from beginning to end." Hyrum suggested that if he could read it to Emma, he could convince her of the truth. "You do not know Emma as well as I do," Joseph warned him, but Hyrum persuaded his brother that it was worth a try.[14]

Joseph had dictated few revelations in Nauvoo, especially in comparison to the torrent of divine words he had brought forth during the earliest years of the church. The revelation on marriage, however, was vintage Joseph Smith. The message presented itself as the words of Jesus Christ, answering a biblical conundrum, in this case why and how patriarchs like Abraham, Isaac, and Jacob had been justified in having many wives and concubines.

The revelation contains the fullest expression of Joseph's connection between marriage and exaltation. Only marriages sealed by priesthood authority—by Joseph or by those to whom he delegated that power—would persist for eternity. Moreover, those who married by this law would "come forth in the first resurrection . . . and pass by the angels and the gods which are set there to their exaltation and glory in all things." They would enjoy "a continuation of the seeds for ever and ever." They would continue to have children and would see their progeny increase. This idea was a sharp departure from Protestant and Catholic conceptions of the afterlife. Many American Christians anticipated the persistence of family ties in the hereafter, but those families were static. For Joseph, humans would do far more than bask in God's glory and enjoy the presence of their loved ones. Those men who did what God required on earth could expand their families, their glory, and their power forever. They would "be gods, because they have no end." That was exaltation.[15]

Men with plural wives could multiply their families to a much greater extent. Abraham took Hagar as a second wife, the revelation continued, "and from Hagar sprang many people." Isaac, Jacob, David, Solomon, and Moses had had many wives and concubines who bore them children. God did not condemn them. He exalted them, and they became gods. Latter-day Saint men had to "do the works of Abraham." For those introduced to it, acceptance of the "new and everlasting covenant" was not optional. The revelation warned that those who "abide not that covenant" would be "damned."

Jesus Christ ended with particular words for both Joseph and Emma. "I seal upon you," the Lord assured Joseph, "your exaltation and prepare a throne for you in the Kingdom of my Father." Emma received a more sobering message. Jesus Christ ordered her to "receive all those that have been given to my servant Joseph," but regardless of whether she obeyed this commandment, he would receive "a hundredfold in this world of . . . wives and children, and crowns of eternal lives in the eternal worlds." She could not veto his marriages. Nor could she indulge herself elsewhere, as she apparently had threatened. Joseph could have multiple sexual partners, but she could not. "I command mine handmaid Emma Smith to abide and cleave unto my servant, and to none else," the Lord insisted. If she committed adultery, Joseph dictated, "she shall be destroyed." Similarly, plural wives who had sex with other men committed adultery and would be "destroyed." Destruction also awaited those women who rejected the "law of the priesthood"—polygamy, in this context—as taught them by their husbands.[16]

The prophet's brother took the revelation to Emma as soon as Joseph finished dictating it. Joseph had been correct about Emma, who gave Hyrum the most "severe talking to" of his life. She "did not believe a word of it," she declared. Later that day, Joseph deeded sixty-eight lots of Nauvoo land to Emma and their children. Emma presumably had demanded this element of financial security in response to Joseph's revelatory insistence that she accept his polygamy. Three days later, Joseph asked Clayton to deed another sixty city lots to Emma, along with a half share of a steamboat.[17]

Emma tried to get rid of the revelation. She badgered Joseph until he agreed that she could destroy it. According to several later accounts, Emma burned it. The prophet acquiesced because his associates had already made a copy.[18]

The reduction of the revelation to ashes didn't put Emma's mind at ease. She visited Eliza R. Snow on July 20. By this point, Emma probably suspected that her friend was also her husband's plural wife. Snow did not record the substance of their conversation, but she commented on Emma's "forbidding and angry looks." Given Emma's other actions that summer, she probably visited Snow to urge her to break off or renounce her sealing to Joseph.[19]

Joseph possessed a boundless confidence that he could overcome opposition. He had endured and surmounted persecutions, lawsuits, and apostasy. Now Joseph collided with someone more implacable than impatient creditors or Missouri politicians: Emma, who would neither back down nor abandon him.

David Rogers, *Portrait of Emma Smith*, 1842.
(Courtesy of Church History Museum)

At the end of July, Cyrus Walker and Joseph Hoge came to Nauvoo as their respective campaigns for a seat in the U.S. House of Representatives drew to a close. Given the Mormon population within the state's newly created sixth congressional district, both candidates presumed that their success hinged on Joseph Smith's endorsement.

David Rogers, *Portrait of Joseph Smith*, 1842.
(Courtesy of Church History Museum)

The prophet already had indicated his support for Walker, the Whig candidate, who backed the authority of Nauvoo courts to issue writs of habeas corpus. Still, Hoge wasn't giving up, and Walker wasn't taking the Mormon vote for granted. The two candidates gave stump speeches, and their supporters published letters on their behalf in the *Nauvoo Neighbor*, a paper edited by apostles John Taylor and Wilford Woodruff. "We would suggest the necessity of unanimity," the editors wrote. "It can answer no good purpose that half the citizens should disenfranchise the other half, thus rendering Nauvoo powerless." The Saints should vote as a bloc.[20]

Joseph attended a speech by Walker, then met with Hoge in his office. As Walker had done a month earlier, the Democratic candidate "acknowledged the power of the Mormon 'habeas corpus,' " Willard Richards recorded. The same day, a letter arrived from one of Ford's allies in Springfield. It assured Joseph that the Democratic governor would shield him from further legal harassment. The letter also squelched a rumor that Ford intended to call out the militia against the Saints.[21]

Ford's late overture presented a dilemma. The Democrats were, on balance, more supportive of the Saints than the Whigs. How could Joseph throw his people's support to Hoge without breaking his word to Walker? The prophet resorted to a bit of political skullduggery. He used his brother as his political mouthpiece. Hyrum Smith told a meeting of several thousand Saints that he had received "a revelation it was wisdom to vote for Hoge." William Law, one of Joseph's counselors in the church's presidency, stood up, denied that God had communicated such a revelation, and stated that he was certain that Joseph supported Walker. The next day, in lieu of a Sunday sermon, Joseph clarified where he stood on the election. He would fulfill his own personal promise to vote for Walker, but he backed his brother. "I never knew Hyrum say he ever had a revelation and it failed," Joseph observed.[22]

Shortly before the election the prophet got into a fight with Walter Bagby, the Hancock County tax collector. Bagby's personality was a mixture of aspirational respectability and frontier roughness. One neighbor called him "a Kentuckian but a first-rate man, a very trusty, correct businessman." The altercation with Joseph stemmed from a dispute over property taxes. Bagby had seized and sold a parcel of land after claiming that Joseph or the church had failed to pay property tax on it. The sale angered Joseph, who maintained that the taxes already had been paid. On August 1, Bagby approached Joseph's carriage as the prophet arrived at the temple. Joseph alleged that Bagby "abused the citizens" of Nauvoo, and the tax collector called him a liar.[23]

Joseph climbed down out of his buggy. Bagby, feeling threatened, moved to pick up a stone. According to his own public admission later in the month, Joseph seized Bagby by the throat "to choke him off." William Clayton recorded that Joseph struck Bagby several times. Daniel Wells, a Nauvoo resident and county justice of the peace, separated the men. Wells was not a church member but was friendly toward Joseph and the Saints. (He was baptized into the church several years later.) Go ahead and fine me, Joseph told Wells. It seems that Wells didn't want to take any action against the prophet. Joseph then rode down to see Bishop Newel K. Whitney, who was also a justice of the peace. Jacob Backenstos, who had witnessed the fight, swore a complaint against Joseph for assaulting Bagby, and Whitney fined him. The amount of the fine is unknown, but Joseph thought it was worth it for the satisfaction of hitting Bagby.[24]

Tensions were high by the time Illinois voters cast their ballots on August 7. The late-breaking Mormon endorsement proved decisive. Hoge lost most counties in the district, but an overwhelming Hancock County majority secured him a seat in Congress. Members of the church won several county offices in another sign of the church's growing political clout.[25]

Newspaper editors and politicians in Illinois had closely scrutinized the statements of church leaders in the run-up to the election. A *"revelation from heaven,"* the *Warsaw Message* complained, "turned a majority against us." Hyrum Smith's revelation had sunk Walker's candidacy. Whigs in and around Hancock County were outraged.[26]

After the election, the church's antagonists began more serious efforts to combat what they saw as Joseph's union of religious and political power. When the several Mormon victors in county-wide races went to Carthage to take their oaths of office, they were met by a mob "armed with hickory clubs, knives, dirks, and pistols." The county commissioners court ignored the menacing crowd and administered the oaths of office.[27]

The next week around two hundred individuals attended a meeting of the "old citizens of Hancock County" in Carthage. Bagby was among the prime movers, as were Thomas Sharp, the former (and future) editor of the *Warsaw Signal,* and Levi Williams, a colonel in the Hancock County militia. The group, which dubbed itself the "Anti-Mormon Party," accused Joseph of "a most shameless disregard for all the forms and restraints of law." One complaint was the prophet's successful use of Nauvoo's habeas corpus authority to evade extradition to Missouri. Another was the fact that Joseph had "committed violence upon" Bagby. The anti-Mormons pledged that if Governor Ford issued another warrant, they would form a posse to assist in Joseph's arrest. They vowed to resist further outrages against non-Mormon citizens of the county, "peaceably if we can, but forcibly if we must." Bagby and his co-conspirators formed a committee to correspond with anti-Mormon organizations across the county. The anti-Mormon meetings, resolutions, committees of correspondence, and threats of violence were all echoes of the church's years in Missouri. Joseph had seen this play before, and it never ended well.[28]

Joseph had nearly thirty plural wives, and a handful of his most trusted male followers had also married plurally. Despite its expansion and despite the rumors, polygamy remained a secret practice, even to some high-ranking Latter-day Saints. After he dictated his revelation on marriage, Joseph gradually took more men into his confidence. The subject of polygamy arose at a summer 1843 meeting of the Nauvoo High Council. With Joseph's permission, Hyrum Smith shared the revelation with its members. The prophet's brother, it turned out, was still a poor advocate for polygamy. Stake president William Marks, along with Austin Cowles and Leonard Soby, rejected the doctrine.[29]

Joseph showed the revelation to William Law, one of his counselors in the church's First Presidency. The Irish-born Law and his wife, Jane, had lived to the west of Toronto when they joined the church in 1836. At the time William Law praised Joseph as "all we could wish a prophet to be." After the Laws moved to Nauvoo, William Law and his brother, Wilson Law, bought land, built a steam mill, and impressed Joseph with their industry and wealth. The prophet tapped both Law brothers for a variety of high-ranking church and civic positions. William Law was unconvinced and distressed when Joseph taught him the doctrine of plural marriage.[30]

By summer's end, therefore, there was a cadre of well-positioned church leaders opposed to polygamy. None of these men broke with Joseph or aired their disapproval in public, but private doubts about Joseph's leadership grew.

Most men and women who accepted Joseph's doctrine found it difficult in practice. William Clayton, for instance, eagerly pursued plural wives. The prophet had sealed his scribe to Margaret Moon, the sister of his first wife, Ruth Moon. Clayton hoped that Sarah Crooks would become his second plural wife. Clayton immediately taught her the doctrine after she arrived in Nauvoo from England, but after an initially positive response, she rejected his proposal.

Even worse for Clayton, Margaret Moon regretted having married him, especially once Aaron Farr, to whom she had been engaged, returned to Nauvoo. Farr found the "shock . . . severe," and Margaret was miserable. Clayton went to Joseph and asked the prophet if the covenant could be revoked. The answer was no. Joseph assured his scribe that "if Aaron went to making any trouble he would defend me to the uttermost." Aaron Farr and his family did make some trouble. According to Clayton, they conspired with William Walker (brother of Lucy Walker, another of Joseph's plural wives) and Emma to bring about Clayton's "downfall." As the summer proceeded, moreover, Clayton's mother-in-law soured on his marriage to Margaret. She no longer wanted the sisters to share a bed with Clayton and was driven to insanity over her daughters' polygamy. She threatened to commit suicide, and, on one occasion, the family found her in the garden on her knees, "deranged" and "delirious." Margaret, meanwhile, told Clayton that she wanted to tell everyone in Nauvoo "all she knew" and then "kill herself." Everyone involved in Clayton's polygamy endured tremendous anguish.[31]

With an utter disregard for the sorrow their prior actions had caused within the family, Clayton and Joseph both wanted to marry Lydia Moon, sister to Margaret and Ruth. Getting wind of Clayton's intentions, Joseph told him that the "Lord had revealed to him that a man could only take two of a family except by express revelation." If a man married more than two sisters, it was bound to lead to "wrangles and trouble." That was no doubt true, especially in light of the "wrangles" caused by Clayton's first plural marriage. Joseph then asked Clayton if he would "give Lydia to him." When Clayton assented, the prophet sent his scribe to Lydia as his intermediary. Lydia turned Joseph down. Quick on her feet, she told Clayton that she had promised her mother not to marry during the latter's lifetime. Joseph rarely gave up after an initial "no," and he visited Lydia a few days later to press his case. Her no meant no. After Joseph's death, though before her mother's, Lydia Moon married one of Clayton's brothers, and later, when widowed, married a second Clayton brother.[32]

Turmoil continued in Joseph's own family. In early August, Emma undertook another trip to St. Louis, off limits to her husband because of outstanding warrants for his arrest in Missouri. While away from Nauvoo, Emma reflected on the events of the last several months and decided to reject "the priesthood [polygamy] in toto." According to Clayton's report, upon her return Emma urged Joseph to renounce polygamy and abandon the covenants he had made with his plural wives. Joseph felt compelled to agree that he would "relinquish all." Emma then suggested that he could retain Emily and Eliza Partridge. Joseph, however, worried that if he kept any plural wives "she would pitch on him and obtain a divorce and leave him." Emma probably wasn't in earnest about a divorce or other forms of public opposition. She did not want scandal. Nevertheless, Joseph took the threat seriously, as Emma was in a singular position to undercut his authority. He told her that he was through with polygamy. Privately, though, he reassured Clayton that he would not "relinquish anything." It was back to secrecy and deception.[33]

For Emma, it was back to suspicion and unwanted discoveries. On August 21, she found two letters from Eliza Snow in one of Joseph's pockets. Emma was "vexed and angry."[34]

The next day Emma and Joseph rode to the home of Lucien and Phebe Woodworth. Joseph proceeded to the temple, probably with Lucien Woodworth. When he returned, he found his wife demanding the gold watch he had given to sixteen-year-old Flora Woodworth. It is likely that when Emma saw the watch, she realized that Flora was among her husband's plural wives. Given by a man to a woman, the watch was a costly romantic token. Joseph had gifted Emma a watch early in their marriage. Now she could see a symbol of Joseph's affection for someone else. According to one story passed down among church members, Emma stomped on the watch with her foot.[35]

Emma berated Joseph on the way home. She was livid that he had concealed the extent of his polygamy from her. According to Clayton, Joseph "had to use harsh measures to put a stop to her abuse but finally succeeded." What were those harsh measures? Did Joseph strike Emma, or threaten to do so? Did he simply browbeat her until he had stilled her voice? No other sources shed light on the fight.[36]

Flora Woodworth was also shaken by the fracas. The next day she went to Carthage and married Carlos Gove, who was not a member of the church. She signed a statement attesting—falsely—that she had reached her eighteenth birthday. Joseph met with Phebe and Flora Woodworth several days after her civil wedding. No records reveal the substance of their conversations, but one of Joseph's other plural wives commented many decades later that the prophet had given his "consent" to the wedding. As far as Emma was concerned, her husband had lost a wife. It was a start.[37]

Watch given by Joseph Smith to Eliza R. Snow. (© By Intellectual Reserve, Inc.)

The inscription on the watch reads, "1844 / JS to ERS / 1887 to JFS."
JFS is Joseph F. Smith, son of Hyrum Smith. (© By Intellectual Reserve, Inc.)

At the end of August 1843, Joseph, Emma, their children, Lucy Mack Smith, and other members of the household began moving into a new residence. The two-story frame building was only one block from their old home, and one block back from the river. Joseph for some time had envisioned a hotel, the Nauvoo House, that would impress visitors with its hospitality and class. Work on the project had been slow, so Joseph intended the new Smith residence to double as a tavern and boarding-house. On September 15, the prophet hung a sign on his new home, naming it the Nauvoo Mansion.[38]

Emily and Eliza Partridge were still with the family when the Smith household moved into the home. According to Emily, Emma repeatedly took the pair aside and told them that they needed to "break [their] covenants." She eventually wore down their resolve. "Joseph asked her," recounted Emily, "if we made her the promises she required, if she would cease to trouble us, and not persist in our marrying some one else." Emma agreed. "Joseph came to us and shook hands with us," Emily continued, "and the understanding was that all was ended between us." She and her sister moved out. Joseph had no contact with them for months. The change in circumstances would not affect their eternal covenants, but the marriages ended on earth. Emma had prevailed again.[39]

Joseph did not relinquish all his wives. Emma did not press her husband to send away Sarah and Maria Lawrence. Perhaps more surprisingly, Joseph married another plural wife who became part of the household. Melissa Lott was the nineteen-year-old daughter of Cornelius Lott, who managed the Smith farm on the eastern outskirts of Nauvoo and was the captain of Joseph's bodyguard. Joseph Smith III recalled Melissa Lott as a tall, beautiful young woman "with dark complexion, dark hair and eyes." She was also a fine singer. On September 20, 1843, the prophet rode to his farm and watched as Hyrum Smith sealed Cornelius Lott to his wife, Permelia. Hyrum then sealed Melissa to Joseph. Melissa later testified that she and Joseph had intercourse on multiple occasions. During the subsequent winter, she lived in the Nauvoo Mansion and cared for Joseph and Emma's children. It is unclear whether Emma knew about the sealing.[40]

Later in the fall, Joseph was sealed to Fanny Young, a widowed, fifty-six-year-old sister of Brigham Young. This sealing is the prophet's final known plural marriage. In all Joseph had been sealed to more than thirty women. The exact number remains uncertain. While Joseph did not cease all contact with his plural wives, there are fewer records of interactions or liaisons with them after the summer of 1843. Emma had constrained, though not fully ended, Joseph's polygamy.[41]

Despite everything that had transpired between them, despite her very real sense of betrayal, Emma had enduring affection for Joseph. She believed in him as a prophet and was deeply attached to his vision. Emma yearned to be at the center of Joseph's most sacred activities, not peripheral to them. Joseph had spoken of making the Relief Society a "kingdom of priests," and he alluded to the eventual inclusion of women in the endowment. Yet so far he had initiated only a set of trusted male followers. And while Emma had been sealed to her husband, so had his other plural wives. Finally, in the fall of 1843, Joseph invited Emma to participate in rituals that eased her sense of alienation from him.

On the evening of September 18, Joseph gathered with eleven men and Emma in the front upper room of their new home. It was a meeting of what participants called simply the "quorum" or the "council," the group of individuals initiated into the endowment. (The group later became known as the "anointed quorum" or "holy order.") At the meeting Joseph and Emma were "anointed and ordained to the highest and holiest order of the priesthood." Apostle Wilford Woodruff termed the new ritual the "Second Anointing." It was another degree in Joseph's priesthood rite, a crowning ordinance for couples.[42]

Joseph by this time was teaching that in order for a man to obtain the fullness of the priesthood, "he must be [anointed] a king and a priest." It was not that anyone would rule a kingdom in the here and now. As Brigham Young explained prior to Joseph's ritual anointing, a man could be "anointed king and priest long before he receives his kingdom." The ritual signified his future eternal reign. He would possess eternal power and glory.[43]

The ordinance contributed to newfound concord between Emma and Joseph. The prophet informed Clayton that Emma had become "quite friendly and kind. She had been anointed, and he had also been anointed king." The ritual differentiated Emma's place in Joseph's life from that of his plural wives. Joseph had formed connections with countless women and families, but, according to later descriptions of the ordinance, Emma would reign alongside her husband as a "queen" and "priestess."[44] The prophet's strategic concessions on polygamy, coupled with his decision to bring Emma into his most sacred rituals, allowed them to move forward.

Emma assisted as other women were initiated into the endowment and joined what Brigham Young termed the "order of the priesthood." She helped prepare the dresses women wore during the ritual. For instance, two days before Jennetta Richards received her endowment, she and her husband went to "see Emma about dress." For the remainder of the fall and winter, those who had been endowed held "prayer meetings" several times a week, and the church's leading couples received their second anointings. Joseph once again had turned to ritual to restore order.[45]

On October 3, 1843, Joseph and Emma "opened" the Nauvoo Mansion by hosting a "luxurious feast" for a hundred couples. In a speech to his guests, Joseph compared himself to the biblical Job, a righteous man who endured worsening afflictions without cursing God. "After Job had suffered and drank the very dregs of affliction," the prophet explained, "the Lord had remembered him in mercy and was about to bless him abundantly."[46] God had given Job wealth, children, and long life as recompense for his suffering. Joseph too had suffered, and Missouri politicians and their Illinois conspirators had tried to deprive him of his liberty, if not his life. He had overcome them. When he looked at his new home, full of his family and his many friends, he found it easy to think that God was now rewarding him. In Joseph's case, however, the worst persecution lay ahead.

CHAPTER TWENTY-NINE

Cool as a Cucumber (1843–1844)

O N DECEMBER 5, 1843, church member Margaret Avery, who
lived about twenty-five miles southeast of Nauvoo, arrived in
the city with distressing news. Her son and husband had
been kidnapped, taken across the river to Missouri, and imprisoned on false charges. Marc Childs, who had stolen a horse in nearby
Clark County, Missouri, pinned his crime on Daniel and Philander
Avery. Like his wife, Daniel Avery was a Latter-day Saint.[1]

It was a shrewd move by Childs to scapegoat the Averys. Anti-
Mormons in Hancock County alleged that Nauvoo courts protected
Mormon criminals from prosecution. The church's opponents accordingly felt that extralegal forms of justice were justified. One of Childs's
partners decoyed Philander Avery to Warsaw, Illinois, where a gang of
Missourians forced him across the river. Several weeks later, Levi Williams, colonel of the Hancock County militia, led a posse that abducted
the elder Avery. Even the *Warsaw Signal*, normally unstinting in its criticism of the church and its prophet, agreed that the seizure of Daniel
Avery was vigilantism, "the arrest being without any legal process."[2]

The kidnappings pointed to a larger danger. Missourians and Illinois
anti-Mormons were working together, and a militia officer had joined a
mob in a vigilante action. The Averys were small fry. Joseph knew that he
was the ultimate target.

A special session of the city council, presided over by Joseph, passed
an ordinance designed to shield him from extradition to Missouri. That

statute threatened anyone who came to Nauvoo in an attempt to arrest
Joseph Smith with life imprisonment unless "pardoned by the governor
with the consent of the mayor." The idea that the governor could pardon
someone only with Joseph's consent was a brazen assertion of Nauvoo's
legal supremacy. With similar brazenness, another city council ordinance
declared that "all writs or warrants issued out of the city" needed approval by Nauvoo's mayor before being executed. In other words, no
constable or posse could arrest any Nauvoo resident without Joseph's
permission.³

Joseph went even further, seeking what amounted to Nauvoo's independence from the State of Illinois. He proposed that the Saints petition
Congress to "receive the city under their protection," federalize the Nauvoo Legion, and lend the city assistance in fortifying itself against possible attack. Nauvoo would be a city-state, its own mini-territory within
the American republic. In the petition, the Saints asked Congress to em-
power Nauvoo's mayor—Joseph Smith—to deploy the legion's troops as
he deemed necessary to repel invaders and quell mobs. He would not
need to consult Thomas Ford. When the petition eventually reached
Washington, it died in committee.⁴

The *Warsaw Message* denounced the ordinances as "utterly regardless
of all law and right and decency." Newspapers farther afield also took
note. "What beautiful legislation!" mocked a letter published in the *New-
York Daily Tribune*, a leading Whig newspaper. "The pardoning power
taken from the Governor! and life imprisonment under a city ordinance!!" It wasn't just that Nauvoo arrogated powers properly belonging
to the State of Illinois. It was that these statutes concentrated power in a
single individual. Joseph was "Prophet, Priest, President . . . General,
Mayor of the Cup, and *Landlord!*" He could reign without restraint.⁵

Joseph projected that power beyond Nauvoo. Church members identified John Elliott, a schoolmaster who lived near Warsaw, as a chief con-
spirator in the kidnapping of Daniel Avery. Aaron Johnson, a church
member and justice of the peace, issued a warrant for Elliott's arrest, and a
Mormon posse went to his home, arrested him, and brought him to Nauvoo. A December 18, 1843, hearing before Johnson took place on the second floor of Joseph's store, with the prophet present. There was ample
evidence that Elliott had participated in the kidnapping, and Johnson remanded his case for trial and set a high bond. Johnson also heard testimony that Elliott had remarked that Joseph Smith "was a bad man . . .
that he would be popped over" to Missouri. The prophet swore a further

complaint against Elliott for a "breach of the peace" and for having used "threatening language" against him.[6]

Aaron Johnson issued a warrant for the arrest of Levi Williams. This was a far more provocative step given Williams's standing in the county. A Nauvoo posse went to arrest Williams and bring him back to the city. Word soon reached Joseph that a crowd had assembled to protect Williams and that "messengers had gone to Missouri to reinforce the mob." The prophet ordered Major General Wilson Law to send a hundred additional men to strengthen Nauvoo's posse. Joseph also instructed Law to prepare the Nauvoo Legion to repel a possible attack.[7]

It was a dangerous moment. Joseph wanted to demonstrate that anti-Mormons could not persecute the Saints without consequences. But if the Saints contributed to the outbreak of violence, anti-Mormons would respond aggressively, and the remaining goodwill or neutrality of politicians such as Thomas Ford would vanish.

Joseph pulled back. First, he told the court that he would "forgive" John Elliott for his threats. He even invited Elliott and his companions to take supper, lodging, and breakfast. The *Warsaw Message* scoffed that the prophet made them pay for it. Regardless, Elliott wasn't moved by the prophet's hospitality. He became more involved in Hancock County's anti-Mormon movement and looked for an opportunity to revenge himself on Joseph.[8]

Meanwhile, as the reinforced Mormon posse approached Williams's residence, they learned that a large group of men armed with rifles had gathered to defend the colonel. The posse prudently returned to Nauvoo for "weapons and help." Joseph decided that the men should not make another attempt at the present time. Eventually, he reasoned, the mob would dissipate, and they could seize Williams with less trouble.[9]

On Christmas Day, Joseph's mood was buoyant. The crisis had passed, and Philander Avery had escaped from Missouri and returned to Nauvoo. (His father Daniel was freed by a judge that same day.) The prophet hosted fifty couples for dinner in the afternoon. He also invited Nauvoo's "young ladies and gentlemen" for an evening of dancing.[10]

An uninvited guest caused a stir at the party. In the midst of the festivities, a man stumbled in. He appeared drunk, and his long and wild hair made him seem "like a Missourian." Joseph told the captain of Nauvoo's newly formed police to "put him out of doors." Then Joseph got a look at the man's face. It was Porter Rockwell, the accused shooter of Lilburn Boggs, back from nine months in squalid Missouri jails.[11]

Orrin Porter Rockwell, ca. 1866. (Courtesy of Church History Library)

The previous spring, Rockwell had escaped his confinement but had quickly been recaptured. Then, in August 1843, a grand jury had decided against indicting Rockwell for the attempted murder of Boggs, but it did indict him for the jailbreak. A trial jury convicted him of the latter charge. The judge in the case was Austin King, who had remanded Joseph and other Saints to prison back in the fall of 1838. King still hated the Mormons, but the jury concluded that Rockwell had suffered enough. Rockwell received a token punishment of five additional minutes in jail.[12]

The *Warsaw Message* reported that Joseph festooned Rockwell with a variety of ribbons "and christened him Lion of the Day." Legend developed that the prophet promised Rockwell that if he imitated Samson and never cut his hair, "no bullet or blade" would harm him. Rockwell sported long locks for several decades. He later killed men in both Illinois and Utah and, despite heavy drinking and a readiness to fight, managed to escape serious harm. He died of a heart attack while awaiting trial on charges of murder.[13]

The return of Rockwell and the Averys meant that God once more had delivered his faithful servants from their enemies. "Missouri was again rid of the brethren," Joseph remarked. The prophet urged his associates to forward evidence of his enemies' illegal machinations to Governor Ford, but he assured them that there was no cause for panic. "Let us keep cool as a cucumber in a frosty morning," he advised. The Nauvoo City Council repealed the most brazen of its recently passed laws, and tensions between the Saints and the anti-Mormons in Hancock County subsided.[14]

Joseph preached calm but worried about disloyalty and division within the church. Disunity had led to the collapse of Mormon Kirtland, and in Missouri, several disaffected church members had betrayed Joseph to his enemies. In late December 1843, Joseph discussed his concerns with the forty members of Nauvoo's newly sworn police force. "I think my life more in danger from some little dough head of a fool in the city than from ... enemies abroad," Joseph asserted. A "Brutus" might betray him.[15]

William Law, Joseph's counselor in the First Presidency, heard that the prophet considered him a "dough head," "Judas," or "Brutus." Law had been among the first men initiated into what became the Nauvoo endowment. Then, in the summer of 1843, the prophet had tried to convince Law and his wife, Jane, of the propriety of plural marriage. They did not accept the principle, but Joseph must have persuaded them to at least keep an open mind. Jane Law received her endowment that fall, and the couple attended prayer meetings of the anointed quorum.

In mid-October 1843, Joseph invited William Law—and perhaps Jane as well—to the farm of John Benbow, about five miles east of the city. One of Joseph's plural wives was present: Maria Lawrence, the prophet's nineteen-year-old ward. Joseph and William Law stayed at Benbow's overnight. Law left convinced and disgusted that Joseph had slept with Maria Lawrence.[16]

The Laws definitively rejected polygamy before the year's end. As William Law wrote in his journal, God's "spirit prevailed ... before the fearful step was taken." He concluded that the "spiritual wife system" was "of the devil," and he told Joseph as much.[17]

Joseph later alleged that his counselor had become upset when he had refused to seal him to Jane for eternity. The prophet explained that the Lord forbade it because Law "was an adulterous person." Joseph further claimed that after this rebuke, Jane Law had found Joseph on the street, invited him into her home, put her arms around him, and asked to be sealed to him instead. When he rebuffed her, she told her husband that "Joseph wanted her to be married to him." Joseph most likely invented the accusations after his alienation from the Laws. Regardless, the subject of plural marriage drove a wedge between the Laws and Joseph.[18]

William Law soon heard rumors that his life was in jeopardy. He went to Joseph, who denied any such intention and invited Law to appear before the city council. The meeting was a confusing affair. Joseph both affirmed his friendship with Law and warned him that he had been talking too freely about the "spiritual wife system," an increasingly poorly kept secret.[19]

Law's alienation was a turning point. Opposition to polygamy—and therefore to Joseph—began to coalesce in early 1844. In addition to William Law, polygamy opponents included William Marks, president of the Nauvoo stake; Leonard Soby, a member of the Nauvoo High Council; Wilson Law, major general of the Nauvoo Legion and William Law's brother; and Francis M. Higbee, whose brother, Chauncey, had been accused of adultery and excommunicated in the spring of 1842. These men still did not want to break with Joseph publicly, but they discussed their discontents with each other.

Joseph tried to intimidate the dissenters. Soby heard from a Nauvoo policeman—Warren Smith, no relation to the prophet—that Law and Marks were traitors. Soby passed on a message to Law. He and Marks should keep clear of Warren Smith. Otherwise, the policeman would shoot them. An alarmed Law again sought out Joseph, this time with his brother Wilson. Joseph told the Laws that they were "fools" and "that he had a good mind to put them (the police) on us anyway."[20]

When the Nauvoo City Council reconvened the following day, Soby, Marks, and Higbee testified. They were encountering men on the street—in some cases members of the police force—who warned them that they were in danger. Joseph said that such tales were ridiculous, but he warned Francis Higbee to "stay at home and hold his tongue, lest rumor turn upon him." Adding insult to the threat, Joseph stated that he would not allow Higbee in his home or to "associate with his females." The prophet added that Higbee stank from a venereal disease.[21]

Joseph accosted William Law on the street a few days later. He accused Law, his wife, and his brother of "telling evil of him." Joseph informed Law that he had been removed from his position in the First Presidency. "Some unpleasant words ensued," wrote Law. "I am glad to be free from him, and from so vile an association." Yet like many men and women who endured a rupture with Joseph, Law was not really "free" from the prophet. He was hurt and angry and not sure what to do next.[22]

Joseph told those close to him that the turmoil amounted to "another tempest in a tea pot." He was rattled by the thought that Law or someone else would betray him to the Missourians, but at home he was relaxed and on good terms with Emma. Early in the new year, Joseph enjoyed a dinner with William W. Phelps, now solidly back in the fold after his Missouri apostasy. The prophet remarked to Phelps that he was fortunate to have a "kind provident wife." Whenever he was hungry, "she would load the table with so many good things" that he would be stuffed. Phelps joked that Joseph should "do as [Napoleon] Bonaparte did" and use a "little table" that would hold only a modest amount of food. The French dictator was known for eating quickly by himself. "Mr. Smith is a bigger man than Bonaparte," Emma retorted. "He can never eat without his friends." Joseph praised the comment as "the wisest thing" he had heard Emma say.[23]

"Friendship is one of the grand fundamental principles of Mormonism," Joseph had preached the previous summer. He joked that he would be happy to be resurrected to either heaven or hell, as long as he was with the Saints. "What do we care where we are if the society be good?" he asked. Joseph loved the company of his friends, but the emergence of new teachings, the prophet's demands for loyalty, and his fear of betrayal tested the bonds of many friendships.[24]

CHAPTER THIRTY

The Kingdom (1844)

T
HE UNITED STATES IN early 1844 was a strange mixture of optimism and foreboding. Late that winter, the Massachusetts minister-turned-lecturer Ralph Waldo Emerson proclaimed that "America is the country of the future." The United States was "a country of beginnings, of projects, of vast designs and expectations."[1]

The nation was at once coming together and tearing itself apart. Railroads allowed people and goods to travel more quickly between cities, and Samuel Morse's telegraph would soon permit the near-instantaneous movement of information across the country. The news early in 1844 revolved around the looming presidential election. President John Tyler had signaled his intention to pursue the annexation of Texas, which would attach the slaveholding republic to the United States. Both the Methodists and the Baptists divided over the issue of slavery in the mid-1840s. It didn't take a prophet to foresee the worsening of sectional tension ahead.

Joseph wasn't what Emerson had in mind when he thought about the American future, but the Mormon prophet's career had been one of many new beginnings and bold projects. At the age of thirty-eight, Joseph remained his customarily audacious self. Dissatisfied with the leading presidential candidates, he announced his own run for the White House as the darkest of dark-horse candidates. He also established yet another new council, a secret political arm of what he understood as the

Kingdom of God on earth. Joseph wanted the new council to plan an expansive, glorious future for the church, possibly in Nauvoo, possibly elsewhere. As the prophet contemplated his next move, he lashed out at those men who opposed both polygamy and his exercise of political power. Dissent, and Joseph's response to it, threatened to tear apart the city and the church.

On a frigid late-January morning, Joseph met with the members of the Quorum of the Twelve Apostles and several other men in the upper floor of his red-brick store. Unlike William Law and William Marks, the apostles had, if anything, become more closely bound to Joseph. Over the prior week, several apostles and their wives had received their second anointings. All of these men had married plural wives.

This evening, however, the apostles had not gathered with Joseph for sacred ordinances. Their purpose was political. The men voted unanimously "that Joseph Smith be a candidate for the next presidency" of the United States.[2]

Joseph had been thinking about the 1844 election for some time. The incumbent, John Tyler, had ascended to the presidency following William Henry Harrison's death. After a series of clashes over policy and personalities, the Whigs expelled "His Accidency" from their party and closed ranks behind perennial presidential candidate Henry Clay of Kentucky. The "Great Compromiser" had seemed sympathetic when Joseph had brought the church's petition to the nation's capital in the wake of the Missouri persecutions. The prophet had not forgotten, and in August 1843 Joseph reportedly declared himself a "Clay man."[3]

Joseph's attachment to Clay proved malleable. In October, the church's *Times and Seasons* urged the Saints to vote for the candidate "most likely to render us assistance in obtaining redress for our grievances." Joseph decided to write Clay and the four leading contenders for the Democratic nomination—John C. Calhoun, Lewis Cass, Richard M. Johnson, and former president Martin Van Buren—to find out whether they would advance the Saints' hitherto unsuccessful quest for redress for their Missouri losses. He reminded the candidates of the Saints' growing political clout. Indeed, it was possible the Mormon vote might prove decisive in Illinois. In 1840, Van Buren had prevailed in the state by fewer than two thousand votes.[4]

Calhoun, Cass, and Clay all replied, but none of them promised to help. Clay expressed sympathy but wanted to enter office "free and unfettered" from any pledges. Cass told Joseph that if Missouri and Congress had re-jected the Saints' petition for redress, he could not see what power the pres-ident could exercise on the matter. Calhoun's reply was the most pointed. The former vice president and current U.S. senator, who had supported the prerogative of South Carolina to nullify federal tariffs, told Smith that the federal government possessed no authority to interpose in a state matter.[5]

The replies angered Joseph. Could a state deprive a portion of its citizens of their liberties with impunity? If a state allowed mobs to ban-ish and plunder one group of citizens, what would protect others from the same treatment? William Phelps, increasingly busy as Joseph's politi-cal ghostwriter, drafted a florid and fervent rebuttal to Calhoun. In it, Jo-seph argued for the supremacy of the national government. "Congress," he declared, "with the president as executor, is as almighty in its sphere as Jehovah is in His." The danger was the local tyranny of mobs abetted by the support or indifference of state governments. Joseph demanded that the national government protect the liberty of his people. It was the mirror opposite of Calhoun's states' rights philosophy. As no other can-didate promised to defend the Saints and support their calls for redress, Joseph decided to run himself.[6]

After the late-January 1844 meeting with the apostles, Joseph and Wil-liam Phelps prepared a platform for his campaign: *General Smith's Views of the Powers and Policy of the Government of the United States*. Joseph sought credibility from the military title despite his inexperience in battle. The pamphlet began with a common political argument. Through partisanship and corruption, the United States had departed from the glory and liberty of its founders. Joseph blamed the decline on Martin Van Buren ("poor lit-tle Matty") and John Tyler ("a pseudo Democratic Whig president"). The Mormon prophet argued that other politicians pandered to faction and party. He, by contrast, would govern on behalf of all Americans.[7]

The most contentious national issue in 1844 was the intersection of slavery and territorial expansion. Eight years earlier, American settlers in Texas had declared their independence from Mexico, and large numbers of southern slaveholders moved there. Many Anglo-Texans understood the establishment of their republic as a stepping stone to American state-hood. By 1844, most Democrats favored the annexation of Texas even at the risk of war with Mexico, while northern Whigs opposed the addition of a slave state.

Joseph's ideas about race and slavery were complex and sometimes contradictory. On the one hand, the Book of Abraham and Joseph's revisions to the Bible suggested that dark-skinned Africans could not hold the priesthood. Nevertheless, Joseph had not interfered with the priesthood ordination of Elijah Able, an African American convert. The Mormon prophet was not a racial egalitarian, though. One of his stated objections to slavery was that slaveholders might compel white "children to mix with their slaves." Joseph favored the separation of the races rather than their social, let alone sexual, integration. As a city, Nauvoo prohibited Black men from voting, holding civic office, and performing military service, and Joseph once fined two Black men for intending to marry white women.[8]

Joseph had developed a consistent opposition to slavery, however. At a December 1843 city council meeting he "suggested the propriety of making all colored people free." This idea found clear expression in his presidential platform. Joseph envisioned a "free people from the east to the west sea" and thus would add Texas, Oregon (claimed by Great Britain), and also Canada and Mexico should they seek union with the United States. Thus, Joseph favored the annexation of Texas, but as a free state. He also proposed a plan of emancipation by which Congress would purchase the freedom of enslaved people with the revenue gained from selling western lands. Slavery would be abolished by 1850 at the latest. Many anti-slavery northerners supported colonization schemes to export freed slaves far from the United States or proposed emancipation in the distant future. By contrast, General Smith would purchase the freedom of enslaved people, and soon.[9]

On February 8, Joseph introduced his platform to a large group of church members who gathered in his red-brick store office and unanimously approved *General Smith's Views*. Mormon leaders mailed copies to Washington politicians, state governors, a host of postmasters, and leading newspapers across the country, and Joseph asked many of his trusted followers to prepare to serve missions boosting his bid for the White House.[10]

"There is oratory enough in the church to carry me into the presidential chair the first slide," Joseph predicted.[11] Joseph probably realized that he would face an uphill struggle to gain a majority in Hancock County, let alone anywhere else in the country. So why run? The most basic reason is that no other candidate had "stepped forward" and promised the Saints redress and protection. Joseph also saw an opportunity to spread his ideas across the country, and an enhanced political profile would help him broker the Mormon vote in the coming election. If nothing else, politics was a welcome diversion from other challenges.

On March 10, George Miller handed the prophet two letters from himself and apostle Lyman Wight. The nearly fifty-year-old Miller, an "irksome personality with real business skills," was bishop of the branch of the church in Black River Falls in the Wisconsin Territory. More than a hundred church members had moved north to mills and logging camps in the Wisconsin "pineries." The "logging saints" and hired men felled the great trees and dragged them to sawmills. Bound into rafts, the lumber then floated to the Mississippi and downriver to Nauvoo.[12]

The letters informed Joseph that by summer 1844 they would have produced enough lumber for both the temple and the Nauvoo House. They had a new proposal for the future. According to Wight, local Menominee and Chippewa leaders wanted to "receive the gospel." The pineries Mormons could preach to them and induce them to relocate to the "beautiful hills and valleys" along the upper Colorado River in Texas. The settlement, Wight and Miller predicted, also would attract slaveholding whites from across the South as well as Cherokee and Choctaw slaveholders from present-day Oklahoma. A Mormon outpost in Texas could also serve as a base for preaching missions to other Native peoples. The church finally would advance the Book of Mormon vision of Lamanite conversions.[13]

The proposal from Wight and Miller intersected with anxieties about Nauvoo's future. The history of persecution in Missouri suggested that harassment and violence would increase in tandem with the church's growth. Joseph could not count on Governor Ford to quell mobs. No aspiring president would protect the Saints, and Joseph knew that in the end, his own campaign was more quixotic than serious. Joseph intended to remain in Nauvoo long enough to finish the temple and to lead church members through its sacred ordinances. Then he was prepared to leave. Joseph already had instructed the apostles to form an expedition to investigate possible locations in Oregon and California where the Saints could form their own government. Upon receipt of the letters, Joseph gathered with the apostles and several other men. They discussed the ideas late into the night and approved the strategy.[14]

The prophet also had a much more radical project in mind for this group of men, who became the core of yet another governing council and inner circle. The prophet swore them to strictest secrecy. Lucien Woodworth added that they should not divulge the council's business to anyone, even their wives. "The man who broke the rule 'should lose his cursed head,' " Woodworth warned. Joseph organized the men "after the pattern of heaven." They formed a semicircle in front of him, seated from oldest to youngest, and they voted in the same order.[15]

Joseph soon announced that by revelation the Lord had revealed the council's name: "The Kingdom of God and his laws, with the keys and power thereof, and judgment in the hands of his servants. Ahman Christ." An earlier revelation had identified "Ahman" as the name of God in the "pure language" spoken by Adam and Eve. Joseph explained that "Ahman Christ" meant "the first man's son." William Clayton, who became the council's clerk, sometimes shortened the council's name to simply "the Kingdom." As the number of its members swelled to around fifty, including a few friendly non-Mormons, Clayton also referred to it as the "Council of Fifty."[16]

Joseph understood the new council as the nucleus of the literal Kingdom of God on earth. One of his early revelations drew on the biblical Book of Daniel to proclaim that "the keys of the kingdom of heaven are committed unto man on the earth." The kingdom was like a "stone hewn from the mountain." It was small, but it would "roll forth until it hath filled the whole earth." Accordingly, the Saints would establish a "theocracy" in Oregon or Texas, with a constitution "according to the mind of God." That heavenly constitution would correct the defects in the U.S. Constitution, which had failed to protect liberty. The Kingdom of God would serve as a "standard" or "ensign" to the nations. The righteous would flock to its banner.[17]

Joseph made a distinction between the kingdom and the church. The First Presidency and other quorums governed church affairs. By contrast, the Council of Fifty "was designed to be got up for the safety and salvation of the saints." It would protect them and—as the kingdom expanded—any other people who lived within its jurisdiction.[18]

The members of the Kingdom bandied about some far-fetched ideas over the coming weeks. They sent a memorial to Congress asking it to authorize Joseph to raise an army of one hundred thousand volunteers to protect American citizens emigrating to Texas, Oregon, and other western lands. (Both houses of Congress and President Tyler rejected the memorial in the spring of 1844.) The council also tapped James Emmett, who had served missions to the Sioux in present-day Minnesota, to undertake "a mission to the Lamanites to instruct them to unite together." Looking east at the same time, Joseph asked the apostles to select men to "preach and electioneer through the different states" in support of his presidential bid.[19]

As they discussed all sorts of future plans, Joseph stressed that they should speak freely and reach decisions by consensus. He did not want to be surrounded by "dough heads," he told them at their first meeting. Council members only partly heeded this request. They expressed a variety of opinions, but they also demonstrated a strong tendency toward sycophancy. As Brigham Young declared, "Revelations must govern." Joseph was their revelator, the earthly conduit for the voice of God. A kingdom needed a king.[20]

Joseph took care to establish decorum and order within the Council of Fifty, but, more broadly, Nauvoo's civic and church affairs were unraveling. In late February, Orasmus F. Bostwick was brought before the Nauvoo mayor's court. Bostwick had joined the city's Masonic lodge but did not belong to the church. According to testimony, Bostwick had been at Joseph's house the previous week when the prophet asked him "if he thought he had any spiritual wives." Bostwick said no but volunteered his opinion that Hyrum Smith had wives all over the city and could sleep "with three or four every night." Bostwick further claimed that for a pittance a man could have what he wanted with "almost any woman in the city." Even though Joseph had raised the topic in the first place, he used Bostwick's comments to make a fresh attempt to clamp down on rumors and dissent.[21]

It wasn't clear that Bostwick had violated any city ordinance, but Joseph fined him $50 anyway. Francis Higbee represented Bostwick in court and told Joseph he would appeal his client's case to the circuit court in Carthage. Joseph accused Higbee of doing so in order to "stir up the mob and bring them upon us." Probably because Higbee's involvement angered him, Joseph wouldn't let the matter drop. He asked William Phelps to eviscerate Bostwick and Higbee in print. The resulting "The Voice of Innocence from Nauvoo" defended the honor of Latter-day Saint women and urged the city's citizens to "kick the bloodthirsty pimp from the pale of social communion." A week later, the prophet's thoughts remained fixed on Bostwick and Higbee. Joseph threatened that if their outrages did not cease, he would "give them into the hands of the mob." Church leaders also gave notice that the Relief Society would hold a meeting at which it would endorse "The Voice of Innocence."[22]

Emma Smith hadn't attended a Relief Society meeting for nearly two years. Given that Joseph had married a number of women in the society, she felt betrayed by a group she had charged with "watch[ing] over the morals . . . of the members of the institution." The Bostwick case, however, gave Emma an opportunity to reaffirm her moral leadership and her opposition to Joseph's polygamy. She read and amended Phelps's essay, and she returned to the Relief Society for discussion of the matter. The upper room of Joseph's store could not accommodate the more than one thousand members of the society, so she presided over four separate meetings. At least during the first session, Joseph was in his office next door. William Clayton noted that Joseph was "weeping and seemed very sorrowful" that morning. Clayton did not explain the source of Joseph's sorrow, but one suspects that the furor over Bostwick renewed tension— at least temporarily—between Mormonism's first couple.[23]

Emma read passages from the Book of Mormon and Doctrine and Covenants that denounced polygamy. She also exhorted the women to "follow the teachings of President Joseph Smith *from the stand.*" In other words, regardless of what Joseph taught in private, women should follow his public instruction. At the last meeting, she stated that "if there ever was any authority on the earth she had it." Emma might have made some private compromises with Joseph, but here she was resolute. The Relief Society approved "The Voice of Innocence," which thanked Joseph for his defense of Hyrum and resolved that "polygamy, bigamy, fornication, adultery, and prostitution . . . be frowned out of the hearts of honest men." The *Nauvoo Neighbor* published the essay later in the month. Joseph had received a public vote of confidence from Emma and the Relief Society, but Emma had orchestrated an equally public rejection of her husband's secret teachings.[24]

During the same meeting at which Joseph excoriated Bostwick and Francis Higbee, the prophet got into a public spat with Charles Foster. Both Foster and his older brother, Robert D. Foster, were physicians. Robert Foster, who was the proprietor of the city's Mammoth Hotel, was a member of the church, while Charles Foster was not. Joseph accused Charles Foster of having penned an anonymous letter published in the *New York Tribune.* The epistle painted a portrait of a power-hungry prophet who defrauded his followers out of their donations for the Nauvoo Temple. Charles Foster responded sharply to Joseph's accusation, and the prophet fined him $10 for making threats and disturbing the meeting. When Robert Foster objected, Joseph threatened to fine him as well.[25]

Animosity between Joseph and the Fosters grew to a fever pitch over the next several weeks. Merinus Eaton, a non-Mormon resident of Nauvoo, informed church leaders that Joseph's opponents had invited him to a clandestine meeting. (The next month Joseph invited Eaton into the Council of Fifty.) Eaton heard Robert Foster claim that Joseph had tried to seduce his wife, Sarah Phinney Foster. The prophet had come while her husband was out and taught her the "spiritual wife doctrine." Then Robert Foster had returned and found his wife dining with the prophet. After Joseph made an awkward exit, Sarah Foster had refused to say what had transpired until her husband threatened to shoot her.[26]

On March 23, Joseph and William Clayton rode to Robert Foster's home. The hotel proprietor was not at home, but they found Sarah Foster at a neighbor's residence. The prophet asked her whether he had taught polygamy to her and whether he had proposed "illicit intercourse with her" while dining with her "during the doctor's absence." She emphatically rejected any hint of impropriety.[27]

It is difficult to know what to make of the strange episode. Had Joseph attempted to seduce Sarah Foster less than a week after clashing with her husband at a public meeting? Yet would Robert Foster have told other men a story that cast doubt on his own wife's fidelity? Had Joseph and his allies manufactured the whole story in order to accuse his opponents of slander? Regardless, Joseph delivered a sermon in which he warned about a cadre of men that had "held a caucus, designing to destroy all the Smith family."[28]

Since the start of the year, Joseph had responded to a relatively small number of dissenters in ways that were erratic and counterproductive. He, or men loyal to him, had warned William Law that his life was in danger. Joseph had turned a private conversation with Orasmus Bostwick into a public confrontation that Emma had used to denounce polygamy. Joseph sometimes had stooped to gratuitous insults, and his incendiary steps, such as the accusations against the Fosters, only added to a sense of crisis. By early April 1844, Joseph was searching for a way to quell growing doubts about his leadership.

On April 6, the Saints in and around Nauvoo gathered for the church's semiannual conference. Joseph told the congregation that he was "never in any nearer relationship to God than at the present time." He would "show before the conference closed that God was with him." Later that day, there was a vicious thunderstorm, followed by a double rainbow. It was auspicious.[29]

Anticipation built overnight, and Joseph spoke to an enormous congregation the next afternoon. The prophet began by referencing the death of King Follett—not a royal figure, simply a church member with the given name King. He had been battered by a falling bucket of rocks while "stoning up a well" and died eleven days later. Follett had joined the church in 1831, endured repeated expulsions in Missouri, and then suffered imprisonment in the spring of 1839. Now he had been crushed in an unfortunate accident.[30]

Joseph's sermon was not a eulogy, however, nor did the prophet offer standard Christian words of consolation. Instead, he told the congregation that before he could address their grief, it was necessary for him to "go back to the beginning of creation," to the nature of God. "What kind of a being is God?" Joseph asked. He staked his prophetic authority on his ability to bring forth a correct and compelling answer to that question. "If I do not do it," he allowed, "I have no right to revelation." Joseph knew that his critics accused him of being a "false teacher" and "false prophet." He would refute the notion. "If I can bring you to [God]," he suggested, "all persecution against me will cease and let you know that I am his servant." Joseph was determined to reassert his prophetic leadership.[31]

"God himself who sits enthroned in yonder heavens," Joseph taught, "is a man like unto one of yourselves." God once had dwelt on an earth. In turn, Joseph told the Saints, "you have got to learn how to be a God yourself." This divine potential within humanity was "consoling to the mourner" in the wake of death. Yes, their earthly bodies would dissolve, but faithful men would "be heirs of God and joint heirs of Jesus Christ to inherit the same powers [and] exaltation." Death was not the end but a necessary step toward eternal glory.

Joseph next returned to one of his favorite biblical passages. According to Joseph's interpretation of the first several verses of Genesis, God had not created the world out of nothing. Instead, he had organized the world out of chaos. Matter was eternal and could not be destroyed. The body's dissolution was not forever. This was a comfort to mourners, but also a spur to action. Living Saints had an "awful responsibility" to their dead, to do the ritual work that would give departed spirits an opportunity to obey the gospel and receive eternal glory. Living Saints could be—had to be—saviors for the dead.

The "King Follett Discourse," as the sermon became known, was not the first time Joseph had publicly taught these principles, but he distilled them with particular clarity on this occasion. Men could become gods. The only thing Joseph held back was exactly what was required in order for humans to achieve exaltation. The prophet alluded to the endowment, but he said not one word about marriage.

Before he finished speaking, Joseph stopped and reflected on his life. He knew what his many detractors said about him. The mockery and the accusations stung. The prophet maintained that he was misunderstood, or simply not understood, and he knew that his claims were incredible. "You never knew my heart," Joseph lamented. "No man knows my history." Joseph insisted that he would be vindicated after his death. Perhaps he sensed the end was near.

Joseph intended to continue on the subject of the resurrection the next day, but his voice was tired. Instead, he briefly disclosed what he termed a "great, grand, and glorious revelation." He noted that there had been "great discussion" within the church about "where Zion is." Joseph's early 1830s revelations had pinpointed Zion to the Jackson County town of Independence. In recent years, though, talk of a return to Jackson County had faded, as had predictions of Christ's imminent Second Coming. Now Joseph broadened Zion's geography. "The whole [of] America is Zion," he proclaimed. The elders would build churches across North and South America. Nauvoo would become a place of pilgrimage. The Saints would not only be baptized for the dead. In order to save their fathers, mothers, siblings, and friends, they also would be anointed and washed "same as for themselves." As the ancient Israelites had journeyed to Jerusalem to perform certain required sacrifices, so the Saints would come to the Nauvoo Temple, perform ordinances for their deceased kin, and return to their homes.[32]

The prophet was clear about his own position. The Latter-day Saints should understand that God had made him "their king and their God." Joseph knew that such talk would strike some as blasphemous, or at least full of hubris. "If you don't like it," he stated, "you must lump it." He wasn't going to soften his tone or change his ways.[33]

The prophet's teachings about the nature of God, men, and creation reaffirmed the trust of some church members in him. "Anyone that could not see in him the spirit of inspiration of God must be dark," commented Joseph Fielding. "They might have known that he was not a fallen prophet." At the same time, the prophet did not win over those who already regarded him as fallen. William Law asserted that Joseph had taught "blasphemous doctrines," including "a plurality of gods." Law alleged that Joseph had presented himself as a "god to this generation." And Law wouldn't lump it.[34]

The members of the Council of Fifty gathered in the newly dedicated Masonic Hall several days after the conference. At one of the council's first meetings, Joseph had appointed a committee to write a constitution. The men had made slow progress. How does one draft a constitution for the Kingdom of God on earth? William Phelps now motioned that Joseph be added to the committee charged with drafting the constitution. After all, Joseph was their divinely appointed lawgiver. Joseph declined. The committee should do its work, and he could correct any errors. Then he explained how he understood their task. "Theocracy," he taught them, was "for the people to get the voice of God and then acknowledge it." It was a twist on the common American understanding of *vox populi, vox dei*. Instead of affirming the will of the people as the voice of God, Joseph called for "the voice of the people assenting to the voice of God." The message was clear. Joseph was God's mouthpiece, his chosen prophet. He was the medium through which the people received divine instruction. Hyrum Smith explained that his brother was akin to Moses and Enoch, only greater. Phelps added that Joseph's work was like that of Jesus Christ.[35]

Finally, Erastus Snow offered a motion that the council receive Joseph as their "prophet, priest, and king," a common description of Jesus Christ's offices. Council members shouted hosannas "to God and the Lamb [Jesus Christ]" as they affirmed the motion.[36]

Joseph explained that they didn't need anything like the "old dead horse's head" of the U.S. Constitution. While speaking, Joseph held a two-foot ruler, one of the "implements" associated with new initiates in Freemasonry. He became so animated that he snapped the ruler in two. Brigham Young commented that the broken ruler symbolized tyrannical government's downfall.[37]

Joseph discarded the idea of a written constitution for the Kingdom. Instead, he wrote a brief revelation on a scrap of paper. "Verily thus saith the Lord," it stated. "Ye are my constitution, and I am your God, and ye are my spokesmen. From henceforth do as I shall command you." The members of the council were the living constitution of the Kingdom of God, with Joseph as their king. In the American republic, however, there was no space for a theocratic kingdom and no place for a biblical prophet.[38]

A few half-hearted attempts at reconciliation between the prophet and the dissidents failed. Hyrum Smith visited William Law to try to bring him back into the fold, but Law made it clear that he would not budge unless Joseph renounced polygamy.[39] Joseph himself initiated conversations with Robert D. Foster and Chauncey Higbee, but no one was ready to apologize. The prophet had had enough. On April 18, a church council "cut off" Foster, Wilson Law, and William and Jane Law for "unchristianlike conduct."[40]

More conflict arose the next week, when yet another set of brothers got into a scuffle with each other. Orson Spencer was a member of the Council of Fifty and a city alderman. His older brother, Augustine Spencer, was not a Latter-day Saint. The Spencer brothers were at odds over their late father's estate, and Augustine Spencer loathed Joseph Smith, whom he accused in letters back east of keeping "six or seven young females as wives." On April 26, 1844, Orson Spencer went to Joseph in the latter's capacity as mayor and complained that his brother had choked him. Without bothering to make out a warrant, Joseph sent Porter Rockwell to arrest Augustine Spencer.[41]

When Rockwell tried to apprehend Spencer, he refused to be taken without a warrant. Rockwell left and returned with city marshal John P. Greene, but Spencer was unmoved. The Foster brothers and Chauncey Higbee were present, and Greene asked for their assistance in making the arrest. They rebuffed Greene, saying that "they would see the mayor damned." Greene went back to Joseph and obtained a warrant.[42]

Everyone proceeded toward the mayor's office. When they reached its steps, Joseph asked Greene to arrest Higbee and the Fosters for their refusal to help make the arrest. Not surprisingly, they resisted, and Joseph "laid hold on the two Fosters at the same time." Charles Foster drew a double-barreled pistol on the prophet, but it was wrenched away, and others on the scene helped Greene detain the men. Joseph fined Augustine Spencer, the Foster brothers, and Higbee $100 each.[43]

Joseph's opponents saw his treatment of the four defendants as further proof of "tyranny." Per the terms of the Nauvoo Charter, the city's mayor functioned as a justice of the peace. When Joseph received a complaint that someone in the city had broken the law, he could have that person arrested and fine him if he judged him guilty. Charles Foster and the others alleged that Joseph had abused his power. Both Spencer brothers had fought, and Augustine Spencer also had sworn a complaint against his younger brother. Why was only one brother fined?[44]

The dissidents began meeting on Sundays, forming what became known as the "new church." William Law was the prime mover in the group, which consisted of men who believed that Joseph had been a prophet but was now "fallen." There was speculation in both Joseph's office and in nearby newspapers that William Law was the new church's prophet, but he rejected the title, stating that "no man can assume the spirit of prophecy." Other leaders in the new church included Wilson Law, Austin Cowles (a former member of the Nauvoo High Council), Francis Higbee, and Robert Foster. The dissidents appointed a committee to visit Nauvoo's families, and they purchased a printing press and made plans to publish their allegations against Joseph.[45]

The imminent danger to Joseph and those loyal to him lay not in "new church" meetings, but in the legal and political threat posed by the dissenters. As illustrated by similar moments in Kirtland and Missouri, there were many ways they could make things difficult and dangerous for Joseph: lawsuits, criminal charges, exposés, and alliances with the region's anti-Mormon agitators. Thomas C. Sharp, who had resumed editing the *Warsaw Signal* in February 1844, filled his paper's columns with letters from the dissenters, rumors of Joseph's misdeeds, and news about the lawsuits.

Francis Higbee was a particularly sharp legal thorn in Joseph's side. Still piqued that Joseph had accused him of having a venereal disease during their early January 1844 argument, Higbee filed a suit for $5,000 in the Hancock County circuit court. A county deputy sheriff arrested Joseph, who promptly obtained a writ of habeas corpus from Nauvoo's municipal court, which then held a hearing on the legality of his arrest. Joseph and others gave lurid testimony about Higbee's sexual escapades, based in part on what they had heard from John C. Bennett. Higbee, they asserted, had contracted syphilis after a liaison with a "French lady," stank from it, and had confessed to seducing women. In other words, Joseph had not slandered Higbee. The prophet included gratuitous aspersions against other dissenters. He testified that he had seen Robert D. Foster "steal a raw hide" and "feel of a woman's bosom in a stage and feel of her backsides." The outcome of the hearing was a given. The court set Joseph free.[46]

Joseph tried to focus on strategies for the church's future. He met with the Council of Fifty on May 6. Lucien Woodworth had just returned from Texas, where President Sam Houston had suggested that the Texas

Congress might grant land for a Mormon settlement. The council resolved that if the United States did not annex Texas, Woodworth should head back to Austin to negotiate further.

The prophet also pushed forward with his presidential campaign. The council selected Sidney Rigdon as Joseph's running mate after overtures to other men foundered. Rigdon and Joseph were finally on better terms again. Joseph had brought his counselor into the Council of Fifty, and Rigdon was initiated into the anointed quorum. Church leaders knew that per the Twelfth Amendment to the U.S. Constitution, electors could not vote for both a presidential candidate and a vice presidential candidate from their own state. Rigdon prepared to move to his native Pennsylvania.[47]

Delegates—mostly church members, but a few non-Mormon allies—came to Nauvoo for a political convention in mid-May. They nominated Joseph Smith and Sidney Rigdon for president and vice president. Joseph missed some of the evening celebration because Emma, two months pregnant, was sick, but the prophet arrived in time for the festive conclusion. After music and speeches, the organizers lit a barrel of tar on fire and shouted the names of the candidates. Joseph was hoisted on shoulders and carried around the fire. Then the band and the crowd escorted the prophet back to his residence. Joseph basked in the adulation, a distraction from opposition to him within and beyond Nauvoo.[48]

The plan was for Mormon elders to organize a convention in each state, which in turn would send delegates to a national convention in Baltimore. The apostles, along with scores of other missionaries, prepared to disperse across the country for what Brigham Young termed "storming the nation."[49]

Just before the Nauvoo convention, Joseph received a visit from two eminent Bostonians, Charles Francis Adams and Josiah Quincy IV. Their families were the epitome of what Oliver Wendell Holmes later dubbed the "Brahmin caste of New England." Adams was the grandson and son of John Adams and John Quincy Adams, respectively. Quincy's father was the president of Harvard and a former congressman. The two men were Harvard-educated lawyers. Adams and Quincy, still at the outset of their own political careers, were on a western tour that had taken them to Cincinnati and St. Louis.[50]

Joseph showed his guests the four mummies and the papyri, and he took them to see the temple, whose architecture Adams found

Nauvoo Temple sunstone, early 1900s. (Courtesy of Church
History Library)

"original—and curious." They saw a workman "laboring upon a huge
sun." The temple walls included thirty pilasters. Each pilaster eventually
had a carving of the moon at its base, was crowned with a two-ton sunstone, and had a star above. Wandle Mace, a foreman during the temple's
construction, explained that carvings represented the church—"clothed
with the sun"—as depicted in the twelfth chapter of the Book of
Revelation.[51]

Quincy and Adams asked Joseph to predict a victor in the coming
presidential election. "I will prophesy that John Tyler will not be the next
president," he ventured, "for some things are possible and some things
are probable; but Tyler's election is neither." Joseph suggested that as the
Saints grew in number, he might one day "hold the balance of power between parties," which would enable his election. Quincy told Joseph that
he already had "too much power to be safely trusted to one man." Joseph
granted the concern. "In your hands or that of any other person, so
much power would, no doubt, be dangerous," he replied. "I am the only
man in the world whom it would be safe to trust with it. Remember, I am
a prophet!"[52]

CHAPTER THIRTY-ONE

Bleeding Hearts (1844)

O N A MID-JUNE 1844 afternoon, Joseph examined Benjamin
West's *Death on the Pale Horse*. An exhibitor had brought a
copy of the painting to Nauvoo, where it was displayed in Joseph's "reading room" above his store. West depicted a macabre scene from the Book of Revelation, in which John of Patmos sees
four horsemen poised to unleash destruction on the earth. "And I
looked," John recorded, "and behold a pale horse: and his name that sat
on him was Death, and Hell followed with him." The dead and dying included women and children.[1]

The subject fit the moment. Mormon settlers in outlying areas were
under pressure from mobs. Joseph worried about himself as well, though
publicly he was resolute. "I despise the idea of being scared to death," he
stated.[2]

The Mormon prophet wasn't predisposed toward gloom. He usually
was confident that he could outfox his enemies, or flee from them if necessary. Suddenly, however, his options narrowed. Joseph did not see how
he and his people could escape the looming destruction.

A few weeks earlier, Joseph had enjoyed a pleasant ride out onto the prairie with Porter Rockwell. A messenger interrupted their idyll with news
that an officer from Carthage had come with a summons for Joseph,
probably in connection with one of Francis Higbee's suits. Joseph "kept
out of the way," according to William Clayton. Later in the day, there

Benjamin West, *Death on the Pale Horse,* 1817.
Oil on canvas, 176 × 301 in. (Courtesy of the Pennsylvania Academy of the
Fine Arts, Philadelphia. Pennsylvania Academy purchase, accession 1836.1)

was word that the officer was hanging about near the Smith residence. Joseph dispatched Clayton to ask Emma whether she would mind if he stayed away from home that night. She minded. Clayton found her "crying with rage and fury because he [Joseph] had gone away." Joseph returned home at dusk when the officer had left.[3]

The substance of the newest legal complaints stoked Emma's rage and fury. Based on testimony from William and Wilson Law, a Hancock County circuit court grand jury in Carthage indicted Joseph for living in adultery and fornication with Maria Lawrence, the prophet's twenty-year-old ward and a member of the Smith household. Other counts specified similar acts with "certain women to the jurors unknown."[4]

The same grand jury indicted Joseph for perjury. This complaint stemmed from a December 1843 crime, in which unknown assailants had entered the Nauvoo home of Richard and Hannah Badham and demanded money. One of the intruders had stabbed Richard Badham in the stomach, nearly killing him. An informant approached Joseph and told him that Alexander Sympson, a non-Mormon resident of Nauvoo, was responsible for the assault. On the basis of an affidavit signed by Joseph, Sympson was arrested. He promptly was acquitted when the Badhams did not recognize him as one of their assailants. Sympson testified that Joseph, in his affidavit, had sworn falsely about him. Robert D. Foster (a business partner of Sympson) and Joseph Jackson (formerly one of Joseph's aides-de-camp in the Nauvoo Legion) also provided testimony in the case.[5]

With news of the indictments circulating in Nauvoo, Joseph delivered a defiant Sunday sermon. He compared himself to the apostle Paul in his afflictions. "I should be like a fish out of water if I were out of persecution," he joked. He vowed that he would "come out on the top at last," then defended himself against the most recent charges. In the Sympson case, Joseph stated that he had merely passed along an accusation and had not sworn falsely. As for "spiritual wifeism," Joseph complained, "why a man dares not speak, or wink, for fear of being accused of this." Who were these women, anyway? Joseph made light of the rumors, but his words revealed frustration. "I never had any fuss with these men until that Female Relief Society brought out the paper against adulterers and adulteresses," he complained, alluding to the "Voice of Innocence." Joseph suggested that the document had pushed several of his critics to conspire against him. Joseph didn't mention her by name, but it was Emma who had spoken so resolutely against polygamy and adultery during the Bostwick affair.[6]

The next day Joseph rode to Carthage on Joe Duncan, one of his horses. It isn't clear why in this instance Joseph chose to face the charges in the county seat rather than secure his freedom by a writ of habeas corpus from Nauvoo's court. It was a more conciliatory approach, though he took enough men with him to deter any attack on his person.

Perhaps because he submitted to the circuit court's authority, several of his antagonists evidenced a desire for peace. Charles Foster approached the prophet when Joseph came within a few miles of Carthage. Willard Richards noted that Foster appeared "more mild than he had done"; the doctor allowed that he may have been influenced by "false reports" about Joseph. Foster's brother, Robert D. Foster, "with tears in his eyes," warned Joseph's party that there were men determined he would not leave Carthage alive. There were rumors that Joseph Jackson had been seen loading his pistol. There was no violence, however. Joseph's cases were deferred to the court's October term, and the prophet agreed to post bail.[7]

Any hope of reconciliation vanished on June 7 when the first issue of the *Nauvoo Expositor* appeared. Edited by Sylvester Emmons, a lawyer and disaffected member of the city council, its publishers included the trio of brothers at the heart of Nauvoo dissent: William and Wilson Law, Francis and Chauncey Higbee, and Robert and Charles Foster.

Joseph's enemies held nothing back. They professed belief in "the religion of the Latter Day Saints, as originally taught by Joseph Smith," but they accused Joseph of having betrayed those principles through a series of "abomination and whoredoms." Joseph and his allies lured pious women to Nauvoo, enticed them to meet in secret locations, proposed that they become Joseph's spiritual wives, and damned them if they rejected him. Polygamy was the most salacious accusation, but the *Expositor* also denounced Joseph's accumulation of political power and his use of habeas corpus to shield himself and his friends from justice. The *Expositor* called on the state legislature to repeal Nauvoo's charter.[8]

The *Expositor*'s editors assured readers that they would "be among the first to put down anything like an illegal force used against any man or set of men." They added, however, that if it were "necessary to make a show of force, to execute legal process, it will create no sympathy in that case to cry out, we are mobbed." In other words, county or state authorities might need a large armed posse to apprehend and prosecute Joseph Smith and other church leaders for their crimes.[9]

Joseph presided over a meeting of the Nauvoo City Council on June 8. The mayor lashed out at his enemies, saying that "if he had kept a whore from Canada here . . . he would have been as good a man as William and Wilson Law." Hyrum Smith alleged that Joseph Jackson had planned to kidnap and elope with his (Hyrum's) daughter Lovina. The dissenters were liars, adulterers, and counterfeiters. Joseph and his supporters argued that the *Expositor* posed an acute threat to the city. Its accusations would foment mobs. "We will be in our graves," Joseph warned, "if the city does not put down every thing which tends to mobocracy." The prophet demanded action.[10]

The city council suspended Sylvester Emmons from its ranks and then met again on June 10 to consider its options. A committee had prepared "an ordinance on libels" that, if passed, would mandate fines or imprisonment for individuals who wrote or published false statements "against the chartered privileges, peace, and good order" of the city.[11]

Joseph insisted on a more vigorous response. He didn't think the threat of fines or jail would dissuade his enemies, who had promised their readers a new issue every Friday. The Nauvoo Charter authorized the council to "declare what shall be a nuisance, and to . . . remove the same." It was a public-health provision, but Joseph argued that the paper was "a greater nuisance than a dead carcass." How should it be removed? Hyrum Smith asserted that men should "smash the press all to pieces and pie [scatter] the type."[12] The council discussed freedom of the press but concluded that it did not include the liberty to publish libels. In the end, though, it wasn't really a question of law. As Joseph and his allies saw it, it was a matter of life and death. Several council members referred to past events in Missouri, including the massacre at Hawn's Mill, and argued that the newspaper's destruction was necessary to avoid a repetition of such evils. The resolution passed.

Joseph promptly ordered the city marshal, John P. Greene, to destroy the press, scatter its type in the streets, and burn any remaining copies of the paper and other "libelous hand bills." The mayor also authorized Greene to "demolish the house" and make arrests in the event of resistance.[13]

The job didn't take long. Greene recruited a posse. According to the secondhand report of William Law, they broke into the office with sledgehammers, carried the press and type into the street, piled papers and furniture on top, and burned everything. The posse then gathered in front of Joseph's mansion, where the prophet assured the men that they had "done right" and that he would never permit "another libelous publication" to be printed in the city.[14]

Joseph's opponents were outraged. "Several of them have said," wrote William Clayton, "that the temple shall be thrown down, Joseph's house burned, and the printing office torn down." The dissenters were also scared, worried that the newly passed libel ordinance would be used to prosecute them, and fearful that church members loyal to Joseph might attack their homes or persons. Jane Law, wife of William Law, was nearing the end of a pregnancy. On June 12, the Law brothers, the Foster brothers, and two other families left the city and went to Burlington, Iowa.[15]

William Law wrote that he had not suspected "men of being such fools." The press's destruction handed the dissenters the legal ammunition they needed. Francis Higbee rushed to Carthage. Thomas Morrison, a Hancock County justice of the peace, issued a warrant for the arrest of Joseph and seventeen other men. The charge was rioting. The next day, Hancock County constable David Bettisworth arrested Joseph and the other Mormon defendants.[16]

The same old legal story played out one last time. Bettisworth intended to take Joseph to Carthage and bring him before Morrison. The prophet was willing to appear before a justice in Nauvoo, but he had no intention of going to Carthage, which he considered the "headquarters of mobocracy." Morrison's warrant specified that Joseph could appear before him "or some other justice of the peace" in Hancock County, though state law permitted the latter course only if the issuing justice was "absent." Joseph obtained a writ of habeas corpus from Nauvoo's municipal court, appeared before the same court that evening, and had his case dismissed. The court dismissed the cases against his fellow defendants the next day and ordered Francis Higbee to pay the court costs.[17]

"The law is again put at defiance," Thomas Sharp's *Warsaw Signal* declared, "and the only recourse left us is to take up arms." Anti-Mormons held meetings in Carthage and Warsaw. They resolved that "the adherents of Smith . . . should be driven from the surrounding settlements, into Nauvoo." The prophet and other top leaders should surrender, and if they did not, "a war of extermination should be waged to the entire destruction, if necessary for our protection, of his adherents." Soon there were reports that hundreds of vigilantes were gathering in Carthage.[18]

Joseph insisted in a letter to Governor Ford that the city's destruction of the *Nauvoo Expositor* press was both legal and done according to "law and good order." The prophet knew that Nauvoo's use of its claimed habeas corpus authority had created the impression that he regarded himself and his associates as above the law. Therefore, he offered to appear before U.S. district court judge Nathaniel Pope, who had ended an earlier attempt to extradite Joseph to Missouri, or before any court in the state capital. Just not Carthage.[19]

On June 15, messengers arrived from the "Morley Settlement," a Latter-day community near the town of Lima, some thirty miles south of Nauvoo. Acting on the anti-Mormon resolutions, a mob headed by Levi Williams had demanded that the Mormon settlers give up their arms until Joseph and other high-ranking church leaders submitted to arrest. The prophet told them "not to give up their arms but to keep them till they died." After the messengers had departed, Joseph commented to his associates that if the mob "did come and begin to destroy," they could then send the sufferers to Governor Ford and "know what he would do." These were shaky grounds for hope. It was that afternoon that Joseph gazed upon Benjamin West's apocalyptic painting.[20]

The next morning, despite a heavy rain, Joseph preached in a grove near the temple. The prophet noted that Jesus's enemies found fault with him

because he claimed to be the divine son of God. Likewise, Joseph's enemies wanted to silence him. "They say like the apostates of old I must be
put down," he observed. Joseph presented himself as a martyr in the
making, persecuted for his belief in a "plurality of gods." It was one of
the "false and damnable doctrines" the *Nauvoo Expositor* had critiqued.

Of course there was a plurality of gods! Joseph insisted that the
creedal understanding of the Trinity was nonsense. "[If] all are to be
crammed into one god," Joseph suggested, "it would make the biggest god
in all the world . . . he would be a giant." But it was not just that God the
Father, Jesus Christ, and the Holy Spirit were separate persons. When
Jesus had laid down his life and then been raised up, he had done so in
imitation of his father. "I learned it by translating the papyrus now in my
house," Joseph explained. "Intelligences exist one above another and there
is no end." Just as Jesus Christ was the Son of God, so it stood to reason
that God also had a father. "When ever did a tree or anything spring into
existence without a progenitor?" Joseph asked. There was an endless
chain of gods and saviors. And men could take their place among them.[21]

In his sermon, Joseph rejected the suggestion that he taught stronger
theological meat in private. There were concepts that he did not share,
however, and not just polygamy. One of those inchoate ideas was that
there was a Mother in heaven alongside God the Father. "In the heavens
are parents single?" Eliza R. Snow asked in a poem published the next
year. "No, the thought makes reason stare." William Phelps also introduced the idea in 1845. Both he and Eliza Snow almost certainly heard
the idea from Joseph. Perhaps the prophet had not fully developed the
doctrine in his own mind, or perhaps he regarded it as too controversial
for public consumption.[22]

There was little time for Joseph or the congregation to contemplate
their future divinity. Jesse B. Thomas Jr., a state circuit court judge, visited Nauvoo that day and gave the prophet some advice. If Joseph would
submit to arrest, he would either be acquitted or bound over to face trial
at a later date. Either way, Thomas predicted, it "would allay all excitement or cut off all legal pretext for a mob." Joseph sent another letter to
Thomas Ford, informing the governor that he would follow Thomas's
guidance. He also encouraged Ford to come to Hancock County in
order to restore peace.[23]

Instead of going to Carthage, however, Joseph and his co-defendants
appeared before Daniel Wells, a non-Mormon justice of the peace in

Nauvoo. Not surprisingly, Wells dismissed the charges against the defendants. The hearing was not what Jesse Thomas had intended. Thomas had wanted Joseph to appear before Thomas Morrison, the justice of the peace who had issued the warrant for the prophet's arrest. As far as Joseph's opponents were concerned, his legal shenanigans made a mockery of Illinois justice.[24]

Joseph soon took another provocative step. On June 18, the Nauvoo Legion assembled in front of his residence. Joseph stood on top of a "graining frame" in his lieutenant general's uniform and proclaimed that Nauvoo was under martial law. He ordered the militia, the police, and other residents to "strictly see that no persons or property pass in or out of the city without due orders." The prophet warned the assembled troops that the mob "waged a war of extermination upon us because of our religion." During the address, Joseph unsheathed his sword and pointed it to heaven. Joseph urged the men before him to protect their wives and children from the mob and, if necessary, to "die like men of God and secure a glorious resurrection." It was a call to defensive holy war.[25]

Governor Ford arrived in Carthage on Thursday, June 20. He gathered reports from both the Saints and their opponents. Church leaders sent him affidavits stating that they had acted lawfully and without violence in the removal of the printing press. Ford was not convinced.

On Saturday, June 22, the governor sent a posse of thirty men with an ultimatum for Joseph. The prophet and his co-defendants should submit to arrest and appear before Morrison. "Nothing short of this can vindicate the dignity of violated law," the governor insisted, "and allay the just excitement of the people." In other words, it was reasonable for non-Mormons to protest Joseph's violation of the law. Ford guaranteed the safety of Joseph and anyone else who agreed to come to Carthage as a defendant or a witness. He also instructed Joseph to release individuals detained under the martial law proclamation. Ford warned that he would call out the militia if Joseph resisted, and the governor added that he might not be able to control their actions. "I have great fears that your city will be destroyed and your people many of them exterminated," Ford concluded. The governor's letter had not included a deadline, but the officers of the posse told Joseph he had until Sunday morning to surrender.[26]

In a midnight response, Joseph agreed to set aside his proclamation of martial law, and he informed Ford that he had disbanded the Nauvoo

William Camm, portrait of Illinois governor Thomas Ford, 1840s. (Courtesy of
Abraham Lincoln Presidential Library and Museum, Springfield, Illinois)

Legion. But the prophet still refused to go to Carthage. After all, as Joseph pointed out, Ford himself had conceded that he lacked the power to control the mob. "*We dare not come,*" Joseph emphasized, repeating the phrase several times. He reminded Ford that anti-Mormons in Hancock County threatened to expel or even exterminate his people, just as the mobs in Missouri had done. The prophet had no illusions that state militia troops would protect the Saints. Just that May, a Pennsylvania militia unit had failed to defend Catholic churches and homes in Philadelphia from the fury of a Protestant mob. Still, Joseph urged Ford to safeguard Nauvoo's women and children.[27]

Then Joseph made hasty preparations to flee. He summoned William Clayton and whispered instructions to him. Clayton should "put the records of the Kingdom into the hands of some faithful man and send them away, or burn them or bury them." Joseph knew that the talk of theocracy and his acclamation as "king" could cause him trouble if the records fell into the wrong hands. Clayton went home, put the records in a box, and buried it in his garden.[28]

Meanwhile, Joseph, his brother Hyrum, and Willard Richards crossed the Mississippi River and took shelter in a cabin near Montrose. Joseph dictated a letter to Emma after sunrise, describing his location simply as "Safety." He gave Emma some financial advice, identifying property that she could sell and individuals to whom she could turn for money. Joseph did not know whether he would see her and his children again, and there had been no time for proper farewells. "I do not know where I shall go, or what I shall do," Joseph wrote. He was considering traveling to the nation's capital, where he could beseech Congress and President Tyler to aid the Saints. "My heart bleeds," he concluded.[29]

Hearts were bleeding in Nauvoo as well. "Some were tried almost to death to think Joseph should leave them in the hour of danger," Vilate Kimball wrote her husband. Many Saints feared that their enemies would descend on Nauvoo at any moment. What if Joseph's judgment had failed him? What if the more dangerous course was flight rather than submission? If the prophet went to Carthage under Ford's protection, could he not post bail, return to Nauvoo safely, and eliminate any pretext for an assault on the city?[30]

Emma was among those who believed that Joseph had erred. She was four months pregnant and worried about her four children. Emma felt abandoned in the midst of imminent danger. William Clayton reported that she "sent messengers over the river to Joseph ... and urged him to give himself up inasmuch as the Governor had offered him protection." Several of the men who went to confer with the prophet were members of the Council of Fifty. John M. Bernhisel, back from a recent trip to Carthage, had met with the captain of the posse and expressed confidence that Joseph would be protected.[31]

According to some reminiscences, the messengers sent by Emma accused Joseph of "cowardice" for saving himself while leaving the people to be destroyed. Joseph purportedly responded "that if his life was of no value to them it was none to himself." In other words, Emma and her allies shamed Joseph into sacrificing his life. The comments reflect later animosity between Emma and Utah church leaders, who blamed her for what happened to her husband.[32]

At the time, though, it wasn't just Emma who held this position. Nearly everyone, including Hyrum Smith, favored return and surrender as a way of saving the city and the church. For a while, Joseph dug in his heels. According to Lucien Woodworth, present during the deliberations, the prophet "was determined not to go back." Eventually, however, Joseph changed his mind. Vilate Kimball attributed the decision to prayer and revelation. On the other side of the river, she wrote, Joseph "stopped and composed his mind, and got the will of the Lord concerning him, and that was, that he should return and give himself up for trial." William Clayton recorded that Joseph now saw "no alternative." He "must either give himself up or the city be massacred by a lawless mob under the sanction of the governor." After sending a letter to Ford explaining his change of mind, Joseph and his companions returned across the Mississippi.[33]

Joseph enjoyed brief reunions and then endured tearful goodbyes with Emma and their four children. There is no evidence that Joseph bid farewell to any of his plural wives. He had had little contact with them since the previous fall.

The prophet rode toward Carthage on Old Charley, his favorite horse. As they neared their destination, Joseph's party stopped at the farm of church members Albert and Sally Fellows, a few miles west of Carthage. John Bernhisel got out of a buggy and walked over to Joseph. "I am going as a lamb to the slaughter," Bernhisel remembered the prophet saying. Joseph may have said something to that effect, but he certainly wasn't a willing lamb. Carthage was the last place he wanted to go.[34]

Colonel James E. Dunn, an Illinois militia officer, arrived at the farm with around sixty mounted troops. Dunn conveyed an order from Governor Ford demanding that the Nauvoo Legion surrender its state arms, including its three cannons. Joseph countersigned the order and accompanied Dunn and his men back to Nauvoo. With great reluctance, men collected the weapons and brought them to the Masonic Hall, where Dunn took possession of them. "Many of the brethren looked upon this as another preparation for a Missouri massacre," observed William Clayton.[35] Just as at Hawn's Mill, the Saints would be unable to defend themselves against a mob attack.

Before setting off for Carthage again, Joseph rode back to his house to say another goodbye to Emma, their children, and his mother. "He appeared to feel solemn and thoughtful," recorded William Clayton, "and from expressions made to several individuals, he expects nothing but to be massacred."[36] Dunn escorted Joseph and the other Mormons into Carthage. That evening, storms arose in the west. "The heavens gathered blackness," wrote Zina Jacobs, one of the prophet's plural wives. The skies flashed with lightning.[37]

As the prisoners proceeded to their hotel, members of the local militia unit, the "Carthage Greys," jeered at them. "Where is the damned prophet?" men yelled. Some troops wanted the chance to shoot the Mormons. Others just wanted a look at the notorious Joseph Smith, whose presence was forcing them to stand guard. Governor Ford shouted from a hotel window that he would have the prisoners appear before the troops in the morning.[38]

Early on Tuesday, June 25, an unexpected legal twist complicated Joseph's hope to post bail and dash home. Constable Bettisworth served the prophet and his brother with unexpected arrest warrants on the charge of treason. Augustine Spencer, whom Joseph had fined a month earlier for fighting with his brother, had made the complaint against the prophet. It was "because we called out the Nauvoo Legion," Joseph explained in a letter to Emma.[39]

Governor Ford came to see the Smith brothers. Along with Brigadier General Miner Deming of the Illinois state militia, he walked them through the crowd. The governor himself led the way, Joseph and Hyrum flanked Deming, and Willard Richards, William W. Phelps, and John Taylor walked behind. Ford and Deming introduced the most important prisoner as "General Joseph Smith." The men of the Carthage Greys were upset by what they considered excessive courtesy. They shouted and hissed at the Smiths. Among those making noise was Walter Bagby, who had fought with the prophet the previous summer.[40]

Soon after Joseph and the others returned to the hotel, news came that the Carthage Greys had revolted. When Ford and Deming explained that the procession had taken place at the request of other troops, order was quickly restored. Bagby went and apologized to Ford and asked the governor if he would shake hands. "Oh yes," replied Ford. "I have just had hold of Joe Smith's."[41]

The prophet projected calm when he informed Emma of the treason charge. "When the truth comes out we have nothing to fear," he assured her. There were still rumors of an impending attack on Nauvoo, possibly by a Warsaw militia regiment commanded by Levi Williams. In response to a request from Joseph, Governor Ford agreed to send a small detachment of troops to guard the city. Joseph informed Emma that both he and Ford would accompany the detachment. They would be reunited, and Joseph believed he would be safe from mobs if he could reach the city of the Saints.[42]

Joseph and his co-defendants went to court later that afternoon to answer the charge of rioting. For reasons that remain unclear, they did not appear before Justice Morrison, but rather before another Carthage justice of the peace, Robert Smith. Justice Smith was the captain of the Carthage Greys. Chauncey Higbee, one of the *Expositor*'s erstwhile publishers, was the prosecuting attorney. The proceedings seemed amicable, though, and the defendants were released on bail until the October term of the county circuit court. They could go home.

Except Joseph and Hyrum. Bettisworth soon arrived with a court order signed by Justice Smith remanding the Smith brothers to jail. In the order, Smith explained that he had postponed their trial on the charge of treason because "material witnesses," including Francis Higbee, were absent. Joseph's lawyers objected that their clients were being jailed without the benefit of a hearing. Governor Ford, however, declined to interfere. Joined by a number of friends who refused to abandon them, Joseph and Hyrum were escorted by Captain Dunn to Carthage Jail. The jailer at first put them in the "criminals' cell" but upon their complaint and Ford's agreement moved them into the more comfortable "debtors' department."[43]

On the morning of Wednesday, June 26, the Mormon prisoners were still fuming, both at what they considered unjust imprisonment and at Ford's neglect of their circumstances. The governor visited the jail around nine thirty. He and the prisoners discussed the *Expositor* case and the new treason charge. Joseph offered to pay compensation for the newspaper's destruction. Ford told the prisoners that the treason case hinged on the intention behind the martial law proclamation. If they had intended to "resist the government of the state," it was treason. If they were attempting to defend themselves, "it was all right." Without any resolution, Ford left by reminding the prisoners that they were under his protection.[44]

In the afternoon, Joseph and Hyrum were taken before Justice Smith. However, in order that witnesses could be brought to Carthage, the judge postponed their hearing, first until noon the next day and then until June 29. The prisoners were returned to the jail and "thrust into close confinement" in the criminals' cell. The news seemed to grow worse with each passing hour. Joseph's lawyers reported that the governor had decided against taking the Smith brothers with him to Nauvoo.[45]

While Ford and the bulk of the militia troops were away, the safety of Joseph and Hyrum rested only on the fifty Carthage Greys left in the city as a guard. Ford had been given repeated warnings that Joseph and Hyrum were in danger of being killed. He made little effort to defend them, however, so Joseph's friends did what they could. They smuggled a small pistol and a six-shooter into the jail.[46]

The next morning, on Thursday, June 27, Joseph dictated a letter to Emma and then added a note in his own hand. The prophet was no longer sanguine about his deliverance. "I am very much resigned to my lot."[47]

John Taylor and Willard Richards stayed with Joseph and his brother, choosing confinement with them over liberty in Nauvoo. The prisoners spent the day outside the cell in the jailer's quarters. At Hyrum's request, Taylor sang "A Poor Wayfaring Man of Grief," a popular hymn. Hyrum asked Taylor to sing it a second time. Meanwhile, Joseph chatted with the guards, one of whom told the prophet he intended to move out of the state if Joseph obtained his freedom and remained in Illinois. George Stigall, the jailer, reported that Latter-day Saint Stephen Markham had been surrounded by a mob in town and had left for Nauvoo. Stigall told the prisoners "they would be safer" back in the cell. Joseph answered that they would go in after supper. "Will you go in with us?" Joseph asked Richards. "Do you think I would forsake you now?" his loyal scribe replied.[48]

Meanwhile, the governor and his detachment of troops reached Nauvoo. Ford went to the Nauvoo Mansion (the Smith residence), shaved, and met with a few aides. He then made a speech to the anxious townspeople who had gathered outside. The governor asked the crowd whether they would obey state laws even if those laws clashed with the orders of their leaders. Nauvoo's men demonstrated their assent by raising their hands. According to William Clayton, however, "every breast was filled with indignation." Ford hastily left the city.[49]

Back in Carthage, the jailer's son told the prisoners that the guards wanted some wine. Joseph gave them money, and they soon procured a bottle of wine, a pipe, and some tobacco. Willard Richards uncorked the bottle. Joseph, Richards, and John Taylor drank, hoping to "revive" their "dull and heavy" spirits. Then they gave the rest to one of the guards.[50]

Someone called for the guard, who started down the stairs. The prisoners heard the sound of rustling below, then cries and several shots. Richards looked out the window and saw a hundred armed men at the jail's entrance. They were led by Colonel Levi Williams. Their ranks included the *Warsaw Signal*'s Thomas Sharp and John C. Elliott, whom a Mormon posse had arrested in connection with the 1843 Avery kidnappings. Others were outwardly respectable men from Warsaw. Jacob C. Davis, for example, held a seat in the Illinois senate.[51]

General Deming had ordered Williams's regiment to march toward Nauvoo in anticipation that they would accompany Ford into the city. The governor, worried that they would initiate violence, disbanded them. Most of the men returned home, but others headed to Carthage. These renegade troops had painted their faces or blackened them with mud and gunpowder. Some turned their militia coats inside out. The Warsaw militia-turned-mob gathered in the woods, alongside a fence, fired three shots as a signal for the attack, and then stormed the jail.[52]

Most of the Carthage Greys were several hundred yards away. The seven or eight men guarding the jail were badly outnumbered by the vigilantes and made little attempt to deter them.

The Smith brothers drew their pistols, and Richards and Taylor brandished canes. But it was an indefensible situation. Dan Jones, a church member who had spent the previous night with the prisoners, recalled that the door to their room "was of pine, common batton, without bolts, lock, or even a latch that would shut." Hyrum and Willard Richards pushed themselves against the door to hold back the mob.[53]

A ball passed through the flimsy door and struck Hyrum in the face. "I am a dead man," he cried. He collapsed on his back and blood pooled around him. Joseph returned fire through what was now a gap between the door and the frame. "Parry them off as well as you can," he urged Taylor. Countless balls whizzed into the room. The surviving prisoners couldn't hold their attackers at bay and so tried to escape. Taylor was shot as he prepared to leap from the east window. The face of his pocket watch shattered, leaving it stopped at 5:16 p.m. He rolled under the bed.

Joseph also intended to jump. At the window, however, the prophet was struck from behind and by a shot fired from below. Those wounds probably would have been fatal. "O Lord, my God!" Joseph exclaimed as he fell to the ground. It was the opening of the Masonic cry of distress, which continues, "Is there no help for the widow's son?"[54]

Many of Joseph's attackers were fellow Freemasons, but no one came to the prophet's aid. Instead, members of the mob propped him up against a well and fired a few more balls into his chest. Joseph Smith was dead.

Epilogue

ORTER ROCKWELL WOKE WILLIAM CLAYTON with news of the murders early on Friday morning. A letter from Willard Richards, himself nearly unscathed in the assault on the jail, had reached Nauvoo. "Joseph and Hyrum are dead," the apostle wrote. "Taylor wounded not very bad." Disbelief quickly gave way to grief. "Sorrow and gloom was pictured in every countenance," noted Clayton.[1]

Many residents of Carthage fled after the murders because they presumed that Mormons would avenge the blood of their prophets. The Saints in Nauvoo, meanwhile, anticipated that the mob would descend on the city and butcher them. Neither fear materialized.

Willard Richards, Samuel H. Smith (the prophet's younger brother), Artois Hamilton (the Carthage hotelier), and eight soldiers accompanied the wagons that brought the corpses to Nauvoo. Thousands of Saints took the hastily built oak coffins into the Nauvoo Mansion. "Joseph looks very natural except being pale through loss of blood," Clayton recorded. Hyrum's face was disfigured from the gunshot that had killed him.[2]

Emma collapsed when she entered the room and attempted to approach the bodies. She finally steadied herself, came and placed a hand on Hyrum's forehead, then made her way to Joseph and sank into an embrace of her late husband. "Joseph, Joseph," she moaned, "are you dead? Have the assassins shot you?" Lucy Mack Smith was shattered by the loss of two sons. Sarah Kimball found her sitting alone in the corner of her bedroom. "How could they kill my poor boys?" she sobbed. "Oh how could they kill them when they were so precious?"[3]

371

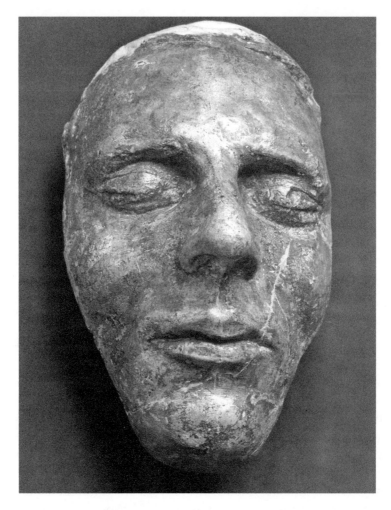

Joseph Smith's death mask. (© By Intellectual Reserve, Inc.)

There was no procession of plural wives into the family residence. At least one such woman visited that day, however. Zina Huntington Jacobs entered the mansion and saw "the lifeless speechless bodies of the two martyrs." The days that followed were, as she put it, "lonely and heart sorrowful." She spent time with women like Louisa Beman and Agnes Coolbrith Smith, friends who shared her polygamy and her grief. She also washed the clothes of Joseph and Hyrum.[4]

On Saturday, June 29, many thousands of Saints came to see the martyrs over the span of five hours. The sight was gruesome, as the warm temperatures caused the bodies to ooze blood and other fluids. A non-Mormon then staying at the Mansion House remembered that tar, vinegar, and sugar were "kept burning on the stove" to mitigate the stench.[5]

The prophet had made plans for what he called "the Tomb of Joseph" to be built somewhere on the south side of the temple block. He wanted his father, his brother Alvin, and his stillborn children to be brought there. "When I die," he requested in 1842, "let me be gathered to the tomb of my father," as the biblical Joseph had been gathered to Jacob's burial place.[6] Church leaders and family members alike, however, worried that mobs would steal and desecrate the corpses. In order to confuse would-be grave robbers, they put bags of sand in the cheap oak boxes and buried them in a cemetery. Then they placed the bodies in "two handsome coffins" and buried them "in a safe place," beneath the unfinished Nauvoo House, in the middle of the night. It would not be Joseph's final resting place.[7]

Once fears of a Mormon reprisal subsided, Joseph's enemies exulted in his death. Thomas Sharp, the *Warsaw Signal* editor who was part of the mob that killed the Smiths, defended the action in print, though without admitting his role in it. "The only alternative then was," he editorialized, "whether the guilty cause, should be removed . . . or whether, we should have waited until renewed aggressions . . . provoke[d] the surrounding country to a general war of extermination." Had the mob not killed Joseph, the Mormon prophet would have escaped from the jail or escaped via court proceedings and would have pursued his campaign of tyranny. The Saints and their enemies would have fought each other. In other words, Sharp reasoned, the sacrifice of two individuals preserved many more lives.[8]

Sharp, Levi Williams, Jacob Davis, and six other men were indicted on charges of murder. Five of the accused stood trial in May 1845. A jury refused to convict them. No one was punished for the crimes.

"Joe and Hyrum Smith were regarded as the only individuals that could hold together the Mormon community," Sharp explained in another justification for the murders. The editor, like many of Joseph's detractors, hoped that the prophet's murder would be his church's death knell.[9]

Especially with Hyrum Smith also dead, it wasn't clear who was in a position to lead the church. The thirty-eight-year-old prophet hadn't outlined any sort of succession plan. Emma Smith wanted William Marks, Nauvoo stake president and a polygamy opponent, to become the church's next president and trustee-in-trust. Sidney Rigdon, the only surviving member of the First Presidency, suggested himself as the church's "guardian." Most of the apostles were in the east at the time of Joseph's murder. After they returned to Nauvoo, Brigham Young, president of the Quorum of the Twelve, asserted that the Twelve possessed the "keys" of priesthood authority, would finish the Nauvoo Temple, and would lead the Saints through long-promised sacred rituals.

Thousands of Saints gathered in August 1844 and heard Rigdon and Young make their cases. A large majority backed Young and the Twelve. The apostles excommunicated Rigdon the next month. They also stripped William Marks, who had supported Rigdon, of his leadership position.

The most bitter divide was that between the apostles and Emma Smith. She and Brigham Young disagreed about everything from polygamy to property to custody of the late prophet's remains. Joseph's financial affairs had remained entangled with those of the church, and Emma, a pregnant widow with four children, worried about her ability to provide for her family. As William Clayton noted a week after the murders, "the situation looks gloomy." Most of Joseph's property holdings were as the church's trustee-in-trust, while his debts were "personal." Worry evolved into wrangling, and relations between Emma and the apostles deteriorated. Young, who recognized that Emma would never accept polygamy, made little attempt to resolve the conflict.

In the fall of 1844, Emma arranged for trusted friends to move the bodies of Joseph and Hyrum from underneath the Nauvoo House onto the old Smith property near the banks of the river. She informed no one, not even Mary Fielding Smith, Hyrum's widow. Young, who had visited Joseph's corpse on at least one occasion, was livid. "I shall demand of Sister Emma who has charge of those bodies to give them up that we may put them where Joseph commanded us." If she refused, there would be future reckonings. "When he wakes up in the morning of the resurrection," Young explained, "he shall talk with them and not with me. The sin shall be upon her head not ours." Emma was unmoved.[10]

Joseph's first wife remained in Nauvoo when the majority of the city's residents followed Young and the other apostles to what became the Utah Territory. Emma remarried in 1847, to Lewis Bidamon, a Methodist. In the early 1860s, she supported the efforts of Joseph Smith

III and William Marks to "reorganize" the church. Until her death Emma denied that her first husband had practiced polygamy, a stance that the Reorganized Church of Jesus Christ of Latter Day Saints (RLDS) retained for many decades.

By the 1920s there was concern that rising river waters might cover the still-unmarked graves of Joseph and Hyrum. RLDS leaders decided to locate, disinter, and rebury the remains. In 1928, a crew discovered two skeletons next to each other and stumbled upon Emma's remains in the process. All three were reburied in a more stable location, with Emma laid to rest between Joseph and Hyrum. A stately granite memorial was placed over their remains in 1951. Researchers believe that the 1928 crew mistook Joseph's remains for those of his brother and vice versa.[11]

Joseph's bones haven't moved for a century, nor has custody of them changed. In 2024, the Community of Christ (as the Reorganized Church renamed itself in 2000) sold the Kirtland Temple and a number of Nauvoo properties—including the red-brick store, the Smith family homestead, the Mansion House, and the Nauvoo House—to the Utah-based Church of Jesus Christ of Latter-day Saints. The deal did not include the Smith Family Cemetery.

Nearly all men and women who achieve prominence or celebrity as religious leaders quickly fade into obscurity. In the early nineteenth century, evangelists such as Lorenzo Dow and Charles Finney converted vastly more people than did Joseph Smith. Few people today would make pilgrimages to their places of birth or death. Some nineteenth-century prophets, such as Nat Turner and John Brown, still resonate, but they exert little religious influence per se. Some Americans enjoy reading Emerson and Thoreau but are unlikely to reorient their lives after finishing *Walden* or "Self-Reliance."

Joseph Smith, by contrast, remains a decisive inspiration for millions of Latter-day Saints around the world. Smith left indelible marks. He brought forth the Book of Mormon, the most widely printed and translated work of American literature. Most of those copies go unread, but millions of people study the Book of Mormon devotionally. Smith fashioned rituals that still shape the activities and mentalities of Latter-day Saints and adherents of other movements that he inspired. Smith also built communities, and even if those communities didn't last, the act of building them brought his people together in ways that endured.

Perhaps even more unusually, Smith remains an object of curiosity and controversy for many non-Mormons. Threatened by Mormon missionaries who proclaim that theirs is the one true church of Jesus Christ, evangelicals have denounced Smith as the progenitor of a dangerous, heretical cult. When Latter-day Saint Mitt Romney ran for president in 2008 and 2012, conservatives, progressives, and pundits asked questions about everything from Smith's prophecies to his plural marriages. Always good for a laugh because of golden plates or polygamy, the Mormon prophet has been lampooned on *South Park* and on Broadway.

Satirical musicals, evangelical films, and critical histories have all failed in their attempt to cut him down to size, however. Smith told the Nauvoo Female Relief Society that "although he had everything bearing him down, standing in his way and opposing," he would triumph in the end. He was "continually rising." Perhaps he was right after all.[12]

No church, archive, or book has been able to constrain Joseph Smith. Whether it was religion, marriage, or politics, he burst through the conventions of his time. Brigham Young once said that when he encountered Mormonism, he couldn't let it go, in part because he couldn't put it in a box, couldn't fully figure it out. The same holds for Joseph Smith. He was a day laborer, visionary, seer, money-digger, glass-looker, translator, revelator, prophet, elder, high priest, president, patriarch, merchant, banker, prisoner, wrestler, real estate speculator, prolific polygamist, lieutenant general, Master Mason, and mayor. He always had another plan grander than the last plan. With Joseph Smith, everything was subject to revision, from the Bible to the church's hierarchy to its sacred rituals. He was never finished, and at least as long as his devotees and their detractors care about his legacy, we will never be finished with him.

Notes

Abbreviations

CCA—Community of Christ, Archives, Independence, Missouri.

CHL—Church History Library, Church of Jesus Christ of Latter-day Saints, Salt Lake City, Utah.

Compton, ISL—Todd Compton, *In Sacred Loneliness: The Plural Wives of Joseph Smith* (Salt Lake City: Signature Books, 1997).

EMD—Dan Vogel, ed., *Early Mormon Documents*, 5 vols. (Salt Lake City: Signature Books, 1996–2003).

Hales, *Polygamy*—Brian C. Hales, *Joseph Smith's Polygamy*, 3 vols. (Salt Lake City: Kofford Books, 2013).

HBLL—Special Collections, Harold B. Lee Library, Brigham Young University, Provo, Utah.

HOYP—Mark Lyman Staker, *Hearken, O Ye People: The Historical Setting of Joseph Smith's Ohio Revelations* (Salt Lake City: Greg Kofford Books, 2010).

JD—*Journal of Discourses by Brigham Young, His Two Counsellors, the Twelve Apostles and Others* . . . , 26 vols. (Liverpool and London: various publishers, 1854–1886).

JMH—*Journal of Mormon History*.

JSJ—Joseph Smith, Jr., Journal (see JSP Journals series).

JSP—Dean C., Jessee, Ronald K. Esplin, and Richard Lyman Bushman, eds., *The Joseph Smith Papers*, 27 vols. (Salt Lake City: Church Historian's Press, 2008–2023). The *Joseph Smith Papers* are published in several multivolume series: Documents (D), Journals (J), Legal Records (LR), Revelations and Translations (R), and Histories (H). Individual volumes are cited by series and volume number. For instance, *Documents*, volume 14 is shortened to D14.

JSP, C50—Matthew J. Grow, Ronald K. Esplin, Mark Ashurst-McGee, Gerrit J. Dirkmaat, and Jeffrey D. Mahas, eds., *Council of Fifty, Minutes, March*

1844–January 1846. First volume of the Administrative Records series of *The Joseph Smith Papers*, ed. Ronald K. Esplin, Matthew J. Grow, and Matthew C. Godfrey (Salt Lake City: Church Historian's Press, 2016).

JSTOM—Kent P. Jackson, Robert J. Matthews, and Scott Faulring, eds., *Joseph Smith's New Translation of the Bible: Original Manuscripts* (Salt Lake City: Deseret Book, 2004).

JWHAJ—*John Whitmer Historical Association Journal*.

LB—Lavina Fielding Anderson, ed., *Lucy's Book: A Critical Edition of Lucy Mack Smith's Family Memoir* (Salt Lake City: Signature Books, 2001).

M&A—*Messenger & Advocate*, Kirtland, Ohio, 1834–1837.

MHC—Manuscript History of the Church, Church Historian's Office, CR 100 102, CHL.

MU—E[ber] D. Howe, *Mormonism Unvailed . . .* (Painesville, Ohio: printed by the author, 1834).

MWP—Mormon War Papers, 1837–1841, Missouri State Archives, Jefferson City, Missouri.

NCHCM—John S. Dinger, ed., *The Nauvoo City and High Council Minutes* (Salt Lake City: Signature Books, 2013).

Park, KoN—Benjamin E. Park, *Kingdom of Nauvoo: The Rise and Fall of a Religious Empire on the American Frontier* (New York: Liveright, 2000).

PWES—Maureen Ursenbach Beecher, ed., *The Personal Writings of Eliza Roxcy Snow* (Salt Lake City: University of Utah Press, 1995).

RS50—Jill Mulvay Derr, Carol Cornwall Madsen, Kate Holbrook, and Matthew J. Grow, eds., *The First Fifty Years of Relief Society: Key Documents in Latter-day Saint Women's History* (Salt Lake City: Church Historian's Press, 2016).

RSR—Richard Bushman with Jed Woodworth, *Joseph Smith: Rough Stone Rolling* (New York: Knopf, 2006).

T&S—*Times & Seasons*, Nauvoo, Illinois, 1839–1846.

WCJ—William Clayton Journal, CHL.

WRJ—Willard Richards Journal, MS 1490, CHL.

WWJ—Wilford Woodruff Journal, MS 1352, CHL. See Dan Vogel, ed., *The Wilford Woodruff Journals*, 6 vols. (Salt Lake City: Signature Books, 2020).

Introduction

1. Historian's Office, Journal, 28 April 1844, CR 100 1, CHL.
2. Joel Hills Johnson, "A Journal or Sketch of the Life of Joel Hills Johnson," n.d., 12, Folder 3, MS 1546, CHL.
3. I am borrowing this metaphor from Sarah Imhoff.
4. Quincy, *Figures of the Past from the Leaves of Old Journals* (Boston: Roberts Brothers, 1883), 377.

5. Shipps, "The Prophet Puzzle: Suggestions Leading toward a More Comprehensive Interpretation of Joseph Smith," JMH 1 (1974): 3–20.

6. For examples, see Lawrence Foster, "Why the Prophet Is a Puzzle: The Challenges of Using Psychological Perspectives to Understand the Character and Motivation of Joseph Smith, Jr.," *Dialogue* 53 (Summer 2020): 1–35; William D. Morain, *The Sword of Laban: Joseph Smith, Jr. and the Dissociated Mind* (Washington, D.C.: American Psychiatric Press, 2005); Robert D. Anderson, *Inside the Mind of Joseph Smith: Psychobiography and the Book of Mormon* (Salt Lake City: Signature Books, 1999); Isaac Woodbridge Riley, *The Founder of Mormonism: A Psychological Study of Joseph Smith, Jr.* (New York: Dodd, Mead, 1902).

7. Relief Society minutes, 28 April 1842, RS50, 55.

8. Mantel, "Why I Became a Novelist," *Guardian*, 3 June 2017, https://www.theguardian.com/books/2017/jun/03/hilary-mantel-why-i-became-a-historical-novelist.

9. Barney, *Joseph Smith: History, Methods, and Memory* (Salt Lake City: University of Utah Press, 2020), 12.

10. Brodie, *No Man Knows My History: The Life of Joseph Smith*, rev. ed. (New York: Knopf, 1971), 84–85; RSR, 97.

11. Melville, *The Confidence-Man: His Masquerade* (New York: Dix, Edwards, 1857), 380. See the discussion in Charles McCary, *Sincerely Held: American Secularism and Its Believers* (Chicago: University of Chicago Press, 2022), 33–36.

12. Laurie F. Maffly-Kipp, "Tracking the Sincere Believer: 'Authentic' Religion and the Enduring Legacy of Joseph Smith Jr.," *Sunstone*, no. 140 (Dec. 2005): 28–36.

Chapter One. Very Low Circumstances (1805–1816)

1. In the paragraphs that follow, I rely most closely on Lucy Mack Smith's reconstruction of her family's history in the mid-1840s, and on Joseph Smith Jr.'s own histories of his childhood. See also Richard L. Bushman, *Joseph Smith and the Beginnings of Mormonism* (Urbana: University of Illinois Press, 1984), chapter 1.

2. Henry W. Bigler, Journal, 19, MS 1853, CHL; Mark L. Staker and Donald L. Enders, *Joseph and Lucy Smith's Tunbridge Farm: An Archaeological and Landscape Study* (Independence, Mo.: John Whitmer Books, 2021), chapter 3.

3. "perfect failure" in LB, 283.

4. See Mark L. Staker and Donald L. Enders, "Joseph Smith Sr.'s China Adventure," JMH 48 (April 2022): 79–105.

5. EMD, 1:659.

6. LB, 299.

7. LB, 257, 277–278.

8. LB, 291–292; Paine, *The Age of Reason: Part the Second* (London: H. D. Symonds, 1795), 16.

9. Shelby M. Balik, *Rally the Scattered Believers: Northern New England's Religious Geography* (Bloomington: Indiana University Press, 2014), 1.

10. LB, 240; *A Narraitve [Narrative] of the Life of Solomon Mack* (Windsor, Vt.: n.p., 1811), 23, 45.

11. LB, 292–294.

12. LB, 295–296.

13. LB, 300; EMD, 2:122. See William Davis, "Reassessing Joseph Smith Jr.'s Formal Education," *Dialogue* 49 (Winter 2016): 1–58, esp. 4–5.

14. LB, 299.

15. LB, 300–301.

16. LB, 304.

17. LB, 306. See LeRoy S. Wirthlin, "Joseph Smith's Boyhood Operation: An 1813 Surgical Success," *BYU Studies* 21 (Spring 1981):131–154.

18. LB, 307.

19. LB, 309.

20. LB, 310; EMD, 1:663–665. See Richard S. Van Wagoner, *Natural Born Seer* . . . (Salt Lake City: Smith-Pettit Foundation, 2016), 55.

21. EMD, 1:668.

22. LB, 311.

23. LB, 311.

24. LB, 317. See also MHC, A-1, 131–132.

25. MHC, A-1, 132.

26. EMD, 1:597.

Chapter Two. Light (1817–1825)

1. Joshua Forman to David Hosack, 13 Oct. 1828, in Hosack, *Memoir of De Witt Clinton* (New York: J. Seymour, 1829), 347.

2. LB, 318; Pomeroy Tucker, *Origin, Rise, and Progress of Mormonism* (New York: D. Appleton, 1867), 12.

3. Jeffrey N. Walker, "Joseph Smith's Introduction to the Law: The 1819 Hurlbut Case," *Mormon Historical Studies* 11 (Spring 2010): 121.

4. Philander Packard Records, MS 23132, CHL. See Donald L. Enders, "Treasures and a Trash Heap: An Early Reference to the Joseph Smith Family in Palmyra," *Journal of Mormon History* 40 (Summer 2014): 201–222; William Davis, "Reassessing Joseph Smith Jr.'s Formal Education," *Dialogue* 49 (Winter 2016): 25–29.

5. LB, 335; Orasmus Turner, *History of the Pioneer Settlement of Phelps & Gorham's Purchase* . . . (Rochester: William Alling, 1851), 213–214.

6. EMD, 3:68; LB, 322.

7. LB, 321.

8. Dan Vogel, *Joseph Smith: The Making of a Prophet* (Salt Lake City: Signature Books, 2004), 33; RSR, 42.

9. "charge" in LB, 349; EMD, 3:426.

10. LB, 324–325.

11. Finney, *Memoirs of Rev. Charles G. Finney* (New York: A. S. Barnes, 1876), 78. See Douglas J. Winiarski, "Seized by the Jerks: Shakers, Spirit Possession, and the Great Revival," *William & Mary Quarterly* 76 (Jan. 2019): 111–150; Spencer W. McBride and Jennifer Hull Dorsey, eds., *New York's Burned-over District: A Documentary History* (Ithaca, N.Y.: Cornell University Press, 2023), part 3.

12. MHC, A-1, 1; E. Latimer, *The Three Brothers: Sketches of the Lives of Rev. Aurora Seager, Rev. Micah Seager, Rev. Schuyler Seager, D.D.* (New York: Phillips & Hunt, 1880), 22; *Palmyra Register*, 28 June 1820, 2. See the discussion in HOYP, chapter 11; D. Michael Quinn, "Joseph Smith's *Experience* of a Methodist 'Camp-Meeting' in 1820," *Dialogue*, E-Paper #2, 12 July 2006.

13. JS, History, 1832, JSP, H1:11; Alexander Neibaur Journal, 24 May 1844, MS 1674, CHL.

14. Unless otherwise noted, the quotations in the subsequent paragraphs are from MHC, A-1, 1–3.

15. See HOYP, 134–135.

16. For two sophisticated treatments of Joseph's early visionary experiences, see Ann Taves, "First Vision Controversies: Implications for Accounts of Mormon Origins," *BYU Studies* 59 (2020): 73–94; Steven C. Harper, *First Vision: Memory and Mormon Origins* (New York: Oxford University Press, 2019).

17. Brodie, *No Man Knows My History: The Life of Joseph Smith*, rev. ed. (New York: Knopf, 1971), 25; RSR, 40.

18. Richard Lyman Bushman, "The Visionary World of Joseph Smith," *BYU Studies* 38 (1997–1998): 183–204.

19. JS, History, 1832, JSP, H1:13.

20. Peter Ingersoll, 1833 affidavit, MU, 232; Butts, 1885 statement, EMD, 2:202. See Mark Ashurst-McGee, "A Pathway to Prophethood: Joseph Smith Junior as Rodsman, Village Seer, and Judeo-Christian Prophet" (M.A. thesis, Utah State University, 2000), chapter 3.

21. LB, 393; "way off" in W[illiam] D. Purple, "Joseph Smith, the Originator of Mormonism," *Chenango Union*, 2 May 1877, 3. Ashurst-McGee, "Pathway," 198–247.

22. Docket entry from 1826 trial published in *Utah Christian Advocate*, Jan. 1886, 1; statements of Christopher M. Stafford and Cornelius R. Stafford, 1885, EMD, 2:195–197.

23. Willard Chase affidavit, 1833, MU, 240–241. On the well digging as a pretense, see Fayette Lapham, "The Mormons," *Historical Magazine*, May 1870, 6. See also Ashurst-McGee, "Pathway," 258–259.

24. When Joseph and his assistants prepared a history of his life and the church for publication, in drafts and in print they identified the angel as Nephi

rather than Moroni. However, in several earlier accounts Joseph and his associates gave the angel's name as Moroni. For the name Nephi, see MHC, A-1, 15; T&S, 15 April 1842, 753. For an early use of Moroni, see *Doctrine and Covenants of the Church of the Latter Day Saints . . .* (Kirtland, Ohio: F. G. Williams, 1835), 180.

25. "literal" in Oliver Cowdery, "Letter IV," M&A, Feb. 1835, 80; "fullness" in MHC, A-1, 5.

26. See Elizabeth Fenton, *Old Canaan in a New World* (New York: New York University Press, 2020); Sonia Hazard, "How Joseph Smith Encountered Printing Plates and Founded Mormonism," *Religion and American Culture* 31 (2021): 137–192.

27. JS, History, 1832, JSP, H1:13–14; MHC, A-1, 6.

28. MHC, A-1, 7. Willard Chase and Martin Harris both stated that Joseph used the white stone in order to discover the plates. See Ashurst-McGee, "Pathway," 286–292.

29. JS, History, 1832, JSP, H1:14. See Larry E. Morris, *A Documentary History of the Book of Mormon* (New York: Oxford University Press, 2019), 13–14.

30. LB, 351–354.

31. JSJ, 23 Aug. 1842, JSP, J2:116.

32. JS, discourse of 13 April 1843, JSP, J2:356.

33. LB, 355.

34. Joseph Smith Sr., Patriarchal Blessing for Hyrum Smith, 9 Dec. 1834, in H. Michael Marquardt, *Early Patriarchal Blessings of the Church of Jesus Christ of Latter-day Saints* (Salt Lake City: Smith-Pettit Foundation, 2007), 12.

35. *Wayne Sentinel*, 29 Sept. 1824, 3. See Samuel Morris Brown, *In Heaven as It Is on Earth: Joseph Smith and the Early Mormon Conquest of Death* (New York: Oxford University Press, 2012), 55.

36. EMD, 1:513; Townsend sermon, "Palmyra May 10th 1818," MS 26361, CHL.

37. LB, 357.

38. H. Michael Marquardt, *The Rise of Mormonism: 1816–1844*, 2nd ed. (Maitland, Fla.: Xulon Press, 2013), 68–69.

39. LB, 323.

Chapter Three. Plates (1825–1827)

1. Joseph and Hiel Lewis Statement, 30 April 1879, EMD, 4:301–302.

2. Docket Entry, 20 March 1826, Chenango County, New York, Justice of the Peace Court, published in *Utah Christian Advocate*, Jan. 1886, 1; "fourteen dollars" in *Elders' Journal* [Far West, Mo.], July 1838, 43.

3. *Laws of the State of New-York* (Albany: Websters & Skinner, 1807), 1:123–124. Jortner, *No Place for Saints: Mobs and Mormons in Jacksonian America* (Baltimore, Md.: Johns Hopkins University Press, 2021), 29–31.

4. Mark L. Staker, "Isaac and Elizabeth Hale in Their Endless Mountain Home," *Mormon Historical Studies* 15 (Fall 2014): 1–105; LB, 430.

5. Articles of Agreement, 1 Nov. 1825, EMD, 4:411–413. On the uncertain provenance of this document, see JSP, D1:344–352.

6. Isaac Hale, affidavit of 20 March 1834, MU, 263.

7. LB, 367–368.

8. LB, 369–372.

9. Docket Entry, 20 March 1826.

10. W[illiam] D. Purple, "Joseph Smith, the Originator of Mormonism," *Chenango Union*, 2 May 1877, 3; William Stafford affidavit, 8 Dec. 1833, MU, 239. See Manuel W. Padro, "Cunning and Disorderly: Early Nineteenth-Century Witch Trials of Joseph Smith," *Dialogue* 54 (Winter 2021): 35–70.

11. "squandering" in Purple, "Joseph Smith"; "glass looker" in EMD, 4:260; "implicit faith" in Docket Entry, 20 March 1826; "designedly" in [Abram W. Benton], "Mormonites," *Evangelical Magazine and Gospel Advocate* [Utica, N.Y.], 9 April 1831, 120. See EMD, 4:94.

12. Linda King Newell and Valeen Tippetts Avery, *Mormon Enigma: Emma Hale Smith* (Urbana: University of Illinois Press, 1994), 1–8. On Emma's Congregational baptism, see Staker, "Isaac and Elizabeth Hale in Their Endless Mountain Home," 56.

13. Isaac Hale, affidavit of 20 March 1834, MU, 263.

14. Isaac Hale, affidavit of 20 March 1834, MU, 263; Joseph Smith III, "Last Testimony of Sister Emma," *Saints' Herald* [Plano, Ill.], 1 Oct. 1879, 289.

15. Isaac Hale affidavit, MU, 264.

16. LB, 345 ("recitals").

17. Willard Chase affidavit, Dec. 1833, MU, 243. See Rich Troll, "Samuel Tyler Lawrence: A Significant Figure in Joseph Smith's Palmyra Past," *Journal of Mormon History* 32 (Summer 2006): 38–86.

18. LB, 375.

19. Joseph Knight Sr., History, 2, MS 3470, CHL.

20. MHC, A-1, 8 ("delivered"), 5 ("two stones"); LB, 385.

21. Knight Sr., History, 2–3; LB, 379.

22. LB, 379–380.

23. LB, 381–382.

24. Knight Sr., History, 3; LB, 393.

25. T&S, 1 March 1842, 707; MHC, A-1, 34.

26. Joseph Smith III, "Last Testimony of Sister Emma," 290; Stowell in *Boston Christian Herald*, 19 Sept. 1832, 2.

27. Bushman, "A Joseph Smith for the Twenty-First Century," *BYU Studies* 40 (2001): 162.

28. Sonia Hazard, "How Joseph Smith Encountered Printing Plates and Founded Mormonism," *Religion and American Culture* 31 (2021): 137–192.

29. Dan Vogel, *Joseph Smith: The Making of a Prophet* (Salt Lake City: Signature Books, 2004), 98–99.
30. See Richard Bushman, *Joseph Smith's Gold Plates: A Cultural History* (New York: Oxford University Press, 2023), esp. chapter 4.
31. I am inspired here by Ann Taves, *Revelatory Events: Three Case Studies of the Emergence of New Spiritual Paths* (Princeton, N.J.: Princeton University Press, 2016), chapter 2.

Chapter Four. Lost in Translation (1827–1828)

1. Joseph Knight Sr., History, 2, MS 3470, CHL. See Martin Harris, 1859 interview, EMD, 2:302–310.
2. Pomeroy Tucker, *Origin, Rise, and Progress of Mormonism* (New York: D. Appleton, 1867), 40; Saunders in EMD, 2:149. See Susan Easton Black and Larry C. Porter, *Martin Harris: Uncompromising Witness of the Book of Mormon* (Provo, Utah: BYU Studies, 2018); Ronald W. Walker, "Martin Harris: Mormonism's Early Convert," *Dialogue* 19 (Winter 1986): 29–43.
3. Saunders in EMD, 2:133; Lucy Harris statement, 1833, MU, 255; "private purse" in LB, 395; "golden Bible" in Martin Harris, 1859 interview. On negative depictions of Lucy Harris by Lucy Mack Smith and other Latter-day Saints, see Quincy D. Newell and Sara M. Patterson, "Mormonism's First Bad Girl: Lucy Harris and the Gendering of Faith and Doubt in the Church of Jesus Christ of Latter-day Saints," *Religion and American Culture* 32 (Fall 2022): 405–434.
4. *Millennial Star* [Liverpool, U.K.], 4 Dec. 1893, 794; "The Three Witnesses," *Historical Record* 6 (May 1887): 218; Harris, 1859 interview.
5. "glass-box" in Harris, 1859 interview; LB, 398–399.
6. Harris, 1859 interview.
7. "unwell" in Joseph Knight Sr., History, 2.
8. Harris, 1859 interview, EMD, 2:310; LB, 401.
9. Mark Lyman Staker and Robin Scott Jensen, "David Hale's Store Ledger: New Details about Joseph and Emma Smith, the Hale Family, and the Book of Mormon," *BYU Studies* 53.3 (2014): 89–92.
10. Isaac Hale, 1834 affidavit, MU, 264.
11. Staker and Jensen, "David Hale's Store Ledger," 99–104.
12. LB, 402. See Don Bradley, *The Lost 116 Pages: Reconstructing the Book of Mormon's Missing Stories* (Salt Lake City: Greg Kofford Books, 2019), 20–21; Michael Hubbard MacKay, Gerrit J. Dirkmaat, and Robin Scott Jensen, "The 'Caractors' Document: New Light on an Early Transcription of the Book of Mormon Characters," *Mormon Historical Studies* 14 (2013): 131–152.
13. JS, History, 1832, JSP, H1:15.
14. Bennet, "Mormonites," *Morning Courier and Enquirer* [New York, N.Y.], 1 Sept. 1831. On Mitchill, see Richard E. Bennett, " 'Read This I Pray Thee':

Martin Harris and the Three Wise Men of the East," *Journal of Mormon History* 36 (Winter 2010): 194–216.

15. See Erin B. Jennings, "Charles Anthon—The Man behind the Letters," *John Whitmer Historical Association Journal* 32 (Fall/Winter 2012): 171–187.

16. MHC, A-1, 9.

17. JS, History, 1832, JSP, H1:15.

18. Anthon to Howe, 17 Feb. 1834, MU, 270–272.

19. LB, 402–404.

20. LB, 404–407.

21. Joseph Smith III, "Last Testimony of Sister Emma," *Saints' Herald* [Plano, Ill.], 1 Oct. 1879, 289–290. See Michael Hubbard MacKay and Gerrit J. Dirkmaat, *From Darkness unto Light: Joseph Smith's Translation and the Publication of the Book of Mormon* (Provo, Utah: Brigham Young University Religious Studies Center, 2015), 67–68.

22. Edward Stevenson, letter of 30 Nov. 1881, *Deseret Evening News*, 13 Dec. 1881, 4.

23. Joseph Smith III, "Last Testimony of Sister Emma."

24. Minutes of 25–26 Oct. 1831, Minute Book 2 ("Far West Record"), 13, LR 7874 21, CHL; Preface to Book of Mormon (1830).

25. Joseph Smith, History, 1832, JSP, H1:15. A revelation Joseph dictated in July 1828 referred to "counsel" Joseph had received from his "directors." The latter term refers to the "spectacles" or seer stones that Joseph had employed during the translation. See Revelation, ca. July 1828, JSP, D1:8–9.

26. Sophia Lewis Statement, 1834, MU, 269; Samuel Morris Brown, *In Heaven as It Is on Earth: Joseph Smith and the Early Mormon Conquest of Death* (New York: Oxford University Press, 2012), 56; Blair Hodges, "In Memory of an Infant Son," *By Common Consent*, 23 Jan. 2013, https://bycommonconsent.com/2013/01/23/in-memory-of-an-infant-son/.

27. LB, 420–423.

28. LB, 418–419.

29. John A. Clark, *Gleanings by the Way* (Philadelphia: W. J. & J. K. Simon, 1842), 247–248. See the discussion in J. B. Haws, "The Lost 116 Pages Story: What We Do Know, What We Don't Know, and What We Might Know," in Dennis L. Largey et al., eds., *The Coming Forth of the Book of Mormon: A Marvelous Work and a Wonder* (Salt Lake City: Deseret Book, 2015), 83–86; Don Bradley, *The Lost 116 Pages*, chapter 4.

30. "wearied" in MHC, A-1, 10; LB, 425.

31. Revelation, ca. July 1828, JSP, D1:8–9.

32. See the analysis in Ann Taves, "First Vision Controversies: Implications for Accounts of Mormon Origins," *BYU Studies* 59.2 (2020): 90–92.

33. Staker and Jensen, "David Hale's Store Ledger"; Joseph Knight Sr., History, 4.

34. Joseph Knight Sr., History, 4.

Chapter Five. Witnesses (1829)

1. Joseph Smith, History, 1832, JSP, H1:16.
2. Joseph Knight Sr., History, MS 3470, CHL.
3. Revelation, ca. Feb. 1829, JSP, D1:13; Presbyterian Church in Palmyra records, EMD, 3:498–501.
4. Revelation, March 1829, JSP, D1:16–19.
5. LB, 433; Joseph Smith, History, 1832, JSP, H1:16.
6. LB, 434–437.
7. Agreement with Isaac Hale, 6 April 1829, JSP, D1:32–33; Oliver Cowdery to William Cowdery, 21 Jan. 1838, in Oliver Cowdery Letterbook, 81, Henry E. Huntington Library, San Marino, Calif. See JSP, D1:23.
8. Cowdery to William W. Phelps, 7 Sept. 1834, in M&A, Oct. 1834, 14; Richard McNemar Diary, Jan. 1831, in Christian Goodwillie, "Shaker Richard McNemar: The Earliest Book of Mormon Reviewer," *Journal of Mormon History* 37 (Spring 2011): 138–145.
9. Revelations, ca. April 1829, JSP, D1:36, 45–47.
10. Revelation, ca. April 1829, JSP, D1:49–50.
11. Revelation, April or May 1829, JSP, D1:40–44.
12. Joseph Knight Sr., History, 5.
13. "establish my church" and "priestcraft" in Revelation, March 1829, JSP, D1:17; "true points" in revelation, ca. spring 1829, JSP, D1:43.
14. 3 Nephi 11:25.
15. Joseph Smith, History, 1832, JSP, H1:10; Cowdery, Oct. 1835 narrative, in Brian Q. Cannon, "Priesthood Restoration Documents," *BYU Studies* 35.4 (1995): 182. See the discussion in Michael Hubbard MacKay, *Prophetic Authority: Democratic Hierarchy and the Mormon Priesthood* (Urbana: University of Illinois Press, 2020), chapter 2, esp. 28–35; Ronald O. Barney, *Joseph Smith: History, Methods, and Memory* (Salt Lake City: University of Utah Press, 2020), chapter 8.
16. Larry C. Porter, *A Study of the Origins of the Church of Jesus Christ of Latter-day Saints in the States of New York and Pennsylvania* (Provo, Utah: Joseph Fielding Smith Institute for Latter-day Saint History, 2000), 91–95.
17. EMD, 5:75. See Porter, *Study of the Origins*, 95.
18. "chamber" in JS to "The Church of Jesus Christ of Latter Day Saints," 7 Sept. 1842, Revelations Collection, MS 4583, CHL; MHC, A-1, 27. See MacKay, *Prophetic Authority*, 54–60.
19. "The New Bible," *Gospel Luminary* [New York, N.Y.], 10 Dec. 1829, 194.
20. MHC, A-1, 25; Edward Stevenson Journal, 22 Dec. 1877, 12, MS 4806, CHL, in EMD, 5:29.
21. MHC, A-1, 25; "Testimony of Three Witnesses," JSP, D1:381–382.
22. LB, 455–456; "Testimony of Eight Witnesses," JSP, D1:387.
23. I am adapting the analysis of Ann Taves, who compares the "materialization" of the plates to the way that the ordinary elements of bread and wine

become the very body and blood of Jesus Christ for many Christians. Taves posits that Joseph's followers "fus[ed] an ordinary material object"—such as pieces of other metal—with "a non-ordinary believed-in object that could only be seen through the eyes of faith." See Taves, *Revelatory Events: Three Case Studies of the Emergence of New Spiritual Paths* (Princeton, N.J.: Princeton University Press, 2016), chapter 2, esp. 43. For many individuals, including some of the witnesses, the presence of the "ordinary material object" was itself unnecessary.

24. Twain, *Roughing It* (Hartford, Conn.: American Publishing, 1872), 130.

25. "delivered them" in MHC, A-1, 8; Cameron J. Packer, "Cumorah's Cave," *Journal of Book of Mormon Studies* 13.1 (2004): 50–57, 170–171; "wagon loads" from Brigham Young, discourse of 17 June 1877, in JD, 19:38.

26. See the discussion in Michael Hubbard MacKay and Gerrit J. Dirkmaat, *From Darkness unto Light: Joseph Smith's Translation and Publication of the Book of Mormon* (Provo, Utah: Religious Studies Center, 2015), chapter 10.

27. LB, 458; revelation, ca. summer 1829, JSP, D1:91.

28. John H. Gilbert memorandum, 8 Sept. 1892, EMD, 2:542–542; Pomeroy Tucker, *Origin, Rise, and Progress of Mormonism* (New York: D. Appleton, 1867), 50–53. See the discussion in MacKay and Dirkmaat, *From Darkness unto Light*, chapters 9 and 10.

29. JS to Oliver Cowdery, 22 Oct. 1829, JSP, D1:97.

Chapter Six. A Choice Seer (1829)

1. *Rochester Daily Advertiser and Telegraph*, 2 April 1830, 2.

2. MHC, A-1, 5.

3. See the discussion in Paul C. Gutjahr, *The Book of Mormon: A Biography* (Princeton, N.J.: Princeton University Press, 2012), 103–104.

4. See Simon G. Southerton, *Losing a Lost Tribe: Native Americans, DNA, and the Mormon Church* (Salt Lake City: Signature Books, 2004); Thomas W. Murphy, "Simply Implausible: DNA and a Mesoamerican Setting for the Book of Mormon," *Dialogue* 36.4 (2003): 109–131.

5. On the latter issue, see Samuel Morris Brown, *Joseph Smith's Translation: The Words and Worlds of Early Mormonism* (New York: Oxford University Press, 2020), 154.

6. Elizabeth Fenton and Jared Hickman, *Americanist Approaches to the Book of Mormon* (New York: Oxford University Press, 2019), esp. 7–9.

7. Latter-day Saint scholars have intelligent answers to many of these objections. See, for example, John L. Sorenson, *Mormon's Codex: An Ancient American Book* (Salt Lake City: Deseret Book, 2013); Brant A. Gardner, *The Gift and Power: Translating the Book of Mormon* (Salt Lake City: Greg Kofford Books, 2011).

8. Mark Twain, *Roughing It* (Hartford, Conn.: American Publishing, 1872), 127.

9. Bloom, *The American Religion: The Emergence of the Post-Christian Nation* (New York: Simon & Schuster, 1992), 81.

10. See Solomon Spalding, *Manuscript Found: The Complete Original 'Spaulding Manuscript,'* ed. Kent P. Jackson (Provo, Utah: Religious Studies Center, 2008).

11. [Jonathan Hadley], "The Gold Bible Society," *New-York Telescope*, 17 April 1830, 1. See Dale Broadhurst's commentary on this article in http://www .sidneyrigdon.com/dbroadhu/NY/telescp1.htm.

12. Joseph Smith III, "Last Testimony of Sister Emma," *Saints' Herald* [Plano, Ill.], 1 Oct. 1879, 289.

13. Laurie F. Maffly-Kipp, "Tracking the Sincere Believer: 'Authentic' Religion and the Enduring Legacy of Joseph Smith Jr.," *Sunstone*, no. 140 (Dec. 2005): 28–36.

14. See Jared Hickman, "The Book of Mormon as Amerindian Apocalypse," *American Literature* 86 (Sept. 2014): 429–461.

15. See Nathan O. Hatch, *The Democratization of American Christianity* (New Haven, Conn.: Yale University Press, 1989), 117–120.

16. MHC, A-1, 3–4.

17. Patrick H. Breen, *The Land Shall Be Deluged in Blood: A New History of the Nat Turner Revolt* (New York: Oxford University Press, 2016), 19. On White, see Ronald L. Numbers, *Prophetess of Health: A Study of Ellen G. White.* rev. ed. (Grand Rapids, Mich.: Eerdmans, 2008), chapter 1.

18. Scholar Wilfred Cantwell Smith explains that "scripture is a human activity." Whether or not divine revelation or inspiration contributes to the process, communities "make a text into scripture, [and] keep it scripture: by treating it in a certain way." Smith, *What Is Scripture? A Comparative Approach* (Minneapolis: Fortress, 1993), 18.

Chapter Seven. Moses (1830)

1. [Abner Cole], "Address of the Carrier, to the Patrons of the *Wayne Sentinel*," 1 Jan. 1831. The piece appears to have been a New Year's Day broadside sent to subscribers with the 31 Dec. 1830 issue of the paper. See Andrew H. Hedges, "The Refractory Abner Cole," in Donald W. Perry et al., eds., *Revelation, Reason, and Faith: Essays in Honor of Truman G. Madsen* (Provo, Utah: Foundation for Ancient Research and Mormon Studies, 2002), chapter 16.

2. LB, 472; *Reflector* [Palmyra, N.Y.], 2 Jan., 13 Jan., and 22 Jan. 1830.

3. LB, 473–475.

4. Agreement with Martin Harris, 16 Jan. 1830, JSP, D1:108.

5. Whitmer, *An Address to All Believers in Christ* (Richmond, Mo.: n.p., 1887), 31.

6. Revelation, ca. Jan. 1830, JSP, D1:111.

7. Hiram Page to William McLellin, 2 Feb. 1848, typescript published in EMD, 5:257–259; Whitmer, *Address to All Believers in Christ*, 31. See Ste-

phen Kent Ehat, " 'Securing' the Prophet's Copyright in the Book of Mormon: Historical and Legal Context for the So-Called Canadian Copyright Revelation," *BYU Studies* 50 (2011): 5–70.

8. Joseph Knight Sr., History, n.d., 6, MS 3470, CHL.

9. Sources from the 1830s and 1840s diverge on whether the organizational meeting took place in Fayette or Manchester. For the latter view, see H. Michael Marquardt and Wesley P. Walters, *Inventing Mormonism: Tradition and the Historical Record* (Salt Lake City: Smith Research Associates, 1994), chapter 7. The baptisms of Joseph Smith Sr. and Martin Harris took place in Manchester, and Lucy Mack Smith dates them to 6 April 1830, "the day on which the church was organized." Joseph Knight Sr. seems to place the baptisms prior to the organizational meeting. What matters is that in early April 1830 a small number of believers organized the Church of Christ, and several of Joseph's closest family members and friends were baptized.

10. JS, History, 1838–1841, Draft 1, JSP, H1:366.

11. Revelation, 6 April 1830, JSP, D1:129.

12. LB, 477; Joseph Knight Sr., History, 7.

13. "cleave" and "age" in the *Reflector*, 30 June 1830, 5–6. Other quotes in MHC, A-1, 40–41. See Stephen Taysom, " 'Satan Mourns Naked upon the Earth': Locating Mormon Possession and Exorcism Rituals in the American Religious Landscape, 1830–1977," *Religion and American Culture* 27 (Winter 2017): 57–94.

14. A[bram] W. B[enton], "Mormonites," *Evangelical Magazine and Gospel Advocate*, 9 April 1831, 120.

15. Minutes of Joel K. Noble, in *Boston Christian Herald*, 19 Sept. 1832, 2.

16. Noble to Jonathan B. Turner, 8 March 1842, Abraham Lincoln Presidential Library, Jonathan Baldwin Turner Papers, MS-BC643, Box 1 (EMD, 4:109). For a summary of the two trials, see Marquardt and Walters, *Inventing Mormonism*, chapter 8.

17. JSTOM, 83–85.

18. "drenched" in Philip L. Barlow, *Mormons and the Bible: The Place of Latter-day Saints in American Religion* (New York: Oxford University Press, 1991), 11; John Fea, *The Bible Cause: A History of the American Bible Society* (New York: Oxford University Press, 2016), chapter 4. On the nature of biblical authority in nineteenth-century America, see Seth Perry, *Bible Culture and Authority in the Early United States* (Princeton, N.J.: Princeton University Press, 2018).

19. *The Sacred Writings of the Apostles and Evangelists of Jesus Christ, Commonly Titled the New Testament* (Buffaloe, Va.: Alexr. Campbell, 1826), 3.

20. Peter Manseau, *The Jefferson Bible: A Biography* (Princeton, N.J.: Princeton University Press, 2020), 6. See also Thomas S. Kidd, *Thomas Jefferson: A Biography of Spirit and Flesh* (New Haven, Conn.: Yale University Press, 2022), 205–213.

21. JSTOM, 88–89.

22. *Ohio Star* [Ravenna], 24 March 1831. See David G. Hackett, *That Religion in Which All Men Agree: Freemasonry in American Culture* (Berkeley: University of California Press, 2014), 112; Samuel Morris Brown, *In Heaven as It Is on Earth: Joseph Smith and the Early Mormon Conquest of Death* (New York: Oxford University Press, 2012), 175. On Hyrum Smith's Masonic affiliation, see Cheryl L. Bruno, Joe Steve Swick III, and Nicholas S. Literski, *Method Infinite: Freemasonry and the Mormon Restoration* (Salt Lake City: Greg Kofford Books, 2022), 37.

23. JSTOM, 94–95.

24. JSTOM, 102; "round" in revelation, 7 Dec. 1830, JSP, D1:220.

25. George M. Marsden, *Jonathan Edwards: A Life* (New Haven, Conn.: Yale University Press, 2003), 133–136.

26. Revelation, ca. July 1830, JSP, D1:162–164.

Chapter Eight. Enoch (1830–1831)

1. Ezra Booth, "Mormonism," *Ohio Star* [Ravenna], 8 Dec. 1831, 1. See Provo Central Stake, General Minutes, 6 April 1856, LR 9269 11, vol. 10, 273, CHL.

2. "spiritually sees" in *Ensign of Liberty*, May 1848, 98. See David Whitmer, *An Address to All Believers in Christ* (Richmond, Mo.: n.p., 1887), 35, 56.

3. MHC, A-1, 51.

4. Revelation, September 1830, JSP, D1:185–186.

5. "powder" in Provo Central Stake, General Minutes, 6 April 1856. See minutes, 26 Sept. 1830, JSP, D1:192.

6. *Millennial Star*, 16 Dec. 1878, 787.

7. Flake interview, 27 April 2006, https://www.pbs.org/mormons/interviews/flake.html.

8. Adam Jortner, *No Place for Saints: Mobs and Mormons in Jacksonian America* (Baltimore, Md.: Johns Hopkins University Press, 2021), 57–59; Michael Hubbard MacKay, *Prophetic Authority: Democratic Hierarchy and the Mormon Priesthood* (Urbana: University of Illinois Press, 2020), 67–70.

9. Revelation, ca. September 1830, JSP, D1:179–180.

10. Bradford King Journal, 28 Nov. 1830, University of Rochester, Rush Rhees Library, Special Collections.

11. David L. Rowe, *God's Strange Work: William Miller and the End of the World* (Grand Rapids, Mich.: Eerdmans, 2008).

12. Revelation, ca. September 1830, JSP, D1:186. On early Mormon apocalypticism, see Christopher James Blythe, *Terrible Revolution: Latter-day Saints and the American Apocalypse* (New York: Oxford University Press, 2020), chapter 1; Grant Underwood, *The Millenarian World of Early Mormonism* (Urbana: University of Illinois Press, 1993). See also William Mulder, *Homeward to Zion: The Mormon Migration from Scandinavia* (Minneapolis: University of Minnesota Press, 1957), chapter 2.

13. Colby Townsend, "Revisiting Joseph Smith and the Availability of the Book of Enoch," *Dialogue* 53 (Fall 2020): 41–72; David G. Hackett, *That Religion in Which All Men Agree: Freemasonry in American Culture* (Berkeley: University of California Press, 2014), 96.
14. Quotations are from JSTOM, 98–109.
15. Revelation, ca. July 1828, JSP, D1:9; revelation, Oct. 1830, JSP, D1:202.
16. *Christian Baptist* [Buffaloe, Va.], 7 Feb. 1825, 156. On Pratt's background, see Terryl L. Givens and Matthew J. Grow, *Parley P. Pratt: The Apostle Paul of Mormonism* (New York: Oxford University Press, 2011), chapter 1.
17. On the movements of the Campbells, Walter Scott, and Barton Stone, see Richard T. Hughes, *Reviving the Ancient Faith: The Story of Churches of Christ in America* (Grand Rapids, Mich.: Eerdmans, 1996), chapters 2–6.
18. Mary Fielding Smith to Mercy F. Thompson, 8 July 1837, Folder 3, MS 2779, CHL; A. S. Hayden, *Early History of the Disciples in the Western Reserve, Ohio* (Cincinnati: Chase & Hall, 1875), 192. On Rigdon, see Richard S. Van Wagoner, *Sidney Rigdon: A Portrait of Religious Excess* (Salt Lake City: Signature Books, 1994).
19. See HOYP, chapters 5 and 6.
20. *The Autobiography of Parley Parker Pratt . . .* (New York: Russell Brothers, 1874), 37.
21. Revelation, 7 Dec. 1830, JSP, D1:223.
22. JS to Hyrum Smith and the church in Colesville, 2 Dec. 1830, JSP, D1:218; LB, 502.
23. Revelation, December 1830, JSP, D1:227.
24. John Whitmer, History, 1831–ca. 1847, JSP, H2:21.
25. Revelation, 2 Jan. 1831, JSP, D1:230–233; *Reflector* [Palmyra, N.Y.], 1 Feb. 1831, 95.

Chapter Nine. Flying High (1831)

1. [Elizabeth Ann Whitney], "A Leaf from an Autobiography," *Woman's Exponent* [Salt Lake City], 1 Sept. 1878, 51.
2. HOYP, 222, 225–228.
3. James Rollins, "A Life Sketch of James Henry Rollins," 1896, 1, typescript in MS 2393, CHL.
4. HOYP, 72.
5. Joel Miller, "Statement," 1885, in *Naked Truths about Mormonism* [Oakland, California], April 1888, 2; Levi Hancock, "The Life of Levi W. Hancock," 79, MS 8174, CHL.
6. "talking" in Reuben P. Harmon, "Statement," 1884, in *Naked Truths about Mormonism*, April 1888, 1; "scoot" in John Whitmer, History, 1831–ca. 1847, JSP, H2:38. See Christopher C. Smith, "Playing Lamanite: Ecstatic Performance of American Indian Roles in Early Mormon Ohio," JMH 41 (July 2015): 131–166; Angela Pulley Hudson, *Real Native Genius: How an*

Ex-Slave and a White Mormon Became Famous Indians (Chapel Hill: University of North Carolina Press, 2015), chapter 2.

7. George A. Smith, discourse of 14 Nov. 1864, JD, 11:4; "fancies" in *Buffalo Bulletin*, 26 Feb. 1831, 2. George A. Smith's report is secondhand, as he was not present in Kirtland at the time. On Peter, see HOYP, 5–8; "Peter," https://exhibits.lib.utah.edu/s/century-of-black-mormons/page/peter#_ftnref2. On scrolls as conduits for revelation, see Adam Jortner, *No Place for Saints: Mobs and Mormons in Jacksonian America* (Baltimore, Md.: Johns Hopkins University Press, 2021), 71.

8. MHC, A-1, 101; "destruction" in Thomas Marsh and Eliza G. Marsh to Lewis and Ann Abott, 1 April 1831, MS 23457, CHL. See JSP, D1:257, n. 95.

9. Hancock, "Life," 81; *Buffalo Bulletin*, 26 Feb. 1831, 2.

10. Revelation, 4 Feb. 1831, JSP, D1:243–244.

11. Revelation, 4 Feb. 1831, JSP, D1:244. See HOYP, 102.

12. Revelation, 9 Feb. 1831, JSP, D1:251–252.

13. Revelation, 9 Feb. 1831, JSP, D1:254–256.

14. JS to Hyrum Smith, 3–4 March 1831, JSP, D1:273; Jared Carter, Journal, 1831–1833, 15, MS 1441, CHL.

15. "disfigured" in *The Autobiography of Parley Parker Pratt . . .* (New York: Russell Brothers, 1874), 65; revelation, ca. 8 March 1831, JSP, D1:283.

16. Eleanor Atkinson, "The Winter of the Deep Snow," *Transactions of the Illinois State Historical Society for the Year 1909* (Springfield, Ill.: State Journal, 1910), 47–62. See Terryl L. Givens and Matthew J. Grow, *Parley P. Pratt: The Apostle Paul of Mormonism* (New York: Oxford University Press, 2011), chapter 2; Ronald E. Romig, "The Lamanite Mission," JWHAJ 14 (1994): 25–33.

17. See John P. Bowes, *Land Too Good for Indians: Northern Indian Removal* (Norman: University of Oklahoma Press, 2016), chapter 3; Max Perry Mueller, *Race and the Making of the Mormon People* (Chapel Hill: University of North Carolina Press, 2017), 65–70.

18. *Painesville Telegraph*, 15 Feb. 1831, 1; *Autobiography of Parley Parker Pratt*, 59.

19. Cowdery to "brethren" in Kirtland, 29 Jan. 1831, in JS to Hyrum Smith, 3–4 March 1831, JSP, D1:272; Cowdery to "brethren" in Kirtland, 8 April 1831, JSP, D1:291–294.

20. Cummins to Clark, 15 Feb. 1831, copy in MS 9625, CHL.

21. Revelation, ca. 7 March 1831, JSP, D1:275–280.

22. JSTOM, 219–220.

23. *Salem Gazette* [Mass.], 24 June 1831, 2; "Last Testimony of Sister Emma," *Saints' Herald* [Plano, Ill.], 1 Oct. 1879, 289.

24. LB, 539–540; John Murdock to children, 20 Jan. 1859, in Autobiography of John Murdock, ca. 1860s, 191–197, MS 1194, Folder 4, CHL.

25. See the discussion in Larry C. Porter, *A Study of the Origins of the Church of Jesus Christ of Latter-day Saints in the States of New York and Pennsylvania*

(Provo, Utah: Joseph Fielding Smith Institute for Latter-day Saint History, 2000), chapter 7.

26. JS to Harris, 22 Feb. 1831, JSP, D1:264; Gilbert, 1 Dec. 1877 interview, EMD, 3:519; *Millennial Star*, 20 Aug. 1859, 545.

27. Jared Carter, Journal, 17.

28. Hancock, "Life," 89–90. See also John Whitmer, History, 1831–ca. 1847, JSP, H2:40; minutes of 3–4 June 1831, JSP, D1:324.

29. Hancock, "Life," 90; Booth to Ira Eddy, 31 Oct. 1831, MU, 189.

30. Revelation, 2 Jan. 1831, JSP, D1:232; Minutes 25 Oct. 1831, JSP, D2:82.

31. Hancock, "Life," 91.

32. Revelation, 6 June 1831, JSP, D1:328–332.

33. Hancock, "Life," 95.

Chapter Ten. Land of Joseph (1831)

1. *Ohio Star* [Ravenna], 17 Nov. 1831, 3; Pierre M. Irving, ed., *Life and Letters of Washington Irving* (New York: G. P. Putnam, 1863), 3:38; "Extract of a Letter from the Late Editor of This Paper," *Ontario Phoenix* [Canandaigua, N.Y.], 7 Sept. 1831, 2.

2. Revelation, 20 July 1831, JSP, D2:7–12.

3. Booth to Partridge, 20 Sept. 1831, *Ohio Star* [Ravenna], 24 Nov. 1831, 1.

4. Edward Partridge to Lydia Partridge, 5–6 Aug. 1831, MS 23154, CHL; "unbelief" in revelation, 1 Aug. 1831, JSP, D2:15.

5. MHC, A-1, 129. See also Phelps, Reminiscence, 21 April 1864, MS 6019, CHL.

6. Booth to I. Eddy, 6 Dec. 1831, *Ohio Star* [Ravenna], 8 Dec. 1831, 1; Council of Fifty minutes, 27 Feb. 1845, JSP, C50:533; Phelps to Brigham Young, 12 Aug. 1861, Revelations Collection, MS 4583, CHL. See Dan Vogel, *Charisma under Pressure: Joseph Smith, American Prophet, 1831–1839* (Salt Lake City: Signature Books, 2023), 78–81.

7. John Whitmer, History, 1831–ca. 1847, JSP, H2:45; MHC, A-1, 139.

8. *Ontario Phoenix*, 7 Sept. 1831, 2.

9. MHC, A-1, 142; Booth to Partridge, 24 Nov. 1831.

10. Cahoon, Diary, MS 1115, CHL.

11. Revelation, 1 Aug. 1831, JSP, D2:20; revelation, 11 Sept. 1831, JSP, D2:65.

12. *The Evening and the Morning Star* [Independence, Mo.], Oct. 1832, 37. See Mark Ashurst-McGee, "Zion Rising: Joseph Smith's Early Social and Political Thought" (Ph.D. diss., Arizona State University, 2008), 237–238.

Chapter Eleven. Pure Language (1831–1832)

1. HOYP, 280.

2. Philo Dibble, "Philo Dibble's Narrative," in *Early Scenes in Church History* (Salt Lake City: Juvenile Instructor Office, 1882), 79. See HOYP, 282–284.

3. HOYP, chapter 24.

4. Minutes, 6 Sept. 1831, JSP, D2:61.

5. Booth to Partridge, 20 Sept. 1831, *Ohio Star* [Ravenna], 24 Nov. 1831, 1.

6. Whitmer, History, 1831–ca. 1847, JSP, H2:45; Campbell in *Millennial Harbinger* [Bethany, Va.], 4 July 1831, 331; bomb in McLellin, Journal, 17 Nov. 1831, in Jan Shipps and John W. Welch, eds., *The Journals of William E. McLellin* (Provo, Utah: BYU Studies, 1994), 47.

7. *Ensign of Liberty* [Kirtland, Oh.], Jan. 1848, 61; McLellin Journal, 26–27 Oct. 1831, 45–46.

8. *Ohio Star* [Ravenna], 20 Oct. 1831, 3.

9. Revelation, ca. 7 March 1831, JSP, D1:280; Whitmer, *Address to all Believers in Christ* (Richmond, Mo.: n.p., 1887), 54–55.

10. Revelation, ca. 2 Nov. 1831, JSP, D2:109; MHC, A-1, 162. See Mark R. Grandstaff, "Having More Learning Than Sense: William E. McLellin and the Book of Commandments Revisited," *Dialogue* 26 (Winter 1993): 23–48.

11. Minutes, 8 Nov. 1831, JSP, D2:123.

12. Minutes, 26 April 1832, JSP, D2:231.

13. See Kathryn Gin Lum, *Damned Nation: Hell in America from the Revolution to Reconstruction* (New York: Oxford University Press, 2014).

14. See Clyde D. Ford, "The Book of Mormon, the Early Nineteenth-Century Debates over Universalism, and the Development of the Novel Mormon Doctrines of Ultimate Rewards and Punishments," *Dialogue* 47 (Spring 2014): 1–23.

15. JSTOM, 454. Quotations from the vision in this and subsequent paragraphs are from Vision, 16 Feb. 1832, JSP, D2:183–192.

16. Campbell, "The Three Kingdoms," *Christian Baptist* [Bethany, Va.], 1 June 1829, 253–257; Colleen McDannell and Bernhard Lang, *Heaven: A History*, rev. ed. (New Haven, Conn.: Yale University Press, 1988), 200–201. See HOYP, 322–323.

17. McDannell and Lang, *Heaven*, 201. See J. B. Haws, "Joseph Smith, Emanuel Swedenborg, and Section 76: Importance of the Bible in Latter-day Revelation," in Andrew H. Hedges et al., eds., *The Doctrine and Covenants: Revelations in Context* (Provo, Utah: BYU Religious Studies Center, 2008), 142–167.

18. JS to Emma Smith, 6 June 1832, JSP, D2:256; JS to William W. Phelps, 27 Nov. 1832, JSP, D2:320. See Samuel Morris Brown, *Joseph Smith's Translation: The Words and Worlds of Early Mormonism* (New York: Oxford University Press, 2020), 32–33.

19. See Brown, *Joseph Smith's Translation*, 25–29.

20. "pure language" in [Thomas A. Marsh], letter of 9 Jan. 1831, in *Hopkinsian Magazine*, 31 Dec. 1831, 285; JSTOM, 97.

21. Sample of Pure Language, ca. March 1832, JSP, D2:215.

22. The following paragraphs rely on MHC, A-1, 205–209; and the analysis and sources in HOYP, chapter 27.

23. Luke Johnson, "History of Luke Johnson, by Himself," *Millennial Star*, 31 Dec. 1864, 835; hair in Levi W. Hancock, "Life of Levi W. Hancock," 130.

24. "disguised" in *Observer and Telegraph* [Hudson, Ohio], 5 April 1832, 3.

25. *Public Discussion of the Issues between the Reorganized Church of Jesus Christ of Latter Day Saints and the Church of Christ (Disciples)* (St. Louis, Mo.: Clark Braden, 1884), 202; Fawn M. Brodie, *No Man Knows My History: The Life of Joseph Smith*, rev. ed. (New York: Knopf, 1971), 119.

26. Benjamin F. Johnson, Letter to George F. Gibbs, 1903, 54–55, MS 1289, CHL. See HOYP, 369–370, n. 69.

27. Murdock, Diary, 1830–1859, May 1832, 19, Folder 2, MS 1194, CHL.

Chapter Twelve. Olive Leaves (1832–1833)

1. See Erin B. Jennings, "The Consequential Counselor: Restoring the Root(s) of Jesse Gause," JMH 34 (Spring 2008): 182–227.

2. Minutes, 10 March 1832, Minute Book 2 ("Far West Record"), 23, LR 7874 21, CHL.

3. Minutes, 26 April 1832, JSP, D2:231–232.

4. Revelation, 26 April 1832, JSP, D2:235–237. See Max H. Parkin, "Joseph Smith and the United Firm: The Growth and Decline of the Church's First Master Plan of Business and Finance, Ohio and Missouri, 1832–1834," *BYU Studies* 46 (2007):5–66.

5. "did not take the trouble" in JS to Emma Smith, 6 June 1832, JSP, D2:249–257; "conspiracy" in JS to William W. Phelps, 31 July 1832, JSP, D2:264.

6. MHC, A-1, 214.

7. MHC, A-1, 215; JS to Emma Smith, 6 June 1832. On Mary Smith's death, see Hyrum Smith, Journal, 29 May 1832, Vault MSS 774, HBLL.

8. JS to Emma Smith, 6 June 1832.

9. MHC, A-1, 209. See also Elizabeth Ann Whitney, "A Leaf from an Autobiography," *Woman's Exponent* [Salt Lake City], 1 Oct. 1878, 71.

10. JS to Edward Partridge et al., 14 Jan. 1833, JSP, D2:373; JS to Phelps, 31 July 1832, JSP, D2:261–271.

11. JS to Phelps, 31 July 1832.

12. "kingdom taken" and "was ours" in Reynolds Cahoon, Diary, 5–6 July 1832, MS 1115, CHL; "devil" in LB, 560–564; reordination in Hyrum Smith, Journal, 28 July 1832; "feelings" in JS to Phelps, 31 July 1832. On the new Rigdon residence, see HOYP, 251.

13. JSJ, Nov. 1833, JSP, J1:18; JSJ, 3 Dec. 1832, JSP, J1:10.

14. HOYP, 251.

15. Revelation, 22–23 Sept. 1832, JSP, D2:293–304. See Matthew C. Godfrey, "A Culmination of Learning: D&C 84 and the Doctrine of the Priesthood," in Scott C. Esplin et al., eds., *You Shall Have My Word: Exploring the Text of the Doctrine and Covenants* (Provo, Utah: BYU Religious Studies Center, 2012), 167–181.

16. Whitney, Statement, 1842, Joseph Smith History Documents, CR 100 396, CHL.
17. JS to Emma Smith, 13 Oct. 1832, JSP, D2:307–314.
18. Brigham Young, discourse of 6 April 1860, transcription of George D. Watt, shorthand by LaJean Carruth, CR 100 912, CHL.
19. Brigham Young, discourse of 3 Sept. 1865, transcription of George D. Watt, shorthand by LaJean Carruth, CR 100 912.
20. Brigham Young, discourse of 20 Nov. 1864, transcription of George D. Watt, shorthand by LaJean Carruth, CR 100 912.
21. See "History of Brigham Young," *Deseret News*, 10 Feb. 1858, 385.
22. Coltrin, Journal, 14 Nov. 1832, 49–50, MS 1443, CHL.
23. Robert Elder, *Calhoun: American Heretic* (New York: Basic Books, 2021), 242.
24. Daniel Walker Howe, *What Hath God Wrought: The Transformation of America, 1815–1848* (New York: Oxford University Press, 2007), 395–410; Elder, *Calhoun*, chapters 11 and 12.
25. Revelation, 25 Dec. 1832, JSP, D2:330–331.
26. Orson Hyde and Hyrum Smith to Edward Partridge et al., 14 Jan. 1833, JSP, D2:374–377.
27. Minutes, 27 Dec. 1832, JSP, D2:333.
28. Revelation, 27–28 Dec. 1832, JSP, D2:345; JS to Phelps, 11 Jan. 1833, JSP, D2:365. Joseph F. Darowski, "Schools of the Prophets: An Early American Tradition," *Mormon Historical Studies* 9.1 (Spring 2008): 1–13.
29. Revelation, 3 Jan. 1833, JSP, D2:347–348.
30. Minutes, 23–24 Jan. 1833, JSP, D2:381.
31. Minutes, 23–24 Jan. 1833, JSP, D2:381–382.
32. Coltrin, Journal, 24 Jan. 1833, 49–50.
33. Minutes, 26 Feb. 1833, Minute Book 2 ("Far West Record"), 34.

Chapter Thirteen. Zion Is Fled (1833–1834)

1. *Reflector* [Palmyra, N.Y.], 30 June 1830, 5; Campbell, "Delusions," *Millennial Harbinger* [Bethany, Va.], 7 Feb. 1831, 91; *Preston Chronicle* [Lancaster, U.K.], 30 June 1838, 3. See J. Spencer Fluhman, *"A Peculiar People": Anti-Mormonism and the Making of Religion in Nineteenth-Century America* (Chapel Hill: University of North Carolina Press, 2012), chapter 1.
2. JS, discourse of 11 June 1843, JSP, D12:380.
3. Revelation, 2–23 Sept. 1832, JSP, D2:295; revelation, 27–28 Dec. 1832, JSP, D2:345.
4. Coltrin, Journal, MS 1443, CHL; "History of Orson Hyde," *Deseret News*, 5 May 1858, 45.
5. School of the Prophets (Salt Lake City), minutes, 3 and 11 Oct. 1883, in Devery S. Anderson, ed., *Salt Lake School of the Prophets, 1867–1883* (Salt Lake City: Signature Books, 2018), 503, 511.

6. Young, discourse of 8 Feb. 1868, transcript of George D. Watt, shorthand by LaJean Carruth, CR 100 912, CHL; Shane A. Smith, "Anti-Tobacco Sentiments in Periodical Literature, 1800–1870," *Historian* 77 (Spring 2015): 37.

7. Stephen Nissenbaum, *Sex, Diet, and Debility in Jacksonian America: Sylvester Graham and Health Reform* (Westport, Conn.: Greenwood, 1980). See W. J. Rorabaugh, *The Alcohol Republic: An American Tradition* (New York: Oxford University Press, 1979), chapter 1. For a distillation of his argument, see Rorabaugh, "Alcohol in America," *OAH Magazine of History*, Fall 1991, 17–19.

8. Revelation, 27 Feb. 1833, JSP, D3:20–21; School of the Prophets (Salt Lake City), minutes, 3 Oct. 1883, 503.

9. Minutes, 18 March 1833, JSP, D3:40–42.

10. Minutes, 18 March 1833, JSP, D3:42.

11. JSP, D3:47; Coltrin, Journal, 23 March 1833. An April 1832 revelation had referred to Kirtland as a "stake to Zion." Revelation, 26 April 1832, JSP, D2:236.

12. Minutes of 2 Feb. 1833, Kirtland High Council Minutebook, 8, MS 3432, CHL; JS to Missouri church leaders, 21 April 1833, JSP, D3:68; L. John Nuttall, Journal, 10 Sept. 1879, in Jedediah S. Rogers, ed., *In the President's Office: The Diaries of L. John Nuttall, 1879–1892* (Salt Lake City: Signature Books, 2007), 26–27. See Bruce W. Worthen, *Mormon Envoy: The Diplomatic Legacy of Dr. John Milton Bernhisel* (Urbana: University of Illinois Press, 2023), 44–45.

13. JSTOM, 442.

14. Revelation, 6 May 1833, JSP, D3:85–91. See the analysis in Nicholas J. Frederick, *The Bible, Mormon Scripture, and the Rhetoric of Allusivity* (Lanham, Md.: Fairleigh Dickinson University Press, 2016).

15. See Terryl L. Givens, *When Souls Had Wings: Pre-Mortal Existence in Western Thought* (New York: Oxford University Press, 2010), esp. chapter 4.

16. Revelation, 1 June 1833, JSP, D3:107–108; Hyrum Smith, 1832–1833 Journal, 7 June 1833, Vault MSS 774, HBLL; cornerstones in MHC, A-1, 330. See Elwin C. Robison, *The Mormon Temple: Design, Construction, and Historic Context of the Kirtland Temple* (Provo, Utah: Brigham Young University Press, 1997), chapter 2.

17. Plat of the City of Zion, June 1833, JSP, D3:124–146.

18. Revelation, 1 Aug. 1831, JSP, D2:20; *The Evening and the Morning Star* [Independence, Mo.], July 1833, 110. See Mark Roscoe Ashurst-McGee, "Zion Rising: Joseph Smith's Early Social and Political Thought" (Ph.D. diss., Arizona State University, 2008), chapter 9. Ashurst-McGee's dissertation led me to many of the sources cited in the following paragraphs. Other excellent studies of the Mormon expulsion from Jackson County include Adam Jortner, *No Place for Saints: Mobs and Mormons in Jacksonian America* (Baltimore, Md.: Johns Hopkins University Press, 2021); Warren A. Jennings,

"The Expulsion of the Mormons from Jackson County Missouri," *Missouri Historical Review* 64 (October 1969): 41–63.

19. "To His Excellency, Daniel Dunklin," *The Evening and the Morning Star* [Kirtland, Ohio], Dec. 1833, 114; *The Evening and the Morning Star* [Independence, Mo.], July 1833, 109, 111; *The Evening and the Morning Star* [Independence, Mo.], 16 July 1833 Extra.

20. "To His Excellency, Daniel Dunklin."

21. *Missouri Intelligencer and Boon's Lick Advertiser* [Columbia, Mo.], 10 Aug. 1834.

22. Vienna Jacques statement, 22 Feb. 1859, MS 3172, CHL; *The Evening and the Morning Star* [Kirtland, Ohio], Dec. 1833, 114.

23. *Missouri Republican*, 9 Aug. 1833, 3; Dunklin to Edward Partridge et al., 19 Oct. 1833, William W. Phelps Collection of Missouri Documents, MS 657, CHL.

24. Daniel A. Cohen, "Passing the Torch: Boston Firemen, 'Tea Party' Patriots, and the Burning of the Ursuline Convent," *Journal of the Early Republic* 24 (Winter 2004): 527–586; David Grimsted, "Rioting in Its Jacksonian Setting," *American Historical Review* 77 (April 1972): 367.

25. Revelation of 6 Aug. 1833, JSP, D3:234.

26. JS to William W. Phelps et al., 18 Aug. 1833, JSP, D3:268–269.

27. JS to Phelps et al., 18 Aug. 1833, JSP, D3:264; Dale W. Adams, "Doctor Philastus Hurlbut: Originator of Derogatory Statements about Joseph Smith, Jr.," JWHAJ 20 (2000): 76–93.

28. Minutes, ca. 3, 21, and 23 June 1833, JSP, D3:103, 117, 120.

29. Kent P. Jackson, ed., *Manuscript Found: The Complete Original 'Spaulding Manuscript'* (Provo, Utah: BYU Religious Studies Center, 1996). See Adam Jortner, "Solomon Spaulding's Indians, or, What the 'Manuscript Found' Really Tells Us," JMH 38 (Fall 2012): 226–247.

30. Adams, "Doctor Philastus Hurlbut," 79–83.

31. JS to Phelps et al., 18 Aug. 1833, JSP, D3:267–268.

32. JSJ, 13 Nov. 1833, JSP, J1:17–18.

33. On the renewal of mob activity, see Roger D. Launius, "A Question of Honor? A. W. Doniphan and the Mormon Expulsion from Jackson County," *Nauvoo Journal* 10 (Fall 1998): 3–17.

34. Partridge, "A History, of the Persecution," T&S, Jan. 1840, 33–36; Partridge to JS, ca. mid-November 1833, JSP, D3:346–351.

35. JS to Edward Partridge et al., 10 Dec. 1833, JSP, D3:377.

36. Revelation, 16–17 Dec. 1833, JSP, D3:389–397.

37. *Painesville Telegraph*, 31 Jan. 1834, 3; Orson Hyde to "brethren" in Missouri, 22 Jan. 1834, JSP, D3:411. On the legal proceedings, this and the subsequent paragraphs rely on David W. Grua, "Joseph Smith and the 1834 D. P. Hurlbut Case," *BYU Studies* 44 (2005): 33–54.

38. B. F. Norris to Mark Norris, 6 Jan. 1834, Burton Historical Collection, Detroit Public Library.

39. Transcript of Proceedings, *State of Ohio v. D. P. Hurlbut*, Geauga County Court of Common Pleas, 9 April 1834, https://www.josephsmithpapers.org /paper-summary/transcript-of-proceedings-circa-9-april-1834-state-of-ohio-v-d-p-hurlbut/1. See the reconstruction of courtroom testimony in Grua, "The 1834 D. P. Hurlbut Case," 38–41.

40. JSJ, 7–9 April 1834, JSP, J1:38; *Chardon Spectator and Geauga Gazette* [Chardon, Ohio], 12 April 1834, 4. See Grua, "The 1834 D. P. Hurlbut Case," 44–49.

41. Oliver Cowdery to John F. Boynton, 10 April 1834, 40, Cowdery Letterbook, Huntington Library, San Marino, Calif.

42. Minutes, 24 Feb. 1834, JSP, D3:456–457; revelation, 24 Feb. 1834, JSP, D3:460.

43. JSJ, 19 April 1834, JSP, J1:41.

Chapter Fourteen. General Smith (1834)

1. Jortner, *The Gods of Prophetstown: The Battle of Tippecanoe and the Holy War for the American Frontier* (New York: Oxford University Press, 2012), 1.

2. Minutes, 3 May 1834, JSP, D4:44; "The Saints," *The Evening and the Morning Star* [Kirtland, Ohio], May 1834, 158.

3. Reuben McBride, Reminiscence, n.d., 1–2, MS 8197, CHL.

4. Dunklin to Gilbert et al., 4 Feb. 1834, Phelps Collection of Missouri Documents, MS 657, CHL. See the discussion in Matthew C. Godfrey, " 'The Redemption of Zion Must Needs Come by Power': Insights into the Camp of Israel Expedition, 1834," *BYU Studies* 53 (2014): 125–146.

5. W. W. Phelps to "brethren," 1 May 1834, JSP, D4:40–42.

6. "History of George A. Smith," n.d., 15–16, George A. Smith Papers, MS 1322, CHL.

7. Martin, 20 May 1834, May–June 1834 Journal, MS 1986, CHL; "side complaint" in JS to Emma Smith, 4 June 1834, JSP, D4:54.

8. Martin, 17 May 1834, May–June 1834 Journal, 4.

9. Martin, 4 June 1834, May–June 1834 Journal, 9; WWJ, ca. 4 June 1834; identification as Zelph in MHC, A-1, 483. Kenneth B. Farnsworth, "Lamanitish Arrows and Eagles with Lead Eyes: Tales of the First Recorded Explorations in an Illinois Valley Hopewell Mound," *Illinois Archaeology* 22 (2010): 25–48.

10. JS to Emma Smith, 4 June 1834, JSP, D4:57; "modern Zelphs" from Samuel Morris Brown, *In Heaven as It Is on Earth: Joseph Smith and the Early Mormon Conquest of Death* (New York: Oxford University Press, 2012), 90.

11. Quotations from minutes, 28–29 Aug. 1834, JSP, D4:129–130. For context, see "History of George A. Smith," 23–24; Levi Hancock, "The Life of Levi W. Hancock," 142–143, MS 8174, CHL.

12. Hancock, "Life," 143–144; Martin, 10 June 1834, June–Nov. 1834 Journal, 5, MS 1986, CHL; "History of George A. Smith," 25.

13. Dunklin to J. Thornton, 6 June 1834, *The Evening and the Morning Star,* July 1834, 176; Charles Coulson Rich, 1834 Daybook, 14 June 1834, WA MSS 404, Beinecke Rare Book and Manuscript Library, Yale University, New Haven, Conn.

14. Martin, June–Nov. 1834 Journal, 7; minutes, 28–29 Aug. 1834, JSP, D4:127–129; "History of George A. Smith," 26–27.

15. "Proposition of the Jackson Committee to the Mormons and Their Answer," 16 June 1834, Phelps Collection of Missouri Documents; anonymous letter of 20 June 1834, in *Daily National Intelligencer* [Washington, D.C.], 23 July 1834, 3.

16. Rich, 1834 Daybook, 19 June 1834; Martin, 19–20 June 1834, June–Nov. 1834 Journal, 9–10.

17. JS et al., statement of 21 June 1834, JSP, D4:65–68.

18. Resolutions of Lafayette County committee, 23 June 1834, JSP, D4:79–80.

19. Revelation, 22 June 1834, JSP, D4:73–77.

20. "History of George A. Smith," 29.

21. *Richmond Palladium* [Ind.], 26 July 1834, 4; *Chardon Spectator and Geauga Gazette* [Ohio], 12 July 1834, 3.

22. JS to Lyman Wight et al., 16 Aug. 1834, JSP, D4:104.

23. Minutes, 11 Aug. 1834, JSP, D4: 100.

24. Minutes, 11 and 23 Aug. 1834, JSP, D4:100, 109.

25. JS to Lyman Wight et al., 16 Aug. 1834.

26. Minutes, 28–29 Aug. 1834, JSP, D4:132–133.

27. M&A, Oct. 1834, 10–11; minutes, 24 Sept. 1834, JSP, D4:174.

28. Cass to Gilbert et al., 1 May 1834, Phelps Collection of Missouri Documents.

Chapter Fifteen. Blessings (1834–1835)

1. "fanatical" MU, 156; JSJ, 30 April 1834, JSP, J1:43; "victims" in *Painesville Telegraph,* 16 Aug. 1833, 3.

2. MU, 19 ("farrago"), 145 ("immediate" and "Pope Joseph"), 161 ("army of Zion").

3. *Doctrine and Covenants of the Church of the Latter Day Saints* . . . (Kirtland, Ohio: F. G. Williams, 1835), preface.

4. *Doctrine and Covenants,* preface.

5. Peter L. Berger, *The Sacred Canopy: Elements of a Sociological Theory of Religion* (New York: Doubleday, 1967).

6. See William Shepard and H. Michael Marquardt, "The Relationship of Oliver Cowdery with Joseph Smith," JWHAJ 38 (Spring/Summer 2008): 95–130.

7. See the commentary in Richard L. Bushman, "Oliver's Joseph," in Alexander L. Baugh, ed., *Days Never to Be Forgotten: Oliver Cowdery* (Provo, Utah: Religious Studies Center, 2009), 4.

8. 5 Dec. 1834 entry, 1834–1836 History, JSP, H1:32–37.
9. See the discussion in JSP, D4:200–202.
10. Irene M. Bates and E. Gary Smith, *Lost Legacy: The Mormon Office of Presiding Patriarch*, rev. ed. (Urbana: University of Illinois Press, 2017), chapters 1 and 2.
11. H. Michael Marquardt, *Early Patriarchal Blessings of the Church of Jesus Christ of Latter-day Saints* (Salt Lake City: Smith-Pettit Foundation, 2007), 11.
12. Marquardt, *Early Patriarchal Blessings*, 11–12.
13. Marquardt, *Early Patriarchal Blessings*, 13–14.
14. Marquardt, *Early Patriarchal Blessings*, 15.
15. Marquardt, *Early Patriarchal Blessings*, 21 (Murdock), 40 (Jackman). See Samuel Morris Brown, *In Heaven as It Is on Earth: Joseph Smith and the Early Mormon Conquest of Death* (New York: Oxford University Press, 2012), 213ff.
16. Marquardt, *Early Patriarchal Blessings*, 531 (Wilson), 43 (Phelps).
17. MHC, B-1, Addenda, Note A; minutes, 14 Feb. 1835, JSP, D4:225. See also Brigham Young, discourse of 7 May 1861, JD, 9:89.
18. Minutes, 14 Feb. 1834, JSP, D4:224–227.
19. Record of the Twelve, 27 Feb. 1835, JSP, D4:252. See revelation, June 1829, JSP, D1:72.
20. Minutes, 1 March 1835, JSP, D4:263, 272. Benjamin E. Park, " 'Thou Wast Willing to Lay Down Thy Life for Thy Brethren': Zion's Blessings in the Early Church," JWHAJ 29 (2009): 27–37.
21. Minutes, 7 March 1835, JSP, D4:284–285.

Chapter Sixteen. Abraham (1835)

1. On Chandler and the mummies, see H. Donl Peterson, *The Story of the Book of Abraham: Mummies, Manuscripts, and Mormonism* (Salt Lake City: Deseret Book, 1995), chapters 1 and 9; S. J. Wolfe with Robert Singerman, *Mummies in Nineteenth Century America: Ancient Egyptians as Artifacts* (Jefferson, N.C.: McFarland, 2009), 96–107.
2. Peter Lacovara, "United States of America," in Andrew Bednarski et al., eds., *A History of World Egyptology* (Cambridge: Cambridge University Press, 2020), chapter 17.
3. *Cleveland Daily Advertiser*, 26 March 1835, 2; Wolfe and Singerman, *Mummies*, 103.
4. *Painesville Telegraph*, 27 March 1835, 3; *Cleveland Whig*, 25 March 1835, 1.
5. Oliver Cowdery to William Frye, 12 Dec. 1835, in M&A, Dec. 1835, 235.
6. William W. Phelps to Sally Phelps, 26 May 1835, William Wines Phelps Papers, Vault MSS 810, HBLL.
7. Certificate, 6 July 1835, JSP, D4:364.
8. *Cleveland Whig*, 25 March 1835; William W. Phelps to Sally Phelps 20 July 1835, in Journal History of the Church, 20 July 1835, CR 100 137, CHL.

9. Cowdery to Frye, 12 Dec. 1835, 235. Peterson, *Story of the Book of Abraham*, chapters 16, 17, and 19; JSP, R4:8.

10. Robert K. Ritner, *The Joseph Smith Egyptian Papyri: A Complete Edition*, rev. ed. (Salt Lake City: Signature Books, 2013), 183, 187–251. See also JSP, R4:3–18.

11. The literature on the Book of Abraham and the larger corpus of Joseph's Egyptian project is vast. I have relied most closely on Samuel Morris Brown, *Joseph Smith's Translation: The Words and Worlds of Early Mormonism* (New York: Oxford University Press, 2020), chapter 6; Robert K. Ritner, *The Joseph Smith Egyptian Papyri*; Dan Vogel, *Book of Abraham Apologetics: A Review and Critique* (Salt Lake City: Signature Books, 2021); Terryl Givens with Brian M. Hauglid, *The Pearl of Greatest Price: Mormonism's Most Controversial Scripture* (New York: Oxford University Press, 2019), chapter 2; Hauglid, " 'Translating an Alphabet to the Book of Abraham': Joseph Smith's Study of the Egyptian Language and His Translation of the Book of Abraham," in MacKay et al., eds., *Producing Ancient Scripture: Joseph Smith's Translation Projects in the Development of Mormon Christianity* (Salt Lake City: University of Utah Press, 2020), chapter 15; and the scholarly apparatus in JSP, R4.

12. "Katumin," in "Valuable Discovery of Hiden Records," JSP, R4:31; Charlotte Haven, "A Girl's Letters from Nauvoo," *Overland Monthly*, Dec. 1890, 623.

13. Book of Abraham manuscript, recorded by William W. Phelps and Warren Parrish, ca. July–Nov. 1835, JSP, R4:219. On the possible dating of this document, see Vogel, *Book of Abraham Apologetics*, 15–32.

14. MHC, B-1, 597.

15. Vogel, *Book of Abraham Apologetics*, chapter 3.

16. JSP, R4:119 ("father of many nations"), 57 ("first seen"), 125 ("first discovered"), 121–123 ("record"). See Brown, *Joseph Smith's Translation*, 215–223.

17. William W. Phelps to Sally Phelps, 11 Sept. 1835, Phelps Papers, HBLL; JSJ, 1 Oct. 1835, JSP, J1:67; JSP, R4:163 ("fifteen"), 169 ("delegated"), 165 ("millions"), 167 ("residence").

18. JSP, R4:163. Kristopher Stinson, "A New Jerusalem: Flavius Josephus in Early America," *Church History* 91 (Sept. 2022): 555–574.

19. Benjamin E. Park, " 'Reasonings Sufficient': Joseph Smith, Thomas Dick, and the Context(s) of Early Mormonism," JMH (Summer 2012): 210–224. See also Fawn M. Brodie, *No Man Knows My History: The Life of Joseph Smith*, rev. ed. (New York: Knopf, 1971), 171–172; John L. Brooke, *The Refiner's Fire: The Making of Mormon Cosmology, 1644–1844* (Cambridge: Cambridge University Press, 1994), 205–207. On the currency of ideas about an infinite and expanding universe, see Matthew Stewart, *Nature's God: The Heretical Origins of the American Republic* (New York: Norton, 2014), chapter 3.

20. Cowdery, JS, et al., to the Twelve, 4 Aug. 1835, JSP, D4:373–378.

21. JSJ, 26 Sept. ("satisfactorily"), 3 Oct. ("ancient"), and 5 Oct. ("School"), JSP, J1:66, 68.

22. Cowdery to Brigham Young, 27 Feb. 1848, Box 39, Folder 11, CR 1234 1, CHL; JSJ, 31 Oct. 1835, JSP, J1:80.

23. JSJ, 7–15 Oct. 1835, JSP, J1:69–72.

24. Minutes, 29 Oct. 1835, JSP, D5:27–28.

25. "rest" in minutes, 29 Oct. 1835, JSP, D5:29; JSJ, 29 Oct. 1835, JSP, J1:77.

26. JSJ, 29 Oct. 1835, JSP, J1:77–78; minutes, 29 Oct. 1835, JSP, D5:229.

27. JSJ, 31 Oct. 1835, JSP, J1:80–81.

28. JSJ, 3 Nov. 1835, JSP, J1:83.

29. JSJ, 8 Nov. 1835, JSP, J1:86.

30. JSJ, 12 Nov. 1835, JSP, J1:96–99.

31. Book of Abraham manuscript A, ca. July–Nov. 1835, JSP, R4:195. Joseph's scribes produced several manuscripts of this material in 1835, which the church published with additional text in 1842. On Abraham's father, see Dan Vogel, *Charisma under Pressure: Joseph Smith, American Prophet, 1831–1839* (Salt Lake City: Signature Books, 2023), 490.

32. David M. Goldenberg, *The Curse of Ham: Race and Slavery in Early Judaism, Christianity, and Islam* (Princeton, N.J.: Princeton University Press, 2003), chapter 12; Stephen R. Haynes, *Noah's Curse: The Biblical Justifications of American Slavery* (New York: Oxford University Press, 2002).

33. JSTOM, 105 ("seed of Cain were black") and 118 ("veil of darkness"); Book of Abraham manuscript A, JSP, R4:197. See Ryan Stuart Bingham, "Curses and Marks: Racial Dispensations and Dispensations of Race in Joseph Smith's Bible Revision and the Book of Abraham," JMH 41 (July 2015): 22–57.

34. M&A, April 1836, 290; "Elijah Able," Joseph F. Smith Papers, CHL, https://www.josephsmithpapers.org/bc-jsp/content/jsp/images/content/pdf/Docs/Able_bio_sketch.pdf. See Russell W. Stevenson, " 'A Negro Preacher': The Worlds of Elijah Ables," JMH 39 (Spring 2013): 165–254.

35. JSJ, 2 and 20 Nov. 1835, JSP, J1:82, 107. See Matthew J. Grey, "Approaching Egyptian Papyri through Biblical Language: Joseph Smith's Use of Hebrew in His Translation of the Book of Abraham," in MacKay et al., eds., *Producing Ancient Scripture*, 394–398.

36. Crosby, "A Biographical Sketch," 13–14, Jonathan Crosby Papers, MS B 89, Utah State Historical Society, Salt Lake City.

37. JSJ, 12 Dec. 1835, 120–121; JS to William Smith, ca. 18 Dec. 1835, JSJ, JSP, J1:131–134.

38. JS to William Smith, ca. 18 Dec. 1835.

39. Hyde to JS, 15 Dec. 1835, JSJ, JSP, J1:124–128.

40. JSJ, 15 and 17 Dec. 1835, JSP, J1:123–128.

41. JSJ, 17 Dec. 1835, JSP, J1:128; JS to William Smith, ca. 18 Dec. 1835.

42. JSJ, 1 Jan. 1836, JSP, J1:140–141.

Chapter Seventeen. Jubilee and Pentecost (1836)

1. JSJ, 1–2 Jan. 1836, JSP, J1:141–142.
2. JSJ, 5–6, JSP, J1:145; Joseph Smith, 1834–1836 History, JSP, H1:167.
3. JSJ, 16 Jan. 1836, JSP, J1:156–160.
4. Jonathan A. Stapley, *Holiness to the Lord: The Latter-day Saint Temple Liturgy* (forthcoming), chapter 2.
5. Oliver Cowdery Sketchbook, 16 Jan. 1836, in Leonard J. Arrington, ed., "Oliver Cowdery's Kirtland, Ohio, 'Sketchbook,'" *BYU Studies* 12 (1972): 416.
6. Revelation, 27 Feb. 1833, JSP, D3:21.
7. Cowdery Sketchbook, 16 Jan. 1836, 416. See Samuel Morris Brown, *In Heaven as It Is on Earth: Joseph Smith and the Early Mormon Conquest of Death* (New York: Oxford University Press, 2012), 157–158.
8. Cowdery Sketchbook, 17 Jan. 1836, 416.
9. William Phelps to Sally Phelps, Jan. 1836, MS 8711, CHL.
10. Cowdery Sketchbook, 21 Jan. 1836, 419; JSJ, 21 Jan. 1836, JSP, J1:166–167.
11. JSJ, 21 Jan. 1836, JSP, J1:167–168.
12. JSJ, 21–22 Jan. 1836, JSP, J1:170–171.
13. JSJ, 28 Jan. 1838, JSP, J1:174–175.
14. *Aurora* [New Lisbon, Ohio], 2 June 1836; JSJ, 17 Feb. 1836, JSP, J1:186.
15. JSP, 17 Feb. 1836, JSP, J1:186.
16. Cowdery Sketchbook, 15 Feb. 1836, 423–424; certificate, 30 March 1836, JSP, D5:216. See Shalom Goldman, "Joshua/James Seixas (1802–1874): Jewish Apostasy and Christian Hebraism in Early Nineteenth-Century America," *Jewish History* 7 (Spring 1993): 65–88.
17. John Corrill, *A Brief History of the Church* [1839], JSP, H2:151.
18. Orton to Roger Orton, ca. early Feb. 1836, in Laurence B. Johnson, ed., *The Pines Letters* (n.p.: n.p., 1854), 21; HOYP, 437.
19. David J. Howlett, *Kirtland Temple: The Biography of a Shared Mormon Sacred Space* (Urbana: University of Illinois Press, 2014), 19–20.
20. M&A, March 1836, 276.
21. M&A, March 1836, 276.
22. M&A, March 1836, 276–277.
23. M&A, March 1836, 277.
24. M&A, March 1836, 278.
25. M&A, March 1836, 280–281; Stephen Post, Journal, 27 March 1836, MS 1304, CHL; JSJ, 27 March 1836, JSP, J1:210–211.
26. Post, Journal, 28 March 1836; M&A, March 1836, 281.
27. Post, Journal, 27 March 1836.
28. JSJ, 29 March 1836, JSP, J1:211.
29. Partridge, Journal, 29 March 1836, MS 892, CHL.
30. JSJ, 30 March 1836, JSP, J1:213.
31. JSJ, 30 March 1836, JSP, J1:214–216.

32. JSJ, 3 April 1836, JSP, J1:219–222.

33. In January 1836, Joseph told a visitor that there were "between 15 hundred and 2,000 [church members] in this branch." JSJ, 21 Jan. 1836, JSP, J1:166.

Chapter Eighteen. Follies (1836–1837)

1. [Caleb M. Peck], "About the Mormons," in B. C. Fowles Vertical File, Western Reserve Historical Library, Cleveland, Ohio. See HOYP, 446.

2. Corrill, *A Brief History of the Church* [1839], JSP, H2:151.

3. Peck, "About the Mormons"; Oliver Olney, *The Absurdities of Mormonism* (Warsaw, Ill.: n.p., 1843), 4.

4. Benjamin F. Johnson to George F. Gibbs, 1903, 26, MS 1289, CHL.

5. I am grateful to David Golding for the dairy maid suggestion.

6. McLellin to Joseph Smith III, July 1872, in Stan Larson and Samuel J. Passey, eds., *The William E. McLellin Papers, 1854–1880* (Salt Lake City: Signature Books, 2007), 488–489; Johnson to Gibbs, 1903, 26.

7. Ann Eliza Young, *Wife No. 19 . . .* (Hartford, Conn.: Dustin, Gilman, 1875), 66; Oliver Cowdery to Warren Cowdery, 21 Jan. 1838, 80–83, Cowdery Letterbook, Huntington Library, San Marino, Calif.

8. Levi Ward Hancock and Mosiah Hancock, "Autobiography of Levi Ward Hancock," 1896, part 3, 63, MS 570, CHL. See the analysis in Don Bradley, " 'Dating' Fanny Alger: The Chronology and Consequences of a Proto-Polygamous Relationship," in Cheryl Bruno, ed., *Secret Covenants: New Insights on Early Mormon Polygamy* (Salt Lake City: Signature Books, 2024), 149–151.

9. Eliza J. Webb to Mary Bond, 24 April 1876, CCA; note by Eliza R. Snow and comments by Andrew Jenson, Box 49, Folder 16, Andrew Jenson Collection, MS 17956, CHL. See the discussion in Hales, *Polygamy*, 1: chapter 5.

10. Eliza J. Webb to Mary Bond, 4 May 1876, CCA. See Don Bradley and Christopher C. Smith, "Of Generations and Genders: Fanny Alger and the Adoptive Origins of Ritual Sealing," in Bruno, *Secret Covenants*, chapter 5. See also Brian C. Hales, "Fanny Alger and Joseph Smith's Pre-Nauvoo Reputation," JMH 35 (Fall 2009): 154.

11. Webb to Bond, 24 April 1876.

12. Levi Hancock, "The Life of Levi W. Hancock," 150, MS 8174, CHL.

13. See Leland H. Gentry and Todd M. Compton, *Fire and Sword: A History of the Latter-day Saints in Northern Missouri, 1836–1839* (Salt Lake City: Greg Kofford Books, 2011), chapter 2; Max Parkin, "A History of the Latter-day Saints in Clay County, Missouri, from 1833 to 1837" (Ph.D. diss., Brigham Young University, 1976), 247ff.

14. M&A, Aug. 1836, 353–355. See the account of the whipping in A. Wilson to Samuel Turrentine, 4 July 1836, in Durward T. Stokes, ed., "The Wilson Letters, 1835–1849," *Missouri Historical Review* 60 (July 1966): 509.

15. Sidney Rigdon et al., to John Thornton et al., 25 July 1836, JSP, D5:260–268.

16. See M&A, Sept. 1836, 372–377.

17. Ebenezer Robinson, "Items of Personal History of the Editor," *Return*, July 1889, 105–106. Robinson published his recollection more than a half century after Joseph's trip, but he was well acquainted with the prophet in the mid-1830s. He had boarded with Joseph, who baptized him in the fall of 1835. See David R. Proper, "Joseph Smith and Salem," *Essex Institute Historical Collections* 100 (Apr. 1964): 88–98; Richard Lloyd Anderson, "The Mature Joseph Smith and Treasure Seeking," *BYU Studies* 24 (1984): 489–560.

18. [Hawthorne], "Peter Goldthwait's Treasure," *Token and Atlantic Souvenir* (Boston: American Stationers, 1848), 37–65 (quote on 43).

19. Revelation, 6 Aug. 1836, JSP, D5:277–278; Oliver Cowdery to William Cowdery, 24 Aug. 1836, M&A, Oct. 1836, 386–393. See Spencer W. McBride, "Joseph Smith's Quest to Secure Religious Liberty for All," *Ensign* [Salt Lake City], Feb. 2019.

20. JS to Emma Smith, 19 Aug. 1836, JSP, D5:282–283.

21. JS to Emma Smith, 19 Aug. 1836.

22. Mortgage to Peter French, 5 Oct. 1836, JSP, D5:295–299; Promissory note to Bailey, Keeler, and Remsen, 12 Oct. 1836, https://www.josephsmithpapers.org/paper-summary/promissory-note-to-bailey-keeler-remsen-12-october-1836/1.

23. Stephen Mihm, *A Nation of Counterfeiters: Capitalists, Con Men, and the Making of the United States* (Cambridge, Mass.: Harvard University Press, 2007).

24. Van Buren, *The Autobiography of Martin Van Buren* (Washington, D.C.: Government Printing Office, 1920), 2:625. See Daniel Walker Howe, *What Hath God Wrought: The Transformation of America, 1815–1848* (New York: Oxford University Press, 2007), chapter 10; Mihm, *Nation of Counterfeiters*, chapter 3.

25. Kirtland Safety Society Bank Stock Ledger, 1836–1837, 13–14, MS 8137, CHL (the original is held at the Chicago Historical Society). See Jeffrey N. Walker, "The Kirtland Safety Society and the Fraud of Grandison Newell," *BYU Studies* 54 (2015): 35–41; D. Paul Sampson and Larry T. Wimmer, "The Kirtland Safety Society: The Stock Ledger Book and the Bank Failure," *BYU Studies* 12 (1972): 427–436. See also the introductions and annotations in JSP, D5, Part V.

26. WWJ, 6 Jan. 1837.

27. Willard Richards to Hepzibah Richards, 20 Jan. 1837, MS 12765, CHL.

28. *Cleveland Daily Gazette*, 12 Jan. 1837, 2.

29. *Painesville Republican*, 19 Jan. 1837, 2. See HOYP, chapter 33.

30. *Ohio Star* [Ravenna], 30 March 1837, 3. See Walker, "Kirtland Safety Society," 50–55.

31. Jessica M. Lepler, *The Many Panics of 1837: People, Politics, and the Creation of a Transatlantic Financial Crisis* (Cambridge: Cambridge University Press, 2013), chapters 2 and 3.

32. M&A, April 1837, 387–388; "streets" in WWJ, 9 April 1837.

33. WWJ, 9 April 1837.

34. WWJ, 13 April 1837. See Walker, "Kirtland Safety Society," 60–69.

35. Emma Smith to JS, 25 April and 3 May 1837, JSP, D5:371–372 ("small"), 374–376 ("pacify"); twenty persons in the household in Mary Fielding to Mercy Thompson, June 1837, MS 2779, CHL.

36. Emma Smith to JS, 3 May 1837.

37. Kirtland Safety Society Ledger, 227–228. See HOYP, 524–526.

38. Pratt to JS, 23 May 1837, JSP, D5:389–391. See Terryl L. Givens and Matthew J. Grow, *Parley P. Pratt: The Apostle Paul of Mormonism* (New York: Oxford University Press, 2011), 97–99.

39. Johnson and Pratt to Whitney and Kirtland High Council, 29 May 1837, JSP, D5:397; minutes, 29 May 1837, Kirtland High Council Minutebook, 230, MS 3432, CHL.

40. M&A, Aug. 1837, 560. See HOYP, 528.

41. Mary Fielding to Mercy Thompson, June 1837.

42. Mary Fielding to Mercy Thompson, June 1837.

43. Joseph Smith History, B-1, 767 and Addendum S. See "Introduction to Seymour Griffith v. Rigdon and JS," in JSP, LR.

44. LB, 597–598; Snow, *Biography and Family Record of Lorenzo Snow* (Salt Lake City: Deseret News, 1884), 20–21. See the analysis in Ronald K. Esplin, "The Emergence of Brigham Young and the Twelve to Mormon Leadership, 1830–1841" (Ph.D. diss., Brigham Young University, 1981), 293–294.

45. Vilate Kimball to Heber C. Kimball, 12 Sept. 1837, MS 12476, CHL. See also Mary Fielding to Mercy Thompson, ca. Aug.–Sept. 1837, MS 2779, CHL; Anson Call reminiscences, ca. 1856, MS 313, CHL.

46. Mary Fielding to Mercy Thompson, ca. Aug.–Sept. 1837.

47. Young in WWJ, 25 June 1857; JS to John Corrill et al., 4 Sept. 1837, JSP, D5:430.

48. William W. Phelps to JS, 7 July 1837, JSP, D5:402. See Stephen C. LeSueur, "Missouri's Failed Compromise: The Creation of Caldwell County for the Mormons," JMH 31 (Fall 2005): 113–144.

49. *Elders' Journal* [Far West, Mo.], Nov. 1837, 27.

50. Minutes, 6 Nov. 1837, JSP, D5:466–468; LB, 596–597.

51. Oliver Cowdery to Warren Cowdery, 21 Jan. 1838.

52. Walker, "Kirtland Safety Society," 79–92.

53. "tenor" and "denies" in Vilate Kimball to Heber Kimball, 19 Jan. 1838, MS 12476, CHL; Marsh to Wilford Woodruff, 30 April 1838, MS 1352, CHL.

54. See the analysis in Don Bradley and Christopher C. Smith, "Of Generations and Genders: Fanny Alger and the Adoptive Origins of Ritual Sealing," in Bruno, *Secret Covenants*, chapter 5.

55. John Smith to George A. Smith, 1 Jan. 1838, MS 1322, CHL. It is possible that church leaders never formally excommunicated Martin Harris. In May 1843, Parley Pratt reported that Harris was "still in the church." Alternatively, he

may have regained his fellowship, or he simply may have continued to express his faith in the church. Pratt to John Van Cott, 7 May 1843, MS 5238, CHL.

56. *Painesville Telegraph*, 5 Jan. 1838, 3; Hepzibah Richards to Willard Richards, 18 Jan. 1838, Willard Richards Papers, MS 1490, CHL; article of agreement, 4 Jan. 1838, MS 24664, CHL; Vilate Kimball to Heber Kimball, 19 Jan. 1838.

57. Revelation, 12 Jan. 1838, JSP, D5:501–502.

58. Hepzibah Richards to Willard Richards, 18 Jan. 1838.

Chapter Nineteen. East of Eden (1838)

1. JSJ, 1 March 1838, JSP, J1:237.

2. JSJ, 1 March 1838, JSP, J1:237–238.

3. Oliver Cowdery to Warren Cowdery, 21 Jan. 1838; Oliver Cowdery to Warren Cowdery and Lyman Cowdery, 4 Feb. 1838, both in Cowdery Letterbook, Huntington Library, San Marino, Calif.

4. Minutes, 26 Jan., 5 Feb., and 10 March 1838, 95–99, 107, "Record Book of Christ's Church of Latter Day Saints" (Minute Book 2, "Far West Record"), LR 7874 21, CHL.

5. Minutes, 12 April, 1838, JSP, D6:84–94.

6. Minutes, 12 April 1838, JSP, D6:91.

7. Revelation, 26 April 1838, JSP, D6:114–118.

8. JSJ, 18 May–1 June, 1838, JSP, J1:271; instructions on priesthood, ca. spring 1835, JSP, D4:317. See Alexander L. Baugh, "The History and Doctrine of the Adam-ondi-Ahman Revelation (D&C 116)," in Craig James Ostler et al., eds., *Foundations of the Restoration: Fulfillment of the Covenant Purposes* (Salt Lake City: Deseret Book, 2016), chapter 9. On the location of the Garden of Eden in Jackson County, see Reed Peck to "Dear Friends," 18 Sept. 1839, 19–20, Huntington Library, San Marino, Calif.

9. Minutes, 28 June 1838, JSP, D6:165–167.

10. Avard et al., to Cowdery et al., ca. 17 June 1838, copy in Box 2, Folder 24, MWP. See the introduction at https://www.josephsmithpapers.org/paper-summary/appendix-1-letter-to-oliver-cowdery-and-others-circa-17-june-1838/1#full-transcript.

11. Reed Peck to "Dear Friends," 18 Sept. 1839, 23–26.

12. JSJ, ca. 4 July 1838, JSP, J1:278; *Ensign of Liberty* [Kirtland, Ohio], March 1847, 8–9.

13. See Alexander L. Baugh, " 'We Have a Company of Danites in These Times': The Danites, Joseph Smith, and the 1838 Missouri-Mormon Conflict," JMH 45 (July 2019): 1–25.

14. Corrill, *A Brief History of the Church* [1839], JSP, H2:166–167; Robinson in JSJ, 27 July 1837, JSP, J1:293. On the Caldwell County militia, see JSP, D6:686–687.

15. *Oration Delivered by Mr. S. Rigdon on the 4th of July, 1838* (Far West, Mo.: Journal Office, 1838).

16. *Return* [Davis City, Iowa], Nov. 1889, 170; *Elders' Journal* [Far West, Mo.], Aug. 1838, 54.

17. Some church members recalled that Joseph interpreted the blast as a sign of impending judgment upon the nation and its constitution. See, for instance, Henry W. Bigler, Journal, 23, MS 1853, CHL.

18. JSJ, 28–29 July, JSP, J1:294. See Leland H. Gentry and Todd M. Compton, *Fire and Sword: A History of the Latter-day Saints in Northern Missouri, 1836–39* (Salt Lake City: Greg Kofford, 2011), 466.

19. "rough" in Bigler, Journal, 22; Swartzell, *Mormonism Exposed, Being a Journal of a Residence in Missouri . . .* (Pekin, Ohio: n.p., 1840), 20–23.

20. JSJ, 10 May 1838, JSP, J1:267–268; Rigdon to Sterling Price, 8 Sept. 1838, MS 2560, CHL. See Steve LeSueur, "Mixing Politics with Religion: A Closer Look at Electioneering and Voting in Caldwell and Daviess Counties in 1838," JWHAJ 33 (Spring/Summer 2013): 184–208.

21. Rigdon to Sterling Price, 8 Sept. 1838; John Lowe Butler, "A Short Account of an Affray," 1859, 1–2, MS 2418, CHL. See Reed C. Durham Jr., "The Election Day Battle at Gallatin," *BYU Studies* 13 (Autumn 1972): 36–61.

22. *Document Containing the Correspondence, Orders, &c., in Relation to the Disturbances with the Mormons . . .* (Fayette, Mo.: Boon's Lick Democrat, 1841), 161.

23. JSJ, 8 and 9 Aug. 1838, JSP, J1:300–301; Joseph Smith, Affidavit, 5 Sept. 1838, JSP, D6:222–225.

24. *Daily Missouri Republican* [St. Louis], 3 Sept. 1838, 2; Peniston, affidavit of 10 Aug. 1838, MS 20139, CHL; JSJ, 16–18 Aug. 1838, JSP, J1:304–305. On the developing conflict between the Saints and anti-Mormons in Daviess County, see Alexander L. Baugh, *A Call to Arms: The 1838 Mormon Defense of Northern Missouri* (Provo, Utah: BYU Studies, 2000), chapter 5.

25. JSJ, 2 Sept. 1838, JSP, J1: 313; Adjutant General B. M. Lisle to David Atchison, 30 Aug. 1838, Box 1, Folder 15, MWP. On behalf of Governor Boggs, Lisle sent similar orders to other militia officers.

26. JSJ, 4 and 7 Sept. 1838, JSP, J1:314, 316–317.

27. See Corrill, *A Brief History of the Church*, JSP, H2:173–174.

28. Petition, 22 Sept. 1838, Box 1, Folder 23, MWP. On the conflict in Carroll County, see Gentry and Compton, *Fire and Sword*, 191–201; Baugh, *Call to Arms*, chapter 6; Keith W. Perkins, "De Witt—Prelude to Expulsion," in Arnold K. Garr and Clark V. Johnson, eds., *Regional Studies in Latter-day Saint Church History—Missouri* (Provo, Utah: BYU Department of Church History, 1994), 261–280.

29. John Murdock, 1 Oct. 1838, Journal, 1830–1859, Folder 2, MS 1194, CHL.

30. H. G. Parks to Atchison, 7 Oct. 1838, in *Document Containing*, 37.

31. Lucas to Boggs, 4 Oct. 1838, Box 1, Folder 29, MWP; *Missouri Republican (For the Country)* [St. Louis], 10 Nov. 1838, 3. See Gentry and Compton, *Fire and Sword*, 201–203.

32. See Gentry and Compton, *Fire and Sword*, 203–205.

33. Albert P. Rockwood, Journal, 14 Oct. 1838, in Dean C. Jessee and David J. Whittaker, eds., "The Last Months of Mormonism in Missouri: The Albert Perry Rockwood Journal," *BYU Studies* 28 (Winter 1988): 21.

34. Warren Foote, Autobiography and Journals, typescript, 11, MS 12206, CHL.

35. Reed Peck to "Dear Friends," 78–79.

36. John Smith, 22 Oct. 1838, 1836–1840 Journal, MS 1326, CHL.; King to Boggs, 24 Oct. 1838, Box 1, Folder 44, MWP; Testimony of Hinkle, 12 Nov. 1838, in *Document Showing the Testimony Given before the Judge of the Fifth Judicial Circuit of the State of Missouri, on the Trial of Joseph Smith, Jr.* (Washington, D.C.: Blair & Rives, 1841), 22. See Gentry and Compton, *Fire and Sword*, 272–280.

37. Marsh affidavit, 24 Oct. 1838, Box 1, Folder 47, MWP.

38. Bogart to Atchison, 23 Oct. 1838, Box 1, Folder 39, MWP. See Baugh, *Call to Arms*, 99–102.

39. Gentry and Compton, *Fire and Sword*, 284–289; Baugh, *Call to Arms*, 102–114.

40. Drusilla Hendricks autobiography, ca. 1877, 20, MS 123, CHL.

41. There are many accounts of the Hawn's Mill Massacre. I have relied on Gentry and Compton, *Fire and Sword*, chapter 10; Baugh, *Call to Arms*, chapter 9.

42. Account of McBride's death in Nathan K. Knight, Autobiographical Sketch, MS 2852, CHL.

43. Amanda Smith, in Tullidge, *The Women of Mormondom* (New York: Tullidge & Crandall, 1877), 126–127.

44. Amanda Barnes Smith, Autobiography, 1858, 6, MS 2409, CHL.

45. Boggs to John B. Clark, 27 Oct. 1838, copy in Box 1, Folder 49, MWP. On the lack of connection between Boggs's order and the massacre at Hawn's Mill, see Baugh, *Call to Arms*, 127; Gentry and Compton, *Fire and Sword*, 337–338.

46. See Baugh, *Call to Arms*, 136–138.

47. Hinkle, Testimony, 12 Nov. 1838, 24.

48. Corrill, *A Brief History of the Church*, 183–187. See Baugh, *Call to Arms*, 140–142.

49. JS to Emma Smith, 4 Nov. 1838, JSP, D6:280; Corrill, *A Brief History of the Church*, 184; Hinkle to Phelps, 14 Aug. 1844, in *Messenger and Advocate of the Church of Christ* [Pittsburgh, Pa.], 1 Aug. 1845, 287.

50. JS, "Bill of Damages," 4 June 1839, JSP, D6:501–502.

51. Hyrum Smith, 1 July 1843 Testimony, 14, Nauvoo Records (1841–1845), MS 16800, CHL.

52. JSJ, 30 Dec. 1842, JSP, J2:198; LB, 656, 672–673. See T&S, July 1839, 6.

Chapter Twenty. Hell Surrounded with Demons (1839)

1. John Smith, Affidavit, 8 Jan. 1840, in Clark V. Johnson, ed., *Mormon Redress Petitions: Documents of the 1833–1838 Missouri Conflict* (Salt Lake City: Religious Studies Center, Brigham Young University, 1992), 540; Andrea G. Radke-Moss, "Silent Memories of Missouri: Mormon Women and Men and Sexual Assault in Group Memory and Religious Identity," in Rachel Cope et al., eds., *Mormon Women's History: Beyond Biography* (Madison, N.J.: Fairleigh Dickinson University Press, 2017), chapter 3.

2. JS to Emma Smith, 4 Nov. 1838, JSP, D6:281; Emma Smith, Deposition, 22 April 1842, in JSP, D6:348, n. 444; John A. Gordon, Declaration to the Clay County Circuit Court, ca. 6 March 1839, JSP, D6:337.

3. JS to Emma Smith, 4 Nov. 1838, JSP, D:280; Lyman Wight, Journal, 4–5 Nov. 1838, in *History of the Reorganized Church* (Lamoni, Iowa.: Board of Publication, 1987), 2:295–296.

4. JS to Emma Smith, 12 Nov. 1838, JSP, D6:291–292.

5. King to Boggs, 24 Oct. 1838, Box 1, Folder 44, MWP.

6. On the hearing, see Gordon A. Madsen, "Joseph Smith and the Missouri Court of Inquiry: Austin A. King's Quest for Hostages," *BYU Studies* 43 (2004):93–136.

7. Testimony of Avard, 12 Nov. 1838, in *Document Showing the Testimony Given before the Judge of the Fifth Judicial Circuit of the State of Missouri, on the Trial of Joseph Smith, Jr.* (Washington, D.C.: Blair & Rives, 1841), 97.

8. JS et al., petition to George Tompkins, March 1839, JSP, D6:345.

9. Bogart to the Postmaster, Quincy, Illinois, 22 April 1839, MS 5704, CHL; "screeching" in JS to Emma Smith, 4 April 1839, JSP, D6:403; JS to Emma Smith, 1 Dec. 1838, JSP, D6:294.

10. JS et al., to Edward Partridge, 20 March 1839, JSP, D6:361; "vomited" in Hyrum Smith, 1 July 1843 Testimony, 22, Nauvoo Records (1841–1845), MS 16800, CHL. See Dean C. Jessee, " 'Walls, Grates and Screeking Iron Doors': The Prison Experience of Mormon Leaders in Missouri, 1838–1839," in Davis Bitton and Maureen Ursenbach Beecher, eds., *New Views of Mormon History: A Collection of Essays in Honor of Leonard J. Arrington* (Salt Lake City: University of Utah Press, 1987), 19–42.

11. LB, 676. See William G. Hartley, " 'Almost Too Intolerable a Burthen': The Winter Exodus from Missouri, 1838–39," JMH 18 (Fall 1992): 11–13.

12. 13 Dec. 1838, "Record Book of Christ's Church of Latter Day Saints" (Minute Book 2, "Far West Record"), LR 7874 21, CHL.

13. JS to Kimball and Young, 16 Jan. 1839, JSP, D6:313–316.

14. Far West Committee minutes, 29 Jan. 1839, MS 2564, CHL.

15. JS et al., Memorial to the U.S. Senate and House of Representatives, ca. Jan. 1840, JSP, D7:169; Mary Audentia Smith Anderson, ed., "The Memoirs of President Joseph Smith," *Saints' Herald* [Independence, Mo.], 6 Nov. 1934, 1416. See Hartley, " 'Almost Too Intolerable a Burthen.' "

16. Hyrum Smith, 1 July 1843 Testimony, 22; Sidney Rigdon, 1 July 1843 Testimony, 23–24, both in Nauvoo Records (1841–1845), MS 16800, CHL. See Jeffrey N. Walker, "Habeas Corpus in Early Nineteenth-Century Mormonism: Joseph Smith's Legal Bulwark for Personal Freedom," *BYU Studies* 52 (2013): 25–28.

17. *State of Missouri v. David Holeman, et al.* [1839], Clay County and Historical Library, Liberty, Mo.

18. "bigots," "till it was mended," "day and night" in Hyrum Smith to Mary Fielding Smith, 16 March 1839, MS 2779, CHL; Wight, Journal, 4 March 1839, in *History of the Reorganized Church*, 2:317; "in chains" in Hyrum Smith, Journal, 17 March 1839, MS 2945, CHL.

19. JS to Emma Smith, 21 March 1839, JSP, D6:374–375.

20. JS to Partridge et al., 20 March 1839, JSP, D6:360–372.

21. JS to Partridge et al., 22 March 1839, JSP, D6:400.

22. JS to Emma Smith, 4 April 1839, JSP, D6:403.

23. Hyrum Smith, Journal, 11 April 1839. See Alexander L. Baugh, " 'We Took Our Change of Venue to the State of Illinois': The Gallatin Hearing and the Escape of Joseph Smith and the Mormon Prisoners from Missouri, April 1839," *Mormon Historical Studies* 2 (Spring 2001): 59–65.

24. Peter H. Burnett, *Recollections and Opinions of an Old Pioneer* (New York: D. Appleton, 1880), 66–67.

25. Burnett, *Recollections*, 67–68. See Baugh, " 'Change of Venue,' " 77, n. 17.

26. Baugh, " 'Change of Venue,' " 75. See JS, promissory note to John Brassfield, JSP, D6:422–426.

27. Testimony of Hyrum Smith, 1 July 1843, 26.

28. JSJ, 30 Dec. 1842, JSP, J2:199.

29. Huntington, Statement, ca. 1855, Joseph Smith History Documents, CR 100 396.

30. $50,000 in MHC, C-1, 924.

31. JS to Emma Smith, 21 March 1839.

Chapter Twenty-One. Keys (1839–1840)

1. Clark, discourse of 6 Nov. 1838, in Joseph Smith, "Letterbook 2," 0–1, MS 155, CHL.

2. Lyndon W. Cook, "Isaac Galland—Mormon Benefactor," *BYU Studies* 19 (Spring 1979):261–284.

3. WWJ, 3 May 1839; minutes, 4 May 1839, JSP, D6:444.

4. Rigdon to JS, 10 April 1839, JSP, D6:408; minutes, 5 May 1839, JSP, D6:447.

5. Jacob G. Bigler, Autobiography, 1907, MS 10735, CHL.

6. Park, KoN, 21–22; Glen M. Leonard, *Nauvoo: A Place of Peace, a People of Promise* (Salt Lake City: Deseret Book 2002), 46–47.

7. Baptism in JSJ, 3 July 1839, JSP, J1:345; Galland to Samuel Swasey, 22 July 1839, CCA.

8. JS, discourse of 27 June 1839, JSP, D6:510. See Benjamin E. Park, "'A Uniformity So Complete': Early Mormon Angelology," *Intermountain West Journal of Religious Studies* 2 (2010): 1–37.

9. "damned Mormons" in Hyrum Smith, 1 July 1843 Testimony, 25, Nauvoo Records (1841–1845), MS 16800, CHL; JS, discourse of ca. 26 June–2 July 1839, JSP, D6:524.

10. JS, discourse of ca. 26 June–2 July 1839, JSP, D6:525–526.

11. JS, discourse of Summer 1839, JSP, D6:542–545.

12. WWJ, 2 July 1839.

13. Huntington, "History of Oliver Boardman Huntington," 53, Box 1, Folder 2, MSS 162, HBLL; Zina Huntington in Edward W. Tullidge, *Women of Mormondom* (New York: Tullidge & Crandall, 1877), 213.

14. WWJ, 22 July 1839.

15. "hole" in JS to Horace Hotchkiss, 25 Aug. 1841, JSP, D8:238; "known" in Elizabeth Haven to Elizabeth H. Bullard, 12 Sept.1839–9 Oct. 1839, MS 941, CHL; minutes, 5 Oct. 1839, JSP, D7:18; "beautiful situation" in T&S, 15 Jan. 1841, 273–274.

16. JS to Emma Smith, 9 Nov. 1839, JSP, D7:56.

17. Emma Smith to JS, 6 Dec. 1839, JSP, D7:75–77.

18. MHC, C-1, 973.

19. Dickens, *American Notes for General Circulation* (London: Chapman & Hall, 1842), 1:272.

20. $500 in MHC, E-1, 1793; *Alexandria Gazette* [Va.], 27 Dec. 1839, 3.

21. JS letter to Hyrum Smith, 5 Dec. 1839, JSP, D7: 69. See Spencer W. Mc-Bride, "When Joseph Smith Met Martin Van Buren: Mormonism and the Politics of Religion," *Church History* 85 (March 2016): 150–158.

22. Alfred Woodward, "Developments of Mr. Joseph Smith Jr.'s Head," JSP, D7:119–124. See Davis Bitton and Gary L. Bunker, "Phrenology among the Mormons," *Dialogue* 9 (Spring 1974): 42–61.

23. Davis to Mary Davis, 6 Feb. 1840, MS 522, CHL. See JSP, D7:177–179.

24. JS et al., Memorial to the U.S. Senate and House of Representatives, ca. Oct.1839–Jan. 1840, JSP, D7:143–174 (quotes on 171, 174).

25. *Daily National Intelligencer* [Washington, D.C.], 29 Jan. 1840, 2.

26. JS to Emma Smith, 20 Jan. 1840, JSP, D7:136.

27. *New York Spectator*, 7 May 1840, 2; JS to Robert D. Foster, 11 March 1840, JSP, D7:228–229.

28. Minutes, 6 March 1840, JSP, D7:215; Elias Smith and JS to Elias Higbee, 7 March 1840, JSP, D7:218; "influential men" and "advocates" in Phebe Woodruff to Wilford Woodruff, 8 March 1840, MS 19509, CHL.

29. Elias Higbee to JS, 26 Feb. 1840, JSP, D7:199; *Journal of the Senate of the United States*, 26th Cong., 1st Sess., 23 March 1840, 259–260.

30. "fop" in JS to Hyrum Smith, 5 Dec. 1839, 70; "burst" in JS, discourse of 1 March 1840, JSP, D7:202; "influence" in minutes, 6 April 1840, JSP, D7:251. See *Peoria Register and North-Western Gazetteer*, 17 April 1840, 2.

Chapter Twenty-Two. Saviors on Mount Zion (1840)

1. JS, discourse of ca. 19 July 1840, JSP, D7:336–340. Population figures from JS to John C. Bennett, 8 Aug. 1840, JSP, D7:372; *Daily Chronicle* [Cincinnati], 26 Aug. 1840, 2. See JSP, D7:311.
2. Vilate Kimball to Heber Kimball, 11 Oct. 1840, MS 18732, CHL.
3. Lorenzo Wasson et al., to David Hale, 12–19 Feb. 1841, JSP, D8:41.
4. Emily Dow Partridge Young, autobiographical sketch, ca. 1887, Andrew Jenson Collection, MS 17956, CHL; Emily Young, Deposition, Temple Lot Transcript, Respondent's Testimony, part 3, 356, Box 1, Folder 15, MS 1160, CHL.
5. JS to Nauvoo High Council, 18 June 1840, JSP, D7:297; minutes, 3 July 1840, JSP, D7:309–310. See Glen M. Leonard, *Nauvoo: A Place of Peace, a People of Promise* (Salt Lake City: Deseret Book, 2002), 54–58.
6. Phebe Woodruff to Wilford Woodruff, 6–19 Oct. 1840, MS 19509, CHL.
7. Phebe Woodruff to Wilford Woodruff, 6–19 Oct. 1840. See Guy Williams, "An Apocalyptic and Magical Interpretation of Paul's 'Beast Fight' in Ephesus (1 Corinthians 15:32)," *Journal of Theological Studies* 57 (April 2006): 42–56.
8. See Johnny Stephenson and H. Michael Marquardt, "Origin of the Baptism for the Dead Doctrine," JWHAJ 37 (Spring/Summer 2017): 138–139.
9. Vilate Kimball to Heber Kimball, 6 Sept. 1840, MS 3276, CHL. See Samuel Morris Brown, *In Heaven as It Is on Earth: Joseph Smith and the Early Mormon Conquest of Death* (New York: Oxford University Press, 2012), chapter 1.
10. Vilate Kimball to Heber Kimball, 6 Sept. 1840; T&S, Sept. 1840, 176.
11. See Jane Neyman, Statement, 29 Nov. 1854, CR 100 396, Joseph Smith History Documents, CHL; Journal History of the Church, 15 Aug. 1840, CR 100 137, CHL.
12. JSJ, 21 Jan. 1836, JSP, J1:168; "hereafter" in *Elder's Journal* [Far West, Mo.], July 1838, 43.
13. Brigham Young to Mary Ann Young, 26 May 1840, George W. Thatcher Blair Collection, MS 15616, CHL, transcript in Ronald O. Barney, "Letters of a Missionary Apostle to His Wife: Brigham Young to Mary Ann Angell Young, 1839–1841," *BYU Studies* 38 (1999): 178–181. See the discussion in Christopher James Blythe, "Ann Booth's Vision and Early Conceptions of Redeeming the Dead among Latter-day Saints," *BYU Studies* 56 (2017): 105–122.
14. MHC, C-1, 1097; LB, 713.
15. LB, 714–723; "ruthless" in JSJ, 23 Aug. 1842, JSP, J2:116. See also Don Carlos Smith to George A. Smith, 28 Dec. 1840, Box 4, Folder 4, George A. Smith Papers, MS 1322, CHL.
16. "Sister Booth's" in Vilate Kimball to Heber C. Kimball, 11 Oct. 1840, MS 18732, CHL; "John Wesley," "released," and "claim" in Phebe Woodruff to

Wilford Woodruff, 6 Oct. 1840; "saviors" in minutes, 3 Oct. 1841, JSP, D8:287. See Ryan G. Tobler, " 'Saviors on Mount Zion': Mormon Sacramentalism, Mortality, and the Baptism for the Dead," JMH 39 (Fall 2013): 182–238.

17. Vilate Kimball to Heber Kimball, 11 Oct. 1840; Phebe Woodruff to Wilford Woodruff, 6 Oct. 1840; William Appleby, Autobiography and Journal, May 1841, MS 1401, CHL.

18. Susan Easton Black and Harvey Bischoff Black, *Annotated Record of Baptisms for the Dead, 1840–1845* (Provo, Utah: Brigham Young University Press, 2002), 6:3356–3357, 3361, 3378–3380.

19. Black and Black, *Annotated Record*, 3:1573, 2016, 5:3352, 2:823; Theodore Calvin Pease, *Illinois Election Returns, 1818–1848* (Springfield: Illinois State Historical Library, 1923), 117; "Nauvoo Baptisms for the Dead in Mississippi River (Sept. 1840–Nov. 1841)," 10, Family History Library, Salt Lake City, https://www.familysearch.org/library/books/records/item/386499-redirection.

20. Franklin D. Richards, Journal, 11 April 1841, typescript in MS 1215, CHL. See Jonathan A. Stapley and David W. Grua, "Rebaptism in the Church of Jesus Christ of Latter-day Saints," *BYU Studies* 61 (2022): 59–96; Jonathan A. Stapley and Kristine Wright, " 'They Shall Be Made Whole': A History of Baptism for Health," JMH 34 (Fall 2008): 69–112.

21. JSJ, 9 July 1843, JSP, J3:55; Vilate Kimball to Heber Kimball, 11 Oct. 1840.

22. JS, discourse of ca. 25 April 1841, https://www.josephsmithpapers.org/paper-summary/discourse-25-april-1841-as-reported-by-julius-alexander-reed/. On Bennett, see Andrew F. Smith, *The Saintly Scoundrel: The Life and Times of Dr. John Cook Bennett* (Urbana: University of Illinois Press, 1997).

23. T&S, Oct. 1840, 186.

24. Ford, *A History of Illinois . . .* (Chicago: S. C. Griggs, 1854), 265; Park, KoN, 55.

25. Park, KoN, 55; Spencer W. McBride, *Joseph Smith for President: The Prophet, the Assassins, and the Fight for American Religious Freedom* (New York: Oxford University Press, 2021), 42–45.

26. Minutes, 3 Feb. 1841, JSP, D8:26; Commission from Thomas Carlin, 10 March 1841, JSP, D8:68.

27. T&S, 15 Jan. 1841, 276.

Chapter Twenty-Three. Sealings (1841–1842)

1. Joseph B. Noble, Deposition, Temple Lot Transcript, Respondent's Testimony, part 3, 395, Box 1, Folder 16, MS 1160, CHL. See Hales, *Polygamy*, 1:227–233; Compton, ISL, chapter 3.

2. Joseph Bates Noble affidavit, 38, Box 1, Folder 46, MS 3423, CHL.

3. William W. Phelps to Sally Phelps, 16 Sept. 1835, Vault MSS 810, HBLL.

4. Disguise and "first sealing" in Franklin D. Richards, Journal, 22 Jan. 1869, MS 1215, CHL; "whisper" in George F. Richards, Journal, 10 June 1883, https://www.churchhistorianspress.org/george-f-richards/1880s/1883 /1883-06.

5. Joseph B. Noble, Deposition, Temple Lot Transcript, Respondent's Testimony, part 3, 396.

6. WCJ, 17 May 1843. See Gary James Bergera, "Identifying the Earliest Mormon Polygamists, 1841–1844," *Dialogue* 38 (Fall 2005): 17–18.

7. See Compton, ISL, chapter 3.

8. "costume" in Ronald O. Barney, ed., *The Mormon Vanguard Brigade of 1847: Norton Jacob's Record* (Logan: Utah State University Press, 2005), 31; T&S, 15 April 1841, 381.

9. Revelation, 19 Jan. 1841, JSP, D7:514–518.

10. *Western World* [Warsaw, Ill.], 7 April 1841, 3; T&S, 15 May 1841, 414.

11. *Warsaw Signal* [Ill.], 19 May 1841, 2.

12. *Warsaw Signal*, 2 June 1841, 2; *Warsaw Signal*, 9 June 1941, 2.

13. *Warsaw Signal*, 9 June 1941, 2; *Wasp* [Nauvoo, Ill.], 23 April 1842, 2–3 ("Devil" and "Fat Turkey"), 30 April 1842, 2 ("Thom-ass Sharp" and "far-famed").

14. See "Introduction to Extradition of JS et al. for Treason and Other Crimes," JSP, LR.

15. T&S, 15 June 1841, 447–449. See Jeffrey N. Walker, "Habeas Corpus in Early Nineteenth-Century Mormonism: Joseph Smith's Legal Bulwark for Personal Freedom," *BYU Studies* 52 (2013): 34–39; John S. Dinger, "Joseph Smith and the Development of Habeas Corpus in Nauvoo, 1841–44," JMH 36 (Summer 2010): 142–144.

16. Don Carlos Smith to Oliver Granger, 11 July 1841, MS 7043, CHL.

17. George A. Smith to Joseph Smith III, 9 Oct. 1869, Journal History of the Church, 20 July 1835, CR 100 137, CHL; Young, discourse of 14 July 1855, JD, 3:266; *Woman's Exponent* [Salt Lake City], 1 March 1877, 148. See Hales, *Polygamy*, 1:234–240.

18. Young, Zina D. H., autobiographical sketch, ca. 1880s, 4, Box 2, Folder 17, MS 4780, CHL.

19. JS to Presendia Huntington Buell, 15 March 1839, JSP, D6:354. See Martha Sonntag Bradley and Mary Brown Firmage Woodward, *4 Zinas: A Story of Mothers and Daughters on the Mormon Frontier* (Salt Lake City: Signature Books, 2000), 106.

20. Henry B. Jacobs to Zina D. Young, 2 Sept. 1852, Box 2, Folder 2, MS 4780, CHL. See Bradley and Woodward, *4 Zinas*, 111–112; Compton, ISL, chapter 4.

21. "angel" in "Joseph, the Prophet, His Life and Mission," *Salt Lake Herald Church and Farm Supplement*, 12 Jan. 1895, 212; "dreams" in *Saints' Herald* [Lamoni, Iowa], 11 Jan. 1905, 29; Ugo A. Perego, Natalie M. Myres, and Scott R. Woodward, "Reconstructing the Y-Chromosome of Joseph Smith: Genealogical Applications," JMH 31 (Fall 2005): 55–56.

22. Compton, ISL, chapter 5.

23. Brigham Young, 6 Jan. 1842, 1837–1845 Journal, CR 1234 1, CHL; Tim Rathbone, "Brigham Young's Masonic Connection and Nauvoo Plural Marriages," CHL. See Compton, ISL, 154; Hales, *Polygamy*, 1:259.

24. WRJ, 17 Jan. 1842; "just across" in JS to George W. Harris, 24 May 1838, JSP, D6:470; "countenance" in *Millennial Star* [Liverpool, U.K.], 24 Jan. 1876, 51. See Compton, ISL, chapter 2; cf. Hales, *Polygamy*, 2:284–286. Hales finds the evidence for Joseph's mortal sealing to Lucinda Harris unconvincing.

25. See unsigned, undated affidavit, 60, Book 1, Folder 5, MS 3423, CHL; unsigned, undated affidavit, 62, Book 2, Folder 6, MS 3423, CHL. The latter affidavit dates the sealing to February 1843.

26. Patty Sessions statement, ca. June 1867, Box 1, Folder 33, MS 3423, CHL.

27. Compton, ISL, chapter 8.

28. "obey," "drawn sword," and "take with me" in Mary Rollins Lightner, "Remarks," 1905, Folder 6, Vault MSS 363, HBLL; "created for him" and "personage" in Todd Compton, *In Sacred Loneliness: The Documents* (Salt Lake City: Signature Books, 2022), 158, 159. See Hales, *Polygamy*, 1:262–270.

29. The more certain sealings between January and August 1842 are: Agnes Coolbrith Smith, widowed; Mary Elizabeth Rollins, married; Patty Sessions, married; Marinda Hyde, married; Elizabeth Durfee, married; Sarah Cleveland, married; Dulcena Sherman, widowed; Eliza Snow, single; Sarah Ann Whitney, single; Martha McBride, widowed. Conflicting affidavits place the prophet's sealing to Sylvia Sessions (married) in February 1842 or February 1843, but the former is more likely given her presence as a witness at her mother's sealing. As discussed above, Lucinda Harris (married) is another probable plural wife. I have relied most heavily on the analysis and documentation assembled by Todd Compton and Brian Hales. The latter dates several fewer marriages to these months.

30. *Saints' Herald* [Lamoni, Iowa], 11 Jan. 1905, 29.

31. RSR, 440. See also the analysis in Jonathan A. Stapley, *The Power of Godliness: Mormon Liturgy and Cosmology* (New York: Oxford University Press, 2018), 19–20.

32. *Saints' Herald*, 11 Jan. 1905, 29.

Chapter Twenty-Four. Upper Rooms (1842)

1. WWJ, 19 Feb. 1842.

2. T&S, 1 March 1842, 703–706. See JSP, R4:8; Robert K. Ritner, *The Joseph Smith Egyptian Papyri: A Complete Edition* (Salt Lake City: Signature Books, 2013), 113–116.

3. JS, discourse of 16 June 1844, transcription by Thomas Bullock, JSP, D15:271.

4. Ritner, *The Joseph Smith Egyptian Papyri*, 263–276.

5. T&S, 15 March 1842. See Samuel Morris Brown, *Joseph Smith's Translation: The Words and Worlds of Early Mormonism* (New York: Oxford University Press, 2020), 252–253.

6. T&S, 15 March 1842.

7. JS, discourse of 30 Jan. 1842, JSP, D9:129. Wilford Woodruff recorded a summary of Joseph's sermon in what he labeled a "Book of Revelations." Woodruff himself, however, was away from Nauvoo that evening. Presumably he obtained notes from another church member present at the meeting. See WWJ, 30 Jan. 1842.

8. WWJ, 19 Dec. 1841.

9. William Morgan, *Illustrations of Masonry* (Batavia: n.p., 1826), 63–94 (quotes on 76–77, 94). See Samuel Morris Brown, *In Heaven as It Is on Earth: Joseph Smith and the Early Mormon Conquest of Death* (New York: Oxford University Press, 2012), 179.

10. WWJ, 15 March 1842; "ancient York Masonry" in minutes of the Nauvoo Lodge, 12, MS 3436, CHL. See Michael W. Homer, *Joseph's Temples: The Dynamic Relationship between Freemasonry and Mormonism* (Salt Lake City: University of Utah Press, 2014), chapter 6.

11. *Juvenile Instructor* [Salt Lake City], 15 Jan. 1892, 67; Linda King Newell and Valeen Tippetts Avery, *Mormon Enigma: Emma Hale Smith*, rev. ed. (Urbana: University of Illinois Press, 1994), 102–104.

12. Sarah Kimball, Reminiscence, 17 March 1882, RS50, 495; Relief Society minutes, 31 March 1842, RS50, 43. On sewing societies in the early 1800s, see Robert Gross, *The Transcendentalists and Their World* (New York: Farrar, Straus & Giroux, 2021), 453–454.

13. Relief Society minutes, 17 March 1842, RS50, 32.

14. Relief Society minutes, 17 March 1842, RS50, 34–35.

15. Relief Society minutes, 17 March 1842, RS50, 31, 33.

16. Relief Society minutes, 24 March 1842, RS50, 38–39. See also JSJ, 24 March 1842, JSP, J2:46.

17. Relief Society minutes, 24 March 1842, RS50, 39–40.

18. Relief Society minutes, 31 March 1842, in RS50, 42.

19. Relief Society minutes, 31 March 1842, in RS50, 43–44.

20. JS and Brigham Young to Emma Smith, 31 March 1842, JSP, D9:308–310.

21. Minutes, 7 April 1842, JSP, D9:344; Brotherton to John C. Bennett, 13 July 1842, in *American Bulletin* [St. Louis], 16 July 1842, 2.

22. JSJ, 10 April 1842, JSP, J2:50; WWJ, 10 April 1842.

23. Clarissa Marvel, 2 April 1842 certificate, RS50, 99; Relief Society minutes, 14 April 1842, RS50, 46.

24. *A Voice from Jerusalem, or a Sketch of the Travels and Ministry of Elder Orson Hyde* (Liverpool: P. P. Pratt, 1842), 34; "hearken" in revelation, 2 Dec. 1841, JSP, D9:8–9; Marinda Hyde, Statement, ca. 1880, MS 23157, CHL; "confidante" in Hales, *Polygamy*. Thomas Bullock, who worked for Joseph Smith as a scribe during the final year of the prophet's life, dated the sealing

to April 1842. See JSP, J3:59–60, n. 265. Marinda Hyde herself dated the sealing to May 1843. See Hyde, affidavit of 8 May 1869, Box 1, Folder 44, MS 3423, CHL.

25. JS to Nancy Rigdon, ca. mid-April 1842, in JSP, D9:416–418. The letter first appeared in the *Sangamo Journal* [Springfield, Ill.], 19 Aug. 1842. For John C. Bennett's allegations about the failed courtship, see also *Sangamo Journal*, 15 July 1842, 2. On the letter, see Gerrit Dirkmaat, "Searching for 'Happiness': Joseph Smith's Alleged Authorship of the 1842 Letter to Nancy Rigdon," JMH 42 (July 2016): 94–119. One argument in favor of the letter's authenticity is that Sidney Rigdon issued a very convoluted and half-hearted denial that Joseph had authored it. Rigdon, letter of 27 Aug. 1842, *Wasp* [Nauvoo, Ill.], 3 Sept. 1842, 3.

26. JSJ, 1 and 4 May 1842, JSP, J2:53.

27. JSJ, 4 May 1842, JSP, J2:53. See Kathleen Flake, " 'Not to Be Riten': The Mormon Temple Rite as Oral Canon," *Journal of Ritual Studies* 9 (Summer 1995): 1–21.

28. Willard Richards, "History of Joseph Smith," Draft, 4 May 1842, CR 100 92, CHL; Young in L. John Nuttall Journal, 7 Feb. 1877, typescript, MSS 790, HBLL.

29. Kimball to Pratt, 17 June 1842, MS 897, CHL; Richards, "History of Joseph Smith."

30. Relief Society minutes, 28 April 1842, RS50, 57.

31. Woodruff to Pratt, 18 June 1842, MS 897.

32. WWJ, 7 May 1842; JSJ, 7 May 1842, JSP, J2:54–55.

33. Relief Society minutes, 28 April 1842, RS50, 55.

Chapter Twenty-Five. World on Fire (1842)

1. JSJ, 29 April 1842, JSP, J2:53.

2. Bennett, *History of the Saints. . .* (Boston: Leland & Whiting, 1842), 256.

3. *Salt Lake Daily Tribune*, 31 July 1887, 6.

4. Jonas to George Miller, 4 May 1842, MS 751, CHL; Nauvoo Lodge minutes, 7 May 1842, MS 3436, CHL; Notice, 11 May 1842, JSP, D10:43.

5. JSJ, 12–13 May 1842, JSP, J2:55–56. See *Warsaw Signal* [Ill.], 29 May 1844, 2.

6. *Daily Missouri Republican* [St. Louis], 12 May 1842, 2. See Morris A. Thurston, "The Boggs Shooting and Attempted Extradition: Joseph Smith's Most Famous Case," *BYU Studies* 48 (2009): 9.

7. WWJ, 15 May 1842.

8. *Hawkeye and Patriot*, 19 May 1842; David Kilbourne to Thomas Reynolds, 14 May 1842, in Warren A. Jennings, "Two Iowa Postmasters View Nauvoo: Anti-Mormon Letters to the Governor of Illinois," *BYU Studies* 11 (Spring 1971): 277.

9. *Quincy Whig*, 4 June 1842, 2; *Wasp* [Nauvoo, Ill.], 28 May 1842, 2.

10. See Spencer W. McBride, *Joseph Smith for President: The Prophet, the Assassins, and the Fight for American Religious Freedom* (New York: Oxford University Press, 2021), 67–68.

11. Minutes, 26 May 1842, JSP, D10:100.

12. JSJ, 19 May 1842, JSP, J2:58.

13. *Historical Record* [Salt Lake City], May 1887, 232.

14. Nauvoo City Council minutes, 19 May 1842, JSP, D10:73–76. See Park, KoN, 110.

15. JSJ, 19 May 1842, JSP, J2:60–61.

16. Relief Society minutes, 19 May 1842, RS50, 66–67.

17. Nauvoo High Council minutes, 20–28 May 1842, in NCHCM, 414–420; testimony of Catherine Warren, 25 May 1842, MS 24557, CHL.

18. JSJ, 26 May 1842, JSP, J2:63.

19. Relief Society minutes, 26 May 1842, RS50, 69–70.

20. Relief Society minutes, 26 May 1842, RS50, 71.

21. Kimball to Pratt, 17 June 1842, MS 897, CHL.

22. WWJ, 18 June 1842.

23. *Wasp*, 25 June 1842, 2–3.

24. *Sangamo Journal* [Springfield, Ill.], 15 July 1842, 2.

25. Bennett letter of 2 July 1842, in *Sangamo Journal*, 15 July 1842, 2; JSJ, 28 June 1842, JSP, J2:71; Rigdon to JS, 1 July 1842, JSP, D10:219–220.

26. Bennett letter of 2 July 1842; *Sangamo Journal*, 29 July 1842, 2.

27. Orson Pratt note of 14 July 1842, MS 16976, CHL.

28. JSJ, 15 July 1842, JSP, J2:75–78.

29. Young to Parley P. Pratt, 17 July 1842, MS 14291, CHL.

30. Snow, affidavit of 7 June 1869, Box 1, Folder 44, MS 3423, CHL.

31. Snow, Journal, 29 June 1842, PWES, 52; Snow, "Sketch of My Life," PWES, 11, 16.

32. Elizabeth Ann Smith Whitney, "A Leaf from an Autobiography," *Woman's Exponent* [Salt Lake City], 15 Dec. 1878, 105.

33. Revelation of 27 July 1842, JSP, D10:313–314.

34. Lucy D. Young, affidavit of 10 July 1869, vol. 2, p. 48, MS 3423, CHL.

35. *Sangamo Journal*, 15 July 1842, 2; 8 July 1842, 2 ("murderer"); Boggs, affidavit, 20 July 1842, https://www.josephsmithpapers.org/paper-summary/lilburn-w-boggs-affidavit-20-july-1842-extradition-of-js-for-accessory-to-assault/.

36. See Thurston, "The Boggs Shooting," 7–13.

37. JS to Carlin, 24 June 1842, JSP, D10:196–200; Carlin to JS, 30 June 1842, JSP, D10:211–213.

38. Minutes, 22 July 1842, JSP, D10:303.

39. Snow, Journal, 29 July 1842, PWES, 52.

40. *State Register* [Springfield, Ill.], 1 July 1842, 2; MHC, C-1, 1356; *Wasp*, 23 July 1842, 2.

41. Nauvoo City Council Minute Book, 5 July 1842, in JSP, D10:236.

42. Ordinance of 8 August 1842, in NCHCM, 101. See John S. Dinger, "Joseph Smith and the Development of Habeas Corpus in Nauvoo, 1841–44," *JMH* 36 (Summer 2010): 135–171; Jeffrey N. Walker, "Habeas Corpus in Early Nineteenth-Century Mormonism: Joseph Smith's Legal Bulwark for Personal Freedom," *BYU Studies Quarterly* 52 (2013): 4–97.

43. Thurston, "The Boggs Shooting," 13–21.

Chapter Twenty-Six. David (1842–1843)

1. JSJ, 16 Aug. 1842, JSP, J2:94.
2. JSJ, 15–17 Aug. 1842, JSP, J2:92–96 ("undaunted" on 94).
3. JS to Newel K., Elizabeth Ann, and Sarah Ann Whitney, 18 Aug. 1842, JSP, D10:439–440; Newel K. Whitney journal entries, 21 and 27 Aug. 1842, in Revelation, 27 July 1842, MS 4583, CHL.
4. Eliza R. Snow, Journal, 18 Aug. 1842, PWES, 54.
5. WWJ, 10 Aug–18 Sept. 1842; JSJ Journal, 21 and 29 Aug. 1842, JSP, J2:99, 122–124.
6. *Affidavits and Certificates, Disproving the Statements and Affidavits Contained in John C. Bennett's Letters* (Nauvoo, Ill.: n.p., 1842), 2.
7. Pratt, letter of 28 Sept. 1842, in *Wasp* [Nauvoo, Ill.], 1 Oct. 1842, 2.
8. JSJ, 21 Aug. 1842, JSP, J2:97.
9. *Sangamo Journal* [Springfield, Ill.], 19 Aug. 1842, 2.
10. *Affidavits and Certificates*, 2.
11. JSJ, 29 Aug. 1842, JSP, J2:123; *Affidavits and Certificates*, 2.
12. *Sangamo Journal*, 23 Sept. 1842, 2.
13. JS to James Arlington Bennet, 8 Sept. 1842, JSP, D11:83; Emma Smith to Sidney Rigdon, 12 Sept. 1842, including a reply from Rigdon to Emma Smith, MS 792, CHL; JSJ, 8 Nov. 1842, JSP, J2:167–168. See William Clayton on behalf of JS to Richard M. Young, 9 Feb. 1843, JSP, D11:400; JSP, D11:200, n. 32.
14. See Dallin H. Oaks and Joseph I. Bentley, "Joseph Smith and Legal Process: In the Wake of the Steamboat 'Nauvoo,'" *BYU Studies* 19 (Winter 1979): 167–199.
15. Relief Society minutes, 31 Aug. 1842, RS50, 93; Snow, Journal, 14 Aug. 1842, PWES, 54.
16. JSJ, 3 Sept. 1842, JSP, J2:125–126.
17. Law to JS, 16 Aug. 1842, in JSJ, J2:106; Butterfield to Rigdon, 20 Oct. 1842, copy in MS 713, CHL.
18. *Journal of the Senate of the Thirteenth General Assembly of the State of Illinois* . . . (Springfield, Ill.: William Walters, 1842), 44.
19. JSJ, 26 Dec. 1842–2 Jan. 1843, JSP, J2:194–214 ("equalization," 212).
20. JSJ, 26 Dec. 1842–2 Jan. 1843 ("horns," 205; "whale ivory," 194).
21. Isaac Newton Arnold, *Reminiscences of the Illinois Bar Forty Years Ago: Lincoln and Douglas as Orators and Lawyers* (Chicago: Fergus, 1881), 6. See Jeffrey N.

Walker, "Habeas Corpus in Early Nineteenth-Century Mormonism: Joseph Smith's Legal Bulwark for Personal Freedom," *BYU Studies* 52 (2013): 53–71.

22. JSJ, 6 Jan. 1843, JSP, J2:235.

23. *Nauvoo Songs* ([Nauvoo, Ill.]: Taylor & Woodruff, 1843).

24. JSJ, 18 Jan. 1843, JSP, J2:246.

25. Quorum of the Twelve minutes, 20 Jan. 1843, JSP, D11:351–353; Brigham Young Journal, Dec. 1843, 1840–1844, Box 71, Folder 3, CR 1234 1, CHL.

26. Quorum of the Twelve minutes, 20 Jan. 1843. See Gary James Bergera, *Conflict in the Quorum: Orson Pratt, Brigham Young, and Joseph Smith* (Salt Lake City: Signature Books, 2002), 33–38.

27. WWJ, 19 [20] Jan. 1843; WCJ, 20 Jan. 1843 ("break the ice").

Chapter Twenty-Seven. Deep Water (1843)

1. "deep water" in WWJ, 14 May 1843.

2. On March 4, 1843, Willard Richards recorded Joseph's visit to the Woodworth home. Richards then crossed out "Woodworth" and replaced it with an abbreviated form of the name in shorthand. He similarly recorded the prophet's same-evening visit to the home of Heber C. Kimball, at which Joseph was sealed to Emily Dow Partridge. JSJ, 4 March 1843, JSP, J2:297, n.567.

3. Wight, Reminiscences, ca. 1890s, MS 405, CHL. As Todd Compton notes, Phebe Woodworth was sealed to Joseph Smith for eternity in the Nauvoo Temple after the prophet's death. The posthumous sealing may indicate that she was also sealed to him during his lifetime. Compton, ISL, 388.

4. WCJ, 21 March 1843; blessing to Sarah Ann Whitney, 23 March 1842, JSP, D12:103–104. On the land purchase, see JSP, D11:447–452.

5. Kingsbury, Diary and Autobiography, ca. 1864, MS 522, University of Utah Special Collections, Salt Lake City; blessing to Joseph Kingsbury, 23 March 1843, JSP, D12:107–108.

6. Marriage Certificate, Joseph C. Kingsbury and Sarah Ann Whitney, 29 April 1843, MS 16824, CHL.

7. JSJ, 11 Feb. 1843, JSP, J2:262; Snow, Journal, 11 Feb. and 17 March 1843, PWES, 64, 66; riding together: JSJ, 19 March 1843, JSP, J2:313. See the discussion in Brian C. Hales, "Emma Smith, Eliza R. Snow, and the Reported Incident on the Stairs," *Mormon Historical Studies* 10 (Fall 2009): 63–75; Maureen Ursenbach Beecher et al., "Emma and Eliza and the Stairs," *BYU Studies* 22 (1982): 87–96.

8. JSJ, 11 and 13 March 1843, JSP, J2:307; Joseph Smith History, Draft Notes, 11 and 13 March 1843, CR 100 92, CHL.

9. JSJ, 18 March 1843, JSP, 2:313.

10. JSJ, 15 March 1843, JSP, J2:309.

11. JS to Rigdon, 27 March 1843, JSP, D12:115–116; Rigdon to JS, 27 March 1843, JSP, D12:117–120.

12. JSJ, 6 April 1843, JSP, J2:329–331.

13. Clayton, affidavit of 16 Feb. 1874, Box 1, Folder 6, MS 3423, CHL.

14. WCJ, 7 and 9 March 1843. On Clayton and Crooks in Manchester, see James B. Allen and Thomas G. Alexander, eds., *Manchester Mormons: The Journal of William Clayton, 1840 to 1842* (Santa Barbara, Calif.: Peregrine Smith, 1974), 31–35, 110. On Clayton's practice of polygamy, see Laurel Thatcher Ulrich, *A House Full of Females: Plural Marriage and Women's Rights in Early Mormonism, 1835–1870* (New York: Knopf, 2017), chapter 4.

15. WCJ, 22, 24, 27 April 1843.

16. Lyman Omer Littlefield, *Reminiscences of Latter-day Saints . . .* (Logan: Utah Journal, 1888), 37–50.

17. Littlefield, *Reminiscences*, 47–48.

18. WCJ, 1 and 2 May 1843; Lucy W. Kimball, deposition of 22 March 1892, 463, Box 2, Folder 1, MS 1160, CHL.

19. T&S, 1 May 1843, 186; Fugate to James Cobb, 30 June 1879, in W. Wyl, *Mormon Portraits, or the Truth about the Mormon Leaders, from 1830 to 1886* (Salt Lake City: Tribune Printing, 1886), 207–208. I am relying on the detailed research presented by Mark Ashurst-McGee and Don Bradley in "'President Joseph Has Translated a Portion': Joseph Smith and the Mistranslation of the Kinderhook Plates," in Michael Hubbard MacKay, Ashurst-McGee, and Brian M. Hauglid, eds., *Producing Ancient Scripture: Joseph Smith's Translation Projects in the Development of Mormon Christianity* (Salt Lake City: University of Utah Press, 2020), 452–523.

20. WCJ, 1 May 1843; Pratt to John Van Cott, 7 May 1843, MS 5238, CHL.

21. *New York Herald*, 30 May 1843, 2; *A Brief Discovery of the Brass Plates Recently Taken from a Mound Near Kinderhook, Pike County, Illinois* (Nauvoo, Ill.: n.p., 1843).

22. WWJ, 14 May 1843 ("more sure"); WCJ, 16 ("three heavens") and 17 ("knowledge is power") May 1843.

23. Benjamin Johnson to George F. Gibbs, 1903, 32, MS 1289, CHL.

24. WCJ, 16 May 1843; Benjamin F. Johnson affidavit, 4 March 1870, Box 1, Folder 45, MS 3423, CHL.

25. Johnson to George F. Gibbs, 1903, 32.

26. Julia Murdock to John Riggs Murdock, 2 Nov. 1858, copy in John Murdock, Autobiography, 190, Folder 4, MS 1194, CHL.

27. Emily Young, Diary and Reminiscences, 1–2, MS 2845, CHL.

28. Emily Young, Diary and Reminiscences, 1.

29. Emily Young, Diary and Reminiscences, 1.

30. Emily Young, affidavit of 1 May 1869, Box 1, Folder 44, MS 3423, CHL; Emily Young, Diary and Reminiscences, 1.

31. Emily D. Partridge Young, deposition of 19 March 1892, 384, Box 1, Folder 15, MS 1160, CHL; Eliza Partridge Lyman, affidavit of 1 July 1869, Box 1,

Folder 20, MS 3423, CHL. See H. Michael Marquardt, "Emily Dow Partridge Smith Young on the Witness Stand: Recollections of a Plural Wife," JMH 34 (Summer 2008): 110–141.

32. Emily D. Partridge Young, deposition of 19 March 1892, 351 ("proper"), 371 (hand).

33. Emily D. Partridge Young, deposition of 19 March 1892, 364–366.

34. Levi Richards Journal, 14 May 1843, MS 1284, CHL.

35. WCJ, 23 May 1843.

36. Young, discourse of 8 Oct. 1866, transcription of George D. Watt, shorthand by LaJean Purcell Carruth, Box 2, Folder 17, CR 100 912, CHL.

37. JSJ, 26 May 1843, JSP, J3:23; Brigham Young, History, Draft, 69, Folder 5, CR 100 475, CHL.

38. "Reminiscence of Mercy Rachel Fielding Thompson." "Reminiscence of Mercy Rachel Fielding Thompson," in Carol Cornwall Madsen, *In Their Own Words: Women and the Story of Nauvoo* (Salt Lake City: Deseret Book, 1994), 195. See JSP, J3:25, n. 89.

39. Catherine Phillips Smith, affidavit of 28 Jan. 1903, Box 1, Folder 36, MS 3423, CHL. See Gary James Bergera, "Identifying the Earliest Mormon Polygamists, 1841–44," *Dialogue* 38 (Fall 2005): 25–29.

40. JS, discourse of 21 May 1843, reported by Levi Richards, MS 155, CHL.

Chapter Twenty-Eight. Anointed (1843)

1. WCJ, 11 Aug. 1843.

2. Helen Mar Kimball Smith Whitney, Autobiography, 1881, in Richard Neitzel Holzapfel and Jeni Broberg Holzapfel, *A Woman's View: Helen Mar Whitney's Reminiscences of Early Church History* (Provo, Utah: Religious Studies Center, Brigham Young University, 1997), 481–487.

3. Heber C. Kimball, Blessing to Helen Mar Kimball, 28 May 1843, MS 23826, CHL. On the subject of Helen's age, compare Craig L. Foster et al., "The Age of Joseph Smith's Plural Wives in Social and Demographic Context" and Todd M. Compton, "Early Marriage in the New England and Northeastern States, and in Mormon Polygamy: What Was the Norm?," both in Newell G. Bringhurst and Craig L. Foster, eds., *The Persistence of Polygamy: Joseph Smith and the Origins of Mormon Polygamy* (Independence, Mo.: John Whitmer Books, 2010).

4. See Hales, *Polygamy*, 2:29; Compton, ISL, 499–501.

5. "breach" in Heber Kimball to Helen Kimball Smith, 10 July 1843, in *Woman's Exponent* [Salt Lake City], 1 Aug. 1882, 39–40; "loved dancing" in *Woman's Exponent*, 15 Nov. 1882, 90; other quotes in Helen Whitney, Autobiography, 486.

6. WCJ, 29 May 1843 ("familiarity"), 23 June 1843 ("snare," "indulge").

7. JSJ, 16 June 1843, JSP, J3:37. See the summary of the case in JSP, D12:357–362.

8. WCJ, 23 June 1843.

9. "shoot away" in WWJ, 30 June 1843; "away" in WCJ, 23 June 1843.

10. "Arrest of Joseph Smith," *Nauvoo Neighbor*, 19 July 1843, 2.

11. WCJ, 30 June 1843.

12. JSJ, 30 June 1843, JSP, J3:43–48.

13. JSJ, 30 June 1843. See Andrew H. Hedges, "Extradition, the Mormons, and the Election of 1843," *Journal of the Illinois State Historical Society* 109 (Summer 2016): 127–147.

14. Quotes from Clayton, affidavit of 16 Feb. 1874, Box 1, Folder 6, MS 3423, CHL. See also WCJ, 12 July 1843; Clayton to Madison M. Scott, 11 Nov. 1871, Box 1, Folder 5, MS 3423.

15. See Laurel Thatcher Ulrich, *A House Full of Females: Plural Marriage and Women's Rights in Early Mormonism, 1835–1870* (New York: Knopf, 2017), 91–92.

16. Revelation, 12 July 1843, JSP, D12:467–478.

17. "talking to" in Clayton, affidavit of 16 Feb. 1874; WCJ, 12 ("a word") and 15 July 1843; deed to Emma Smith et al., 12 July 1843, JSP, D12:481–483.

18. See, for example, Brigham Young, discourse of 29 Aug. 1852, in *Deseret News—Extra* [Salt Lake City], 14 Sept. 1852, 25. Emma later denied having burned the revelation. Edmund C. Briggs, "A Visit to Nauvoo," *Journal of History* 9 (Oct. 1916): 462. See Linda King Newell and Valeen Tippetts Avery, *Mormon Enigma: Emma Hale Smith*, rev. ed. (Champaign: University of Illinois Press, 1994), 154. Emma denied that her husband practiced or taught plural marriage, which if true would foreclose the existence of a revelation on the subject.

19. PWES, 20 July 1843, 80.

20. *Nauvoo Neighbor*, 2 Aug. 1843, 2.

21. Richards to Brigham Young, Aug. 1843, Box 41, Folder 28, CR 1234 1, CHL; Mason Brayman to JS, 29 July 1843, JSP, D12:503–507.

22. "wisdom" in Richards to Young, Aug. 1843; Thomas Ford, *A History of Illinois . . .* (Chicago: S. C. Griggs, 1854), 318; "never knew" in JSJ, 6 Aug. 1843, JSP, J3:73.

23. James W. Brattle to Charles Brattle, 5 July 1844, in Brattle Family Correspondence, Beinecke Library Special Collections, Yale University, New Haven, Conn.; WCJ, 1 Aug. 1843.

24. WCJ, 1 Aug. 1843; "choke him off" in JSJ, 13 Aug. 1843, JSP, J3:78; complaint in Jacob B. Backenstos, deposition of 1 Aug. 1843, Folder 14, Newel K. Whitney Papers, MS 9670, CHL. See MHC, D-1, 1714. See "Introduction to *State of Illinois v. JS for Assault and Battery*," in JSP, LR.

25. Theodore Calvin Pease, *Illinois Election Returns, 1818–1848* (Springfield: Illinois State Historical Library, 1923), 140.

26. *Warsaw Message*, 6 Sept. 1843, 2.

27. JSJ, 12 Aug. 1843, JSP, J3:75.

28. JSJ, 12 and 19 Aug. 1843, JSP, J3:75, 82; *Warsaw Message*, 13 Sept. 1843, 1.

29. No contemporary minutes of the council meeting are extant, but several men present—both supporters and critics of the revelation—described the proceedings in later statements. For example, see *Nauvoo Expositor*, 7 June 1844, 2; David Fullmer, affidavit of 15 June 1869, Box 1, Folder 44, MS 3423, CHL.

30. William Law to Isaac Russell, 10 Nov. 1837, MS 6066, CHL. See Lyndon W. Cook, "William Law, Nauvoo Dissenter," *BYU Studies* 22 (Winter 1982): 47–72.

31. WCJ, 22 July ("shock"), 26 July, 27 July ("trouble"), 13 Aug. ("deranged"), 18 Aug. ("downfall"), 19 Aug. ("all she knew" and "kill herself") 1843.

32. Quotes from WCJ, 15 Sept. 1843. See also WCJ, 17 and 21 Sept. 1843.

33. WCJ, 16 Aug. 1843.

34. WCJ, 21 Aug. 1843.

35. WCJ, 23 Aug. 1843; Hales, *Polygamy*, 2:104–105. See Jennifer Reeder, "Eliza R. Snow and the Prophet's Gold Watch: Time Keeper as Relic," JMH 31 (Spring 2005): esp. 125–127.

36. WCJ, 23 Aug. 1843.

37. Marriage Certificate of 23 Aug. 1843, in Hancock County, Ill., Marriage Certificates, #750, Family History Library Film 004661406, https://www.familysearch.org/search/catalog/196973/; WCJ, 26 Aug. 1843; Melissa Willes statement, 27 June 1887, Box 49, Folder 16, Andrew Jenson Papers, MS 17956, CHL.

38. JSJ, 15 Sept. 1843, JSP, J3:99.

39. Emily Dow Partridge Young, autobiography and journal typescript, 2–3, MS 2845, CHL.

40. "The Memoirs of President Joseph Smith," *Saints' Herald* [Independence, Mo.], 18 Dec. 1834, 1614; JSJ, 20 Sept. 1843, JSP, J3:102; Melissa Lott Willes, affidavit of 20 May 1869, Box 1, Folder 44, MS 3423, CHL; Melissa Lott Willes, deposition of 19 March 1892, esp. 100, 105–106, Box 1, Folder 11, MS 1160, CHL.

41. Compton, ISL, chapter 30.

42. "Holy order" in Heber C. Kimball, Journal, 20 March 1845, MS 627, CHL; "holiest" in JSJ, 28 Sept. 1843, JSP, J3:104; WWJ, 28 Sept. 1843.

43. WWJ, 6 Aug. 1843.

44. WCJ, 19 Oct. 1843.

45. Brigham Young, 1840–1844 Journal, 29 Oct. 1843, Box 71, Folder 3, CR 1234 1, CHL; WRJ, 30 Oct. 1843. The term "prayer meeting" appears regularly in Richards's journal.

46. JSJ, 3 Oct. 1843, JSP, J3:105–106; *Nauvoo Neighbor*, 4 Oct. 1843, 3.

Chapter Twenty-Nine. Cool as a Cucumber (1843–1844)

1. See the summary in JSP, D13:295–297.

2. Affidavit of Daniel Avery, 28 Dec. 1843, JSP, D13:429–434; *Warsaw Message*, 3 Jan. 1844, 2.

3. Nauvoo City Council ordinances, 8 and 21 Dec. 1843, JSP, D13:344–345, 423.
4. Nauvoo City Council minutes, 8 Dec. 1843, JSP, D13:340–341; memorial, ca. 16 Dec. 1843, JSP, D13:376–393. See the discussion in JSP, D13:374–376.
5. *Warsaw Message*, 17 Jan. 1844, 1; *New-York Daily Tribune*, 27 Jan. 1844, 1.
6. *Nauvoo Neighbor*, 20 Dec. 1843, 2–3.
7. JSJ, 18 Dec. 1843, JSP, J3:1147.
8. JSJ, 18 Dec. 1843, JSP, J3:147; *Warsaw Message*, 3 Jan. 1844, 1.
9. JSJ, 19 Dec. 1843, JSP, J3:147–148. See also WCJ, 19 Dec. 1843.
10. JSJ, 25 Dec. 1843, JSP, J3:151; *Nauvoo Neighbor*, 13 Dec. 1843, 2.
11. JSJ, 25 Dec. 1843, JSP, J3:151.
12. Harold Schindler, *Orrin Porter Rockwell: Man of God, Son of Thunder* (Salt Lake City: University of Utah Press, 1966), chapter 5; Heman C. Smith, "Mormon Troubles in Missouri," *Missouri Historical Review* 4 (July 1910): 249–251.
13. *Warsaw Message*, 10 Jan. 1844, 1; See Schindler, *Rockwell*, 102.
14. JSJ, 26 Dec. 1843, JSP, J3:152; Nauvoo City Council minutes, 29 Dec. 1843, JSP, D13:443.
15. Nauvoo City Council minutes, 29 Dec. 1843, JSP, D13:443–444.
16. JSJ, 11 Oct. 1843, JSP, J3:112; WCJ, 11 Oct. 1843; indictment, 24 May 1844, Hancock County Circuit Court, MS 3464, CHL. See Park, KoN, 178, 309, n. 34.
17. William Law, Journal, 1 and 8 Jan. 1844, in Lyndon W. Cook, ed., *William Law: Biographical Essay, Nauvoo Diary . . .* (Orem, Utah: Grandin Book, 1994), 37, 46–47. For evidence for and against the authenticity of this diary, see Benjamin E. Park, "William Law's Diary and the Perils of Suspect Sources," JMH 48 (April 2021): 123–127.
18. Alexander Neibaur, Journal, 24 May 1844, MS 1674, CHL; JSJ, 30 Dec. 1843, JSP, J3:154.
19. Nauvoo City Council minutes, 3 Jan. 1844, in NCHCM, 203–204.
20. Law, Journal, 4 Jan. 1844, 41–42.
21. "rumor turn" in Nauvoo City Council minutes, 5 Jan. 1844, in NCHCM, 209; "associate" in Law, Journal, 5 Jan. 1844, 45–46.
22. Law, Journal, 8 Jan. 1844, 46.
23. JSJ, 4 Jan. 1844, JSP, J3:156–157.
24. JSJ, 23 July 1843, JSP, J3:65–66.

Chapter Thirty. The Kingdom (1844)

1. Emerson, "The Young American," *Dial* [Boston, Mass.] 4 (April 1844): 492.
2. JSJ, 29 Jan. 1844, JSP, J3:169–170. See Spencer W. McBride, *Joseph Smith for President: The Prophet, the Assassins, and the Fight for American Religious Freedom* (New York: Oxford University Press, 2021), chapter 6.
3. *Pittsburgh Weekly Gazette*, 15 Sept. 1843.
4. T&S, 1 Oct. 1843, 344; JS to Calhoun, 4 Nov. 1843, JSP, D13:251–52.

5. Clay to JS, 15 Nov. 1843, JSP, D13:274; Cass to JS, 9 Dec. 1843, JSP, D13:356–357; Calhoun to JS, 2 Dec. 1843, JSP, D13:307.

6. JS to Calhoun, 2 Jan. 1844, JSP, D14:26.

7. *General Smith's Views of the Powers and Policy of the Government of the United States* (Nauvoo, Ill.: John Taylor, 1844), 11.

8. JSJ, 30 Dec. 1842, JSP, J2:197. See W. Paul Reeve, *Religion of a Different Color: Race and the Mormon Struggle for Whiteness* (New York: Oxford University Press, 2015), chapter 4.

9. Nauvoo City Council minutes, 21 Dec. 1843, JSP, D13:419; *General Smith's Views*, 11 ("free people"). More in keeping with conservative white antislavery northerners, Joseph suggested in March that freed slaves could be sent to Mexico, "where all colors are alike." JSJ, 7 March 1844, JSP, J3:198.

10. WWJ, 8 Feb. 1844; JSJ, 27 Feb. 1844, JSP, J3:184.

11. JSJ, 29 Jan. 1844, JSP, J3:170.

12. Matthew J. Grow and Brian Whitney, "The Pinery Saints: Mormon Communalism at Black River Falls, Wisconsin," *Communal Societies* 36 (Dec. 2016) 153–170; "irksome" in Melvin C. Johnson, "Wightites in Wisconsin: The Formation of a Dissenting Latter Day Community (1842–1845)," JWHAJ 32 (Spring/Summer 2012): 63–78.

13. Wight et al., to JS et al., 15 Feb. 1844, JSP, D14:172–178.

14. JSJ, 10 March 1844, JSP, J3:201; Council of Fifty minutes, 10–11 March 1844, JSP, C50:20–45. See JSJ, 20 Feb. 1844, JSP, J3:180.

15. Council of Fifty minutes, 11 March 1844, JSP, C50:42–43.

16. Council of Fifty minutes, 14 March and 5 April 1844, JSP, C50:48, 81.

17. Revelation, 30 Oct. 1831, JSP, J2:93; Council of Fifty minutes, 11 March 1844, JSP, C50:40–42.

18. Council of Fifty minutes, 18 April 1844, JSP, C50:128.

19. Council of Fifty minutes, 21 March 1844, JSP, C50:58–60.

20. Council of Fifty minutes, 10 March and 5 April 1844, JSP, C50:39, 82.

21. John Scott, Affidavit of 26 Feb. 1844, MS 16800, CHL.

22. JSJ, 26 Feb. and 7 March 1844, JSP, J3:184, 191, 198; "The Voice of Innocence from Nauvoo," RS50, 154.

23. Relief Society minutes, 17 March 1843, RS50, 36; WCJ, 9 March 1844.

24. Relief Society minutes, 16 March 1844, RS50, 130–131 (emphasis added); "Voice of Innocence," 156; *Nauvoo Neighbor*, 20 March 1844, 2.

25. *New York Daily Tribune*, 27 Jan. 1844, 1; JSJ, 7 March 1844, JSP, J3:193–194. See Charles Foster's account in *Warsaw Signal*, 25 April 1844, 3.

26. *Nauvoo Neighbor*, 17 April 1844, 2.

27. WCJ, 23 March 1844.

28. JSJ, 24 March 1844, JSP, J3:207.

29. WWJ, 6 April 1844; Historian's Office, Journal, 6 April 1844, CR 100 1, CHL.

30. JSJ, 7 April 1844, JSP, J3:216; Nauvoo Lodge Minute Book, 10 March 1844, MS 3436, CHL.

31. JS, discourse of 7 April 1844 (Thomas Bullock), JSP, D14:316–327. Several church members took detailed notes as Joseph spoke. In this and the following paragraphs, I quote from the record made by Thomas Bullock, the church's official "reporter" at the conference.

32. JS, discourse of 8 April 1844 (Thomas Bullock), JSP, D14:353–355.

33. JS, discourse of 8 April 1844 (Thomas Bullock), JSP, D14:355.

34. Andrew F. Ehat, " 'They Might Have Known That He Was Not a Fallen Prophet': The Nauvoo Journal of Joseph Fielding," *BYU Studies* 19 (Winter 1979): 148; Lyndon W. Cook, ed., *William Law: Biographical Essay, Nauvoo Diary* . . . (Orem, Utah: Grandin Book, 1994), 49.

35. Council of Fifty minutes, 11 April 1844, JSP, C50:92–94.

36. Council of Fifty minutes, 11 April 1844, JSP, C50:95–96.

37. Council of Fifty minutes, 11 April 1844, JSP, C50:101.

38. Council of Fifty minutes, 25 April 1844, JSP, C50:135–137. See JSP, C50:130.

39. Law, Journal, ca. early April 1844, 48.

40. JSJ, 18 April 1844, JSP, J3:231–232.

41. LB, 741; Parley P. Pratt to JS, 3 May 1844, JSP, D14:441. On the Spencer brothers, see Richard W. Sadler and Claudia S. Sadler, "Augustine Spencer: Nauvoo Gentile, Joseph Smith Antagonist," *Mormon Historical Studies* 12 (Fall 2011): 27–46.

42. JSJ, 26 April 1844, JSP, J3:236–237; "damned" in *Nauvoo Neighbor*, 1 May 1844, 2–3. For a summary of the case, see JSP, D15:54–59.

43. *Nauvoo Neighbor*, 1 May 1844.

44. *Warsaw Signal*, 8 May 1844, 3.

45. *Warsaw Signal*, 15 May 1844. See also JSJ, 28 April and 7 May 1844, JSP, J3:239, 245–246.

46. Nauvoo Municipal Court minutes, 8 May 1844, MS 16800, CHL.

47. Council of Fifty minutes, 6 May 1844, JSP, C50:158.

48. *Nauvoo Neighbor*, 22 May 1844, 2; JSJ, 17 May 1844, JSP, J3:253.

49. BY and WR to Reuben Hedlock et al., 3 May 1844, copy in CR 1234 1, CHL.

50. See John J. Hammond, "Re-examining the Adams-Quincy May 1844 Visit to Nauvoo," JWHAJ 30 (2010): 66–95; Jed Woodworth, "Josiah Quincy's 1844 Visit with Joseph Smith," *BYU Studies* 39 (2000): 71–82.

51. Henry Adams, "Charles Francis Adams Visits the Mormons in 1844," *Proceedings of the Massachusetts Historical Society* 68 (1952): 285–286; Quincy, *Figures of the Past from the Leaves of Old Journals* (Boston: Roberts Brothers, 1883), 389–390; Wandle Mace, Autobiography, 120, MSS 786, HBLL.

52. Quincy, *Figures*, 397.

Chapter Thirty-One. Bleeding Hearts (1844)

1. See Noel A. Carmack, "Of Prophets and Pale Horses: Joseph Smith, Benjamin West, and the American Millenarian Tradition," *Dialogue* 29 (Fall

1996): 165–176; Alex Beam, *American Crucifixion: The Murder of Joseph Smith and the Fate of the Mormon Church* (New York: Public Affairs, 2014), 128–130.

2. JS, discourse of 16 June 1844, reported by Thomas Bullock, JSP, D15:272.

3. WCJ, 21 May 1844.

4. Indictment, 24 May 1844, Hancock County Circuit Court, MS 3464, CHL.

5. For the details of the case, see *Nauvoo Neighbor*, 13 Dec. 1843, 2; *Warsaw Signal*, 7 Feb. 1844, 2; *Warsaw Signal*, 25 April 1844, 3. See "Introduction to *State of Illinois v. Sympson, Sympson v. JS*, and *State of Illinois v. JS for Perjury*," JSP, LR.

6. JS, discourse of 26 May 1844, JSP, D15:46–54.

7. JSJ, 27 May 1844, JSP, J3:263–265.

8. *Nauvoo Expositor*, 7 June 1844.

9. *Nauvoo Expositor*, 7 June 1844.

10. Nauvoo City Council minutes, 8 June 1844, NCHCM, 240–250.

11. Nauvoo City Council minutes, 10 June 1844, NCHCM, 265.

12. Act to Incorporate the City of Nauvoo, 16 Dec. 1840, JSP, D7:486; Nauvoo City Council minutes, 10 June 1844, NCHCM, 254–258.

13. JS to Greene, 10 June 1844, *Nauvoo Neighbor*, 17 June 1844, 3.

14. William Law, Journal, 10 June 1844, in Lyndon W. Cook, ed., *William Law: Biographical Essay, Nauvoo Diary . . .* (Orem, Utah: Grandin Book, 1994), 56; JSJ, 10 June 1844, JSP, J3:277.

15. WCJ, 11 June 1844; Law, Journal, 11–14 June 1844, 56–57.

16. Law, Journal, 10 June 1844, 55.

17. JS to James Arlington Bennet, 20 June 1844, JSP, D15:339; warrant, 11 June 1844, JSP, D15:247; JSJ, 12–13 June 1844, JSP, J3:279–281; WCJ, 12 June 1844. See JSP, D15:241, n. 28.

18. *Warsaw Signal*, 14 June 1844 Extra; JSJ, 13 June 1844, JSP, J3:281.

19. JS to Ford, 14 June 1844, JSP, D15:259–262.

20. WCJ, 15 June 1844. This entry is part of a more detailed 14–22 June 1844 journal kept by Clayton, separate from the standard entries for those dates. Its text is copied at the beginning of the second volume of Clayton's journal.

21. JS, discourse of 16 June 1844, report by Thomas Bullock, JSP, D15:264–274; "false and damnable" in *Nauvoo Expositor*, 7 June 1844.

22. T&S, 15 Nov. 1845, 1039. See Terryl L. Givens, *Wrestling the Angel: The Foundations of Mormon Thought* (New York: Oxford University Press, 2014), chapter 12; Linda Wilcox, "The Mormon Concept of a Mother in Heaven," *Sunstone* 5 (Sept.–Oct. 1980): 78–87.

23. JSJ, 16 June 1844, JSP, J3:286–287; JS to Ford, 16 June 1844, JSP, D15:288.

24. *Nauvoo Neighbor*, 21 June 1844 Extra. See Anson Call, Autobiography, 26, MS 313, CHL.

25. JSJ, 18 June 1844, JSP, J3:290–291; WCJ, 18 June 1844. This entry is part of Clayton's more detailed 14–22 June 1844 journal. For Joseph unsheathing his sword, see MHC, F-1, 119.

26. Ford to JS, 22 June 1844, JSP, D15:384–392.

27. JS to Ford, 22–23 June 1844, JSP, D15:402–409. See Zachary M. Schrag, *The Fires of Philadelphia: Citizen-Soldiers, Nativists, and the 1844 Riots over the Soul of a Nation* (New York: Pegasus, 2021), esp. 9–13.

28. WCJ, 22–23 June 1844. I have expanded the abbreviations that Clayton employed, as in "r[ecords] of [the] k[ingdom]."

29. JS to Emma Smith, 23 June 1844, JSP, D15:411–412.

30. Vilate Kimball to Heber Kimball, June 1844, MS 6241, CHL.

31. WCJ, 23 June 1844; JS to Ford, 23 June 1844, JSP, D15:415–416.

32. Hosea Stout, Nauvoo Legion History, in Dan Vogel, ed., *History of Joseph Smith and the Church of Jesus Christ of Latter-day Saints: A Source- and Text-Critical Edition* (Salt Lake City: Smith-Pettit Foundation, 2015), 8:37.

33. Woodworth to Hosea Stout, 29 Oct. 1855, CR 100 396, CHL; Vilate Kimball to Heber C. Kimball, June 1844; WCJ, 24 June 1844.

34. T&S, 15 July 1844, 585; Bernhisel to George A. Smith, 11 Sept. 1854, CR 100 396, CHL.

35. WCJ, 24 June 1844.

36. WCJ, 24 June 1844.

37. Zina Huntington Jacobs, Journal, 24 June 1844, in Maureen Ursenbach Beecher, "'All Things Move in Order in the City': The Nauvoo Diary of Zina Diantha Huntington Jacobs," *BYU Studies* 19 (Spring 1979): 292.

38. Cyrus Wheelock to George A. Smith, 29 Dec. 1854, CR 100 396, CHL.

39. Warrant, 24 June 1844, JSP, D15:466; JS to Emma Smith, 25 June 1844, JSP, D15:470.

40. WRJ, 25 June 1844; James W. Brattle to Charles Brattle, 5 July 1844, in Brattle Family Correspondence, Beinecke Library Special Collections, Yale University, New Haven, Conn.

41. Brattle to Charles Brattle, 5 July 1844. See also Thomas Ford, *A History of Illinois . . .* (Chicago: S. C. Griggs, 1854), 342–343.

42. JS to Emma Smith, 25 June 1844.

43. "material witnesses" in T&S, 1 July 1844, 562; "cell" and "department" in WRJ, 25 June 1844.

44. WRJ, 25 June 1844.

45. "close confinement" in WRJ, 25 June 1844.

46. John S. Fullmer to George A. Smith, 27 Oct. 1854, and Cyrus Wheelock to George A. Smith, 29 Dec. 1854, both in CR 100 396, CHL.

47. JS to Emma Smith, 27 June 1844, JSP, D15:499.

48. WRJ, 27 June 1844; Hyrum requesting hymn in LaJean Purcell Carruth and Mark Lyman Staker, eds., "John Taylor's June 27, 1854, Account of the Martyrdom," *BYU Studies* 50 (2011): 59.

49. WCJ, 27 June 1844.

50. Quotes in John Taylor, "The Story of Carthage Jail," 1856, Draft Histories, CR 100 92, CHL. See also WRJ, 27 June 1844.

51. The most detailed accounts of the murders at Carthage Jail draw from the firsthand memories of Willard Richards and John Taylor. See JSJ, 27 June 1844, JSP, J3:327–329; *Nauvoo Neighbor*, 30 June 1844 Extra; Richards and Taylor to Reuben Hedlock, 9 July 1844, MS 1490, CHL; *Nauvoo Neighbor*, 24 July 1844, 3; T&S, 1 Aug. 598–599. Church leaders prepared an account that John Taylor included in the 1844 edition of the church's Doctrine and Covenants. See *Doctrine and Covenants* . . . (Nauvoo, Ill.: John Taylor, 1844), 444–445. William Clayton wrote an early secondhand account in his journal. See WCJ, 28 June 1844. James W. Brattle, a member of the Carthage Greys, provided a non-Mormon eyewitness account. See James W. Brattle to Charles Brattle, 5 July 1844.

52. See Dallin H. Oaks and Marvin S. Hill, *Carthage Conspiracy: The Trial of the Accused Assassins of Joseph Smith* (Urbana: University of Illinois Press, 1975), 19; Beam, *American Crucifixion*, 174–176.

53. Jones to Thomas Bullock, 20 Jan. 1855, 6, MS 153, CHL.

54. T&S, 15 July 1844, 585.

Epilogue

1. Richards, letter of 27 June 1844, Box 3, Folder 3, MS 1490, CHL; WCJ, 28 June 1844.

2. WCJ, 28 June 1844.

3. *Deseret Evening News*, 27 Nov. 1875, 2. The reminiscence is from B. W. Richmond, a non-Mormon physician staying at the Mansion House at the time of the murders; Sarah Kimball to Sarepta Heywood, n.d., MS 8708, CHL.

4. Zina Huntington Jacobs, Journal, 28 and 30 June 1844, in Maureen Ursenbach Beecher, " 'All Things Move in Order in the City': The Nauvoo Diary of Zina Diantha Huntington Jacobs," *BYU Studies* 19 (Spring 1979): 293.

5. *Deseret Evening News*, 27 Nov. 1875, 3.

6. JSJ, 23 Aug. 1842, JSP, J2:117.

7. WCJ, 29 June 1844. See Joseph R. Johnstun, " 'To Lie in Yonder Tomb': The Tomb and Burial of Joseph Smith," *Mormon Historical Studies* 6 (Fall 2005); 163–180; Lachlan Mackay, "A Brief History of the Smith Family Nauvoo Cemetery," *Mormon Historical Studies* 3 (Fall 2002):240–252.

8. *Warsaw Signal*, 10 July 1844, 2.

9. *Warsaw Signal*, 10 July 1844, 2.

10. Minutes of 7 Oct. 1845, CR 100 318, CHL. See Johnstun, "Tomb," 177–178.

11. Mackay, "Brief History."

12. Relief Society minutes, 28 April 1842, RS50, 55.

Index